FINALIST FOR THE NATIONAL JEWISH BOOK AWARD

FEAR

ANTI-SEMITISM IN POLAND AFTER AUSCHWITZ

AN ESSAY IN HISTORICAL INTERPRETATION

JAN T. GROSS

Praise for *Fear*

"Compelling . . . Gross builds a meticulous case."
—*Publishers Weekly* (starred review)

"A necessary book."
—*Kirkus Reviews* (starred review)

"Imaginative, urgent, and unorthodox . . . an important book."
—*The New York Sun*

"[*Fear's*] tone is measured, its moral calculations nuanced . . . [Gross] grounds his facts meticulously in historical records, official documents, court testimony, letters, memoirs and interviews. . . . This traumatic book doesn't just establish the particulars of atrocity, it deepens our grasp of the causes."
—Cleveland *Plain Dealer*

"This is a brilliantly written history that combines narrative power with analytical depth. Gross treats his readers with respect, offering every possible interpretation of the evidence before offering his own (often withering) judgment. The word 'genius' is carelessly thrown around these days, but with *Fear*, Gross genuinely deserves the accolade."
—*The Jewish Chronicle*

"A brave and extraordinary book . . . Read Gross and weep." —*The Advocate*

"A bombshell book that is sure to generate bitter debate."
—*The News & Observer*

"*Fear's* anguishing exposé is brilliantly scholarly, analytical, sober, yet compellingly readable."
—*The Australian*

"In his new book, Jan T. Gross proposes a strikingly original, conscientiously documented reinterpretation of the anti-Semitic terror that broke over the heads of Jewish survivors in post–World War II Poland. This brilliant, courageous book about Poles and Jews is deeply disturbing: It should be required reading for anyone concerned about the European past—and our common future."
—TONY JUDT, director of the Remarque Institute at New York University and author of *Postwar: A History of Europe Since 1945*

FEAR

ANTI-SEMITISM
IN POLAND
AFTER
AUSCHWITZ

An Essay in
Historical Interpretation

JAN T. GROSS

RANDOM HOUSE TRADE PAPERBACKS
NEW YORK

2007 Random House Trade Paperback Edition

Copyright © 2006 by Jan T. Gross

Published in the United States by Random House Trade Paperbacks,
an imprint of The Random House Publishing Group,
a division of Random House, Inc., New York.

RANDOM HOUSE TRADE PAPERBACKS and colophon
are trademarks of Random House, Inc.

Originally published in hardcover in the United States by Random House,
an imprint of The Random House Publishing Group,
a division of Random House, Inc., in 2006.

The photograph on page 1 is © 2007 David Seymour Estate/Magnum Photos

Insert photographs are courtesy of the Jewish Historical Institute in Warsaw, Poland.

The poem on pages 256–57 is from the book *The Song That Never Died:
The Poetry of Mordecai Gebirtig*, translation and Introduction by Simcha Simchovitch,
published by Mosaic Press. Copyright 2001. Reprinted by permission
of Mosaic Press, Oakville, Ontario, Canada.

ISBN 978-0-8129-6746-3

Library of Congress Cataloging-in-Publication Data

Gross, Jan Tomasz.
Fear: anti-Semitism in Poland after Auschwitz / Jan T. Gross.
p.   cm.
Includes index.
ISBN 978-0-8129-6746-3
1. Antisemitism—Poland—History—20th century.
2. Pogroms—Poland—Kielce—History—20th century.   3. Jews—Persecutions—Poland—
Kielce.   4. Holocaust, Jewish (1939–1945)—Influence.   5. Communism—Poland.
6. Poland—History—1945–1980.   7. Kielce (Poland)—
Ethnic relations.   I. Title.
DS146.P6G76 2005
305.892'4043809045—dc22   2005052913

Printed in the United States of America

www.atrandom.com

246897531

Book design by Carole Lowenstein

Thus, prima facie, all this looks like elaborate nonsense, but when many people, without having been manipulated, begin to talk nonsense, and if intelligent people are among them, there is usually more involved than just nonsense.

—HANNAH ARENDT, "Personal Responsibility
Under Dictatorship"

On April 30, 1997 . . . Rwandan television showed footage of a man who confessed to having been among a party of *génocidaires* who had killed seventeen schoolgirls and a sixty two-year-old Belgian nun at a boarding school in Gisenyi two nights earlier. It was a second such attack on a school in a month; the first time, sixteen students were killed and twenty injured in Kibuye.

The prisoner on television explained that the massacre was part of a Hutu Power "liberation" campaign. . . . During [this] attack on the school in Gisenyi, teenage girls who had been roused from their sleep were ordered to separate themselves—Hutus from Tutsis. But the students had refused. At both schools, the girls said they were simply Rwandans, so they were beaten and shot indiscriminately.

—PHILIP GOUREVITCH, *We Wish to Inform You
That Tomorrow We Will Be Killed with Our Families*

CONTENTS

INTRODUCTION

The origin of this book, as is so often the case, is in another book. Years ago I read a volume of documents edited by Miriam Hochberg-Mariańska, a wartime member of an organization called Żegota, which on behalf of the Polish underground was helping Jews hiding from Nazi persecution. Hochberg-Mariańska was Jewish but she had what at the time were known as "good" looks, which meant that she could pass for an ethnic Pole. She worked in the Kraków branch of Żegota, and was very courageous.[1]

After the war, she traveled all around Poland on behalf of the Central Committee of Polish Jews, also a risky business then, to look for Jewish children who had been placed with Polish families. Many of these children had been orphaned, or relatives who had miraculously survived the war did not quite know where to look for them. This was one of many important tasks at the time for the remnants of Polish Jewry—to retrieve its surviving dispersed and lost youth.

Hochberg-Mariańska was instrumental in this effort and soon published a slender book describing the fate of a few children and their rescuers.[2] In the introduction to this volume she noted that several courageous Poles who had saved Jewish children declined to have their identities revealed in print. Presumably to clear up the matter, she then wrote a sentence that completely threw me off: "I don't know if anyone living outside Poland will understand and accept the fact that saving a life of a defenseless child pursued by murderers can bring the rescuer shame or unpleasant consequences."[3]

I was living in Poland at the time, and this certainly did not make any sense to me. Why would those who would later be honored as the Righteous Among Nations not want their role as rescuers of Jews to be known?* Why were they afraid to be recognized for what they had done in their own communities? Since then, having read a number of memoirs by rescued Jews, I have come to realize that it was a ubiquitous phenomenon.

Perhaps the best-known episode of this sort can be found in Marcel Reich-Ranicki's memoirs. For decades now one of Germany's most influential literary critics, with an acerbic wit and erudition both admired and feared by the greatest of German writers, Reich-Ranicki as a boy moved from Poland to Germany only to be sent back in the forced expulsion of Polish Jews by the Nazis in 1938. He spent the early war years in the Warsaw ghetto, working for a time as a translator for the chairman of the Judenrat. He then hid, together with his wife, on the so-called Aryan side.

The relevant fragment of his bestselling memoirs, describing a moment after liberation, goes as follows: "We were about to leave when Bolek said: 'I have a drop of vodka here, let's drink a little glass.' I could sense that he had something else to say to us." Reich-Ranicki thus sets up the farewell scene, when he and his wife were leaving the apartment of the Polish couple who had saved their lives. "He was speaking slowly and seriously. 'I implore you, don't tell anyone that you were with us. I know this nation. They would never forgive us for sheltering two Jews.' Genia remained silent. I deliberated for a long time as to whether I should quote this frightening remark here. But, on the other hand, we have never forgotten that it was two Poles to whom we owe our lives—Bolek and Genia."[4]

Personal documents from the period leave no doubt that this same realization came as a shock to numerous survivors, while fear together with tangible persecution marred the lives of many rescuers after the war. "In conclusion of my story," writes Dr. Henryk Stecki, "I also want to

*Yad Vashem, or the Martyrs' and Heroes' Remembrance Authority, was established in Israel in order to perpetuate the memory of victims of the Holocaust. Article 9 of its founding law (passed in 1953) mandates the Authority to perpetuate the names "of the high minded righteous who risked their lives to save Jews." The Department for the Righteous Gentiles was established at Yad Vashem "to award honors to persons recognized as belonging to Hasidei Ummot ha-Olan [literally, "the pious ones of the nations of the world"—a rabbinic term denoting righteous Gentiles], who risked their lives to rescue Jews in the Holocaust" (*Encyclopedia Judaica*, vol. 16, p. 698).

mention that after I returned to Kraków, some 2–3 weeks following my departure from the village where I stayed last, it became known that I was a Jew. Already after this area got liberated I was threatened there with death, and the good, innocent [*"Bogu ducha winni"*] people who gave me shelter were threatened with flogging and having their house set on fire."[5]

Regina Almowa's husband served as an officer in the Polish army before the war. After an *Aktion* in Przemyśl she found herself in desperate straits.* "All acquaintances and good friends completely failed me," she writes in her deposition before the Jewish Historical Commission after the war. "[I]n the end I remembered the family of my husband's commanding officer and I was kept there for about 10 days. The younger lady probably would have kept me longer, but her mother was very nervous, so I decided that I must leave their house. I will always keep a recollection of this woman, but I will not mention her name because under the present circumstances I would risk exposing her to contempt from her compatriots. I find this all the time to be the case that people who saved the Jews do not want their fellow citizens to know about it."[6]

In the Memorial Book of the Ostrołęka Jews, a righteous Gentile named Przechodzień is commemorated with gratitude by the Holcman sisters. "He really helped us a lot, until peasants from nearby villages started to persecute him, called him 'a Jewish knave,' cursed him, and even threw stones at him," they wrote. "After the liberation we found out that he was murdered."[7]

An ethnographer who conducted almost two hundred interviews in the 1970s and 1980s with Polish villagers for her study about the image of the Jew in Polish folk culture never had any difficulty drawing people out on the subject.

The exception was the village of Mulawicze. In several successive homes I was received coldly when I asked the first question. When I got to the house of the village administrator, for a long time I carried on a general conversation with him until finally, after breaking the ice, I got to the point. Even here I encountered incomprehensible resistance, but in the end I managed to start the interview. At a certain moment the respondent

---

*In the jargon of the period, a Nazi sweep through a designated locality aiming to round up Jews for extermination was called an *Aktion*, in Polish, *akcja*, an action. The term is customarily used now in Holocaust literature.

said: "During the war, this boy with three fingers missing walked around the village; people helped him, and thanks to this he survived the war. . . ." Following this, in the greatest secrecy he revealed to me the name of his neighbor who had concealed a Jewish boy. . . . This woman, illiterate, living in poverty, saddled with four children and a sick husband who died shortly after, unhesitatingly took on her shoulders a risk which could have cost the lives of her entire family. The entire village . . . took responsibility for his survival. The village administrator gave warnings of visits by the Germans, who were stationed in the village school. Thanks to this collective effort the boy survived the war. What is most surprising in this whole matter is the concealing of this event to that day. In a certain sense, Mulawicze had still not ceased to conceal "Wintluk."[8]*

Why did Poles who assisted their Jewish neighbors in a time of mortal peril become social outcasts in their own communities after the war? Why would a remote village fearfully conceal its wartime rescue of a Jewish orphan? Whence anti-Semitism in Poland "after Auschwitz"? This book, in essence, should be viewed as an attempt to answer such questions.

I write here a narrowly focused story, and my subject is circumscribed. It is framed by the Holocaust and Communism, two landmarks of Eastern European Jewish experience. The latter serves as a boundary not solely because events described here take place while Communists were consolidating their rule over Eastern Europe, but also because local attitudes toward the Jews were refracted through the prism of the putative relationship between Jews and Communism. Indeed, the still dominant interpretation of postwar anti-Semitism in Poland attributes it to Jewish responsibility for the "Sovietization" of the country. Customarily this line of argument is referred to as "Judeo-Communism," or *żydokomuna*.

What I am about to tell in *Fear* involves overturning strongly held stereotypes and peeling off layers of prejudice. Wartime and postwar anti-Semitism in Poland has never been examined for what it was, but has always been conflated in the minds of Jews and Poles alike with something else, and conveniently deproblematized. In a well-known

---

*What comes to mind, by contrast, is the village of Chambon in France, which celebrates its collective wartime rescue of Jewish fellow citizens, has several websites, books written about it, a documentary film, a foundation.

quip by the onetime Israeli prime minister Yitzhak Shamir, Poles suck anti-Jewish hatred with their mothers' milk. In the Polish Catholic imagination, Jews are God-killers, they use the blood of Christian children for matzo, and they are also Communist. Both views are untenable in the light of common sense or empirical evidence. But to challenge and examine them in order to acquire a better understanding of postwar anti-Semitism, one has to move carefully.

The nature of prejudice is to make unwarranted totalizing claims, whereas understanding advances through elucidation of careful distinctions. These are directly opposed mental exercises. And if one tries to argue prejudice away by the usual procedure of testing hypotheses (that is, by pointing to alternative explanations, or false deductions, or limitations in the empirical evidence) one enters a kind of discourse where the prejudice's basic premise is already accepted. Instead of naming the bad faith from which the prejudice sprouted, we end up framing the argument, half-apologetically, as if we granted that the prejudicial claim were empirically derived. Yet simply to identify bad faith underlying a prejudice does not explain it away, either.

Since we cannot hope to find a direct way out of a tangled web of layered fictions and facts in a single push, I wondered what could be the best manner to present my inquiry. The answer emerged in the process of writing—as a circuitous effort of successive approximations. When trying to take apart a pile of elements that are loose yet wedged against one another, one may not produce a persuasive "either-or" story laid out in a chronological sequence. Instead, we must poke the pile repeatedly from many directions and at different angles, or else important residue will always remain. What I offer here, therefore, is not diachronic but analytical history. I go back and forth in time over different aspects of events bearing on understanding the phenomenon of postwar anti-Semitism in Poland. The flow of events is marked and distinct in the book, but it is also refracted in successive attempts to problematize issues from a perspective that is slightly but constantly changing. Furthermore, the text is in dialogic relationship with the footnotes, sometimes closing off and sometimes opening up alternative interpretive vistas.

I want readers turning the pages to experience from time to time a sense of discomfort. It is all to the good to feel compelled occasionally to go through a page or a chapter over again, querying the soundness of argument or the clarity of exposition, or else to move forward briskly in order to read in a rush what comes next, just to see if what so far has appeared odd and fragmented could possibly make sense as the story unfolds. I think it does in the end. But this is not a "nice" story and we should not be smoothly eased into it. I would not know how to lead anyone gently through it, anyway.

In what follows I make an effort to disentangle anti-Semitism in Poland after Auschwitz from various phenomena with which it has been conflated. I describe it in the dual context of the Holocaust and the imposition of Communist rule on Eastern and Central Europe. At the risk of running ahead of myself, let me simply assert here what emerges in the conclusion of the book by way, I believe, of a comprehensively documented story: it was widespread collusion in the Nazi-driven plunder, spoliation, and eventual murder of the Jews that generated Polish anti-Semitism after the war, not the alleged postwar Jewish collusion in the imposition of Communism on the Poles. Far from championing Jewish "interests" of any kind, the Communist authorities in Poland ignored the suffering of Poland's Jewish citizens at the hands of their neighbors both during and after the war. The Communist Party aimed to distance and insulate itself as much as it could from the "Jewish question" in order to gain a modicum of legitimacy in the eyes of the Polish population, and adopted what at best can be described as an attitude of benign neglect in matters Jewish. When Stalin's increasingly aggressive anti-Semitism factored in, the implicit social contract between Communist authorities and the newly subjugated Polish society—that they mutually benefited from considering the wartime fate of Polish Jews a nonissue; that they would not scrutinize what exactly happened to the Jews during the war; and that they would encourage and facilitate departure from the country by the remainder of Polish Jewry—became a given. My sense is that this was an implicit "give" for the "take" of power, which the Communists grabbed at the Soviet Union's and their own behest.

Here follows a quick guide to the organization of the book. In the first chapter, my intent is to convey the sense of betrayal widely shared among the Poles as a result of the experience of the Second World War and its political aftermath. In the chapter's closing pages, readers will find a narrative encapsulating the main events leading to the subjugation of the Polish society by the Communist Party, and turning the country into a satellite of the Soviet Union against the will of the majority of the Poles.

In chapter 2, I discuss a wide range of anti-Jewish practices in postwar Poland, including the commodification of Jews resulting from wartime plunder. I further argue that not only society at large but also the administrative apparatus and the judiciary in Communist Party–dominated Poland manifested what must be recognized as institutionalized anti-Semitism.

In chapter 3, I present a detailed description of the most violent anti-Semitic episode in postwar Europe (certainly, the culmination of anti-Jewish violence in Poland at the time)—the pogrom in Kielce. In chapter 4, I discuss reactions to the pogrom among various milieus of the Polish population, while all along drawing observations concerning the place of Jews in the moral economy of postwar Polish society.

In chapter 5, I reflect on how the Holocaust and the behavior of the lower strata of Polish society toward the Jews has been registered in the collective consciousness of Polish intelligentsia.

In chapter 6, I sketch the historical antecedents of a belief widely held by Poland's population and its historians, that Jews have a special affinity for Communism. I examine the resulting notion of "Judeo-Communism" (*żydokomuna*) in its applicability to the interwar period, and the framing of the so-called Jewish question by Stalin and the Soviet Communist Party during the war and immediately thereafter. Finally, I examine the myth of Judeo-Communism and how it related to political practices of the Communist regime in Poland in the immediate postwar period. And in my conclusions I attempt to pull together various interpretive strands elucidated earlier in the book.

FEAR

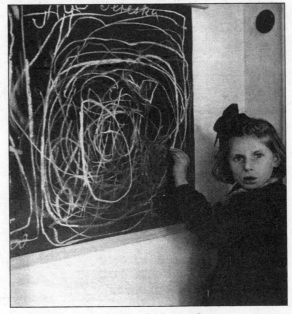

A girl named Tereska, drawing a house.

I

POLAND
ABANDONED

WARS IN EUROPE have simultaneously been periods of social revolutions, and the Second World War is a good case in point.[1] Indeed, one could argue that in Eastern Europe the entire decade from 1939 to 1948—despite the clear divide of 1945, which saw the defeat of the Third Reich—was one continuous epoch of radical transformation toward a totalitarian model of society, imposed first by the Nazis and then by the Soviets.[2]

While the war, it is true, had an enormous impact on every European society, producing both a new map of Europe and a new paradigm of European politics, Poland's case was unique among the belligerent countries because of the scale of devastation and upheaval under the impact of Nazi occupation from 1939 until 1945 (supplemented by the Soviet annexation of eastern Poland from September 1939 until June 1941).* As a

---

*On August 23, 1939, Nazi Germany and the Soviet Union concluded a treaty of nonaggression, known in historiography as the Ribbentrop-Molotov Pact after the names of the foreign ministers who signed the document in Moscow. A week later, on September 1, 1939, World War II began. As agreed between the signatories, the Red Army marched into Poland soon after the German attack. In the secret protocols attached to the August treaty, the Soviet Union reserved for itself a "sphere of interests" including Bessarabia, Estonia, Latvia, and the better part of Poland. The original demarcation line between the Nazi and Soviet zones of occupation—splitting the capital city, Warsaw, in half along the Vistula River—appeared in the September 25, 1939, issue of the main Soviet newspaper, *Pravda*.

On September 28 in Moscow, the German-Soviet Boundary and Friendship Treaty was signed and a somewhat modified territorial division of recent conquests was agreed upon. Stalin settled for only half of Poland's territory and drew the frontier eastward,

result of the war, the country suffered an unprecedented demographic catastrophe. It lost its minorities—Jews in the Holocaust, and Ukrainians and Germans following border shifts and population movements after the war. A third of its urban residents were missing at war's end. Poland's elites in all walks of life were wiped out. More than half of its lawyers were no more, along with two fifths of its medical doctors and one third of its university professors and Roman Catholic clergy. It lost its choice civil servants, army officers, and sportsmen. Several million people were displaced, either because they were deported, or because their domiciles were destroyed, or because the frontiers were changed. Somewhere between 4.5 million and 5 million Polish citizens lost their lives during the war (including 3 million Polish Jews), and several million more experienced imprisonment, slave labor, or forced resettlement.* The scale of material devastation matched the volume of population loss and trauma. Virtually every family in Poland was victimized in one way or another, and many catastrophically.

Particular devastation was suffered by Poland's Jews, an ancient community that was physically destroyed as a result of the war. No more than 10 percent survived the Nazi onslaught—some in German camps, some hiding among Gentile neighbors, most in the Soviet interior, where they fled or had been deported earlier by the Soviet secret police. While half of Poland's prewar territory was under Soviet control from mid-September 1939 through June 1941, a direct result of collaboration between Hitler and Stalin at the time, more than one million Polish Jews (out of the total of approximately 3.5 million) lived in the Soviet zone.

---

following what used to be known as the Curzon Line (a demarcation line suggested by the British foreign secretary, Lord Curzon, in a message to the Soviet foreign minister, Chicherin, during the Polish-Bolshevik War of 1920). In exchange for giving up a good chunk of Poland, including half of the capital city, he consolidated his grip on the Baltic states by bringing Lithuania, Latvia, and Estonia into the fold. Two secret protocols were included with the treaty. The first one amended the boundaries agreed upon in August; the second, barely two sentences long, eliminated for the next two years the anti-Nazi Communist underground in Poland: "Both parties will tolerate in their territories no Polish agitation which affects the territories of the other party. They will suppress in their territories all beginnings of such agitation and inform each other concerning suitable measures for this purpose." We need to know these preliminaries to begin our story, which is embedded in the war experience of Poland's inhabitants.

*The often quoted estimate of total demographic losses—6 million—advanced immediately after the war was certainly an exaggeration. *Dzieje Najnowsze* devoted an entire issue to the study of Polish casualties during the Second World War. An eminent economic historian, Czesław Łuczak, surveying the present state of research in the introduction to the issue, proposed a more likely total of 5 million—2 million Polish non-Jews and 2.9 to 3 million Polish Jews (pp. 12, 14). I am grateful to Professor Antony Polonsky for this reference.

Some 100,000 to 120,000 Jews were deported in 1940–1941 and forcibly settled in the Soviet interior, as part of broader repressive measures aiming at Sovietization of this area. It was the irony of Jewish fate that being subjected to Soviet repression had saved many Jews from death at the hands of the Nazis. In Polish historiography, the Jewish fate was usually presented as a separate story from that of the rest of Polish society. There was a kernel of truth in this approach, since the Nazis did indeed single out Jews for "special treatment," but it conveniently enabled historians to pass in silence over the complex phenomenon of interaction between Polish Jews and their non-Jewish neighbors throughout the period of German occupation. Polish neighbors had witnessed up close the extermination of the Jews, and they often availed themselves of the opportunities afforded by their attendant spoliation. The story of this opportunistic complicity with the Nazis is only now being told in Poland, and I plot it into the narrative as we go along since it provides a crucial background for understanding postwar anti-Semitism.[3]

The Underground State

Despite the violence of foreign invaders, it will be noted in the historical annals that Polish society confronted the horrors of the Soviet and Nazi occupations with heroism and resilience. According to Nazi racial doctrine, Poles were considered "subhuman" (*Untermenschen*). Unlike the Jews, however, the Poles were not scheduled for extermination but were relegated in the Nazi vision of the "New Order" in Europe to the status of slaves fit only for utilization as physical labor. In response to policies of occupation that denied them rights and material resources necessary for survival, Polish society mounted the most formidable and complex resistance movement that the Nazis had to face anywhere in occupied Europe.

In addition to an underground military organization, the Home Army (Armia Krajowa, AK), which at its peak boasted over 300,000 sworn-in members, an elaborate network of institutions was set up in occupied Poland, which together came to be known as the Underground State (Państwo Podziemne). This "state" included clandestine versions of prewar political parties and a shadow government administration (Delegatura) headed by a representative of the legal Polish government-in-exile, which resided first in Angers and then, after the defeat of France in 1940, in London. A skeleton parliament functioned in the underground, bringing together representatives of the four main political parties—the National Democratic Party, the Peasant Party, the Polish Socialist Party, and the Labor Party, liberal in outlook—who regularly consulted with one another and the government delegate. Political leaders, the government, and the army command in London maintained contact with the home country through a clandestine network of couriers and radio operators.

The Underground State was funded by the government-in-exile, from London. Apart from supplying secret military and political organizations, this money was also used to sustain civil society, including, for example, an illegal school system, a welfare network, and an organization, Żegota, that was set up in 1942 in order to aid Jews who were hiding from the Nazis. More than 2,000 underground newspapers and magazines were put out in Poland at one time or another during the occupation. Several made only an ephemeral appearance, with limited circulation, but others were published continuously for a number of years. The most important weekly of the Home Army, the *Information Bulletin* (*Biuletyn Informacyjny*), reached a hefty circulation of 43,000 copies. During the period of its most intense activity, the Warsaw office of the Bureau of Information and Propaganda of the Home Army used five tons of paper monthly.[4]

Henri Michel, the doyen of French historians of the resistance, could hardly be suspected of playing to a domestic audience when he concluded that the Polish underground had enjoyed a strength and a scope unparalleled in Europe.[5] The story first became known in the English-speaking world when one of the most courageous couriers of the underground, Jan Karski (who brought direct evidence to Prime Minister Winston S. Churchill and President Franklin D. Roosevelt that the Nazis were exterminating European Jewry), wrote his slightly fictionalized *Story of a Secret State*.* It became a bestseller soon after its publication, by Houghton Mifflin, during the winter of 1944–45.[6]

The Underground State was the product of a broad mobilization of societal energies. It came about as a result of myriad individual initiatives, which were then institutionalized and put in a broader organizational framework. One could have expected that such a remarkable

---

*Film and television audiences all over the world remember a lengthy interview with Jan Karski from Claude Lanzmann's film *Shoah*, in which he describes the circumstances of his mission and meetings with leading politicians in England and the United States, whom he informed about the tragic fate of the Jews.

collective achievement would provide a good foundation for postwar reconstruction. But it was not to be. As a by-product of Great Power politics and the division of postwar Europe into spheres of influence, all the efforts and sacrifice that had gone into the creation of this contested realm, this civil society that had defied a ruthless regime of occupation, were soon dismissed as a misguided and wrongheaded enterprise. Once Poland had been liberated by the Red Army in 1944–45, any earlier association with the so-called London underground was labeled a stigma and a liability by the emergent Communist organizers of the public order. Soon after liberation the Home Army was portrayed in propaganda posters as "a spittle-bespattered dwarf of reactionary forces" (*"AK—zapluty karzeł reakcji"*) and its veterans had to either hide their past or else risk arrest, internment, censure, or humiliation.* How did this situation—which led to a pervasive sense of historical injustice among a significant majority of the Polish population—come about?

Discovery of the Katyń Mass Graves

In the concluding stages of the Second World War, the Germans were being pushed out of Poland by the rapid advance of the Red Army. For the leaders of Poland's Underground State, this was far from a desirable outcome. The Soviet Communists were regarded as the historic enemies of Polish independence. Twice since the October Revolution of 1917, they had asserted their ambitions of westward expansion in military terms. In 1920, the course of the Polish-Soviet war "miraculously" turned at the outskirts of Warsaw, with fighting continuing until the eventual peace

---

*On September 15, 1944, the Political Bureau of the Polish Workers' Party (as the Communist Party was known at the time) accepted the following text of a declaration that Home Army soldiers were supposed to sign: "I, . . . , having been sent to an internment camp on suspicion of negative attitude towards the only legal organizations of the Polish state—the KRN and the PKWN [Communist Party–sponsored organizations, whose genesis I later explain] and the supreme command of the Polish army, declare from my own unforced and free will the following: 1. I appreciate the activity of the KRN and PKWN as indispensable for our nation and in my further work I will remain loyal and obedient to all their regulations, as befits a Polish soldier; 2. I understand and condemn the abominable activity of the leaders of the AK and other affiliated organizations, who helped the Hitlerite occupier, and weakened the Polish army and the unity of the Polish nation by their diversionary activity . . ." and so on, in the same spirit, for two more paragraphs, promising in the end to aid "the KRN and PKWN" in combating these "pernicious influences" (Krystyna Kersten, *Rok pierwszy*, p. 49).

I wish to acknowledge my gratitude to Tim Snyder and Marci Shore for their efforts to come up with an English translation of the bizarre phrase *zapluty karzeł reakcji*. We settled after a long discussion on "spittle-bespattered dwarf."

treaty of Riga.* And in 1939, the Red Army invaded Poland in collusion with Hitler, resulting in Soviet occupation of approximately half of Poland until June 1941. When Nazi Germany launched its assault on the Soviet Union in the summer of 1941 and the USSR finally joined the Allied cause, the Polish government-in-exile renewed diplomatic relations with the USSR.

The Soviet Union initially buckled before the onslaught of the Nazi war machine and welcomed all the assistance and friends it could muster. A period of intense Polish-Soviet engagement ensued. A treaty was signed between the two governments, and several hundred thousand Polish citizens were "amnestied" in the Soviet Union. A welfare network was established in the USSR to provide for the needs of destitute Polish citizens just released from labor camps and forced settlement in the Soviet interior. At designated assembly points, able-bodied men could join units of a new Polish army, which the Soviets agreed would be formed on their territory.†

But as the fortunes of war gradually turned and as the Soviet Union proved a formidable member of the anti-Nazi coalition, Churchill and Roosevelt developed an ever greater sympathy with Soviet territorial claims and security guarantees in postwar Europe. During their Big Three meeting with Joseph Stalin in Teheran late in 1943, they agreed that after the war the Soviet Union's border could be moved far to the west, at Poland's expense, roughly to the Curzon Line. In this manner, without consulting or informing the Polish government-in-exile in London, they sanctioned a territorial expansion reminiscent of what the Soviet Union had acquired as a result of the Ribbentrop-Molotov Pact in 1939.

As an emboldened Stalin began to maneuver for a postwar settlement that would eventually lead to the Communist subjugation of East-

---

*In Polish folklore and historiography, Józef Piłsudski's counteroffensive, which pushed the Bolsheviks back from Warsaw, has been referred to as "the miracle on the Vistula" ("cud nad Wisłą"). August 15, the day he opened the counteroffensive, was celebrated during the interwar years as a national holiday in Poland.

†Prime Minister General Władysław Sikorski signed the treaty with the Soviet Union in the face of vigorous protests by leading Polish politicians in London. The reason for their opposition was Stalin's refusal to guarantee Poland's territorial integrity in its prewar borders by renouncing the territorial acquisitions made by the Soviet Union in 1939. The pretext for Soviet reluctance was that the population of the occupied territories had allegedly expressed a sovereign wish to join the Soviet Union in a referendum held on October 22, 1939. (On the manner in which this "referendum" was conducted, see my *Revolution from Abroad*, chapter 2.) Nevertheless, Sikorski decided that he must sign the treaty without delay, for while territorial disputes could be settled in the future, hundreds of thousands of Poles lingering in Soviet captivity were in danger of death each day from mistreatment and destitution. To save their lives he thought he had to act immediately.

ern Europe, Polish-Soviet relations soured. Indeed, the deterioration had begun even before the Teheran conference. In the spring of 1943, the USSR severed diplomatic relations with the Polish government following the discovery of mass graves in Katyń.

Back in 1941 and 1942, when the Polish army was being organized in the Soviet Union by General Władysław Anders,* Polish authorities could not locate thousands of officers who had served in the eastern part of the country during the September 1939 campaign and who had been taken prisoner by the Soviets. Polish envoys repeatedly asked the Soviet authorities to find these men and release them promptly, if only because they were needed to staff the newly created military units, but to no avail. All traces of several thousand men—many identified by already released colleagues or by family members with whom they had corresponded briefly from captivity—vanished around the spring of 1940. In one of the most absurd and cynical dialogues of the war, Prime Minister Sikorski, most amicably received on his first visit to the Kremlin by Joseph Stalin, got the Soviet leader visibly concerned about the fate of the missing men. In the end, after Sikorski's repeated inquiries concerning their whereabouts, Stalin feigned incredulity that not everybody had been freed despite the amnesty decreed by the Soviet government. When Sikorski insisted that he had a list of several thousand officers who had been held in captivity by the Red Army and had not been released, Stalin replied, "It is impossible. They must have escaped." "Where could they escape?" demanded a surprised General Anders. "Well, perhaps to Manchuria," retorted Stalin without missing a beat.[7]

Then, in the early spring of 1943, in the vicinity of a little hamlet called Katyń, inside a former Soviet secret police (NKVD) compound, a German communications unit disinterred from a mass grave the remains of executed Polish officers. They had been buried in uniform, many with bullet holes in the back of their skulls, and personal documents and letters from home stuffed in their pockets. It is now known that on March 5, 1940, the Soviet Politburo had issued an order to have these men executed. Stalin's signature, together with those of Molotov, Voroshilov, and Mikoyan, appears on the document.[8] On the basis of this decision, 21,857 people (some 15,000 of them POWs) were put to death. Of this number, 4,421 were executed and buried in the mass grave at Katyń. The story remained a closely held secret by the Soviet leadership, which denied any

*Hence its shorthand designation as "Anders' Army."

complicity in the crime until April 1990, when President Mikhail Gorbachev made a tacit admission of Soviet responsibility. Finally, on October 14, 1992, President Boris Yeltsin passed copies of the 1940 Politburo decision to the Polish president, Lech Wałęsa.

Back in 1943, the Nazis used the discovery as a scoop in their anti-Bolshevik propaganda campaign. The Polish government-in-exile called on the International Red Cross to appoint a commission to carry out an exhumation and to issue an expert opinion about when, and therefore by whom, the crime had been committed. But no one really doubted that for once the Nazi regime was telling the truth. The Soviet government, which all along decried the purported German discovery as a hoax contrived by the Germans to mask their own war crimes, broke off diplomatic relations with Poland on April 25, 1943.

From that point on, the Soviets played an intricate game in order both to change postwar Polish frontiers *and* to install a regime in Poland to their own liking. On the one hand, they used diplomacy and the Big Three consultative process to achieve the desired results. On the other hand, they carefully scripted the moves of the Communist-sponsored underground in Poland.

The Destruction of Warsaw

The most ruthless and telling expression of Stalin's determination to subjugate Poland and destroy patriotic opposition to Communist rule after the war was his refusal to assist the Warsaw insurgents in the summer of 1944. The Home Army launched the Warsaw Uprising (as the episode is called in Polish historiography) on August 1, 1944. It followed a period of German rout by a months-long Soviet offensive. Columns of disheveled German soldiers and civilians had streamed through Warsaw's streets for weeks. The sound of guns from the approaching Russian front could be heard in the city. The rank-and-file of the Home Army was itching for a fight. As the front line got nearer to the Vistula River, the Home Army command was anxious to liberate the capital city *before* the Soviets could enter it in pursuit of the Nazis.*

Without coordinating the move with the Soviets, the Home Army began the insurrection. Warsaw's insurgents foresaw a combat of a few

---

*As was called for in AK's plan Burza ("Tempest"), directing that retreating Germans be challenged wherever possible in order to assert the authority of Poland's legitimate government and establish a skeletal administration prior to the arrival of the Red Army.

days' duration. By then, however, the Wehrmacht was already regrouping to organize a line of defense along the river. As the Soviets halted their advance, the insurgents were left to battle the Germans for almost two months. The Red Army, poised across the Vistula, let the Germans slaughter Home Army soldiers and civilian inhabitants of the city alike. Almost a quarter of a million people perished in the hostilities. The flower of Poland's anti-Nazi underground movement was killed, and the city was reduced to a pile of rubble.

In the initial stages of the uprising, the Soviets pretended that nothing of significance was going on in the city. Later, when the fact of the combat in Warsaw could no longer be denied, Stalin refused landing rights to Allied airplanes flying supply missions from bases in Italy—several hundred miles over enemy territory—to the beleaguered city. Winston Churchill's memoirs capture the story in dramatic detail. On August 14, Churchill sent a telegram to his foreign secretary, Anthony Eden: "It will cause the Russians much annoyance if the suggestion that the Polish patriots in Warsaw were deserted gets afoot, but they can easily prevent it by operations well within their power. It certainly is very curious that at the moment when the Underground Army has revolted, the Russian armies should have halted their offensive against Warsaw and withdrawn some distance. For them to send in all the quantities of machine-guns and ammunition required by the Poles for their heroic fight would involve only a flight of 100 miles. I have been talking to [Air Marshal] Slessor, trying to send all possible assistance from here. But what have the Russians done? I think it would be better if you sent a message to Stalin through Molotov referring to the implications that are afoot in many quarters and requesting that the Russians should send all the help they can."

Two days later, on August 16, the American ambassador was called in to the Soviet Foreign Ministry by Molotov's deputy, Andrei Vyshinsky, who "explain[ed] that he wished to avoid the possibility of misunderstanding, [and] read out the following astonishing statement: 'The Soviet Government cannot of course object to English or American aircraft dropping arms in the region of Warsaw, since this is an American and British affair. But they decidedly object to American or British aircraft, after dropping arms in the region of Warsaw, landing on Soviet territory, since the Soviet Government do not wish to associate themselves either directly or indirectly with the adventure in Warsaw.' "⁹

Churchill was livid, exchanging messages with Roosevelt on this subject every day. But neither man was prepared to challenge Stalin and take a decisive stand. In his memoirs, the American diplomat and historian George Kennan identified the Soviet response toward the Warsaw Uprising as a critical event that

> more than anything that occurred to that point, brought the Western governments face to face with what they were up against in Stalin's Polish policy. For if the inactivity of the Red Army forces as they sat, passive, on the other side of the river and watched the slaughter by the Germans of the Polish heroes of the rebellion was not yet eloquent enough as an expression of the Soviet attitude, then the insolent denial by Stalin and Molotov to Ambassador Harriman of permission for use of the American shuttle base in the Ukraine to facilitate the dropping of arms and supplies to the beleaguered Poles . . . left no room for misunderstanding. I was personally not present at this fateful meeting with Stalin and Molotov; but I can recall the appearance of the ambassador and General Deane as they returned, in the wee hours of the night, shattered by the experience. There was no doubt in any of our minds as to the implications of the position the Soviet leaders had taken. This was a gauntlet thrown down, in a spirit of malicious glee, before the Western powers. What it was meant to imply was: "We intend to have Poland, lock, stock, and barrel. We don't care a fig for those Polish underground fighters who have not accepted Communist authority. To us, they are no better than the Germans; and if they and the Germans slaughter each other off, so much the better." . . . It has been my opinion, ever since, that this was the moment when, if ever, there should have been a full-fledged and realistic political showdown with the Soviet leaders.*

The "Lublin Poles," or the Soviet Politics of the Faits Accomplis

Soon after the Red Army, in pursuit of the withdrawing Germans, crossed the prewar Polish-Soviet border in early January 1944, the Polish

---

*Just as the uprising began in Warsaw, Polish Prime Minister Stanisław Mikołajczyk spent ten days in Moscow. He went there from London to work out a formula for future collaboration with the Soviets and Polish Communists. "Had dinner last night at the British embassy with the Polish Prime Minister, Mikołajczyk, and the members of his entourage," Kennan jotted down in his diary. "I wished that instead of mumbling words of official optimism we had had the judgment and the good taste to bow our heads in silence before the

government-in-exile could no longer assert its authority over the liberated areas of Poland. The Soviets kept arresting locally based Home Army units and networks of the Government Delegate's administrative apparatus as the front moved westward. Soviet-sponsored organizations, the National Council for the Country (Krajowa Rada Narodowa, KRN) soon followed by the Polish Committee of National Liberation (Polski Komitet Wyzwolenia Narodowego, PKWN), were given a free hand to fill the power vacuum and appoint their own administration.

The KRN was established by the underground Polish Communist Party on December 31, 1943. This was the first in a series of institutions duplicating the London-affiliated Underground State and, allegedly, representing a broad spectrum of Polish society. In reality it was a "Potemkin village," a national council entirely controlled by the Communist Party.* Several months later, on July 20, 1944, the PKWN was established in Moscow and the Soviets authorized it to organize the administration of the liberated Polish territories.

The independence of Communist-ruled Poland dates symbolically from July 22, 1944. In the "Polish People's Republic," the most important national holiday was celebrated in commemoration of the "July 22 Manifesto" (or "July Manifesto"), issued by the PKWN in the city of Lublin and proclaiming the country's independence.[†] On December 31, 1944, the National Council transformed the PKWN into a provisional government, which was immediately recognized by the Soviet Union. In this manner a series of faits accomplis was produced in Poland while the legitimate government was still far away in London.

Ever since the Red Army's entry into Polish territory, the Communist Party had a virtual monopoly on the use of coercion necessary to impose political order. Initially the Soviet security services, the NKVD, bore the brunt of ferreting out and neutralizing the remnants of the London government–affiliated underground. Some 60,000 people were arrested by the NKVD before the summer of 1945 and up to 20,000

---

tragedy of a people who have been our allies, whom we have helped to save from our enemies, and whom we cannot save from our friends" (George F. Kennan, *Memoirs, 1925–1950*, p. 210).

*See, for example, the memoirs of the American ambassador to Poland, Arthur Bliss Lane, who notes the establishment of the Communist-controlled Socialist, Peasant, and Christian Labor Parties, even though "parties with these identical names had existed in Poland for years" (Arthur Bliss Lane, *I Saw Poland Betrayed: An American Ambassador Reports to the American People*, p. 112).

†Actually the "July 22 Manifesto" was issued on July 21 and in a different place, namely in the little village of Chełm near Lublin.

Home Army soldiers were deported into the Soviet camps.[10] In time,
by 1944–45, a homegrown Polish apparatus of public security began
to take over these responsibilities. It was first called the Resort of Public Security, but was soon relabeled the Ministry of Public Security
(Ministerstwo Bezpieczeństwa Publicznego, MBP).*

The western Allies kept pressuring the Polish government in London to seek accommodation with the Soviets and with the Polish Communists whom the Soviets championed. Facts on the ground could no
longer be ignored. On January 17, 1945, the Red Army began its final
push to Berlin, crossed the Vistula River in force, and liberated Warsaw.
The Yalta Conference was held three weeks later, in early February, with
Churchill, Stalin, and Roosevelt in attendance. As Anthony Eden wrote
in his memoirs, it was decided there to put an end to the intolerable situation "with the Russians recognizing one Polish Government in Lublin
and ourselves another in London."[11] The Americans and the British insisted on the formation of a new provisional government, which in addition to the so-called Lublin Poles would also include Stanisław
Mikołajczyk, the Peasant Party leader from London, as well as other
"moderate" Polish politicians from abroad. Such an interim government
would then be entrusted with organizing, as soon as possible, free elections in Poland.[†]

The Symbolism of "Yalta"

"This war is not as in the past," Stalin told a young Yugoslav communist
leader, Milovan Djilas, in 1945; "whoever occupies a territory also im-
poses his own social system. . . . It cannot be otherwise."[12] And much like
its tragic fate in 1939, the postwar destiny of Poland was also decided by
outside powers.

*The MBP's most politicized and feared branch was the Security Service, colloquially
called the Bezpieka or UB, deployed all over the country through a network of Public Security Offices (Urzędy Bezpieczeństwa Publicznego). Twice as numerous as the UB was the
ubiquitous regular police force, or Citizens' Militia (Milicja Obywatelska, MO), also subsumed under the Ministry of Public Security. A uniformed quasi-military branch of the Security Service, the Internal Security Corps (Korpus Bezpieczeństwa Wewnetrznego, KBW),
and an auxiliary police force, the Ochotnicze Rezerwy Milicji Obywatelskiej (ORMO)
(Voluntary Reserves of the Citizens' Militia), were also available. As needed, regular army
units could be deployed to quell disturbances, or to assist in large-scale cleanup operations
(primarily by the KBW) against larger groups of armed anti-Communist resisters or the
Ukrainian nationalist insurgency, the UPA, which was active in the southeast of the country.
†Here is a relevant fragment from Charles Bohlen's memoirs: "[A]t a meeting of the
Foreign Ministers at Stalin's villa, the formula for Poland was finally agreed to. The key para-

Western leaders had few illusions concerning Stalin's intentions toward Eastern Europe. Indeed, they recognized the Soviet Union's security interests in the area as legitimate, and granted Stalin the prerogative
of ensuring that local regimes did not include politicians hostile to the
USSR. But with this caveat, Roosevelt and Churchill wanted to believe
that their efforts to bring freedom to Eastern Europe were not in vain.
Both statesmen also had an audience at home that needed to be persuaded of the same. In just such a moment of wishful thinking (I'd like to
believe it was not pure cynicism) Churchill addressed the House of
Commons on February 27, 1945, upon his return from Yalta: "The impression I brought back from the Crimea, and from all my other con-
tacts, is that Marshal Stalin and the Soviet leaders wish to live in
honourable friendship and equality with the Western democracies. I feel
also that their word is their bond. I know of no Government which
stands to its obligations, even in its own despite, more solidly than the
Russian Soviet Government. I decline absolutely to embark here on a
discussion about Russian good faith."[13]*

In all fairness, the discussions over the fate of Poland proved very
difficult. "The Polish question" occupied most of the agenda of the Yalta
Conference, was brought up at seven out of eight of its plenary meetings,

---

graphs in the final agreement on Poland, which became a subject of bitter controversy, read
as follows: 'A new situation has been created in Poland as a result of her complete liberation
by the Red Army. This calls for the establishment of a Polish Provisional Government which
can be more broadly based than was possible before the recent liberation of Western Poland.
The Provisional Government which is now functioning in Poland should be reorganized on
a broader democratic basis with the inclusion of democratic leaders from Poland itself and
from Poles abroad. This new government should then be called the Polish Provisional Government of National Unity. . . . This Polish Provisional Government of National Unity shall
be pledged to the holding of free and unfettered elections as soon as possible on the basis of
universal suffrage and secret ballot. In these elections all democratic and anti-Nazi Parties
shall have the right to take part and put forward candidates' " (Charles E. Bohlen, *Witness to
History, 1929–1969*, p. 191).

*The famous piece of paper on which Churchill, a few months earlier in Moscow, wrote
down the Balkan countries and jotted percentages of relative "predominance" there after the
war by Russia and the other Allies did not, for obvious reasons, include Poland. Which was
just as well, for the agreement also proved as flimsy as the half-sheet of paper it was sketched
on. Only for Greece did Churchill get his numbers right, and even that came at the price of
costly British military intervention in a bloody civil war: "I wrote out on a half-sheet of
paper, Rumania: Russia—90%, the others—10%; Greece: Great Britain (in accord with
USA)—90%, Russia—10%; Yugoslavia: 50%–50%; Hungary: 50%–50%; Bulgaria: Russia—
75%, the others—25%. I pushed this across to Stalin, who had by then heard the translation.
There was a slight pause. Then he took his blue pencil and made a large tick upon it, and
passed it back to us. It was all settled in no more time than it takes to set down" (Winston S.
Churchill, *Triumph and Tragedy*, p. 227).

and is remembered as the most difficult and time-consuming subject by many participants who later wrote important memoirs.* Great Britain went to war over Poland, which was its oldest and most faithful ally. It was a matter of British honor—as Churchill repeatedly stated and was in turn reminded of during subsequent debate on the Polish question in the House of Commons—to ensure freedom and sovereignty for Poland in the postwar world.

Even though final arrangements concerning Poland's postwar boundaries and government were worked out also at meetings held in Teheran and in Potsdam, for the Poles, as a puzzled young British journalist discovered almost four decades after the events, "Yalta" remained the shorthand symbolic point of reference. "When I first came to Poland I kept hearing a very strange word. 'Yowta,' my new acquaintances sighed, 'yowta!,' and conversation ebbed into melancholy silence. Did 'yowta' mean fate, I wondered, was it an expression like 'that's life'?"

" 'Yalta' (Polish pronunciation 'yowta') is where the story of Solidarity begins," writes Timothy Garton Ash in the introduction to his brilliant report on the birth, during the summer of 1980, of the Solidarity movement that eventually, ten years later, brought the downfall of Communism in Eastern Europe. " 'Yalta' for the Poles means that, after their army had been the first to resist Hitler, after Britain had gone to war in defense of Poland's independence and Polish servicemen had fought courageously in defense of Britain after some six million of their compatriots (one in every five citizens of the pre-war Polish Republic) had died in the war—after all this, their country was delivered up by their western allies, Britain and America, into the famously tender care of 'Uncle Joe' Stalin."[14][†]

The unwillingness of the Polish government-in-exile to make an accommodation with Stalin's demands finally wore out the country's Western allies. Prime Minister Stanisław Mikołajczyk, more amenable to the requirements of postwar Realpolitik than his cabinet colleagues, resigned his position on November 24, 1944.[‡] By April, under

---

*"The British record contains an interchange on this topic of nearly eighteen thousand words between Stalin, Roosevelt, and myself," noted Churchill in *Triumph and Tragedy* (p. 365). "The most difficult question of all at Yalta was Poland," wrote Ambassador Charles E. Bohlen in his memoirs (*Witness to History,* p. 187; see also pp. 188–92). And see Anthony Eden, *The Memoirs,* pp. 597–99.

†Garton Ash uses the once accepted figure of 6 million dead for Poland's losses during the Second World War.

‡Mikolajczyk was named prime minister of the Polish government in London on July 14, 1943, after the death of General Sikorski.

Churchill's prodding, he was already prepared to return to Poland as a leader of an independent Peasant Party. In June, he was negotiating in Moscow the composition of a "Provisional Government of National Unity," in which a handful of politicians from London would be given portfolios.

The agreement concluded on June 23, 1945, was signed under a bad omen—two days after Mikołajczyk's colleagues, the sixteen leaders of the Polish underground, were tried and sentenced in Moscow to long prison terms.* But the symbolism of the trial served only as a background to a message communicated to Mikołajczyk directly: that he was going back to Poland at the sufferance of the Communists, to be the window dressing for a show they intended to run as they pleased. In a moment of candor during negotiations leading to the establishment of the Provisional Government of National Unity, the Polish Communist leader Władysław Gomułka put it succinctly and without equivocation: "You can shout all you want that blood of the Polish nation is being spilled, that NKVD rules Poland, but this will not turn us back from our path, *władzy raz zdobytej nie oddamy nigdy*"—"Once we have taken power, we will never give it up."[15]

Mikołajczyk's Peasant Party (which adopted the name Polish Peasant Party [Polskie Stronnictwo Ludowe, PSL]) was given 55 seats in the provisional parliament, the KRN, numbering 288 deputies altogether, while Mikołajczyk himself was named second deputy prime minister and the minister of agriculture and land reform. Another of his party colleagues, Władysław Kiernik, got the Ministry of Public Administration. But the real power in the state and a real source of patronage in the countryside were located somewhere else, outside the prerogatives of ministries headed by Peasant Party politicians. The Ministry of Public Security, taken firmly in hand by the Communist Stanisław Radkiewicz, was

*Winston Churchill offers a background and a telling description of the "Trial of the Sixteen" in his memoirs: "At the beginning of March 1945 the Polish Underground were invited by the Russian Political Police to send a delegation to Moscow to discuss the formation of a united Polish Government along the lines of the Yalta agreement. This was followed by a written guarantee of personal safety, and it was understood that the party would later be allowed, if the negotiations were successful, to travel to London for talks with the Polish Government in exile. On March 27 General Leopold Okulicki, the successor of General Bór Komorowski in command of the Underground Army, and two other leaders, had a meeting in a suburb of Warsaw with a Soviet representative. They were joined the following day by eleven leaders representing the major political parties in Poland. No one returned from the rendezvous. On April 6 the Polish Government in exile issued a statement in London giving the outline of this sinister episode. The most valuable representatives of the Polish Underground had disappeared without a trace in spite of the formal Russian offer of safe-conduct...."

the enforcement arm of the state, independent of the Ministry of Public Administration. Land redistribution that truly benefited recipients (an urgent social problem in Poland, where poverty in the countryside and demand for land reform were among the most salient issues of the inter-war period) was carried out primarily in the so-called incorporated ter-ritories, the western part of Poland, which before the war had belonged to Germany. A separate Ministry of Incorporated Territories had been established for the purpose of supervising integration of this area with the rest of the country, and the first secretary of the Communist Party (the PPR), Władysław Gomułka, was in charge of it. By 1949 peasants had received from the state over 6 million hectares of land (4.4 million in the newly incorporated territories), distributed to enlarge some 250,000 small individual holdings and create 800,000 new family farms.[16]

On June 27, 1945, Stanisław Mikołajczyk returned to Warsaw to a tu-multuous reception. On July 5, the United States, Great Britain, and France officially recognized the Provisional Government of National Unity. As provided for in stipulations of the Yalta Conference, the Pro-visional Government was supposed to hold within a year "free and unfet-tered elections" in Poland. Mikołajczyk bargained that the United States and Britain would be able to hold Stalin to his promise and extract the fulfillment of this commitment.

From then on, the Communist takeover developed as a three-pronged offensive. In the first place it aimed at the destruction, primarily through police terror, of the post–Home Army network of illegal orga-nizations. Second, the Communists maneuvered to crush the legal oppo-sition, the PSL, through propaganda, manipulation of the electoral process, and direct physical intimidation. And third, they strove to ren-der ever more groups in society dependent on the state, in which all power, in time, was monopolized by the Communist Party.

"On May 18 Stalin publicly denied that the arrested Polish leaders had even been in-vited to Moscow, and asserted that they were mere 'diversionists' who would be dealt with according to 'a law similar to the British Defence of the Realm Act.' The Soviet Government refused to move from this position. Nothing more was heard of the victims of this trap until the case against them opened on June 18. It was conducted in the usual Communist manner. The prisoners were accused of subversion, terrorism, and espionage, and all except one ad-mitted wholly or in part the charges against them. Thirteen were found guilty, and sentenced to terms of imprisonment ranging from four months to ten years, and three were acquitted. This was in fact the judicial liquidation of the leadership of the Polish Underground which had fought so heroically against Hitler. The rank and file had already died in the ruins of Warsaw" (Churchill, *Triumph and Tragedy*, pp. 497–98).

The Decommissioning of the London-Affiliated Underground

On January 19, 1945, two days after Warsaw was liberated by the Red Army, the Home Army was dissolved. We will not fight against the Soviets, its commanding general, Leopold Okulicki, said in his last order to AK soldiers, but we will never accept Soviet domination of Poland, either: "I am giving you the last order. Conduct your further work and activity in the spirit of regaining state independence and so as to safeguard the Polish population from annihilation. Try to act as leaders for the Nation and in the spirit of implementing Polish independence. In this activity each of you must be his own commander. . . . [E]mpowered to do so by the President of the Polish Republic, I release you from your oath and dissolve the ranks of the Home Army." Okulicki was soon arrested by the Soviet secret service; he died in a Soviet prison following conviction in the infamous "Trial of the Sixteen" in Moscow.

By that time, the entire organizational framework of the underground—in the best of circumstances highly decentralized, fluid, and dependent on local conditions and personal relationships—had fallen apart. The Central Command of the Home Army, decimated during the Warsaw Uprising and itself hunted by the Soviet secret police and by the security services of the Communist-dominated Polish state, tried to decommission its members, streamlining their return to civilian life under a regime they were alienated from. Leaders of the underground feared that many Home Army soldiers would continue clandestine activities on their own, or follow the lead of the right-wing splinter groups that opted for sabotage and armed struggle against the nascent Communist regime.[17]

The Home Army went through a series of organizational transformations and name changes (Nie; Delegatura Sił Zbrojnych; Wolność i Niezawisłość), scaling down and redirecting its main focus from armed resistance to civilian, propaganda-oriented work. Colonel Jan Rzepecki, commanding officer of the AK's influential Bureau of Information and Propaganda (BiP) during the war, was appointed delegate of armed forces and became the chairman (*prezes*) of the AK successor group Liberty and Independence (Wolność i Niezawisłość; WiN) in September 1945. He was a brilliant officer and intellectual, liberal and left-leaning in his political outlook, who had assembled in BiP an outstanding group of colleagues. Now he faced the impossible task of converting a clandestine military organization into a civilian opposition movement, which couldn't be legalized and which counted among its most important tasks the reining in of the most radical forms of opposition to the new regime.

There was no ready-made formula for what a successor organization to the Home Army should be or how it ought to act. How to prevent the radicalization of opposition to Poland's nascent new regime, so that young people would not waste their lives in hopeless armed struggle that would rapidly demoralize any "outlaws" who chose to remain "in the forest"?[18] After five years of brutalizing and incapacitating occupation everyone yearned to resume normal work, a professional life, an interrupted education. People wanted to rebuild destroyed homes, communities, and institutions, and to pick up and go on with their personal lives; of this, the postwar baby boom was ample proof.

Rzepecki understood that a successor organization to the Home Army could not work against the desire for normalization, even though the AK's enemies, the Communists, were assuming overall control of this process. Thus, all that remained for the AK's successor organization was to wait until political circumstances changed, either because of a decisive falling-out between the United States/Britain and Stalin (some thought that a war between the Western democracies and the USSR was inevitable), or because the Polish Communists would have to bow to the results of the upcoming "free and unfettered" elections provided for in the Yalta agreement. In the meantime—that is, until the United States went to war with the USSR (which mercifully never came to pass) or until the Communists allowed free elections in Poland (which never came to pass, either)—the lives of hundreds of thousands of young patriotic men and women were at stake. Rzepecki did his best to steer them away from a head-on collision with the new regime, but he could devise no clear formula to show the way.

The rank and file of the Home Army fell victim, as it were, to superior forces of history and had to confront a predicament not of their own making. Clearly this was a fate they did not deserve. One can see a reflection of these powerful dilemmas in a moving address Rzepecki gave to former soldiers of the Home Army on July 24, 1945, the long and short of which can be summarized in one sentence from Okulicki's last order back in January: from now on, "you are your own commanders."* This

---

*"The sixth year of open struggle that the Home Army waged against the German invasion brought for you heavy blows and disappointments. The play of large international

was a phrase later identified by Home Army veterans as an appropriate epitaph for their destiny in postwar Poland.

Not surprisingly such advice, albeit well-meaning, could not stem the tide of chaos nor put a stop to individual dramas. Nor could it rein in various hotheads, misfits, and self-serving opportunists who committed deeds they portrayed as the actions of bona fide underground cells. A secret bulletin of the Polish Interior Ministry describing illegal antistate organizations active in the years 1944–1956 lists fifty-two "armed groups" called "AK" all over Poland, and an additional twenty-eight "AK" entries under a separate category of "illegal youth organizations." Some had as few as four members, some several dozen. Altogether about 1,700 illegal organizations bearing different names are enumerated in the bulletin's alphabetical index.[19] The two letters "AK," in short, appeared on many a leaflet issued by enterprising individuals and were likewise liberally flaunted by the Communist secret police which attributed to the Home Army many a deed committed by impromptu, desperate, rogue, or criminal groups or individuals.

In November 1945, Rzepecki was arrested. The secret police had penetrated various cells of the organization. They seemed to know everything about his activity. He promptly made up his mind that further

---

forces brought about the dissolution of your ranks, releasing you from the service, and led to the liquidation of the government and those centers of political leadership in the country which led you into combat. Effectively, the leading role in reconstruction of the Fatherland has been assumed by the Provisional Government of National Unity. Bad faith, however, maliciously distorts to this day the truth about your multi-year sacrifices and your intentions; it maligns your efforts and deprives you in practice of the full possibility to openly participate in the reconstruction of the Fatherland without having to renounce, dishonorably, your honest soldiers' past. To boot, by promoting the same watchwords of progress, freedom, and independence which were written on your banners, it implements in practice their distorted version. You, in the meantime, are physically and morally persecuted and denounced as 'reactionary tools' and spoilers harming the task of reconstruction. . . .

"In such difficult circumstances there is only one unfailing path to follow—the path of truth and fidelity to the ideals of individual liberty and national independence; ideals for which it is always worthwhile to bear sacrifice. Do not pay attention to malicious words, but scrutinize deeds and hard facts. What agrees with your ideals is good, irrespective of where it is coming from. What harms their realization is wrong, and should be condemned. You will meet on this path all truly democratic Polish social forces. By following such a path you are making the most worthy and lasting contribution to Poland's reconstruction. . . .

"If your personal situation allows it, if thoughtless persecution by the security apparatus does not close off this path to you, join in legal endeavors to reconstruct Poland in all the fields, while remaining faithful to democratic principles dear to every soldier of the Home Army: freedom of the individual citizen, independence of the nation. To struggle for the realization of these principles is your duty and your right, which cannot be taken away from you by any Pole who considers himself a democrat."

clandestine activity by the WiN was senseless, and agreed to cooperate with the authorities on the condition that his subordinates who willingly renounced clandestine work would not be punished.

Monopolization of Power by the Communist Party

The immediate postwar years were a period of social upheaval on a monumental scale, which rendered ever more segments of the population dependent on the state. Up to 7 million Germans had either fled or been deported from the newly incorporated territories in the west. Half a million Ukrainians were sent to the Soviet Union by mid-1946, and another 150,000 were resettled internally in 1947. More than a million Poles were repatriated by the end of 1946 from the border areas incorporated into the Soviet Socialist Republics of Ukraine, Lithuania, and Belorussia, while another quarter million returned from the Soviet interior (more than half of this last group were Polish Jews). In 1945–46, 2 million people settled in the new western provinces, and by 1950, 6 million people were living there. As stated earlier, the Communist leader, Władysław Gomułka, was in charge of the ministry supervising settlement in the west, a bountiful source of patronage to his party. With land reform benefiting landless and land-hungry peasants decreed by the state; with expropriation of industrial, banking, commercial, and real estate private property turning the state into the largest employer; with legislation imposing full state control over welfare, education, media, health services, and every other organization—the etatization of society was in full swing. The Communists merely had to be sure to expand their monopoly control over all levers of power in the state. And this they did.

The most intricate aspect of the political endgame involved taking control of the electoral process, whose purity, in theory, was guaranteed by the Western powers qua signatories of the Yalta agreements. The PPR—the Communist Party—knew that it did not have enough social support to win an open and honest electoral contest. Free elections held in Hungary in September 1945 gave an absolute majority (57 percent) to the Smallholders Party, anti-Communists representing the peasants; the results in Poland, given the personal popularity enjoyed by Mikołajczyk, would have been even more lopsided. So, as the first step in dealing with this problem, the Communist-dominated National Council (the KRN) proposed to hold a "referendum" instead, and thereby postpone the elections.

The referendum held on June 30, 1946, was crafted to show that the Polish population approved in their broad outlines the changes in boundaries and regime brought about at the end of the war. Three questions were put to a yes-or-no vote and the government mounted an aggressive propaganda campaign urging a "Three times yes" (*Trzy razy "Tak"*) vote to indicate support for the direction in which the Communist Party was leading the country.

"The Referendum ballot"—I am quoting from Stanisław Mikołajczyk's important book *The Rape of Poland*—"contained three deceitfully chosen questions. The wording was innocent enough: (1) Are you in favor of the abolishment of the Senate? (2) Are you for making permanent, through the future Constitution, the economic system instituted by the land reform and nationalization of the basic industries, with maintenance of the rights of private enterprise? (3) Are you for the Polish Western frontiers as fixed on the Baltic and the Oder and Neisse? Examining these, we of the Peasant Party felt we might use the first question as a weapon for a gigantic demonstration against the police state. . . . We decided to vote 'No' on the first question. . . . The Polish Peasant Party slogan became, 'If you vote "Yes" on the first question, you are giving a vote of confidence to the police methods of the Provisional Government.' "[20]

The "Three times yes" propaganda was accompanied by intimidation and thwarting of the Peasant Party's campaign efforts. Arthur Bliss Lane recalled that "the Peasant Party had to resort to word of mouth to advise its members of party policy."[21] But in the end a massive government-organized fraud occurred when counting the ballots. A specialized group of NKVD officers came to Poland to orchestrate falsification of some 6,000 protocols from electoral commissions. Documents found in the archives half a century later show that 25 percent of voters answered "yes" to the first question, 44 percent to the second question, and 68 percent to the third. But official results published by the government almost two weeks after the referendum announced that 68 percent of the voters answered "yes" to the first question, 77 percent to the second, and 91 percent to the third.[22]*

---

*Through some "freakish turn of events," as Mikołajczyk put it, the real results of the referendum (83 percent "no" votes in response to the first question) were printed in an official announcement in Kraków, causing "Communist propaganda mills thereafter to proclaim Cracow 'a reactionary city, which must be punished' " (Stanisław Mikołajczyk, *The Rape of Poland*, p. 164).

It was in this period of heightened political tension, when mobilization for and against the government was carried out all over the country by the regime and its legal opposition, and when intimidation and manipulation of the public was resorted to with particular intensity, that the most deadly episode of anti-Jewish violence in postwar Poland took place. On July 4, 1946, several dozen people were killed in a pogrom of Jews in the town of Kielce. Ambassador Bliss Lane called chapter 16 of his memoirs "Referendum and Pogrom," implicitly linking the two events, which occurred only four days apart. Anti-Communist commentaries explicitly linked the Kielce pogrom and the referendum, attributing the assault on the Jews to a deliberate Communist provocation. Allegedly, it aimed to divert the world's attention from the true results of the referendum and the rigged vote count.

Such claims, however, have no basis in historical evidence.[23] On the other hand, the referendum certainly provided a good practice run for the Communist authorities on how to prepare and organize elections. It also showed that the Communists effectively controlled the state apparatus and could deploy it to serve their own particularistic ends.

The date for the elections was set for January 19, 1947. Using the façade of "blocs" or "united fronts" that they effectively controlled was at the time still the favorite political strategy of East European Communists. And in August, on the initiative of the Polish Socialist Party (PPS), allied with the Communists, Mikołajczyk was solicited to enter into such an electoral "bloc" with all the other "progressive" parties in Poland. Participants in the bloc would draw up one list of candidates, with mandates apportioned between parties according to an agreed-upon formula. Instead of competitive elections, the public would thus effectively be invited to participate in a plebiscite, lending legitimacy to a coalition agreed upon in advance by the politicians.

In the August negotiations, the PSL was offered 25 percent of the seats in the new parliament, as much as the Communist Party, the PPR, would retain. The remaining 50 percent were to be distributed among the Socialist Party (22 percent); a pro-Communist splinter of the Peasant Party called the Stronnictwo Ludowe (12 percent); the pro-Communist Stronnictwo Demokratyczne, or Democratic Party (8 percent); and a pro-Mikołajczyk Stronnictwo Pracy, or Christian Labor Party (also 8 percent). Aware that his share of electoral support was far greater, and that the badly outnumbered PSL could not count on parliamentary support of critical members of the PPS, Mikołajczyk requested a 40 percent share of parliamentary seats as his price for joining the bloc. The negotiations soon collapsed.

The Communists then pulled out all the stops in a vicious and intense electoral campaign. Scores of Peasant Party activists were murdered in unexplained circumstances. One hundred sixty-two candidates from PSL lists, and thousands of local organizers, were arrested under various pretexts. Half a million citizens, PSL sympathizers, were struck from lists of eligible voters. In ten electoral districts—out of fifty-two nationwide—PSL lists were arbitrarily invalidated by the electoral commission, which was controlled by the Communists. Such intimidation went on until election day, when state employees and factory workers arrived at polling stations in organized columns to vote openly for "list number 3" of the government bloc. And in the end, the vote count was carried out by methods well honed during the referendum.

When all the votes were "counted," electoral protests filed (and dismissed), and results tabulated, the PSL and its allied Christian Labor Party got 10 percent of the mandates. Mikołajczyk resigned from the cabinet the day the results were officially announced.

From then on the official opposition, the PSL, was fair game for the repressive apparatus of the state and for government propaganda. Mikołajczyk vividly describes "the tightening vise" in a chapter of his memoirs under this title. He stood his ground for several months, speaking out in the parliament and shoring up the weakening spirit of his supporters. But the writing on the wall could no longer be ignored as intimidation, arrests, and trials of Peasant Party leaders multiplied. In September 1947, a conference of nine countries' Communist parties was held in Szklarska Poręba in Poland, marking the tightening of the vise throughout the entire Soviet bloc. Stalin's main ideologist, Andrei Zhdanov, set the course in a tough speech. From now on, East European Communists were no longer interested in hiding behind a façade of coalition. They went on to impose a monopoly of power through the undisguised hegemony of one-party regimes.[*]

In mid-October, Mikołajczyk, apprised of his imminent arrest, contacted the American embassy. On October 21—together with two other leading activists, Stefan Korboński and Kazimierz Bagiński, and the two men's wives—he was spirited out of the country.[24]

---

[*]Creating in short order and throughout Eastern Europe "geographically contiguous replica-regimes," as one student of Stalinism put it (Ken Jowitt, "Moscow 'Centre,'" *East European Politics and Societies*, p. 311).

Over the next year, the Communist Party consolidated its monopoly over various milieus and cultural institutions. A series of political trials of regime opponents was held. The Communist Party itself executed a sharp turn, casting off First Secretary Władysław Gomułka in a dramatic September 1948 plenary meeting of the Central Committee, and replacing him with Bolesław Bierut. Gomułka was accused of "nationalist deviation," of advocating "a national road to socialism"; from now on only "one road" to socialism, emulating the Soviet experience, was politically correct. Symbolically the consolidation of Stalinism in Poland may be dated to mid-December 1948, when the PPR and the PPS held a Unity Congress that yielded the Polish United Workers Party (Polska Zjednoczona Partia Robotnicza, PZPR). The Communists thus swallowed the historical Socialist Party and went on to rule the country, claiming to be the unique representatives of the working class, for the next forty years.

The Landscape After the Battle

In fulfillment of years' worth of dreams, the nightmare of Nazi occupation lifted in Poland during the winter and spring of 1944–45. To be sure, this Poland was a different country: reduced in size by one sixth, moved westward (with 47 percent of its prewar territory now incorporated into the Soviet Union and close to one third acquired at the expense of prewar Germany), with nearly a fifth of the population dead as a result of the war. The end of the war did not bring the return of social peace and political stability. By the time a Stalinist regime was firmly established in 1948, the country had experienced massive population movements, a social revolution, and monopolization of political power by the Communist Party. Separated from these events by the Cold War and decades of competition between the Soviet Bloc and the West, we may think in hindsight that the Communist takeover of Poland in 1945 was a foregone conclusion. And perhaps it was. But it required time and skills to be implemented, and there were always actors involved in the process who bet on and worked for alternative outcomes, against heavy odds.

Memoirs and diaries from the period record outpourings of vital energy and enthusiasm that somehow overcame the loss and mourning due to war's devastation. But the pure joy of liberation was laced for many with a sense of betrayal. Why did their sacrifice on behalf of a common cause count for nothing now? Powerful symbols and heroic deeds were publicly ridiculed. Institutional rewards were withheld from those who only yesterday, in the general estimation, had been the most deserving. It was very easy for ordinary people to make a contribution, since literally everything needed to be rebuilt, repaired, or constructed anew, and yet many Poles didn't quite know what to do with themselves.

The Communists went on to practice a new kind of totalitarian politics in postwar Eastern Europe. Little wonder that political actors in Poland were unable to find an effective response, when the most powerful men in the world proved unable to restrain Stalin's ambitions to subjugate the area. Wrote Churchill to Marshal Stalin on April 29, 1945:

> After all, we have joined with you, largely on my original initiative, early in 1944, in proclaiming the Polish-Russian frontier which you desired, namely, the Curzon Line, including Lvov for Russia. We think you ought to meet us with regard to the other half of the policy which you equally with us have proclaimed, namely, the sovereignty, independence, and freedom of Poland, provided it is a Poland friendly to Russia. . . . There is not much comfort in looking into a future where you and the countries you dominate, plus the Communist Parties in many other States, are all drawn up on one side, and those who rally to the English-speaking nations and their associates or Dominions are on the other.[25]

But the Communists were not prepared to meet anybody halfway. They didn't care about symbols, or about giving comfort to their erstwhile allies. They wanted a monopoly of power in Eastern and Central Europe. Stalin wanted a change of frontiers *and* complete dominion over Poland, as well as of other countries in Eastern Europe liberated by the Red Army. And he engineered the takeover by a combination of ruthlessness, cunning diplomacy, and clever politics pursued by local Communist parties.[26]

The Communist Party successfully outmaneuvered and subdued the legal opposition, the Peasant Party under the leadership of Stanisław Mikołajczyk; prevailed against the overwhelming weight of public opinion, which viewed Communism as an alien ideology; and overpowered the Catholic church, which ruled the hearts and minds of the Polish people. The new government pursued a comprehensive program of industrial and agricultural reforms while coping with the daunting tasks of reconstruction. It also had to follow policy changes emanating from Moscow, while embroiled in internal factional and personal conflicts. Tensions within Communist parties all over Eastern Europe would soon bring a wave of arrests and purge trials imitating the earlier "Great Terror" in the Soviet Union. As Eastern Europe was entering its own period of high Stalinism, Communist activists could feel embattled, indeed endangered, in more ways than one. What about the Jews in the context of postwar Polish politics, then? The rest of the book is devoted to a discussion of this very problem. But before we immerse ourselves in the subject we may find it useful to keep the following in mind.

As stated earlier, over 90 percent of the 3½ million Jews who lived in Poland before the war were killed during the Holocaust. The Jewish population of postwar Poland peaked briefly at around 200,000 in the summer of 1946—a small minority in a country of over 20 million at the time—and then promptly declined in a wave of rapid outmigration.* Anti-Jewish violence, which claimed somewhere between 500 and 1,500 lives during those years, also does not appear numerically out of scale. This was a period of civil war in Poland, and the Communist camp alone mourned the loss of 15,000 dead.† Since the Communist authorities gave as good as they got, the combined toll—made up of anti-Communists, ethnic Germans who were being resettled by the millions from the western portions of the country, and Ukrainians whose national aspirations were being crushed in the eastern voivodeships by a combined force of Soviet and Polish security detachments—ran into several tens of thousands of victims. Not surprisingly, anti-Jewish hostility in postwar Poland was not on the forefront of anyone's agenda but the Jews'.

For it is only in hindsight that the general public, as well as historians, have identified the Holocaust as a theme of universal and central

*Since there was simultaneously a constant outflow of Jews from Poland throughout 1945 and early 1946, one can estimate that altogether about a quarter million Jews had been in Poland in the immediate postwar period. More Polish Jews who survived the war in the Soviet Union were able to return to Poland only after 1956. Many of these promptly emigrated to Israel.

†During the meeting of Communist parties in Szklarska Poręba, in September 1947, Władysław Gomułka deplored the death of "14,876 people" in combat with "reactionary forces" (Gennadi Bordiugov and Gennadi Matveev, et al., eds., *SSSR-Polsha: Mekhanizmi podchinyenya, 1944–1949*, p. 231). A 1988 study gives a somewhat higher estimate, of 18,000 "who perished in the defense of progress and democracy" in the years 1944–1948 (Zenon Jakubowski, *Milicja obywatelska 1944–1948*, p. 432).

significance for the self-understanding of Western civilization. We should remember that the experience of European Jews during the war, or immediately thereafter, was not a subject promptly taken up either by the public or by historiographies of host societies *anywhere* on the Continent.*

But even at this time, when people were busy putting their personal and professional lives back together from scraps while the material and political worlds they knew lay in ruins, the upper crust of Polish intelligentsia reacted with horror and disbelief to manifestations of popular anti-Semitism. Theirs was a cri de coeur in response, especially, to the Kraków (August 1945) and Kielce (July 1946) pogroms, which I describe later. They saw with clarity that anti-Semitism in Poland after Auschwitz signaled a moral failure which touched some core of the collective being. "No longer an economic issue, it is no longer a political issue either," wrote Wincenty Bednarczuk in one of the most important political-literary weeklies of the time, *Odrodzenie,* on September 9, 1945, one month after the pogrom in Kraków. "It is a moral problem pure and simple. Today it is not a question of saving the Jews from misery and death, it is a problem of saving the Poles from moral misery and spiritual death."[27]

These voices soon petered out, submerged on one side by the deep freeze of Stalinism, which stifled all discussion, and on the other by lack of similar concerns among the general public. When most Jews had fled

*As Pieter Lagrou puts it in his important study, "Despite their antagonisms, the anti-fascist and anti-totalitarian memories shared one major feature: they systematically obscured the specificity of the genocide. The anti-fascist discourse assimilated all victims of fascism with anti-fascists. The genocide was not recognized as distinct from the overall anti-fascist martyrdom. . . . A commemoration of the genocide as such had threatening implications which made it incompatible with the reconstruction of national self-esteem. . . . Besides, it is revealing that the requirements for patriotic memories in recovering nations are very similar to the requirements for a patriotic memory in an emerging nation. As the research of Idith Zertal and Tom Segev illustrates, the memory of genocide was incompatible with national affirmation and also threatened the national identity of victorious Israel" (Pieter Lagrou, *Legacy of Nazi Occupation: Patriotic Memory and National Recovery in Western Europe, 1945–1965,* pp. 285–86).

Amos Oz writes on the status of Holocaust survivors in Israel at that time: "We generally treated [them] with compassion and a certain revulsion: miserable wretches, was it our fault that they chose to sit and wait for Hitler instead of coming here while there was still time? Why did they allow themselves to be led like sheep to the slaughter instead of organizing and fighting back? And if only they'd stop nattering on in Yiddish, and stop telling us about all the things that were done to them over there, because that didn't reflect too well on them, or on us for that matter. Anyway, our faces here are turned toward the future, not the past" (Amos Oz, *A Tale of Love and Darkness,* pp. 13–14).

Poland, the Holocaust became a nonsubject in Polish historiography, while "the Jews" became a lingering obsession in Polish political life—like a severed limb, radiating pain throughout the body long after it had been lost.*

*Virtually every postwar political crisis in Poland has been refracted in the public domain through the prism of "the Jewish question." The title of Paul Lendvai's book about the 1968 "March events" in Poland—an anti-Jewish witch hunt carried under the rhetorical cover of an "anti-Zionist" campaign in a country where there were at the time maybe 50,000 or 60,000 mostly completely assimilated Jews, in a total population of 35 million—became a staple phrase capturing this mysterious phenomenon: *Anti-Semitism Without Jews.*

An earlier political crisis of de-Stalinization, the so-called October events of 1956, also had a Jewish subtext in the perception of general public and political aficionados. The most emblematic and widely discussed political analysis of the crisis appeared in an article written by a sociologist, Witold Jedlicki, and entitled "Chamy i Żydy," or "Oafs and Jews."

The first free presidential elections in Poland after 1989, in which Lech Wałęsa and Tadeusz Mazowiecki (the first Solidarity-designated prime minister of Poland) were the main contenders, took place under a cloud of suspicion whether Mazowiecki was indeed "a real Pole," and a Star of David was scribbled on his election posters all over Poland. This is but a handful of center-stage political examples illustrating how the rhetoric of Jewish conspiracy permeates political discourse in Poland. A popular weekly, *Wprost,* reported in its January 18, 2004, issue that in a nationwide survey of public opinion, 40 percent of the respondents declared that the country—which essentially all the Jews have left by now—is still being governed by Jews.

2

THE UNWELCOMING OF JEWISH SURVIVORS

AT FIVE P.M. ON AUGUST 10, 1944, while the war was still going on and more than half of Poland's territory was still under German occupation, in the city of Lublin where two and a half weeks earlier the July Manifesto had been proclaimed, a group of Jews assembled. They set up a committee to help the remnants of Polish Jewry that had survived the war. What would soon become the Central Committee of Polish Jews (Centralny Komitet Żydów w Polsce, CKŻP)—an umbrella organization including representatives of several prewar Jewish political parties—was first called the Committee to Help Jews (Komitet Pomocy Żydom).

In the committee's very first protocol, produced on the following day, we read that the Jews of Włodawa needed help because they were being "attacked by destructive elements."[1] The group's second meeting, on August 13, was devoted to a general discussion of "security," or rather the lack thereof, for the Jewish survivors. Should both the Polish and the Soviet (military) authorities be alerted that there were "elements inimical toward the Jews," or should this be kept en famille, with only Polish officials so informed? Should mayors of already liberated towns be asked to issue proclamations addressed to the Polish population requesting that it be friendly toward its Jewish fellow citizens? Should Catholic clergy be informed about threats and lack of security experienced by the Jews? And how to do all or any of this without making matters worse for Jews and creating an atmosphere of excessive panic?[2]

Protocol Number 3, from August 14, begins with a Dr. Gelbart reporting on a conversation he had on this matter with a member of the National Council for the Country (Krajowa Rada Narodowa, KRN), the proto-parliament already in existence. Gelbart told the assembled reassuringly that "for the moment Jews were not being threatened in Lublin," but added the cautionary postscript that "loud conversations [presumably in Yiddish] and gathering in groups in the street should be avoided."[3] The next day's protocol again refers to a constant flow of pleas for help by Jews from the provinces.

The war was still going on. Germany had not yet been defeated. The area had barely been liberated from a long and exceedingly brutal occupation that had caused suffering to virtually every Polish family. And local people were already after the remnants of Jewish survivors.

Viewed from the perspective of a Jewish observer well versed in current politics, the wave of anti-Jewish violence seamlessly following the tragedy of the Holocaust appeared entirely out of place. It was certainly counterintuitive. The cream of Polish intelligentsia was utterly baffled by the explosion of postwar anti-Semitism in the country. Jews returning from camps or, later, from forced exile in the USSR, when told about the dangers that awaited them upon return—told that they risked being killed if they went back to their native villages—absorbed the unexpected news as a rude awakening.[*]

One could assume that the Nazis' espousal of anti-Semitism should have given it a sufficiently bad name after the war. In addition, the preeminence of Communist and Socialist parties in the politics of the era should have contributed to the marginalization of anti-Semitism, turning it into a mere anachronism. Jews were at this point de facto fully enfranchised and equal in citizenship rights, and scores of Communists from a Jewish background who had always played important roles in the movement had already been entrusted with positions of responsibility in the emerging administration. A plausible argument could be made that if

---

[*]"Thus I awaited the liberation. From camp I went back to Poland. I wanted to go to Klementów, but on the way I met acquaintances who told me not to go back, because Poles killed 5 Jews there after liberation. I went to Łódź" (Żydowski Instytut Historyczny [ŻIH], 301/1184, Sala Ungerman). A young woman, Liba Tiefenbrun, returning from camp to Tarnów in May of 1945, got off the train and "my first question to a railwayman was, Are there still any Jews in town? He said that there are a few, but that they are afraid and have to hide. I got frightened" (ŻIH, 301/1182). For a listing of several sources where people express surprise and fear at the news, see, for example, Natalia Aleksiun, *Dokąd dalej? Ruch syjonistyczny w Polsce (1944–1950)*, pp. 83, 84.

the survivors only found enough energy and inner resources to reconstruct Jewish life, the larger institutional framework and political tides would readily accommodate their efforts. Many, undoubtedly, thought so.* An eminent actor of the Yiddish theater, Jonas Turkov, recalls about the period the euphoria of conversations and meetings with other Jewish artists. As a committed Yiddishist he set about working on the reconstruction of Jewish cultural institutions.[4] Of course, a fundamental issue arose repeatedly in all the discussions: could there be a continuation of Jewish life and culture after the destruction visited on Polish Jews by the Nazis? But as it turned out, Jewish survivors were confronted with an altogether different question in the end: would the reestablishment of a Jewish civic presence after the war in Poland be tolerated by their Polish fellow citizens?

While the Zionist youth saw it as an urgent matter to get all Jews out of Eastern Europe and ready for settlement in Palestine when circumstances permitted, the experience of the Holocaust per se did not impel Jewish survivors to flee from Poland en masse right away. The flow of Jewish refugees with the Brikha, as the clandestine Zionist rescue effort would be called, swelled with the rhythm of postwar anti-Jewish violence. Many who left within a year or two after the liberation—perhaps most, since there is of course no way to gauge such numbers—were persuaded to do so primarily by their postwar experience of physical endangerment and social ostracism.[5]

Turkov's inclination to answer yes to the question whether Jewish life and culture could resume in Poland after the Holocaust was sustained by the hope associated with the prospect of return of more than 200,000 Polish Jews (no one knew exactly how many) who had survived the war in the Soviet Union. Indeed, many of those repatriated from the USSR who were directed upon arrival to the newly incorporated territories in Lower Silesia established a number of thriving communities there. Even though more Jews resided in the area than anywhere else in Poland, anti-Jewish assaults were much less frequent there. This was due, it seems to me, primarily to the fact that almost all the Poles and Jews settled there were newcomers, as these terri-

---

*"The Voivodeship office in Szczecin," wrote Natalia Aleksiun, "in one of its memoranda from 1946 noted that 'already when en route from the USSR the Jewish population—one could say while it was still in the railroad cars—created a number of political parties, unions, and associations'" (Aleksiun, *Dokąd dalej?*, p. 7).

tories had been part of Germany before the war. Consequently, nobody was "returning home" and the context of competing claims over property was missing.[6]

But from the beginning the thoughts and conversations of Turkov (and many others like him) were marred by a growing awareness of looming physical violence against the Jews. As early as September 1944 he was taken aback by unsolicited advice from a Jewish acquaintance in the Security Service that he ought to continue using his wartime-assumed Polish identity and not revert to his real name. Turkov asked why he should keep on hiding, and heard in reply that the "narcotic of anti-Semitism had still not dissipated."[7] Like many others, he tried to convince himself that this was a transitory phenomenon, due to the general anarchy following a devastating war. But as time passed and the violence did not abate, it was increasingly more difficult to maintain his resolve. Despite Turkov's deep immersion in the reconstruction of Jewish community life, the elite role he played in the CKŻP, and his initial enthusiasm, he gave up after a year and left the country in October 1945. A majority of Jewish survivors of the Holocaust in Poland and those who returned after the war from the Soviet Union would end up doing likewise.

Anti-Jewish Violence

It didn't necessarily take a Jewish Committee activist to notice that Jews were an endangered species in Poland after the war. "It is an undeniable fact," wrote Jan Kowalczyk, the Kraków voivodeship "commissar for productivization of the Jewish population," to the Presidium of the District Commission of the Labor Unions (an entirely "Polish" venue), "that the living conditions of the Jewish population in county towns are extremely difficult. Because of the terror of reactionary elements [a phrase often encountered in the official language of the time] the Jewish population runs away from those locations in order to save their lives and concentrates in larger towns."[8]

An eminent French Catholic intellectual, Emmanuel Mounier, visited Poland in late spring 1946 and was impressed with what he had seen. A friendly and unprejudiced commentator, he was nevertheless struck deeply by the intensity of anti-Semitism and noticed

a sudden stiffening of demeanor among everybody as soon as the subject [of Jews in Poland] is raised. Arguments which are being put forth, without understanding that they belong to a used-up arsenal of international anti-Semitism, diffuse hostility[,] and acts of violence that take place find, whatever one might say, a kind of complicity. . . . Earlier [before the war] an isolated Jew had nothing to fear in the countryside. Today, on the other hand, he cannot live there in security. . . . There have been over a thousand killings of Jews in the last nine months. . . . Assaults are less frequent in cities, but there are some. After what they had lived through, Polish Jews are gripped with terror. Survivors think only about leaving, and in fact many leave for Palestine or for the west.[9]

From very early on, county and voivodeship Jewish Committees kept urging the Jewish population to move to larger towns, but even there Jews were not safe, as the August 1945 pogrom in Kraków and the July 1946 pogrom in Kielce would soon demonstrate. How many Jews altogether were killed in this period is difficult to estimate. The most careful, conservative figures range between 500 and 600; more widely accepted estimates put the total at around 1,500.*

Of course, many people were being killed in Poland during those years. There was a civil war of sorts as Communists consolidated their grip on power. The expulsions of ethnic Germans from the incorporated territories in the west were exceedingly brutal and resulted in the death of many thousands. The suppression of Ukrainian nationalists in the east likewise cost many human lives. But Jews were not a category of the population officially targeted for suppression. If anything, the opposite was supposed to be the case, as Jewish Committees kept sending information about murderous assaults and urgent appeals for help to

---

*The most conservative estimate is made in a careful study by David Engel in "Patterns of Anti-Jewish Violence in Poland, 1944–1946" (*Yad Vashem Studies*, 26, 1998). He argues there that the number of Jewish victims as it is usually placed, "at 1000–1500, seemed . . . too high." Engel estimates that the total number of casualties would fall in the range of 500–600 (personal communication). Other estimates, for instance by the late Dr. Lucjan Dobroszycki and by Józef Adelson, opt for higher numbers.

Engel's scholarship is impeccable, but I think he errs too far on the side of caution in this case, if only because so many murders must have remained unreported. Just by way of example, one may consult Alina Cała's 1984 interviews, when the issue of postwar murders of Jews came up: "[Q: Did they look for the murderer?] You've got to be kidding; in those times no one was concerned about individual murders." In another interview she was also told, "There was no investigation, but that is how the times were" (Alina Cała, *The Image of the Jew in Polish Folk Culture*, pp. 216, 217). Furthermore, as I point out later in this book, the militia and the Security Service systematically ignored anti-Jewish violence in their reporting.

the powers that be. "In the files of MAP's Political Department there are
many reports and complaints about acts of murder and plunder committed against Polish citizens of Jewish nationality," read a memo from the
Ministry of Public Administration (MAP) to the Ministry of Public Security (MBP), dated September 29, 1945. "But we have no information
whatsoever about actions undertaken by the state authorities to put an
end to these. Since this information is indispensable for us, we request
that MAP be informed by the Ministry of Public Security what has been
done in the matter and with what results."[10]* Unlike the killings of Germans or even Ukrainians, the killings of Jews by the Poles after the war
could not be subsumed under some overall concept of retribution for war
crimes.

Killings of Jews were occasionally carried out with deliberate cruelty
and they often involved entire groups or families, including women and
children. But what really made the murders of Jews a social phenomenon
apart was that they were anticipated—as punishment is anticipated in a
case of transgression. Time and again, returning Jews were greeted in
their native towns on arrival with an incredulous: "So"—followed by
their first name, as they usually were on a first-name basis with their Polish neighbors—"you are still alive?" And before long they got an un-
ambiguous hint, or a piece of good advice—to clear out, or else. "The
story of their experiences during the past six months," wrote H. J. Fish-
bein, director of a UN Relief and Rehabilitation Administration team in
Berlin in the spring of 1946, "is a monotonous one as it is repeated by all
refugees coming out of Poland. They tell of letters received from a Polish
organization known as AK. . . . These letters threaten the Jews with outright murder if they continue to live in that locality."[11]

There was no high politics behind these threats, or good advice,
whatever one wants to call them and wherever they came from. The
scarce Jewish survivors, going back to their hometowns in a usually fruit-

*One finds no answer to this memorandum in the holdings of the Archiwum Akt
Nowych. The reason, I'm afraid, is not that it has been misfiled or lost. It may be impossible
to prove a negative, but one can still make inferences from the absence of evidence where
one should expect to find it. A reader of various Security Service memoranda, minutes of
important meetings, and periodic listings of priorities and urgent tasks—whether produced
at the central level of the Ministry of Public Security in Warsaw or in the voivodeship offices
of the Security Service—will be struck by their ignoring of anti-Jewish violence as a specific
problem, which needed to be addressed as a distinct and urgent matter. Even in the aftermath of the Kielce pogrom (and I have more to say about this in chapters 4 and 5) the issue
did not come up at the periodic top-level conference of the MBP's leadership with voivodeship Security Service commanders.

less search for relatives or family belongings, had nothing to do with the establishment of Communist rule in Poland after the war; if they had, Communism would have collapsed in the country long before 1989, because Jews promptly fled the villages and small towns for a few big cities. And soon thereafter, in a mass exodus, they fled Poland altogether.

Jews were frequently advised privately about looming danger— Szmul Wasersztajn, whose deposition helped to uncover the story of the Jedwabne murders, for example, was saved in this manner after the war.* Apparently, there was widespread prior knowledge about impending killings among people in a town who weren't necessarily part of a conspiracy. We read reports indicating that the spectacle of plundering, assaulting, and killing Jews did not draw censure or criticism from casual spectators. On the contrary, accidental witnesses are found to have made derogatory comments, shared a laugh, or on occasion helped the assailants.†

It appears that people frequently knew the murderers of Jews, and they spoke about the killings in a detached, matter-of-fact manner that caught the attention of an ethnographer forty years after the war. Alina Cała conducted her interviews about Jews who had once lived in the area with villagers in eastern and southeastern Poland in 1984. Out of ninety interviewees, twenty-seven mentioned some episode in which a Jew or several Jews had been killed after the war, and they often cited in their narrative the names of the perpetrators. Furthermore, as Cała put it, "even those who had severely condemned the Nazi persecutions judged

---

*The story of the murder of the 1,600 Jews of Jedwabne on July 10, 1941, by their Christian neighbors was brought to public attention in Poland with the publication of my book *Sąsiedzi, historia zagłady żydowskiego miasteczka.* It came out in Poland in May 2000, one year before its English-language edition. For an excellent summary of the public controversy around this issue, calendarium, and a comprehensive selection of texts published by various authors during the discussion, see Antony Polonsky and Joanna Michlic, eds., *The Neighbors Respond: The Controversy over the Jedwabne Massacre in Poland.*

†On February 8, 1946, an underground outfit of WiN overwhelmed the militia and the UB outpost and for several hours took over the town of Parczew, near Lublin. The operation was planned in order to plunder the local Jews and restock the unit's dwindling supplies. Dozens of Jewish businesses and homes were ruined in the process, and four Jews were killed. The diary of the unit's commander, which ultimately ended up in police files, includes a long entry on the day's events (hence we know that they came especially to plunder the Jews) and in it is the following passage: "When local people realized what was going on, even though shots were fired, they came out happily into the streets to see 'the forest boys.' Youth from Parczew, primarily local high school students, energetically helped us to search for the Jews, to load the trucks, etc." (Alina Cała and Helena Datner-Śpiewak, eds., *Dzieje Żydów w Polsce 1944–1968: Teksty źródłowe,* p. 39). For casual bystanders' reactions to the killings of Jews, see also chapter 3.

the postwar murders tolerantly or even justified them."[12] Killings of
Jews, in other words, were not a secret cloak-and-dagger operation. They
were, by all appearances, a form of social control.* If Jews remained in
their hometowns despite the warnings, if they traveled by train knowing
the risks (it was public knowledge that Jews traveling by rail might be
pulled off the train and killed), then—in the moral economy of postwar
life in Poland—they had nobody to blame but themselves.

On the 3rd of October [1946] at 7 in the evening I boarded a
train from Warsaw to Kraków. I was accompanied by my husband Henryk Lieberfreund and Amalia Schenker. We rode in a
compartment with a couple more passengers, including a nun. A
candle was burning. We traveled peacefully until we reached
Kamińsk station near Radomsko. In the meantime the candle
burned out and passengers were sleeping in darkness. During
the stop in Kamińsk a man in civilian clothes, wearing a cap with
an eagle sign and toting a submachine gun, entered the compartment. He checked the passengers one by one with a flashlight.
When he reached my sleeping husband, he pulled off the coat
covering him and said, "I got you, kike, heraus, heraus,
aussteigen."† My husband drew back, unwilling to get off the
train, and the man pulled him by the arm but could not budge
him. Then he whistled and immediately another man appeared,
whom I did not see very well, accompanied by the conductor. I
started screaming terribly, and then the first assailant began to
push and pull me using the words "heraus, aussteigen." I pulled
myself away, in the meantime the train began to move, and the
assailant pushed my husband off the train and jumped after him.
I continued to scream and I don't know what happened afterward. I wish to add that nobody's documents were checked, not

---

*As Cała tries to come to terms with the phenomenon of postwar murders of Jews and
the way they resonated in public memory, she writes, "It seems inadequate to explain them
only by the demoralization caused by the occupation, and banditism, which unquestionably
was prevalent for a long time. The scope of these crimes suggest that they belong to the category of a cultural phenomenon" (Cała, *The Image of the Jew*, p. 219). She calls them a "cultural
phenomenon" because, as she puts it, "it is impossible to find a rational reason for this behavior, for there were none" (ibid.).

†The man accosting Lieberfreund was not a German, but in a deliberate mockery he
borrowed from the vocabulary of the Nazi period—a phrase German gendarmes used when
arresting passengers on the train. In the same way, the German word "Jude" would often be
used to mock the Jews after the war.

even my husband's. *Other passengers and the conductor did not pay much attention to the whole episode; quite the opposite, they laughed and behaved rather improperly* [emphasis mine]. One man sitting next to my husband was accosted by the assailant with the words "You Jew." But he stated that he could show documents that he was not a Jew, and he was left alone.*

The Takeover of Jewish Property by Polish Neighbors

What was the nature of the tension between the two groups? The answer to this query—a part of the answer, in any case—was self-evident to many a Polish observer at the time. One of the paramount underlying reasons of conflict between Poles and Jews after the war had to do with the illicit transfer of material property from Jewish ownership during the war. Polish society was uniquely affected by the Holocaust in that the mass killings of Polish Jews created a social vacuum that was promptly filled by the native Polish petty bourgeoisie. Sociologically this was, in a manner of speaking, a natural process. There were more than 3 million Jews in Poland, most of them lower-middle-class; when they were wiped out by the Nazis, the local population moved in to occupy their social space. Now the new incumbents were a social stratum with vulnerable status (if only because a Communist revolution was in the offing), traditionally anti-Semitic in outlook, politically conservative, and full of re-

---

*ŻIH, CKŻP, Centralna Komisja Specjalna, box 1–2, pp. 156–58. The story of Henryk Lieberfreund's murder is unusually well documented; for the most part, murders on the railroad left little trace in the archives. By pure coincidence I also know the subsequent story of the Lieberfreund family, whose surviving members settled after the war in Switzerland and in the United States. The archives of the Central Special Commission contain, in addition, an unsigned memorandum entitled "Information," dated three days after the abduction of Lieberfreund near Kamińsk, and providing the following background story: "On the Kraków–Warsaw line trains go through Kamińsk about fifteen minutes after Radomsko. The railroad line cuts through this village situated in a wood, with houses built along the track. The inhabitants of these houses before the war, during the war, and now live for the most part off the passing trains. This was especially true of the coal transports that passed thereby. Almost all the people in the vicinity made a living from coal pushed off these trains, especially at night. In two of these houses, one right next to the station and the other a one-story house farther down, there lives a bunch of people whose central figure is a woman of dubious reputation. . . . They party at night and drink and from time to time they stake out a passing train in expectation of some spoils. Jewish passengers are now victimized by these bands, for they can be easily intimidated with a gun, taken off a train, robbed of their cash and possessions in a forest, where all of this is taking place, and then they can be made to disappear; thus one gains an easy living for oneself and one's companions. This area should be carefully watched and put under observation" (ibid.).

sentment. Many Polish observers contemporaneously noted this group's "reactionary" mental outlook. But whether one puts this in a sociological language of social mobility or uses some other objectivizing rhetoric, the long and short of the story was that before being killed during the German occupation, Jews were plundered by the Nazis, and the local population in various ways benefited in the process. Often by foul play. "We knew in the country an entire social stratum—the newborn Polish bourgeoisie," writes the September 9, 1945, issue of the Polish weekly *Odrodzenie,* "which took the place of murdered Jews, often literally, and, perhaps because it smelled blood on its own hands, it hated Jews more strongly than ever."[13]

Given their pariah status under the Nazis, Jews were taken advantage of by the surrounding population in a multitude of transactions. But property transfer from Jewish to Polish ownership was marked not only by opportunistic exploitation, but also by outright plunder, associated with mass killings of the Jews by the German occupiers. During the course of the "final solution," as Jews were rounded up for deportation or execution in one locality after another, the Polish population grabbed as much as it could of what material goods had been left behind. The story was repeated all over Poland. In the well-known diary of Dr. Zygmunt Klukowski, from Szczebrzeszyn, we read how "a lot of [peasants with] wagons came from the countryside and stood waiting the entire day for the moment when they could start looting. News keeps reaching us from all directions about the scandalous behavior of segments of the local population who rob emptied Jewish apartments. I am sure our little town will be no different."[14]

Jews were also directly murdered by Poles who wanted to acquire their property. Mass killings in the Podlasie region, of which the murder in Jedwabne was but one episode, were accompanied by widespread and thorough plunder of Jewish property.* It would be more difficult to name

---

*After the Jedwabne murders were brought to public attention, a newly created entity called the Institute of National Memory (IPN) opened a broad inquiry to clarify the matter and, if they could still be found, bring the guilty to account. The results of the IPN investigations, carried out by a dozen legal experts and historians, were published in an encyclopedic two-volume compendium over 1,500 pages long, including sources and commentaries and entitled *Wokół Jedwabnego,* Paweł Machcewicz and Krzysztof Persak, eds. During a thorough two-year-long investigation of the Jedwabne murders, researchers at the institute combed through their extensive archives and discovered that sixty-one cases from the Białystok district court alone were brought after the war against defendants accused of participation in killings of local Jews. It appears that Polish assaults against the Jews in the summer of 1941 were common throughout the Białystok voivodeship, that killings went on for several months, and that they engulfed a vast territory including some two dozen townships

those townspeople who did *not* plunder Jewish houses while their inhabitants were being incinerated in a large barn on the outskirts of Radziłów,
an eyewitness to the murders told a journalist sixty years later. Everybody
seemed to be in the streets grabbing what they could. Symbolically most
evocative in this respect were probably the calls of pogrom organizers in
Wasilków, "who were running around and screaming: 'Don't break anything, don't rip it up, all this is already ours' " (*"w czasie pogromu przywódcy
biegali i krzyczeli: 'Nie łamać niczego, niczego nie rozrywać, to wszystko i tak jest już
nasze' "*).[15]

Jews were a source of wealth also after they had been killed by the
Nazis. Murder sites were dug up after the war in search for valuables.
Michał Kalembasiak and Karol Ogrodowczyk visited the site of the Treblinka extermination camp on September 12, 1945, and took perhaps the
earliest photographs of the site after the war. The entire area was scarred
with holes, several meters deep, with human bones scattered all around.
People sifting through the mounds of ashes didn't bother to answer when
asked what they were doing. The area was large and the scale of the excavations enormous. Thousands had to have worked in the fields to produce
this lunar landscape. "I want to add," Kalembasiak and Ogrodowczyk
stated in a signed deposition for the Jewish Historical Commission in
Warsaw, "that mutual relationships in the Treblinka area are simply incredible [*"panują niesamowite stosunki"*]. People who enriched themselves
with gold dug up from the graves, by night plunder their own neighbors.
We were terrified because in a peasant hut some dozen meters from the
house where we spent the night, a woman was tortured with live fire to
reveal the place where she was hiding gold and valuables."[16] The writer
Rachela Auerbach called one of the chapters of her book about the Treblinka extermination camp "The Polish Colorado, or About the Gold
Rush in Treblinka." She also saw the killing fields, with mounds of ashes
of Jewish victims, dug up and unprotected when she visited the camp in
November 1945.* "Numerous plunderers with shovels are everywhere.
They dig, they search, pulling out bones and body parts. Maybe something could still be found," she writes, "maybe a golden tooth?"[17] On the
site of the Bełżec camp, local peasants dug deeper, below the layer of

---

and produced thousands of victims (see Paweł Machcewicz's introduction to the *Wokół
Jedwabnego* volumes).

*Rachela Auerbach visited Treblinka on November 7, 1945, as part of an official delega-
tion organized by the Main Commission of the Investigation of Hitlerite Crimes. She published her book about Treblinka, including a report from the visit, in Yiddish as *Oif die felder
fun Treblinka*.

ashes that had been sifted through earlier by the Nazis using grain-threshing machines confiscated from Polish farmers. In the mudlike residue of decomposing bodies ("*trupia maź*") they looked for skulls, which they carried home—so that the neighbors digging alongside them could not tell whether they had found anything of value—where they searched for tooth caps made of gold.* The scale of the Treblinka excavations was unique, but the practice of digging up Jewish remains from the sites of mass murder to strip them of valuables was common.

Local people came to perceive Jews as a resource that could be harvested when an opportune moment arrived. The murderous pogrom in Radziłów in July 1941 was preceded by the arrival of peasants from Wąsosz, who had killed and plundered their own Jews two days earlier, but the locals chased them away. An elderly peasant whom Anna Bikont interviewed nearly sixty years after the events recalled that "when people from Wąsosz came our people said, 'Buzz off, you have no business plundering our Jews,' because Wąsosz was seventeen kilometers from Radziłów. But when people from Konopki came to rob, it was only four kilometers in distance, so they were not chased away."[18] Evidently, a town's Jews were for the town's people to plunder.

Occasionally Jews left some property with their Polish neighbors, and when they proved trustworthy the practice helped to save the life of many a Jew who then went into hiding. But honesty was not the norm, and survivors often discovered that they could not reclaim their property after the war, even from acquaintances. The legal department of the CKŻP kept records of numerous suits filed in courts by Jewish survivors for restitution of property. "During the occupation in 1942," writes Jochweta Rozenstein in a characteristic example, "I left for safekeeping with citizen Ludwika Chrapczyńska in Ożarów two eiderdowns and four pillows. Citizen Chrapczyńska refuses to return my property. . . ."[19] And the complaint closes with a sentence that appears in numerous filings of this sort: "Please adjudicate the case, even if I am absent." For already in May 1945, when this complaint was filed in the city court, Jews were running away from Poland, fleeing for their lives to, of all places, Germany.

*Personal communication from Agnieszka Grudzińska, who as translator interviewed scores of local inhabitants in Bełżec during production of the documentary film *Bełżec* by Guillaume Moscovitz (first shown at an international conference, "*Les Juifs et la Pologne [1939–2004]: Aspects Multiformes du Passé,*" held in Paris, on January 13, 2005). The threshing machines used to sift human ashes were eventually returned to the peasants, and in one courtyard, where such a machine, in a state of disrepair, was still standing, the documentary film crew was told the story by the owner.

Safe Among the Germans—Ruth Gay's book about Jewish life in DP camps—is largely about Polish Jews who fled their mother country after the war.[20] The most detailed numbers about the Zionist-organized flight from Poland through February 1947, provided by Yohanan Cohen, put the total of those who left in this period at 127,722. In addition, Cohen estimates that between 11,500 and 16,500 Jews escaped on their own.* Altogether this was about half of the westward migration of Polish Jews at the time, as some 150,000 to 175,000 were repatriated to Poland during this period from the Soviet Union. Many of the repatriates, discouraged by the circumstances they encountered upon return, continued their journey by fleeing Poland with the Brikha.[21]

Irrespective of how personal disputes over bedding or furniture were resolved by the courts, it is telling that the few returning Jews had to use the courts to press such claims. On the other hand, we can also appreciate the sense of bad luck among the likes of Chrapczyńska (the woman unwilling to hand back two eiderdowns and four pillows in Ożarów). Why did "her" Jew have to come back from the dead while all the others, most of the others in any case, had disappeared and wouldn't bother the neighbors who also stocked up on Jewish stuff?

One would wish for a climate of compassion, especially among close acquaintances, toward the few returnees whose communities and families had just suffered an unspeakable calamity. But compassion was absent. Indeed, there was no social norm mandating the return of Jewish property, no detectable social pressure defining such behavior as the right thing to do, no informal social control mechanism imposing censure for doing otherwise. This is why Jews who dared to pursue the matter had to resort to the courts.

Jewish property had been taken by people all around, and it was not

---

*Yohanan Cohen, *Operation "Brikha"—Poland, 1945–1946*, p. 468. Cohen provides a detailed monthly breakdown, which shows fluctuations in the number of Jewish refugees following the rhythm of waves of persecution. The highest monthly figures were for July, August, and September 1946 (i.e., immediately following the Kielce pogrom): respectively, 18,835; 30,800; and 11,180. The Zionists had a quiet agreement with the Polish authorities (the deputy defense minister, General Marian Spychalski, was a key person in helping to arrange it) who turned a blind eye and allowed Jews to leave surreptitiously through several border crossings, provided that no valuables or sought-after political opponents of the regime be smuggled out of the country and that the agreement be kept secret (see, for example, David Engel, *Beyn Shichrur*, pp. 134, 135; Michał Rudawski, *Mój obcy kraj?*, pp. 178–97). There was also legal emigration by Jews, who applied for emigration passports individually. Between 1949 and 1952, Cohen estimates, 39,000 Jews left Poland legally (p. 471). These figures do not account for the period between March 1947 and December 1948. Altogether, more than 200,000 Jews left Poland in the immediate postwar years.

a specifically Polish behavior by any means; Heda Kovaly recounts the
same phenomenon in a moving book about Czechoslovakia.[22] But there
had been many more Jews in Poland than anywhere else, many more had
been killed, and therefore the phenomenon was much more widespread.
Naturally, among the Jews there were also swindlers profiting from
postwar circumstances. They filed false inheritance claims or milked
acquaintances—who lived abroad and were frantically seeking any news
of family members—under the pretense that they were caring for their
relatives.[23]

A courageous miller's wife from Radziłów, Chaja Finkelsztajn, left a
searing memoir in Yad Vashem about the mass murder of Jews in her
hometown on July 7, 1941, and about the subsequent years when she was
in hiding with her family among the peasants. On several occasions (in
one instance, just as the mass killing was unfolding in Radziłów) the so-
called good local people came to her asking that she turn over to them
whatever possessions she still had, since she and her family would surely
be killed. And it was only right—Chaja's interlocutor argued without
malice—for the good people who knew the Finkelsztajns to get posses-
sion, or else the killers would be rewarded.[24] To a Jewish man trying to
find a hiding place with a peasant acquaintance near Węgrów, the latter's
son-in-law said matter-of-factly: "Since you are going to die anyway, why
should someone else get your boots? Why not give them to me so I will
remember you?"[25] Miriam Rosenkranz had a moment of déjà vu during
the pogrom in Kielce "when the horror of the ghetto came back to me
and this scene when I worked with sorting down [feathers] and we were
about to go back to the ghetto, and they were saying that that's the end,
that they were deporting us for sure, and then this woman, Joseph's wife,
looked at my feet, 'Really, you could leave me your boots Missy.' 'But
Mrs. Joseph, I am still alive.' 'Well, I wasn't saying anything, only that the
boots are cool.' "[26]

One could even identify a normative order of sorts regulating access
to plundered Jewish property. The governing rule was simple: those who
were more intimately involved with dispossessing the Jews had a better
claim on the goods than anyone else. Thus, when Helena Klimaszewska,
from the village of Goniądz, went to nearby Radziłów to get an apartment for her in-laws—she knew there were vacancies there after the Jews
had been killed—she was rebuffed by a certain Feliks Godlewski (she
told the story during a deposition at his trial after the war) who reproached the claimants for not having been there when people were

needed to kill the Jews, and only showing up later to ask for apartments. "You could have killed 10 Jews and you would have gotten a house," she quoted him as saying at the time. Her mother-in-law protested that the family had made a contribution on that day as her grandson, Józef Ekstowicz, was the one who had climbed on the barn where the Jews were assembled and doused its roof with gasoline.[27] Communal Jewish property, such as cemeteries and synagogues, was in large measure devastated after the war as the local people carted away tombstones, bricks, roofs, anything useful for their own construction projects.

There was pronounced tension, invidious comparison, and envy among lower-middle-class Poles after the war concerning which families had enriched themselves, and how much, at the expense of the Jews. It was assumed that people who sheltered Jews had enriched themselves handsomely (which was often the case). Indeed, this was one of the reasons why the future Righteous Among Nations wanted to keep their wartime assistance to Jews a secret from their neighbors. If found out, in addition to being stigmatized as "Jew lovers," they risked being identified as potential targets for robbery—a frightening prospect among those who had hidden Jews on principle, for the presumption of Jewish wealth and cunning was so pervasive that if nothing was found in their household they might be tortured by bandits to reveal the hiding place of the putative Jewish treasures that they didn't have. When the village head in one of the places where the Finkelsztajns were hiding learned about their whereabouts, he requested that they move on: not because he feared German reprisals against the village but because, he argued, if they stayed for a long time the peasant who was hiding them would excessively enrich himself.*

*Yad Vashem, 03/3033-1636/255. The original of Chaja Finkelsztajn's testimony was only partially translated by the IPN, and the segment recounting their peregrinations after the Radziłów Jews had been killed was not included in the volume. A similar exchange is recounted by Shraga Feivel Bielawski from the vicinity of Węgrów where he was trying to find a hiding place at the house of a peasant with whom he used to do business: "He thought for a moment and replied, 'This is a time when everyone is paying attention to everyone else's business. If my neighbors or friends knew that I was hiding Jews, I would be in big trouble. They would think I had made a lot of money from the Jews and would report me to the Germans'" (Shraga Feivel Bielawski, *The Last Jew from Węgrów*, p. 72). Yet another conversation along the same lines was overheard by a Jewish boy, Emanuel Kriegel, hiding in a peasant's house near Buczacz: "Our landlady was visited by the banderist [member of a Ukrainian nationalist organization] Turbota Michał and one Pole, his helper, to see her daughter. The banderist boasted that he had killed 40 Jews in the forest, and he pressed our landlady to admit that she kept Jews at her place because she had money—and it was known that whoever has money must be keeping Jews. But our landlady did not confess" (ŻIH, 301/196).

So the scanty returnees were usually met with hostility. On October 11, 1945, Major Irving Heymont, who ran the Landsberg DP camp at the time, wrote in a letter to his wife: "It seems that many Jews from Poland are drifting into the camp. Most of them, I am told, returned to Poland after being liberated from concentration camps to meet persecution again. Their attempts to repossess their pre-war property met with violent opposition from the present owners. The local police forces, according to new arrivals from Poland, often take no action and even join in preventing former owners from regaining their property."[28]

Simply put, socialization into anti-Semitic ideology by the most numerous prewar political parties and the Catholic church, in addition to the demoralization of wartime, combined with the existence of a broad stratum of beneficiaries in Poland who for economic reasons resented and actively opposed the return of Jews to their towns and villages after the war.* Numerous observers, including highly placed functionaries of the Polish Underground State, anticipated this turn of events and viewed it as a natural and desirable outcome of the German occupation. Return to the status quo ante and resumption by Jews of their economic role from before the war was an impossibility, reported Roman Knoll, the head of the Foreign Affairs Commission in the apparatus of the Government Delegate. The non-Jewish population had taken over Jewish positions in the social structure, he wrote in 1943, and this change is final and "permanent in character. . . . Should Jews attempt to return en masse people would not perceive this as a restoration, but as an invasion, which they would resist even by physical means."[29] In July 1945 another distinguished politician of the London-affiliated underground, Jerzy Braun, conveyed his observations about the growing anti-Semitism in Poland[†]:

---

*Sometimes, people wanted to restore a semblance of normality to their shattered lives. "After the war people lived here in fear," recalled Stanisław Ramotowski, who married a local Jewish woman he fell in love with named Rachela. "On one occasion about two years after the war, my wife wanted to buy back an oak family dresser [from someone living nearby who had it in his house]. She could have had a better one, but this was a family heirloom. And somebody didn't like it. We found a piece of paper stuck to our house door saying that we were sentenced to death. At that time the NSZ [National Armed Forces] gave out a lot of such sentences in our area. They stole, they beat people up, they killed. I went to my own people, because I was a member of the AK [Home Army]. And then AK made them rescind the sentence. And so we survived" (Gazeta Wyborcza, April 1, 2001). But not many Jews could draw on such local networks. Ramotowski was an ethnic Pole; he saved and married Rachela during the war, and continued to protect her at considerable personal risk.

†Braun was called the last Government Delegate, as he was entrusted with closing down the civilian apparatus of the London government–affiliated underground in Poland after the former Government Delegate was arrested by the NKVD.

"Today there is no place for a Jew in small towns or villages. During the past six years (finally! [emphasis in the original]) a Polish third estate has emerged which did not exist before. It completely took over trade, supplies, mediation, and local crafts in the provinces. . . . Those young peasant sons and former urban proletarians, who once worked for the Jews, are determined, persistent, greedy, deprived of all moral scruples in trade, and superior to Jews in courage, initiative, and flexibility. These masses . . . are not aware what an important historic role they play by conquering for Poland a new territory, formerly occupied by aliens. Those masses will not relinquish what they have conquered. There is no force which could remove them." It was understandable that Jews who survived the onslaught but could not return to their hometowns "leave ruined and broken telling the rest of the world that Poles are anti-Semites." But what they take for anti-Semitism, Braun concludes, is "only an economic law, which cannot be helped."[30]

How large these "masses" were, we cannot tell with certainty. But in November 2004 a young Polish historian published an important text on the subject in the Catholic weekly *Tygodnik Powszechny*. There had to be no fewer than half a million "successors" to Jewish property in little towns and villages, he estimated. Given that peasant and small-town families were larger than urban families, one could multiply this number by five to gauge the number of people subjected to the resulting "demoralization."[31]

The Takeover of Jewish Property by the Polish State Administration

Not only individuals but also the Polish state administration was involved in the disposition of Jewish property. A series of rules, regulations, and decrees was published from 1945 temporarily placing "abandoned [ownerless] and formerly German properties" (*"majatki opuszczone i poniemieckie"*) in the trusteeship of the state. The constantly evolving character of laws during this period left room for arbitrary implementation.*

---

*"Currently legislation is constantly changing, and every citizen has to understand this," said Justice Rudnicki, the head of the Łódź Court of Appeals, during a September 8, 1945, conference in Warsaw. "For example, regulations concerning abandoned property or the apartments' assigning commissions are constantly evolving. . . . The executive organ may therefore easily make a mistake and carry out regulations differently than the lawmaker had intended" (AAN, MAP B-876, *"I konferencja naczelników władz i urzędów niezespolonych w województwie warszawskim,"* p. 14). This was also the time when a succession of decrees concerning

The category of "abandoned" property applied primarily to "formerly Jewish" (*pożydowska*) possessions. And since Jews made up one third of Poland's urban population; since Jewish religious communities (*Izraelickie Gminy Wyznaniowe*) — the *kehillot* — had ceased to exist as legal entities and no successor had been designated under the law; since the majority of Polish Jews and their descendants had been killed, "formerly Jewish" property represented, despite the deliberate destruction and plunder of Jewish community buildings and properties during the war, a sizable body of real estate which was placed, de facto, under the control of the local state administration.* The archives of the Ministry of Public Administration include ample correspondence illustrating the procedures adopted by local authorities for disposition of this stock.[32]

In principle, the local official who made the determination of how to assign "abandoned" property (a county prefect or a town's mayor) had to consult with the Ministry of Public Administration. He — I did not find a single woman occupying the requisite administrative position — would write for permission either directly, or through the Trusteeship Bureau of the Main Liquidation Office (Biuro Powiernicze Głównego Urzędu Likwidacyjnego), to the Department of Denominations (Departament Wyznaniowy) in the Socio-Political Office (Wydział Społeczno-Polityczny) of the MAP. It would be also with the Socio-Political Office of the MAP that the Jewish Committees would lodge protests against decisions of local authorities which they found objectionable.

Now, the reality on the ground was much more layered and confusing. What used to be a synagogue or a Jewish community building might have been put to different use during the German occupation — as a warehouse for the local agricultural cooperative, for example, or a firehouse, or whatever — and if it suited everybody around all would remain as before. Or else, powerful actors on the scene could elbow their way into a choice piece of "ownerless" real estate no matter what. So, in Wrocław (Breslau), for example — the Central Jewish Committee complained to the MAP on June 28, 1945 — the local militia took over the synagogue

---

restitution of private property was promulgated, until the laws nationalizing banking as well as large and medium industry were passed in January 1946.

*"The immense holdings of kehillot all over Poland, along with the property of many Jewish associations, societies, foundations, etc., remained in the State Treasury. It must be emphasized that this took place long before strictly Socialist measures, like the total nationalization of industry and commerce, were introduced in Poland" (Lucjan Dobroszycki, "The Jewish Community in Poland, 1944–1947: A Discussion of Postwar Restitution." In Yisrael Gutman and Avital Saf, eds., *She'erit Hapletah, 1944–1948, Rehabilitation and Political Struggle,* p. 14).

building on Waalstrasse 5/9, even though the mayor had already assigned it to the Wrocław Jewish Committee.* In Tarnów, in the fall of 1945, the Polish army ordered Jewish residents and community institutions out of a building in the center of town on Goldhammera Street which they had already renovated.† In Katowice, a former Jewish community building with two prayer rooms, a ritual bath, and other cultic facilities, was assigned for editorial offices to a local daily newspaper, *Trybuna Robotnicza (The Workers' Daily)*, by "Marshal Rokossowski."‡ In Włodawa the only synagogue building that was left for use by the local Jews (and which the Jewish Committee started to renovate) was taken over on April 12, 1946, by the Włodawa Committee of the Polish Workers' Party.[33]

In all these instances, there were Jewish organizations to raise objections and challenge improper or arbitrary assignment of synagogues or *kehillot* buildings. But there was no one to speak up in the vast majority of localities where all Jews had been killed or only a few remained, unsure whether they should stay put or leave for good and too intimidated to challenge local powers on any issue.§ Indeed, from a legal standpoint, a crucial factor in making a determination of how to dispose of "formerly Jewish" communal property was the number of Jews still living in a given locality.

---

*"We implore the Ministry of Public Administration to order the Citizens' Militia to vacate the building" (AAN, MAP, B-2613, p. 131).

†While the matter was still being contested, with various offices sending memos back and forth arguing the merits of different claims, the army posted a guard in front of the building who engaged in all kinds of mischief including "dancing, screaming, and singing, under the doors of a prayer-hall during morning prayers in order to disrupt the service and make fun of praying Jews." Ample documentation of the matter can be found in the United States Holocaust Memorial Museum Archives (RG 15.020 M, reel 5). The quote is from a protocol concerning the events of November 4, 1945.

‡Marshal Konstantin Rokossowski was a Soviet war hero, whom Stalin left in charge of the Polish military as minister of defense. The building in Katowice, at 7 Mickiewicza Street, was first occupied by a unit of the Red Army; hence, perhaps, *Trybuna Robotnicza's* subsequent claim that it was assigned the building by Rokossowski.

It is clear from the correspondence that the Jewish Committee in Katowice, where there was a large and growing Jewish community, first complained about this matter to the voivodeship office in the fall of 1945. But the paper could not be dislodged from its offices. One year later, in September 1946, the Ministry of Public Administration wrote to the voivode's office suggesting that if *Trybuna Robotnicza* was still in the same location (and the voivode believed that it should remain there), the editorial board should ask the proper authorities for permission because their justification for taking occupancy of the building "does not constitute a legal title to do so." In the end, in April 1948, the paper settled the matter with the Jewish religious congregation in Katowice by agreeing to pay rent for the building (AAN, MAP, B-2613, pp. 112–15).

§Sometimes local Jews protested the assignment of a synagogue in their town—when the synagogue in Strzyżów was rented out for a mill, for example, or when the one in Białobrzegi, sold by the city for its bricks, was being dismantled—but they wrote protest letters

The Ministry of Public Administration published a regulation (*Okólnik* no. 3) in the first issue of its *Official Monitor* (*Dziennik Urzędowy* MAP) on February 6, 1945, in which the prewar *kehillot* were declared nonexistent and all their properties were put in the trusteeship of the State, pending further legislation. Jews were allowed to establish a "Jewish Religious Association" in any locality where ten or more worshipping Jews so desired, but this association was explicitly barred from claiming the right to succeed to the *kehillot* properties. However, the *Okólnik* stipulated, the property of former Jewish Religious Communities was "in the first place designated for use by Jewish cultural, welfare, etc., associations"; and the *Okólnik* also directed that any new user of Jewish community buildings should respect their original purpose.*

A good example of how such matters could (and should) have been handled can be found in the MAP's correspondence concerning the conversion of a vacant synagogue in Sokółka into a public high school. In late November 1948, the Sokółka county prefect filed a request in the matter with the Białystok voivodeship office; the voivodeship, in turn, requested permission from the MAP's Department of Denominations in mid-January 1949; on March 1, the MAP wrote to the Main Jewish Religious Council, an umbrella rabbinical organization in Poland, requesting an opinion, and in mid-June received a reply from the Central Committee of Polish Jews who, in consultation with the council, gave consent for Sokółka city authorities to convert the building into a high school. "As equivalency for the said building we suggest that the City Council order a clean-up of the local Jewish cemetery, if one is needed, and maintain care of the cemetery in the future."[34]

This was a *legis arte* solution, respectful of legislative intent, for the MAP was not obliged to consult with any Jewish institution on the proposed conversion. Indeed, for the most part the Department of Denominations decided such requests on its own: "because of the absence of the Jewish population of Kolno and in view of the urgent local need, MAP does not object to renting out the building of the Kolno synagogue to an agricultural cooperative and to the volunteer fire company, with the pro-

---

from far away (Katowice and Łódź, in these cases) after fleeing the hometowns where their lives had been threatened (AAN, MAP, B-2613, pp. 76–78; B-2612, pp. 25, 26).

*Rabbi David Kahane, who headed the Jewish Religious Association, protested in a detailed memorandum sent to the MAP on October 21, 1947, against the "constant profanation of Jewish cemeteries in the country, which are being arbitrarily converted into parks, public squares, or landfills" (AAN, MAP, B-2617, p. 44).

viso, however, that the building should not be used for purposes which would clash with its previously sacral character (movie house, dance hall, or performance space)."[35]

The MAP fought some battles over proposed uses of synagogue buildings—there is a particularly interesting correspondence with the county prefect from Włodawa, who insisted on converting one of the local synagogues into a movie house (there was no space in town to show political propaganda films, he argued cunningly), while the 250 Jews who still resided in the city protested vehemently—but the main, and ultimately the only, issue bearing on whether permission for alternative use would be granted was how many Jews had remained in a given locality.[36] Time and again, just as in the opening sentence of the letter granting permission to rent out the Kolno synagogue, local authorities justified their requests by pointing out that no more Jews resided in their township. And all it took for the MAP to give its consent was simply to recognize that fact.

As Jews were pushed out of provincial towns and the countryside by anti-Semitic terror, as they converged in a few larger cities or left Poland altogether, local authorities found themselves in charge of more and more real estate, which they could dispose of to suit local needs. Whether local bureaucrats personally nurtured an anti-Jewish animus or not—and many of them did, as we will see later in this chapter—the institutional logic placed them in the same box with local residents who wanted to get rid of the Jews for assorted personal reasons.* The state apparatus of People's Poland may have been at odds with the local population at the time of Communist consolidation of power. But on some issues their outlook and interests converged.

*In a relatively early exchange of correspondence (December 1945) with the MAP, Rabbi Kahane wrote a bitter reply concerning the proposed conversion of a synagogue in the town of Raciąż: "In reply to your memorandum concerning the transfer of the Raciąż synagogue building to the City Council, we state as follows. The synagogue building is a sanctified place, dedicated to God's worship, and it is a religious profanation to put it to some other use. And if truly, as is claimed, no more Jews live in Raciąż today, then we must note that only during the past few weeks were the last Jewish inhabitants of Raciąż bestially murdered; it would be a success for the reactionary elements if the building was now given up for some other use. We are of the opinion that this building should be cleaned up and preserved as a monument, at least for as long as the present generation is alive" (AAN, MAP, B-2613, p. 144).

Prosecution of Crimes Committed Against Jews

As we already know, the history of Polish Jewish relations during the war involved not only the takeover of property, but also murder. Sala Ungerman returned from the camp not to her native Klementów—where, as she was told, "Poles killed five Jews after the liberation"—but to Łódź. A lot of Jews settled there at the time but Ungerman could not find any family members except a sister of her sister-in-law. "She told me that my brother's child was in the hamlet Bogoria, in Opatów county, with a Pole named J.K. He was childless, he killed my brother and my sister-in-law, and did not want to return the child. . . . This Pole treats the child well and wants under no condition to return her. It is possible that he killed the parents in order to keep the child. My brother and his wife also had a lot of money on them. The little girl is four years old, her name is Halinka Ungerman, I don't know what they call her now. I went to see a prosecutor, but nothing can be done at present."[37]

Certainly something could have been done, if only the prosecutor wanted to and witnesses were ready to testify. But officers of the law were uninterested in prosecution of wartime crimes against the Jews, while the witnesses or family members who most often initiated such suits fell victim to intimidation. People might be dissuaded, as Sala Ungerman was, from filing charges altogether—because it took a long time to set the process in motion, while many were hurrying to leave the country, or because wartime culprits occupied positions of influence in local administrations after the war.* But even people who were ready to act encountered obstacles. I came across a story narrated by a woman who had personally witnessed the murder of her family during the war and survived by a miraculous coincidence, and another story by a man who had been shot repeatedly, gravely wounded, and then left for dead by his would-be killer. They discovered that their efforts to seek justice after the war were thwarted by the inertia of law enforcement institutions and that local public opinion was easily mobilized against them. In one case, the arresting policeman ended up getting drunk with the suspect and

---

*Killers of Jews might be occasionally identified by Jews who had survived the war in the local militia, or in the Security Service—see, for example, Jonas Turkov, *Noch der befrajung—zichroines*, pp. 178–79; Rudawski, *Mój obcy kraj?*, pp. 166–67; personal communication from Professor Georges Mink, Paris, spring 2002.

warned him of the impending arrest so that he could escape. In another, court proceedings were turned into a farcical interrogation of the accuser, who was queried whether, on the critical night when he allegedly murdered her family, the suspect had his mustache coiffed in the English style or wrapped around at the tips. In the end, both Natalia Mącznikowa, née Kleinplac, and Icek Lerner, the plaintiffs in these cases, had to run for their lives; Lerner fled Poland altogether, and Kleinplac moved with her family to Lower Silesia.*

That witnesses in postwar trials were intimidated and compelled or induced to give false testimony exculpating the murderers of Jews is evident also from a broad inquiry, involving dozens of cases, conducted by the Institute of National Memory (Instytut Pamięci Narodowej, IPN) in 2000–2002. After the IPN began its thorough two-year investigation of the Jedwabne murders, researchers at the institute combed through their extensive archives. The IPN took custody of documents from various organizations, including what was known as the Main Commission for Investigation of Hitlerite Crimes. In these holdings are the files of many cases that were tried in the late 1940s and early 1950s under the so-called August laws (passed in August 1944), which made collaboration with the German occupiers a crime. They are known collectively as *"sierpniówki,"* "August cases."

Scholars had assumed that *sierpniówki* for the most part referred to prosecution of individuals who had signed the *Volksliste* (German national list), declaring themselves ethnic Germans, during the occupation, or who had served in the so-called "dark blue" Polish police organization, subsumed under the German authority. But after the Jedwabne investigation began, the IPN experts discovered that sixty-one

---

"Zaznaczam, że w Sądzie mnie, mojemu mężowi i powolanym przez nas 5-ciu świadkom zadawano pytania prowokacyjne, pozwalano sobie na różne kpiny i dočinki. Na przykład pytano mnie czy Salam krytycznej nocy kiedy groziła mi śmierć nosił wąs strzyżony po angielsku czy też kręcony" (ŻIH, CKŻP, Wydział Prawny, 303/XVI/307). "I want to stress that my husband, myself and 5 witnesses we presented were asked provocative questions in Court, we were laughed at and mocked." (The story about the mustache follows.) In the end, the accused, one Salam, was acquitted and charges were brought or were about to be brought against the Mącznik family (who had saved Kleinplac and another Jewish family) for alleged murder of the Jews. "The atmosphere [in the courtroom in Pińczów], as Natalia Mącznikowa put it, "was pogrom-like." Lerner's testimony, sent from Stockholm to the Jewish Historical Institute in Warsaw, can be found in Yad Vashem under YV, 033/768. See also a long plea from Perl Herman to CKŻP in Warsaw to send an observer to the trial of one Stanisław Szymlet, a Volksdeutsch responsible for murdering scores of Jews in the Brzeżany ghetto. The atmosphere in the courtroom in Koszalin, Herman complained, was exactly as Natalia Kleinplac described it in Pińczów (ŻIH, CKŻP, Wydział Prawny, 303/XVI/305, 23.X.1948).

cases from the Białystok district court alone had been brought under the "August laws" against defendants accused of participation in killings of local Jews. And new files continue to reemerge from the archive. In the Lublin district court an IPN researcher found more than a hundred trials held after the war on similar charges.[38]

These postwar trials are most revealing in two respects. First, they document the scope of Polish assaults against the Jews in the summer of 1941 throughout the Białystok voivodeship. We know now that killings went on for several months, and that they engulfed a vast territory including some two dozen townships and resulted in thousands of victims. The second most striking aspect of those documents is the evident reluctance of the judiciary to prosecute culprits after the war. Apparently, there was a "culture" in the judiciary to slow down, sideline, narrow the focus, and generally obstruct the prosecution of such cases.

Professor Andrzej Rzepliński, a leading legal scholar from Warsaw University, was commissioned by the IPN to evaluate the 1949 Jedwabne murder trial from a legal standpoint. Rzepliński's detailed, expert analysis of the trial proceedings and the investigation runs to over one hundred printed pages.[39] Here I shall quote from his brief interview on the subject for the daily *Gazeta Wyborcza* of July 19, 2002.

Rzepliński first described the circumstances that led to the indictment of the Jedwabne murderers. In December 1947, a Jew from Jedwabne who had emigrated to Montevideo before the war wrote to the Central Committee of Polish Jews in Warsaw:

"We have information that they [the Jedwabne Jews] were killed by the Poles, not by the Germans. And we know that those Poles have not yet been brought to justice, that they still live in the same village." The letter somehow reached the Ministry of Justice, which in February 1948 ordered the prosecutor in the Łomża district court to investigate the matter.

The prosecutor's office in Łomża did not react for the next three weeks. And during the following ten months nothing was done in the judicial sense, though probably behind-the-scenes negotiations went on. Suspects in the case were arrested only in January 1949. The Łomża law enforcement apparatus—the prosecutor's office, the police, the security service (UB)—as well as the Łomża county committee of the Communist Party and the Catholic diocese, must all have known about the events in

Jedwabne. But the investigation started only after Warsaw made the request.

Eight functionaries from the security service office in Łomża conducted the investigation. They were very young, and without professional qualifications: only one had a high school diploma. These investigators tried to limit the case as much as possible from the beginning. For example, a witness might say something like "The following people took part in murdering the Jews," and then only one name would be written into the record. Presumably, when the witness started to list other names, the investigator changed the subject.

During questioning, witnesses specifically identified over ninety people as participants in the crime. Most of these no longer lived in Jedwabne, or were deceased. But not one of those who were still alive was interviewed as a witness. The local priest was not interviewed either. And he should have been asked why he didn't appear during the pogrom with a crucifix and the sacrament—he knew very well what needed to be done to convert this mob into a controllable crowd that could be dispersed. None of the Poles who saved some Jews, Antonina Wyrzykowska, for example, were deposed either.

Question: The main trial started on May 16, 1949, in the Łomża district court, and sentence was pronounced the next day. How could such an immense crime be judged in such a short time? Answer: This, frankly speaking, is utterly unimaginable to me. During two days of deliberations (about sixteen hours altogether) the court heard testimony from twenty-two accused and fifty-six witnesses. Seventy-eight people! If the time is subtracted that is needed for various necessary procedures in a court of law, including reading of the indictment and other documents and final speeches, this leaves about six minutes per person.

This haste was a deliberate ploy on the part of the presiding judge (the panel comprised one professional judge and two auxiliary judges) to make sure that witnesses said as little as possible. The prosecutors agreed to it, and the defense lawyers certainly thought it advantageous to their clients. Neither the prosecutors, nor the counsel for the defense, nor the two auxiliary judges asked any questions! The defense lawyers recognized that if they remained silent the trial would end sooner and their clients would get lighter sentences. The witnesses usually repeated the same line—some variation on "I hardly saw anything at all"—even though they had given copious depositions during the preliminary interrogation.

The vast majority of the witnesses testified for the defense. They usually stated that they saw any given accused far from the crime scene. One woman who had said during pretrial interrogation that the accused, Laudański, boasted about killing two or three Jews retracted her testimony in court. She probably feared the Laudański family more than she feared the secret police.

Not one among the people prosecuting and involved with the case knew the topography of Jedwabne. There was no court visit to the crime scene. This was used by the accused and their witnesses to spin tales about what was where. A distance which in reality could be walked in five minutes took twenty or thirty minutes to cover in their testimonies. No exhumations were ordered. In a sense, in this trial there were no victims. The crime allegedly consisted of the local inhabitants chasing the Jews out into the market square and holding them there under guard for a little while. There was nothing about burning of Jews in the trial sentence. The sentencing and its justification were embarrassingly unprofessional: not because of the judge's lack of legal qualifications, but as a result of the tactic he adopted—to limit as much as possible the scope of the case, the number of the accused, and the accusations against them.

The presiding judge, Antoni Małecki, was from a peasant background. He came from the area and probably shared the prejudices of the local people. I have a particular bone to pick with him. The prosecutors in the case were very young, having been appointed after some basic legal tutorials, typical for the Stalinist judicial system. But Małecki was a prewar judge, with twenty years of experience on the bench. He had to know what he was doing.

Question: Was this a political or a criminal trial? Answer: It was a political trial, in the sense that the whole case was deliberately scaled down—some people beat up some other people, but in the end it was not entirely clear who did what to whom, and for what reason. I think that the decision to so circumscribe the case was made somewhere in the voivodeship offices of the

Communist Party. A big trial could provide no political benefit, because there was no way it could be demonstrated that the Germans had killed the Jews in Jedwabne. Indicting a large group of Poles for the murder of Jews could result in a political scandal. Well over a hundred people should have been brought to justice, according to my calculations.

In my deepest belief those ten Poles who were found guilty drew convictions for only a fraction of what they had actually done. And all of this after a glaringly unprofessional trial— unprofessional not because legal know-how was lacking, but as a result of reluctance, due to anti-Semitic prejudice, to bring to light all the circumstances of the crime.

We can understand now why Rzepliński prefaced his interview with the words: "Over my lifetime, I have analyzed some fifteen hundred criminal cases, and none has made such a big impression on me as the trial connected to Jedwabne."[40]

But it was not an unusual trial as far as indictments involving the murder of Jews were concerned, not some accidental miscarriage of justice. The case went through two appeals and the legal cover-up cum incompetence was never challenged in superior courts. To the contrary, the Jedwabne murder trial appears a paragon of thoroughness in its treatment of evidence, compared with dozens of trials held well into the 1950s in the Białystok regional courts, where the issue of killings of Jews by their neighbors came up. I say "where the issue of killings of Jews by their neighbors came up" because in these trials (just as in the Jedwabne trial) the killing was often a tangential, sideline matter, disposed of en passant, with the main accusation and investigation focusing on some other transgression. Twelve convictions were obtained in the Jedwabne murder trial of the twenty-two accused. In the sixty-one trials reviewed by IPN historians, ninety-three Poles were indicted and seventeen were eventually convicted (there were more convictions initially, but some were overturned on appeal). To repeat: this was the judicial disposition of a wave of killings that lasted several months, engulfed a vast territory including some two dozen townships, and resulted in hundreds and possibly thousands of Jewish victims meeting death at the hands of their Polish neighbors.[41]

Anti-Jewish Bias in Local Administration

A state administration acts rather slowly, as we know, and it does not issue memoranda in response to individual interventions. Thus it is fair to assume that the Ministry of Public Administration must have received a good number of complaints before circulating a memorandum entitled "In the Matter of Attitudes Toward Citizens of Jewish Nationality" to all of Poland's voivodes, to district plenipotentiaries, and to the presidents of Warsaw and Łódź. Dated June 5, 1945, the memorandum was issued barely one month after the capitulation of Nazi Germany:

> The Ministry of Public Administration has been appraised that voivodeship and county authorities, as well as offices of general administration, do not always apply the necessary objectivity when dealing with individuals of Jewish nationality. In the unjustifiably negative attitude of the said authorities and offices when handling such cases, and especially when making it difficult for Jewish returnees to take apartments which belong to them, a highly undemocratic anti-Semitic tendency rather clearly comes to the surface. The Ministry of Public Administration calls attention to this undesirable phenomenon and emphasizes that all loyal citizens of the Polish Republic, irrespective of nationality and religious denomination, should be treated the same, and they ought to be helped within the boundaries of existing law. Therefore the Ministry of Public Administration implores you to make sure that authorities and offices within your jurisdiction abide by the recommendations of this memorandum.[42]

For all its toned-down and somewhat wooden language, the document calls attention to a distinct and disturbing phenomenon as the supervisory organ of state administration identifies and calls into question the anti-Jewish bias of its own employees. Their bias was particularly detrimental to the welfare of affected citizens at a time when the state apparatus was crucial for the distribution of virtually all basic necessities required to reestablish people's war-shattered existence. An item from the State Archives in the Kraków voivodeship may help to shed light on how this "undemocratic anti-Semitic tendency" of the state administration actually manifested itself in the lives of ordinary people.

At the beginning of July 1945 in Chrzanów, "a registration clerk at the Citizens' Militia office requested that Citizen Schnitzer Gusta [i.e., Gusta Schnitzer], who had returned from a camp, prove her identity by bringing a witness who would vouch for her identity and attest that she lived in Chrzanów before the war. When Citizen Schnitzer Gusta presented to the clerk at the said office as her witness the Chairman of the County Jewish Committee in Chrzanów, Citizen Bachner Lesser [i.e., Lesser Bachner], the said clerk stated in the presence of the witness that he had no confidence in the presented witness and that he would trust only a witness of non-Jewish extraction and that he would register Citizen [Schnitzer] only when she presented such a witness."[43]

Such an episode, which at first glance may seem no more than a trivial nuisance, captures a crucial moment in the life of postwar Polish citizens. So many documents had been lost, so many offices and records destroyed, so many people compelled to change or move away from their original place of residence that it became necessary to authenticate each and every claim, beginning with one's own identity. Local bureaucracy at various levels, the courts, and professional associations that were understaffed, poorly equipped, and virtually unsupervised exercised broad discretion in processing all kinds of requests for "registration." A bias of the sort Citizen Schnitzer encountered could effectively ban Jews from settling in a given locality, thwart development of an institution, or bar Jews in a given area from gainful employment or access to much needed resources. Thus, beginning with March 1, 1945, in the town of Ostrowiec, for instance, at the whim of a certain Mr. Stawecki, Jews were denied permission to receive a daily meal in the local welfare office. As most of Ostrowiec's Jewish residents had just returned from various German camps and were utterly destitute, for many this was their only meal. "Please, Mr. Mayor," pleaded the local Jewish Committee in a memorandum, "undo the injustice and restore the right to dinner at the RGO [the name of the wartime welfare office] to Jews."[44]

True, Ostrowiec was an unusually difficult town for Jews to get by in—at some point the city council even called representatives of the Jewish Committee and requested that all Jews be sent to work in a mine—but it was not the only place where local authorities were frankly unwelcoming to Jews. The Ministry of Public Administration sent a reprimand, for instance, to the Kielce voivodeship office: "In Jędrzejów the county *starosta* (the head of county administration), Feliks, turns down all cases brought to him by Jews; [and] the same situation prevails in Chęciny and Chmielnik."[45] The county prefect in Radom repeatedly refused to receive a Jewish delegation that came to discuss various complaints until the Ministry of Public Administration sent him a gentle admonition "begging the Citizen Prefect to take note that as a state functionary he has to have an equal attitude toward all citizens irrespective of their race, ethnicity, or religion."[46] In the summer of 1945 the county office denied Jews permission to take residence in Biała Podlaska when they fled into town from the surrounding area, fearing for their lives.* In Międzyrzec the conflict between the municipal authorities and the Jews got out of hand to the point that an outside "intervention" was necessary to restore a modus vivendi.† While "during its July 1945 meeting in Jodłów the Peasant Party resolved to remove the Jews from town altogether and the resolution was carried out."[47]

Clearly, in the perception of local authorities from many townships in Poland, Jews were a distinct, "special problem" category of the popula-

---

*When Jews from Biała Podlaska pleaded with the voivodeship Jewish Committee in Lublin to intervene and try to get the ban revoked, the voivode's office in Lublin forwarded their complaint to the county prefect in Biała Podlaska. Six weeks later, the *starosta* explained to the voivode in writing that "almost all the Jews in town are black marketeers and therefore I denied residence permits to some" (Archiwum Państwowe w Lublinie [APL], Urząd Wojewódzki [UW], Wydział Społeczno-Polityczny, 50, 25.X.1945, and 6.XII.1945).

In general, Biała Podlaska and the vicinity were exceedingly perilous for Jews after the war. I found two reminiscences of victims who had been wounded in unrelated but eerily similar circumstances. Elias Magid, a tailor, was promised sewing machines in the Jewish Committee in Lublin for a tailors' cooperative he was about to establish in Międzyrzec. He traveled by train, and at night near the Łuków station three men struck up a conversation with him; when they realized he was a Jew, they threw him off the train while it was going at full speed. Magid lost both legs and spent nine months recovering in a hospital (ŻIH, 301/2019). In another episode Jakub Modliński and Izrael Zylbersztejn were returning on June 29, 1945, to Biała Podlaska from Lublin with a load of relief supplies for the Jewish Committee. They changed trains in Łuków and boarded a cargo train for Biała Podlaska. A young Jewish woman on the way to Międzyrzec, Rywka Starec, boarded the same wagon along the route, as did two men wearing railroad men's caps. Zylbersztejn, Modliński, and Starec were absorbed in a conversation when the two men pulled handguns and started shooting at them. They killed Modliński and grievously wounded Zylbersztejn, who jumped off the train and survived; Starec was discovered dead, with a cut throat, upon the train's arrival in Międzyrzec (APL, UW, Wydział Społeczno-Polityczny, 50, 7.VII.1945).

†During its plenary meeting on April 15, 1945, the Lublin Jewish Committee discussed the situation in Międzyrzec, where about two hundred Jews resided at the time. "In order not to inflame the situation the local Jewish Committee restrained the Jews from trying to regain their property, of which they had been robbed by some of the local Christians. . . . At the beginning the mayor was unfriendly toward the Jews. He didn't allow a Jewish doctor to establish himself in town. The militia didn't respond when Jewish houses were severely vandalized. Following some complaints, a representative of the Security Service came to town and he smoothed things over between Jews and Poles. A so-called 'agreement' [*ugoda*] was even signed. Now things have quieted down" (ŻIH, CKŻP, Wydział Organizacyjny, 304/3). The very term *ugoda* has a solemn significance in Polish, pointing to social distance between the parties. One can use it synonymously with "treaty" to designate an agreement between states.

tion that remained in an adversarial relationship with the rest of local inhabitants. And apparently, in the eyes of many a local bureaucrat, they
had to be dealt with accordingly.

Dr. Shlomo Herszenhorn, then in charge of the government office
dedicated to providing assistance for the Jewish population, made an inspection tour in February 1945 and noted a spectrum of attitudes among
local officials. In Kraków, he reported, the top echelon of the administration was well disposed toward the Jews but "the attitude of subordinate
authorities was bad." In Łódź the attitude of local authorities was "not
bad." In Radom, despite pressure from the higher-ups, the executive or-
gans of the administration "were not friendly, [were] even hostile." In
the Lublin voivodeship the local administration appeared to Herszenhorn "generally correct" in its attitudes except in Chełm Lubelski and
Krzczonów, where "street round-ups of Jews for compulsory labor were
a frequent occurrence."[48]

Such "bad" or "hostile" attitudes on the part of local officials could
turn every transaction, every piece of paper needed in order to go on
with daily life, into a Kafkaesque nightmare. "How can you do this for a
Jew?" a Polish-looking female employee of the Lublin Jewish Committee
was reproached by a clerk in the City Court. (The committee employee
had come to fetch a birth certificate for a Jew stationed in a faraway army
outpost.) When a Mr. Zyskind's request for some certificate in another
office in Lublin was denied on the grounds that such documents were no
longer issued, he noticed that "another citizen, of Polish nationality, who
simultaneously requested the same, got it right away." Zyskind was a no-
nonsense man, a former partisan, and he went to the manager in a huff
and got the desired document.[49] But how many people's lives were made
chronically difficult as a result of such practices? Or consider the complaint of a Mrs. Nassowa, who was taking care of Jewish orphans and obtained a ration coupon for twenty liters of cod-liver oil from the head
medical officer in the Lublin city administration, Dr. Rupniewski. "I
want to inform the [Jewish] Committee that today," she wrote on December 9, 1945, "while carrying out my official duties I was confronted
with the following anti-Semitic act by an employee of the Lublin Health
Center." Nassowa and a friend took a horse-drawn cart, a *droshki,* to the
health center with a big container to collect the precious supplement for
the vitamin-deficient winter diet. But the woman in the health center
to whom she handed the coupon flatly refused to give her the oil. "So this
is why I was trudging for three months to collect fish oil, so that Jewish

children would get it. I won't give them any fish oil," the woman said.*
No such episode by itself amounted to very much, but multiplied a thou-
sandfold every day of the week they made the already difficult life of the
affected community a constant struggle.

Jews were always loyal citizens. They traditionally viewed the state as
a guardian against potential aggression by xenophobic neighbors. They
certainly considered the Communist-dominated government a natural
ally, given the hostility of the social environment. But in the end, the
state apparatus is staffed by ordinary people. And evidently it did reflect
the shared mind-set of the population concerning the undesirability of a
Jewish presence in postwar Poland.

Upper echelons of the administration tried repeatedly to remedy
the situation. The Ministry of Public Administration urged the Lublin
voivodeship office in March 1945 to impress on subordinates that the
provisional government had restored Jewish citizens to full equality before the law and was determined to combat anti-Semitism. "Unfortunately this political line of the government is not being followed or is not
fully accepted at every level of public administration."⁵⁰ One month later,
on April 27, 1945, the voivode sent an appropriate circular to all county
offices. Whether they changed their ways as a result is rather doubtful,
since there were no sanctions attached to such reminders. But for the
most part, lower-rung subordinates replied according to expectations,
with matter-of-fact and reassuring memos.†

A few months later, on April 12, 1946, the Lublin voivode was again
imploring county prefects to tame the wave of anti-Semitic incidents.

*The woman finally agreed to fill the request, but only if Dr. Rupniewski assigned an-
other barrel of fish oil to the health center. Nassowa went back to city hall, got a second
coupon, and collected her fish oil from the main pharmacy on Narutowicza Street. It took her
a full day, instead of an hour, to get the fish oil for the children (ŻIH, CKŻP, Wydział Organizacyjny, 304/22, "Do Wojewódzkiego Komitetu Żydów Polskich w Lublinie," 9.XII.1945).
†Occasionally, however, a county *starosta* might adopt a tone of defiance, as did the one
from Włodawa, who first tried to ignore the matter altogether and finally wrote back in September, after five months and repeated prodding, to claim that no organized anti-Semitic
incidents ever took place in the county. He admitted that people generally disliked the Jews,
but "the reason for this attitude is that jews [lowercase in the original] during the first
months of independence were too aggressive vis-à-vis everybody else. The attitude toward
other nationalities especially among those [Jews] employed in the militia and in the Security
Service was openly hostile. Several months ago two aryans [2-ch aryjczyków] perished by the
hand of a jewish militiaman, and such facts do not produce harmonious coexistence in a
democratic spirit. It is comforting that the number of citizens of Jewish nationality in the
Militia was reduced and that the rest have a somewhat more positive attitude toward everybody else" (APL, UW, Wydział Społeczno-Polityczny, 50, 10.IX.1945).

The higher in the state hierarchy one looked, the more sympathy and understanding could be found for the plight of Jewish citizens. The MAP was sending memoranda to the voivodes. The voivodeship offices passed these along and acted on complaints of local Jewish Committees by urging lower-level bureaucrats to comply with and enforce the law. In conversations with top state officials, representatives of the CKŻP found many concerned listeners. The commander of the militia, General Franciszek Jóźwiak, was very upset by reports of anti-Jewish bias among his subordinates and issued a stern order in July 1945 to combat anti-Semitism and assist Jews in peril.[51]

But these assorted top-down appeals for fair treatment of Jewish citizens lacked any enforcement protocol, so they amounted to little more than goodwill gestures appealing to the consciences of administrative personnel. And in the meantime ordinary citizens had to deal with low-ranking local bureaucrats who were usually prejudiced.

With a full agenda of urgent tasks before the state bureaucracy, influential people and institutions soon got tired of listening to Jewish complaints. During a meeting of the CKŻP's Presidium held two and a half weeks before the pogrom in Kraków, on July 24, 1945, Adolf Berman, the left-wing Zionist Party leader, reported that the parliamentarians of the National Council of the Country (KRN) were no longer interested in Jewish issues. "One can detect in the statements of all the parties a negative attitude [*niechęć*] to speeches by Jewish representatives as well as to Polish representatives who address Jewish matters."[52]

Immediately after the pogrom in Kraków, Hersh Smolar and Szymon Zachariasz—members of the CKŻP's Presidium and old Communists who had been in the Party longer than almost anyone else in Poland—went to see their "junior" Party colleague, the minister of public security, Stanisław Radkiewicz, who awaited them with two dossiers piled on his desk. One dossier contained reports documenting physical assaults against Jews, and the other, much thicker, was filled with files describing armed attacks against the militia. In part, the minister's attitude only illustrated an understandable ranking of enforcement priorities. But Smolar left Radkiewicz's office chagrined that the authorities were now downplaying the issue of anti-Jewish violence.[53] Evidently yet another branch of the state administration, the Ministry of Public Security, was shunning the Jews. Ignoring the vulnerability of Jewish citizens, the MBP did not respond to evidence from all over the country pointing to the ubiquity of anti-Jewish assaults.

Employment Discrimination

While the special needs of the Jewish population were being ignored by
the agencies responsible for security, the negative "profiling" of Jews (as
we would put it today) by different segments of the state and local administration interfered with their other vital pursuits. It put obstacles in
the way of gainful employment of Jewish artisans, for example, as registration of Jewish cooperatives by the Central Cooperative Administration, Społem, got routinely bogged down. During the April 6, 1945,
meeting of the Presidium of the Central Committee of Polish Jews, one
of its members reported that "nearly all the voivodeship committees"
voiced complaints about local authorities' refusal to register Jewish production cooperatives (*"spółdzielnie wytwórcze"*), which therefore could not
legally open for business.[54] As a result of subsequent CKŻP intervention,
the steering committee of the Supervisory Council of Cooperatives in
the Polish Republic (Zarząd Główny Związku Rewizyjnego Spółdzielni
Rzeczypospolitej Polskiej) instructed its local branches that "matters
brought [before them] by Jewish production cooperatives be treated on
an equal footing with those brought by Polish cooperatives, without giving them preferential treatment or making things especially difficult."[55]

A follow-up memorandum in the CKŻP's files indicates that the
steering committee's intervention produced desirable effects, and scores
of cooperatives were soon legalized in Łódź, Kraków, Tarnów, Warsaw,
and Częstochowa. This apparently emboldened the CKŻP to approach
the Department of Crafts in the Ministry of Industry with a request to
instruct local Chambers of Crafts (Izby Rzemieślnicze) to authorize special procedures for the verification of professional licenses for Jewish
craftsmen. Under existing rules, local guild associations could provide re-
placement licenses on the basis of sworn testimony by two members of
the profession. The CKŻP petitioned that local Jewish Committees also
be empowered to certify witnesses' signatures on sworn affidavits, to
make up for the refusal of administration officials to accept such affidavits from Jewish witnesses.[56]

Along with obstacles faced by Jewish institutions, individual Jews
were occasionally branded as such by zealous local bureaucrats and then
faced discrimination when they sought gainful employment. In one of
the flagship weeklies of this period, *Kuźnica,* the following item appeared

on October 14, 1945: "The Third Reich is no more. Nobody knows what happened to Hitler. Himmler and Goebbels took poison. But Jewish identity cards have reappeared—in the reborn, democratic Poland. Let's be precise. It's not so much identity cards as labor certificates issued by the Regional Labor Office in Dąbrowa Górnicza. One such document is in front of us now—certificate No. 102466, issued on July 5, 1945. One month after the mysterious disappearance of Adolf Hitler, on this certificate, right next to the Polish seal of the Dąbrowa Górnicza City Government, a round stamp is visible with the letter 'J'—Jew. . . . Who are the people responsible for this horrendous Hitlerite scandal in a Polish state institution?"*

Nine months later, at the other end of Poland in Szczecin, during a high-level conference with the voivode and the heads of all the main enterprises in town, the Jewish Committee representative read a long list of complaints concerning job discrimination. The most glaring case, he stated, concerned City Tramways (the Szczecin public transit company), "where despite our interventions no Jews were given employment."⁵⁷

Occasionally a deep emotional response was triggered in the Jewish community when the state bureaucracy made categorical distinctions between Jews and non-Jews. The town office in Chrzanów at some point began sending daily requests for laborers to the Jewish Committee, demanding on July 5, 1945, for example, that "twelve persons of female sex be designated for washing the dirty linen of Red Army soldiers." In the eyes of the Jewish Committee filing the complaint, that the town office did not honor its promise to pay the workers mattered less than the fact of its issuing the request in a manner "emulating the methods of the occupiers, which makes the Jewish Committee responsible if the labor contingent does not appear in the designated time and place. Such requests are issued only to the Jewish population, through the committee. In this manner, the town office in Chrzanów perpetuates traditions established by the occupiers, who communicated with the Jewish population with the help of the Judenrat."⁵⁸

---

*"The Labor Office explains this novel manner of stamping certificates by 'technical reasons' pertaining to registration. What kind of reasons could these be? As far as we know, the same rules for registration apply to Jewish and non-Jewish citizens. As far as we know, the same principles are binding in the Ministry of Labor and Social Welfare as in the rest of the country stipulating complete equality of citizens, including Jews" (*Kuźnica,* October 14, 1945).

Labor relations between the Jewish population and various institutions of the Polish state were volatile. And while the reasons for high unemployment among the Jews in Poland immediately after the war were undoubtedly varied, one contributing factor was institutionalized discrimination.*

Anti-Semitism in Schools

The Jewish population was in constant flux after the war, coming back from German camps or returning from exile in the USSR, moving from place to place, searching for relatives and a safe place to live, or fleeing Poland altogether. None of this made it easy for the children to attend school. In a few locations where more Jews had settled—in Łódź, Warsaw, and Lower Silesia, for example—Jewish schools were established. But scores of Jewish children ended up in regular Polish state schools where, as a rule, they met with hostility.† The range of experiences var-

---

*An undated summary report by the CKŻP's Department for Productivization from the year 1945 affords a glance into the circumstances of Jewish "experts" or "professionals" (somewhat ambiguous in its generality, the Polish word used in the document—*fachowcy*—may refer equally to plumbers, tailors, accountants, or engineers) in various towns and voivodeships. In Kraków, of 1,388 "experts" registered with the committee, 166 worked in "state, local, and social institutions," while 422 were employed in private establishments. In Przemyśl, 9 out of 265 "experts" worked in "state and local institutions," and 74 in private capacity. Among the 1,225 "experts" from the city of Kielce and the Kielce voivodeship as a whole, only 13 had found employment in "state, local, and social institutions," while 599 worked in cooperatives and on their own. In Warsaw, 166 out of 488 committee-registered "experts" were employed in "state or communal institutions," 15 worked in cooperatives, and 146 in an individual capacity, while in Częstochowa, with 490 "experts," only 7 were employed in "state and communal institutions," 31 worked in cooperatives, and 960 people (in Częstochowa an unusually high number of Jews—around 5,000—had survived in local labor camps associated with the armaments industry) worked in various private workshops (ŻIH, CKŻP, Wydział Produktywizacji, 303/XII/6, "Wydział dla Spraw Produktywizacji. Sprawozdanie z Działalności").

†If not too many Jewish children were directly affected by discrimination in schools, it is because so few had survived the war. Young Jews had perished at unusually high rates. We can see this clearly when comparing the relative size of the Jewish population in different age brackets in 1931 (when the last prewar census was taken) and 1947. Those between ages 5 and 9 made up together 11.6 percent of the total Jewish population in Poland in 1931, but only 5.3 percent in 1947. For the 10-to-14 age bracket the corresponding numbers are 8.4 percent in 1931 and 4.4 percent in 1947, and for ages 15 through 19, 9.6 percent in 1931 and 4.8 percent in 1947 (Irena Hurwic-Nowakowska, *Żydzi Polscy [1947–1950]*, p. 30). This important book was Hurwic-Nowakowska's doctoral dissertation, written under the supervision of professor Stanisław Ossowski. Her study was based on personal interviews and a survey sent out in the spring of 1948 to all Jews over 18 years of age who were registered with Jewish Committees in Warsaw, Łódź, and Dzierżoniów—altogether, almost 19,000 people. Six thousand mailings were returned by the post office because it was unable to find the addressee. Of the 13,000 questionnaires that had reached their destination, 817 were completed and returned to the author.

ied, sometimes amounting to little more than an aura of contempt, unaccompanied by physical violence. But for people who had miraculously survived years of Nazi persecution, even this could be difficult to bear.*

In the Otwock orphanage, which she visited on November 12, 1945, Zofia Nałkowska (a great Polish writer and a public figure of considerable influence at the time) came upon children who did not look Jewish at all. Interestingly enough, a *maître à penser* of socialist realism independently made an identical observation. Jan Kott, whose business was typically with highbrow intellectuals and sharp ideological polemics of the day, began a piece entitled "Paris' Week" by reporting on a conversation he had with Louis Aragon about André Malraux. And then, uncharacteristically, he continued: "I am going 30 kilometers from Paris to visit a house where Jewish orphans from Poland were placed. A villa, like any other, standing in the garden; and children, like any other children. No, just like Polish children: the little ones with blond hair and blue eyes romping around on the lawn."[59] Nałkowska thought she had mistakenly gone to the wrong place. But then, she wrote in her *Diaries,* she realized that "this is why they survived, in camps, in hovels, in basements, in ruins where they were hiding."[60]

The editor of Nałkowska's *Diaries* provides a long footnote describing in detail the tribulations of the orphanage's children, who were "physically and spiritually wounded and required special pedagogical and therapeutic care. They had to have their citizen's rights restored, documents issued, sometimes new names provided. Their fears had to be overcome; they had to be sent to school, which from the start proved almost an impossibility. No school in Otwock would enroll Jewish children, for fear that they would be tormented by other pupils. In the end, in School Number 3, an additional second grade was opened for all the

---

*Samuel Bak from Wilno, later a world-famous painter, found himself in Łódź at the conclusion of the war. He went to school there in the autumn of 1945. "The most troubling moments came during recess, when the teachers were out of the hearing range," Bak writes in his memoirs. "My classmates would come up to me, sniff me out and murmur that for 'a regular kike' I smelled not too bad. There was no attempt at physical violence, no pushing, pulling, or kicking, but the overt anti-Semitism of a few boys, nonchalantly tolerated by all the others, started to annoy me greatly. I tried to ignore it for several days, but the anguish I felt every morning on leaving for school soon made me speak about it to Mother. 'We do not need this,' she said," and pulled him out of school right away (Samuel Bak, *Painted in Words,* p. 398). But few had the necessary resolve and resources to act so swiftly and decisively. Mrs. Bak sent her son for a while to study painting with a professor of fine arts and shortly thereafter, by way of Brikha, they left the country for the Landsberg DP camp seeking "safety among the Germans." Of course most Jewish children had no special talents or resources, or doting parents, to shield them from the company of threatening peers.

Jewish children, but even this did not save them from beatings and persecution."*

Most Polish Jews, as we know, moved to larger urban agglomerations. Otwock is near Warsaw, so a large group of Jewish children and the orphanage were in place to press their case with the local authorities. But those who remained in the provinces, usually because of a family business they had to attend to, were left to fend for themselves and either kept children at home or sent them to local schools.

Mejer Cytrynbaum was trying to recover a house and a large three-door oak armoire he had left for safekeeping with Polish peasants during the war. The efforts kept him near his native village. A memo from the Ostrowiec branch of the Jewish Committee to the voivodeship Jewish Committee in Lublin described the circumstances of the "four children of citizen Mejer Cytrynbaum aged twelve, ten, eight, and seven. For two and a half years these children hid in an underground bunker, without light or fresh air; one of them is sick with joint inflammation. After liberation they settled in Denków [where the family was from] but because of the hostile attitude of the local population (threats to their life) they were compelled to move to Ostrowiec. Because there are no [Jewish] schools in this district, the children cannot study. Sending them to a Polish school is totally out of the question ["posłanie do szkoły polskiej jest zupełnie niemożliwe"]. This state of affairs has a negative influence on the children's health and intellectual development, but the Committee has no chance whatsoever of doing anything about this."[61]

Unlike the Cytrynbaum children, Michał Głowiński, whose assimilated family had been settled in town for generations, went to a neighborhood primary school in his native Pruszków. Just like everybody else, the young Głowiński was made to attend classes where the Catholic religion was taught by an anti-Semitic priest. But Michał's real nemesis was a certain Szymański, a classmate who harassed him incessantly with anti-Semitic slurs and threatened to beat him up after graduation.

The end of the school year finally came, and as Michał was happily

*Zofia Nałkowska, Dzienniki, p. 118. A report by the Kraków voivodeship Jewish Committee about its activities at almost the same time—from February through August 1945—reports similar circumstances affecting Jewish children in an orphanage in Zakopane. "The attitude of Polish society in Zakopane—with the exception of a few individuals—is very inimical toward Jewish children. Similarly, the children of the local people, raised in German schools, have an unfriendly attitude toward Jewish children" (ŻIH, CKŻP, Wydział Organizacyjny, 304/34, "Sprawozdanie z działaności WKŻ w Krakowie za czasokres od 1 lutego 1945 do 31 sierpnia 1945").

trudging home with his diploma in his bag and the cheerful prospect before him of a two-month vacation he was jumped by Szymański and an
associate on a deserted street. "I didn't even think of defending myself,"
he writes in *The Black Seasons*.

> Instead I cringed. . . . I'm unable today to reconstruct reliably
> what I felt then; yet I do know that it was one of those situations
> in which I felt that my world was collapsing, that something was
> happening to deprive the world of sense and to direct it in its en-
> tirety against me. It was a great shock, not only in a strictly phys-
> ical sense—in total I received only a few blows, and would surely
> have received more had an unknown man not come to my de-
> fense and driven away the assailants. It was a shock in a deeper
> sense, because that sudden attack allowed me to see—or so I
> thought—that I would always be alienated, that neither in
> Pruszków nor anywhere else would I ever find a place for myself.
> I felt the shock as an extension of the occupation, which I still
> carried inside myself. . . . At once I understood that Szymański
> was not beating me because we had some kind of accounts to set-
> tle from school. . . . He was dispensing justice, he was acting from
> higher motives. After all, I was a God-killer. . . . Getting home
> was not easy. I reacted to the unexpected assault with uncontrol-
> lable, hysterical tears. I was unable to stop them, violent sobbing
> overcame me, and I began to wail. My behavior couldn't go un-
> observed by passersby, all the more so due to its vivid contrast
> with the cheerfulness of the other children, who were happy that
> the school year had ended. . . . I was crying because a great and
> undeserved injury had been done to me. For after all I knew that
> I had not killed Jesus, I was astounded that such a thought could
> have come into someone's head. . . . And thus the episode con-
> cluded. That is, it concluded as a concrete event, since seen from
> another perspective, it endured in me for years, defining my be-
> havior and my ways of seeing the world.[62]

The underlying drama of anti-Semitic encounters, the real inde-
cency of anti-Semitism after the war, consisted in its inevitable mapping,
in the minds *of the Poles and the Jews alike,* into the horrors of the Nazi occupation that had just played out ("I felt the shock as an extension of
the occupation, which I still carried inside myself"). This is why the elite

Polish intelligentsia was so shocked and scandalized by the recurring postwar manifestations of popular anti-Semitism. But for the Jews, these were not merely an intellectual and moral puzzle to parse in disbelief and to reflect upon. They were a trauma, which could be rendered with artistic elegance by a masterful writer from the distance of several decades, or else come out as the scream of a tormented child who could no longer bear the return of suffering.

"I witnessed the most characteristic reaction of a hurt child in the orphanage in Zakopane," writes Miriam Hochberg-Mariańska in the preface to her book which led me to begin this inquiry.

> A nine-year-old boy, always full of life and good spirits, cried inconsolably one afternoon, and it was impossible to calm him down. In the end, utterly overcome with grief and on the brink of emotional collapse, he started to speak about the death of his family, as if it had just happened. Sobbing, he kept repeating that his father and mother and little sister had been murdered, that he was alone in the world, that he had nobody, nobody, nobody. . . . We were astonished by this sudden eruption of despair several months after he had come to the orphanage. But the next day everything became clear. He was regularly insulted, ridiculed, and brutally attacked by a few boys at school, and the teacher listened passively to slurs that were addressed to him. He didn't want to complain to the principal. But his suffering had to generate a reaction, and in the atmosphere of injustice and rejection he felt totally abandoned.
>
> All of this brought about a situation which, despite our efforts, could not be avoided: the isolation of Jewish children. This was unfortunate, but we had to provide them with some respite and calm. If a child in school or at play is called Jew, Jew, Jew, we know that this is a shout older than Hitlerism. But a child who remembers nothing, or very little, from before the war will always find in it the echo of that other call: *Jude, Jude, Jude.*[63]

Accumulated wartime experiences were as much at the root of Jewish children's reactions as they were at the root of their Polish schoolmates' behavior. This was a period of intense public discussion of the war, a subject involving massive human suffering, and society urgently needed to look forward and sort out the options that lay ahead. Even under the best of circumstances the fate of Jews could be but one subject among many, and probably not the most pressing, but matters Jewish still came up in numerous contexts.* What would happen to the young generation, how the war had affected youth, and how the educational system should address these matters was one of the burning issues of the day.

In the framework of this discussion, the issue of anti-Semitism among the young was broached in the most striking manner by Irena Chmieleńska's article "Wartime Children." In the influential political-literary weekly *Kuźnica*, on December 9, 1945, Chmieleńska described a wartime research project to assess the impact of German occupation on the children of Warsaw.† Her article gave a bleak assessment of children's moral condition, which had been radically transformed during the war, Chmieleńska argued, because of exposure to two closely related phenomena—the black market and, as she put it, "the Jewish matter" (*"sprawa żydowska"*).

Children were demoralized during the war and they exhibited ruthless egoism. What mattered above anything else, in their view of the world, was to take advantage of every opportunity for material gain. Considerations for another person's welfare, honesty, fairness, were all dismissed as "stupidity."‡

A German shot at *"Jude,"* and a child shouted *"Jude"* whenever he met one. . . . That somebody else was beaten up or killed, not him, not his family, that he could watch this calmly with a feeling of personal safety, gave such a child a sense of pride—he felt better, untouchable vis-à-vis those who in his presence, and to his delight, were being humiliated. A German gendarme enjoyed it,

*A thorough and profound discussion of postwar anti-Semitism took place on the pages of most prestigious cultural weeklies in the aftermath of the Kraków and Kielce pogroms—see, especially, pp. 128–133.

†Her responsibility was to collect data and evaluate the consequences of wartime conditions on children's ethical notions. Regrettably, all the original materials, including her interviews, were burned during the Warsaw Uprising, and she presented but a general summary of her findings.

‡Young boys, ten to thirteen years old and sometimes even younger, "spent entire nights watching by ghetto walls and blackmailing Jews who were climbing over. . . . I spoke with a 10-year-old boy from an upper-class intelligentsia family. He was a child from a so-called good family. He said that the Germans were right to destroy the Jews because now 'We have more food; earlier Mommy and I were doing worse.' Asked if he thought it would be just as fair to kill him and his mother so that some Jewish child and his mother had more to eat, he replied calmly, after giving the matter 'serious consideration,' that he would not consider this right 'because, you see Miss, everybody is an egoist and has to think first about his own interest, and it is better for me that way.' . . .

and a Polish child enjoyed it. The Germans accustomed our children and us grown-ups as well to concepts of differentiating between human beings and people who were less than human. A Jew belonged to a different category from a human being. A well-known question asked by a small child was widely written about in the underground press: "Mommy, was it a human being that was killed or a Jew?" . . . I cannot forecast the future moral development of children who during their formative years, when moral and ethical notions crystallize, were taught that it is all right to kill a few million people.

It is not surprising that aggressive anti-Semitism showed up in the behavioral repertoire of Polish children after the war. This was the reason, evidently, why no school in Otwock dared to accept Jewish orphans, for fear that they would be mistreated by Polish pupils. For the same reason a joint meeting of the Kielce voivodeship committees of the PPS and PPR condemned "mass participation of Boy Scout youths in the day of the pogrom" ("*masowy udział młodzieży harcerskiej w dniu pogromu*") and called for "suspending local Boy Scouts' leadership because many Boy Scouts were involved as instigators during the pogrom" ("*za liczny udział harcerzy w roli podżegaczy do ekscesów*").[64] Anti-Semitism in schools was not invented by the children. As Michał Głowiński wrote in his sad reminiscences, "The cruelty of an epoch is concentrated and reflected in the cruelties of children who mirror the villainy committed in the adult world."[65]

Whether at work or in a government office, in the street, on a train, or in a classroom, Polish Jews encountered hostility. It was ubiquitous and universal. The truly assimilated ones could avoid it for the most part. The highly educated, too, were somewhat shielded by their elite status. For some, there was the cover of anonymity. And, of course, Jews were not subjected to direct government-mandated policies of discrimination. But, for the reasons enunciated above, few who had survived the war by "passing," and under false identity, returned to their real names after the war. The moment of liberation did not set the Jews free to re-

---

"I knew an eleven-year-old girl who observed from her window a section of the road that led to a place where Jews, discovered in the vicinity, were executed. When she saw someone taken to be killed she ran out of the house and stood up on her toes to watch the executions. She told me once, a few hours after one such occurrence, with great excitement—not with compassion, God forbid, but with excitement—'First they put them like this; a whole family was there; this mother cried so much; the German first shot the children,' etc." (Irena Chmieleńska, "Wartime Children").

veal themselves. As a rule, reports Hurwic-Nowakowska on the basis of her survey conducted in the spring of 1948, they also tried to keep their own children ignorant about Jewish family roots.[66]

A Pogrom That Wasn't

On a short list of anti-Semitic outbursts in postwar Poland one may occasionally find a mention of the pogrom in Rzeszów. It took place on June 12, 1945, the first episode in a sequence of increasingly violent public manifestations of anti-Jewish sentiment. But while the Kraków (August 11, 1945) and the Kielce (July 4, 1946) pogroms have their literature, the one in Rzeszów does not.

This is in part, perhaps, because it did not cause such extensive physical harm to the Jews: no one was killed, apparently, and the beatings inflicted did not injure as many people as in Kraków or Kielce.* More important for interested historians, "the main bulk of materials" collected in the case of one Jonas Landesmann, who had been arrested there under suspicion of murdering a nine-year-old girl, Bronisława Mendoń, were lost in "unexplained circumstances."[†] In any event, the episode

---

*The killing of a Jew was mentioned in two somewhat unrelated circumstances in the context of the pogrom in Rzeszów. Sonia Poloński, interviewed by the Yale Fortunoff Project, attributes one killing to Soviet soldiers, who were allegedly brought by Poles to the place where the body was found and told that Jews had killed Christian children (Fortunoff Archive, T-1681). In another, much more coherent testimony, the Red Army soldiers are credited with protecting a building and providing a truck to get some Jews out of town (Fortunoff Archive, T-1014). The other killing related to the pogrom is described in a summary report prepared by the Jewish Historical Commission on June 16, 1945, a few days after the Rzeszów events. The killing took place in Tarnów, however, where a group of Jews running away from Rzeszów had been arrested at the request of the Rzeszów Railroad Militia. The Security Service, Urząd Bezpieczeństwa, in Tarnów carried out the arrests and, according to the testimony of several Jews who had been detained, "treated them worse than during the German occupation. Women were searched in a manner incompatible with public decency . . . and one Jewish woman was shot to death there in unexplained circumstances. Coming back from a camp she stopped in Rzeszów, then with the above group of Jews she escaped from Rzeszów and met with the tragic fate that she was spared in a German concentration camp" (ŻIH, "Sprawozdanie w sprawie wpadków zaszłych w Rzeszowie w dniu 12 czerwca 1945," 301/1320).

The report also lists the names of half a dozen Jews who had been beaten (adding that "many others" had suffered a similar fate), including one person hospitalized in Kraków.

[†]The vice minister of internal affairs, "Comrade Świtała," was so informed on June 19, 1968 (Instytut Pamięci Narodowej, Oddział w Rzeszowie [IPN-Rz]-062/5). In the political calendar of Communist Poland, "March 1968" stands for an anti-Semitic purge organized at the instigation of the secret police—that is, the Ministry of Internal Affairs. The campaign was in full swing in June of that year and one may wonder what possible use Świtała had in mind for the files of this case.

lingers somewhere at the edges of collective memory even though many an episode of multiple killings of Jews that took place at the time in Poland has been entirely forgotten.

The reason for this, in part, may have been that Rzeszów is a large city. That Jews were vulnerable to assaults in small towns and villages was accepted at the time as a matter of course. But an outburst of collective violence that involved a large number of participants, in the seat of a voivodeship, was memorable also because it induced fear among a good many Jews. Indeed, as many as two hundred Jews left town immediately afterward.

The "events" in Rzeszów went on from the early morning hours of June 12 until well into the afternoon. Sufficient numbers of city inhabitants were involved to warrant publishing a special edition of *Dziennik Rzeszowski* (*The Rzeszów Daily*) that evening announcing under a banner headline that a nine-year-old girl whose mutilated body had been found on Tanenbauma Street was in all likelihood the victim of sexual murder. People were warned not to heed "provocation" by "post-Hitlerite agents" promoting slogans of "racial hatred"—a rather hollow-sounding admonition, given that "the militia was spreading the wildest rumors," which were circulating all over town, about ritual murder performed by "Jews who needed blood [transfusions, to fortify themselves] after returning from camps."[67]

Several Polish families lived on the ground floor and the second floor of number 12 Tanenbauma Street. The rest of the building served as a residence and a community house for Jews transiting through Rzeszów. Fourteen single men shared a few apartments on the third floor. They had all returned to Rzeszów from wherever the destiny of war had cast them. Jonas Landesmann, for instance, came back from a Soviet labor camp near Arkhangelsk.* He shared an apartment, previously occupied by Rabbi Leib Thorn, with a *shokhet* (a kosher butcher) who had returned from Auschwitz and a merchant who had been liberated from a camp in

---

The folder at the Institute of National Memory in Rzeszów includes a memorandum from a Captain Siatko, deputy head of the investigation department, to the prosecutor's office, dated June 14, 1945. It lists eight people whose depositions were included with the report, but the depositions are missing from the file (IPN-Rz-062/5; 92/IV, 14.VI.45).

*He had been liberated in December 1944, having served a five-year sentence for illegally crossing the Soviet border while escaping the Germans in 1939. Landesmann returned to his native Rzeszów right away and found no one alive from a family which, besides his wife and child, had included his parents, five married brothers with children, seven sisters with their husbands and children, etc. (ŻIH, 301/1581).

Częstochowa. Late at night on June 11, a squad of militiamen burst into their apartment swearing at the occupants and accusing them of murdering Polish children.

In the incomplete files of the investigation of Landesmann, we learn what triggered the chain of events: a complaint brought to the police by a Jan Woźniak, also a resident at Tanenbauma 12, who went to the basement to fetch some wood that evening and spotted a bag with schoolbooks bearing the name Bronisława Mendoń. He knew that the girl was missing, he said, because his mother was helping her after school and had earlier mentioned her disappearance. So he went to the militia precinct office to report his finding.

Woźniak apparently returned in the company of eight policemen, including the county militia commander, Lieutenant Grzeszek, and his chief of investigation, Corporal Opiekun.* With the top brass of the precinct involved in the investigation from the start, they went into the basement and found the mutilated body of a girl, the skin stripped off her face and deep lesions on her arms and legs, as if someone had been trying to reach for her veins.

When the militia searched the rabbi's apartment they found traces of blood in a bucket (Landesmann later explained that it came from a chicken slaughtered earlier by the *shokhet*), the *shokhet*'s knife, a bloodstained shirt, and also "a page from the copybook of the murdered girl on the bed of Jonas Landesmann," as well as "a piece of red cloth similar to that of the skirt of the murdered girl."[68†] Landesmann and two other Jews were then brought to the basement of the building to look at the corpse. "The militiamen claimed that her blood was sucked out for ritual purposes," Landesmann later testified before the Jewish Historical Commission, "and that the previous occupant of the apartment, Rabbi Leib Thorn, now a captain and a military chaplain in Warsaw, was implicated in this case."[69‡]

By morning the whole area was under siege by an angry crowd. Several buildings were surrounded by uniformed police, and Jewish inhabitants were pulled out of their apartments and assembled under guard.

---

*The meaning of Lieutenant Grzeszek's name in Polish is "a small sin," while the name Opiekun means "a guardian."

†Captain Siatko's report of June 14, which I mentioned earlier, identifies the apartment where the search was conducted as "Rabbi Thorn's apartment" (IPN-Rz-062/5).

‡The exact timing of the search of Landesmann's apartment is difficult to pin down. A confusing scene involving all the Jewish residents of the third floor lasted for several hours.

The head of the local Jewish Committee showed up on the scene to try to clear up matters with the militia, but seeing the hostility of the crowd he withdrew. In the meantime the local militia, including the railroad police, were rounding up Jews all over town and arresting Jewish passengers on trains passing through Rzeszów.[70]

By ten A.M., a considerable array of police "was bringing Jews from almost all Jewish apartments into the police precinct in Rzeszów. Jews were led through town accompanied by the combative attitude of our militiamen and also Catholic passersby, who were throwing stones at the Jews."[71] Several people were beaten up. The militiamen as well as the passersby were clubbing the Jews, and in the meantime Jewish apartments were being plundered. A man named Sam N. saw the procession of rounded-up Jews passing under his windows, right next to the police precinct. They were being beaten and jeered at by the surrounding crowd.[72]

Later in the day, a superior authority ordered the immediate release of Jews from the custody of the county militia. This authority may have been the Security Service, or the Rzeszów voivodeship commander of the militia, Colonel Franciszek Księżarczyk, or the NKVD.* The Jews went back to their homes (some escorted by the military, because of hostile crowds milling in the street) and many left town on the same day.[73] All the residents of the third floor of Tanenbauma 12 left Rzeszów immediately, except Jonas Landesmann. He chose to remain for a day or

---

In a summary "Report on the events that took place in Rzeszów on June 12, 1945" by the Jewish Historical Commission, reference is made to an army officer, a Jew, who happened to be spending the night in one of the apartments and who drew a firearm and forced the militia to wait until morning before performing the search. In any case, Landesmann's deposition and the report agree that Jewish inhabitants of the building were taken into custody and brought over to the police precinct only in the morning (ŻIH, 301/1320). Whoever prevented the Jews from being taken out of the building at night must have feared for their lives.

*Sam N., who had befriended a Jewish Red Army officer stationed in town, called him as soon as he saw the forced march of Jews, and a detachment of Soviet soldiers arrived soon after. The Jews were released and escorted back to the house on Tanenbauma Street, he told an interviewer forty years later, and on the next day the Soviet officer provided two trucks and a military escort, drove them full of Jews from the community house on Tanenbauma Street toward the Slovak border, and advised the Jews to leave the country. Landesmann states in his deposition that the NKVD ordered the release of the Jews; the Jewish Historical Commission's memorandum attributes the release to the intervention of Colonel Księżarczyk; while a local prosecutor writes in a memorandum that Jews "had been freed on the say-so of the Security Service" ("zostali zwolnieni samowolnie przez organa bezpieczeństwa") (See Fortunoff Archive, T-1014; ŻIH, 301/1581, 301/1320; IPN-Rz-062/5, "Do Ministerstwa Sprawiedliwości. Nadzór prokuratorski," 1.IX.1945).

two to get his affairs in order. It took him three months to get out of town.

A girl had been murdered, and someone decided to put the blame on the Jews. In some fashion the county militia must have been involved in the plot—sending top brass to conduct the initial search; finding blood-stained cloth and a page of the girl's notebook conveniently placed on Landesmann's bed; proceeding to arrest all the Jews in town—all these actions suggest that the culprits had been designated in advance. The flow of events was cut short by the order to release the summarily arrested Jews. But a murder had been committed, and on June 14 an arrest warrant was issued for all the inhabitants of the third floor of Tanenbauma 12. The only one on whom the militia could lay their hands was Jonas Landesmann. When he objected during his arraignment that "a Polish king had issued a decree prohibiting suspecting Jews of ritual murder," the prosecutor replied that he was "suspected of a sexual murder."*

From the beginning, the prosecution did not really bother to investigate the murder case. It did not try to uncover who was responsible for setting off the anti-Jewish riots, either. Landesmann was questioned only at his arraignment and never again called for interrogation. Only one additional witness was deposed after his arrest, and her testimony "did not add anything meaningful which could contribute to finding the perpetrators." True, only one of the inhabitants of the third floor of Tanenbauma 12 was arrested, while everybody else "left Rzeszów on the same day for unknown destinations, and were perhaps hiding." But then, "if not all of them then almost all of them are certainly innocent" (*"jeśli nie wszyscy to prawie wszyscy są niewątpliwie niewinni"*). By September 1, the Institute of Expertise for the Judiciary (Instytut Ekspertyzy Sądowej) in Kraków—where the bloodstained evidence samples had been sent for analysis—had not yet reported its findings. In any case, the prosecutor—who noted all of the above in a long memorandum to the Ministry of Justice on September 1, 1945—was of the opinion that the anticipated results would "not bring the solution of the murder closer."

In fact, the prosecutor continued, Investigative Judge Buhartyk, who had been assigned the case, went on vacation and the file was passed to Judge Sakowski, who actually gave it to his law clerk (*aplikant egzaminowany*), Bury. But then Bury went on vacation, and Sakowski reported

---

*The prosecutor placed him in preventive detention for two months and Landesmann was finally released three months later, on September 12 (ŻIH, 301/1581).

"that his health is poor and that he plans to take a vacation too."[74] Since the two-month limit on preventive detention was already up, the prosecutor wanted to know whether he should keep the suspect in jail. The Ministry of Justice in Warsaw made a wise decision and twelve days later Landesmann was freed. He left town immediately and on October 5 gave his deposition in Kraków before the Jewish Historical Commission. It details the circumstances of his incarceration in Rzeszów.

Landesmann was arrested on June 14. On his arrival at the prison office he "left 11,000 złoty in deposit, [which] the clerk said . . . must be payment from the organization for committing the murder. As I was escorted to the prison cell, the guards and prisoners on work duty called after me, 'Cannibal, murderer of Polish children,' while at the same time they kicked and hit me." And for the next two months Landesmann was tortured and humiliated by prisoners and prison staff alike.* When he complained to a deputy warden conducting an inspection that he was sick and being beaten by other prisoners, this official, responsible for the prison "politico-educational department," retorted that it must be because he was too fat. Not surprisingly, when Landesmann finally managed to see a doctor, the latter asked incredulously, "Are you still alive?"

Finally, when the term of his preventive detention came to an end he requested an interview with the prosecutor.[75] "How much longer am I going to suffer like this?" asked Landesmann when called to the man's office. "He said that my case was in the hands of the investigating judge, that by the end of the month a decision should be made whether the investigation would go on, that the bloodstained shirt had been sent for analysis as well as the sheet of paper from the child's copybook. When I complained about how much they were torturing me, he said that this was not his business, that it concerned the Security Service and the prison administration. When I asked why I had been chosen as a victim, he comforted me that if I was set free my conscience would be clear, while those Jews who fled would have a guilty conscience."[76]

This is not a story about rogue prison guards and violent prisoners, but about a joint project that the entire institution was involved in. The

---

*"I spent seven days in quarantine in transition cell no. 19 and the guard opened it several times a day to let in some guys who beat me up. After seven days they took me to the bathhouse and disinfected my things. The disinfection took an hour. In the meantime they let in prisoners from ten cells who, along with the guards, beat me until I passed out. They revived me with kicks in the stomach.

torture of Jonas Landesmann was probably a unique endeavor in which prisoners and guards, openly and zestfully, were engaged together.

When reading through the 1945 files of the Rzeszów militia and the Security Service we come upon statistical compilations and reports and in particular a volume of "Situational Reports" sent by the Rzeszów voivode-ship command of the Citizens' Militia to the "Politico-Educational De-partment at the Headquarters of the Citizens' Militia in Warsaw.". They were meant to inform the headquarters of "the important events" (*"raport ważniejszych wydarzeń"*) in the voivodeship. In the report numbered 9 and dated June 20, 1945, "for the period from June 10 through June 20," not a word appears about the anti-Jewish riots in Rzeszów. Nor can one find any mention of the June 12 events in Rzeszów in the volume of periodic reports by the Security Service.[77]

Evidently, an anti-Jewish riot was a nonevent in the eyes of those who administered law and order. No one bothered to pursue or identify the instigators of those events, or the officers of the law whose profes-sional (mis)conduct incited the passions of the mob. That cops and rob-bers jointly abused a Jew; that the police rounded up all Jews in town on the basis of a prejudice (what else could it have been, since the Jews in Rzeszów and vicinity could not *all* have been suspected of the murder?); that the crowd in the streets beat Jews and taunted them in the presence of and in collusion with the police—all this, evidently, was within the boundaries of tolerable behavior. Jews might be assaulted not only when they were trying to retrieve private property (and it was "understood" that they were at considerable personal risk while doing so),* or in the context of anonymous and socially tolerated violence—on the trains, for

---

"Then they took me to cell number 26, where common criminals and murderers were kept. The guard introduced me as the murderer of a Polish child. Then these criminals decided to conduct an investigation. The elder of the cell ordered me not to move. . . . They heated a needle red and stuck it under my nails. Then they hung me up with a belt until I turned blue. When I started to scream they put a blanket over my head and suffocated me. . . . Prisoners dropped hot ashes from their smoked cigarettes on my clean-shaven head and it was covered with burns. . . .

"At night, the guards on duty used to open the cell door and kick me [Landesmann was made to sleep on the cement floor near the excrement bucket]. One guard's name was Daniel, the other's Bębenek. . . . He brought me to cell number 30, where only AK members were imprisoned, and they beat me and kicked me until I fell unconscious and then they threw me out into the corridor."

Guards ordered him to report every half hour as "Jonas Landesmann, prisoner under investigation, murderer of children" (ŻIH, 301/1581).

*Jews knew this very well and it was a recurring theme in their conversations then, as well as in their reminiscences afterward.

example, or when murdered in their place of residence following prior semipublic warnings—but also in an overt, collective, violent display of social control. Unlike lynching, however, which also brought together an entire community (including law enforcement personnel), violent social control such as in Rzeszów was not intended to cow a designated minority into submission, but to get rid of it altogether. As a result it had a deadly potential, which we will see come to full realization a year later, during the pogrom in Kielce.

Two sisters, Jewish orphanage in Otwock, 1947.
PHOTOGRAPH BY JULIA PIROTTE (ŻIH, J-16)

Children at play, Jewish orphanage in Śródborów, 1946.
PHOTOGRAPH BY JULIA PIROTTE (ŻIH, J-19)

Children eating a meal, Jewish orphanage in Bielawa (Lower Silesia), 1945–46.
(ŻIH, F-1965)

Study period,
Jewish orphanage in Otwock, 1947.
PHOTOGRAPH BY JULIA PIROTTE
(ŻIH, J-18)

A girl making cheese,
Jewish orphanage in Otwock, 1947.
PHOTOGRAPH BY JULIA PIROTTE
(ŻIH, J-17)

Studying Polish in a Jewish school in Bielawa (Lower Silesia), 1945–46.
(ŻIH, F-1925)

Studying Hebrew in a Jewish school in Bielawa (Lower Silesia), 1945–46.
(ŻIH, F-1921)

Youths dancing the hora at a summer camp.
PHOTOGRAPH FROM THE ALBUM "FROM THE HALUTZ YOUTH MOVEMENT IN POLAND,
GORDONIA–MAKABI–HATZAIR, ŁÓDŹ, 1947" (ŻIH, F-2221)

Volleyball game on a farm in Pilawa.
PHOTOGRAPH FROM THE ALBUM "FROM THE HALUTZ YOUTH
MOVEMENT IN POLAND, GORDONIA-MAKABI–HATZAIR,
ŁÓDŹ, 1947" (ŻIH, F-2197)

A farm cooperative near Wrocław.
PHOTOGRAPH DEPOSITED BY MICHAŁ GRYNBERG (ŻIH, F-1994)

Workshop in a farm cooperative in Lower Silesia.
PHOTOGRAPH DEPOSITED BY MICHAŁ GRYNBERG (ŻIH, F-1990)

A kibbutz in Bielsko, 1946–47.
PHOTOGRAPH FROM THE ALBUM "FROM THE HALUTZ YOUTH MOVEMENT
IN POLAND, GORDONIA-MAKABI–HATZAIR, ŁÓDŹ, 1947" (ŻIH, F-2206)

Executives of the Association of Jewish Students in Wrocław.
(ŻIH, F-1935)

Rabbi Colonel Dr. David Kahane (in uniform).
FROM THE COLLECTION OF WILLIAM BEIN (ŻIH, J-06)

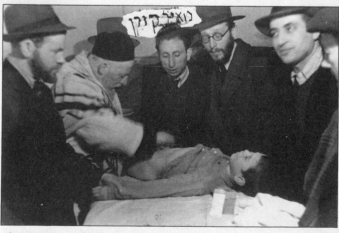

The circumcision of Szmuel Bunem, a boy who was released—after payment from Agudas Yisroel—by the Polish family who had kept him through the war.
(ŻIH, J-10)

Armed guard of the Wrocław voivodeship Jewish Committee, 1945–46.
(ŻIH, F-1928)

3

THE
KIELCE POGROM:
EVENTS

THE FLOODGATES of widespread anti-Jewish urban violence were really opened in Kraków, the ancient capital of Poland, two months after the Rzeszów pogrom. The August 11, 1945, events in Kraków were also incited by a rumor of ritual murder. A Polish mob initially assaulted the synagogue where Jews had allegedly killed a Christian child, and then pursued Jews throughout the neighborhood and in other parts of town. Scores of police were among the assailants. An indictment brought against twenty-five people soon after the pogrom named five soldiers and six militiamen.[1]*

It is not clear how many Jews were killed in Kraków—estimates vary from one to five victims. Dozens were grievously wounded. Stanisław Hartman was visiting someone that day in the hospital on Kopernika Street. "Militamen kept bringing people drenched in blood by horse-drawn drozhkis. Listening to what nurses were saying was even worse than looking at the wounded—We won't keep them here. We'll dress their wounds and let them go away. 'Dress their wounds,' but how do I capture the tone of their voices . . . ?"[2] By coincidence, a Jewish woman,

---

*In this chapter many people are identified by name. Among the most frequently mentioned are the following: Henryk Błaszczyk, a boy whose false accusation triggered the events; Walenty Błaszczyk, his father; Major Kazimierz Gwiazdowicz, the deputy commander of the Kielce voivodeship Citizens' Militia (MO), i.e., the regular police; Colonel Wiktor Kuźnicki, the Kielce voivodeship commander of the Citizens' Militia; Major Władysław Sobczyński, the Kielce voivodeship commander of the Security Service (UB), i.e., the secret police.

Hanna Zajdman, who was wounded during the pogrom and brought to the hospital on Kopernika Street, left an account of her experience with the Jewish Historical Commission on August 20, 1945: "I was carried to the second precinct of the Militia, where they called for an ambulance. There were five more people over there, including a badly wounded Polish woman. In the ambulance I heard the comments of the escorting soldier and the nurse, who spoke about us as Jewish scum whom they had to save, and that they shouldn't be doing this because we murdered children, that all of us should be shot. We were taken to the hospital of St. Lazarus on Kopernika Street. I was first taken to the operating room. After the operation a soldier appeared who said that he would take everybody to jail after the operation. He beat up one of the wounded Jews waiting for surgery. He held us at gunpoint and did not allow us to take a drink of water. A moment later two railroadmen appeared and one said, 'It's a scandal that a Pole does not have the civil courage to hit a defenseless person,' and he hit a wounded Jew. One of the hospital patients hit me with a crutch. Women, including nurses, stood behind the doors threatening us, saying that they were only waiting for the surgery to be over in order to rip us apart."[3]

The synagogue where it all started, as well as many Jewish apartments and stores, were plundered. Unlike in Kielce, however, where the discipline of these units disintegrated, the Security Service and a military detachment brought into town were able to stem the spread of violence once they were deployed in force. Hartman, who by the time he wrote his memoirs was among the most eminent Polish mathematicians, recalled two pogroms he had witnessed during his lifetime: the one in Lwów in the summer of 1941 (after Nazi troops occupied the city), and the one in Kraków in the summer of 1945. And even though the violence of the 1941 pogrom in Lwów, where several thousand Jews had been killed, was incomparably greater, "the second one," he wrote, "was more horrible."[4]

The psychological impact of anti-Jewish mob violence in independent Poland—for someone who was out of touch with the public mood that thus manifested itself—was profoundly shocking. Many of the best representatives of the Polish intelligentsia reacted at the time with disbelief and unmitigated despair to the events in Kraków. Evidently, if a pogrom could take place in a city renowned for its cultural treasures, museums, and universities, then Jews were vulnerable to mass violence anywhere in Poland.

The Taste of Cherries

On July 1, 1946, an eight-year-old boy from Kielce, Henryk Błaszczyk, disappeared from his home.[5] He had hitched a ride to see playmates in a village twenty-five kilometers away, where the family had lived until barely six months earlier, and because he liked the cherries grown by a former neighbor.[6] When he did not come home that evening his parents got worried, and by eleven o'clock they reported him missing to the police. Two days later, around seven P.M., the boy returned, loaded with cherries.

Later in the evening Walenty Błaszczyk, Henryk's father, went back to the police precinct where he had originally reported the boy's disappearance. He informed the officer on duty that his son had been kidnapped by Jews, from whom he had managed to escape. As he was seriously drunk when he showed up in the police station, and as it was already eleven P.M., Błaszczyk was sent away and told to come back the next morning to file a report.[7]

The Opening Phase

About eight A.M. on July 4, Walenty and Henryk Błaszczyk, accompanied by a neighbor, Jan Dygnarowicz, returned to the police precinct at number 45 Sienkiewicza Street. They walked by the Jewish Committee's building at 7 Planty Street (situated only 150 meters from the police station) where the young Błaszczyk had allegedly been kept in the basement. It was a large building, which housed various Jewish institutions operating in Kielce and where up to 180 Jews (over half of Kielce's Jewish residents at the time) were sheltered in mid-1946.* The boy, after some prodding, fingered a small man in a green hat standing nearby as a person who gave him a package to carry into the building, where he was then seized. When this story was related to the commander of the police precinct, Sergeant Zagórski, he ordered that the Jew in a green hat be

---

*The number of residents in the building fluctuated, as many people were merely passing through town; hence the inability to identify several victims of the pogrom who were recent arrivals. Such multifunctional Jewish community centers—where a local Jewish Committee, a dining facility, a prayer room, or a dormitory to accommodate homeless or transiting Jews would be located—were common at the time in larger cities in Poland.

brought in for questioning. A policeman named Stefan Sędek, from the investigating division, took over.

The Błaszczyks, father and son, with their neighbor Dygnarowicz, as well as a few police investigators in plain clothes, went back to the building on Planty to detain the man. On the way, the group told passersby that the boy had been kidnapped by Jews and escaped, and that they were about to arrest the Jews and liberate other Polish children held in the building. A crowd began to assemble.

Kalman Singer, the man in the green hat, was brought over to the precinct under escort, where he was promptly beaten up by a policeman named Zając. The head of the Jewish Committee in Kielce, Dr. Seweryn Kahane, also went to the police station, worried that "a misfortune might come about" if the arrested Jew was not let go. Dr. Kahane was received by Sergeant Zagórski. Kahane pleaded for Singer's release: the boy could not have been kept in the cellar against his will, he pointed out, because the building had no cellar. The Silnica creek ran nearby and the ground was too wet.

At the time, Zagórski was busy lecturing foot patrolmen about hygiene. Briefly interrupting this, Zagórski explained to Kahane that Singer was going to be questioned to clarify the matter. Then he went on with the lecture, Kahane returned to the building at Planty 7, and Singer was kept in the precinct.[8]

Soon a second group of five plainclothesmen and nine uniformed police marched to the building on Sędek's orders to search and secure it.[9] They were followed by a crowd of civilians, with whom the policemen were talking back and forth about kidnapped Polish children. The crowd was shouting that Jews had killed a Christian child (*"za milicjantami szli gromadą przechodnie wykrzykując, iż Żydzi tej nocy zamordowali dziecko"*).[10] In effect, those who left the precinct house on the morning of July 4 to search the building at Planty 7 were not a police patrol on assignment, but a posse. And, true to form, they behaved like one.*

---

*Policeman Sędek was arrested on the evening of July 4 and questioned the next day about his decision to send a large group of uniformed police to check on Błaszczyk's allegations. "Question: How many policemen did you send to Planty Street? Answer: Together with the boy I sent 3 plainclothes agents and 8 or 9 policemen in uniform. Question: Why did you send 8 or 9 uniformed policemen to Planty Street? Answer: I sent 8 or 9 uniformed policemen especially for guard duty so that people would not assemble at the place of the event. Question: Your answer indicates that you were perfectly aware that a crowd might assemble there. Answer: Yes, I knew very well that the presence of a larger group of uniformed policemen might draw a crowd. Question: If you knew that surrounding the house where

Assault on the Building at Planty 7

Until about nine A.M., only the local precinct was involved in handling the Błaszczyks' complaint. The voivodeship deputy commander of police, Major Kazimierz Gwiazdowicz, was then informed over the phone about the ongoing investigation and promised to come over shortly. Sometime between nine and nine-thirty, the commander of the Security Service, one Sobczyński, got alerted that a crowd was gathering near the building at Planty 7, and that police were investigating a complaint about a kidnapped Polish child. He sent some officers with a small guard detachment to the building, then called Major Gwiazdowicz from the regular police and told him that this was a *prowokacja,* a false accusation deliberately meant to stir unrest, and a matter for the Security Service; the uniformed police, Sobczyński said, should be pulled out.[11]

In the meantime, the crowd outside Planty 7 was growing. People were agitated, gawking at the police who were searching the premises for children and for weapons, which Jewish residents were ordered to surrender, while making sure that no Jews escaped from the building. When they established that Planty 7 had no basement, a policeman named Szeląg gave young Błaszczyk a dressing-down in front of the building for telling a fib. Those who saw this were outraged: the police were trying to cover up the crime![12] As Officer Mucha of the Security Service, accompa-

the Jews were living would draw a crowd, why did you send such a large group of uniformed police? Answer: I only knew that the boy had escaped from a basement, I didn't know that the basement was at the Jews'. Question: So, you only knew that he escaped from a basement, but whose basement it was you didn't know? Answer: Yes, I didn't know anything else, only that he escaped from a basement. Question: If a child escaped from a basement at his father's would you also send twelve people to carry out an investigation?" (Stanisław Meducki and Zenon Wrona, eds., *Antyżydowskie wydarzenia kielecki 4 lipca 1946 roku,* vol. I, pp. 234–35).

Sędek was lying. Everybody at the precinct "knew" that the boy had escaped "from the Jews." That was, in a manner of speaking, the whole point. The purpose of such naïve dissembling would be difficult to fathom unless Sędek had something to hide. In a later interrogation on July 31, he revealed, I believe, what he was trying to cover up: "I got no instructions from [the precinct commander] Zagórski about the number of plainclothesmen and policemen to send over. I sent those who volunteered to go" (*"Wysłałem tych, którzy zgłosili chęć pójścia, t.j. 'na ochotnika' "*) (Meducki, *Antyżydowskie,* vol. I, p. 239). This, most plausibly, is exactly what happened: after Błaszczyk told the story of his son's disappearance, whoever was in the precinct went after the Jews (and to rescue the children, of course).

nied by a small detachment of uniformed agents, approached Planty 7, he "saw 5 or 6 policemen with shotguns observing the attic, as if someone was about to escape from the building."[13] Inside, Dr. Kahane was on the phone to Sobczyński asking for help and demanding that the police searchers be withdrawn. Mucha also got on the phone to Sobczyński. He was told that the army and firemen were being called in to disperse the gathering crowd. Two carloads of Security Service personnel pulled in front of the building and about a dozen agents moved to detain some of the policemen present. An altercation resulted, with the crowd rooting for the policemen, three of whom were taken away by Security Service agents.[14]*

Now people outside the building began throwing rocks and inching toward the building; Officer Mucha again called Sobczyński demanding urgent intervention. When he could not get through, he left Planty 7 through an adjacent schoolyard to go seek help in person. In the meantime Kahane's deputy in the Jewish Committee, Chil Alpert, called the Soviet military adviser stationed in town only to be told "that they don't have units in Polish uniforms and don't want to send soldiers in Russian uniforms, or the Poles will be saying that Russians were murdering them."[15]

In the "Chronicle of the Tragedy" prepared by Meducki and Wrona, the timeline entry for "10:00—10:30 A.M." begins with the following paragraph: "The army made an appearance in front of the Jewish building: forty soldiers from the KBW [the Corps of Internal Security], thirty from the 4th regiment of the 2nd Infantry Division, five officers from the intelligence department, and thirty military policemen and soldiers from the city garrison. The crowd momentarily calmed down when soldiers arrived. Some soldiers and policemen entered the Jewish building. Second Lieutenants Marian Rypyst and Jędrzejczak called on the Jews to surrender their weapons. Six or seven handguns were collected. Not all residents turned in their weapons, saying that they had permits to carry. Depositions concerning the events that followed are contradictory."[16]

As a matter of fact, the depositions are not contradictory. They differ as to details and emphasis, but one could hardly expect anything else given the chaos and mayhem they describe. They do converge as to substance, however, whether coming from Jewish victims, law enforcement

---

*Henryk and Walenty Błaszczyk were probably at this point taken into custody by the Security Service as well.

personnel on the scene, or the perpetrators and witnesses interrogated during the trials.

When the army arrived, recalls Chil Alpert, the Jews in the building "sighed with relief, convinced that this was our rescue. And shooting began. But directed at us, not at the assailants."[17] A Security Service agent present on the scene later surmised that the soldiers "did not have clear orders" when they arrived at Planty 7. In any case, the first wave of deadly violence was unleashed as uniformed representatives of the state—the police and the military—intervened *against* the Jews, and as their intervention promptly degenerated into a murderous assault.

Witnesses do not agree who fired the first shot—a policeman, a soldier, or, as some suggest, one of the Jewish residents—but, like a starter's signal, it spurred those present on the scene to deadly violence. "The police and the military," we read in the July 18 report submitted to the PPR's Central Committee by a group of Communist Party officials who arrived in Kielce during the pogrom, "were not disciplined. Instead of quelling the disturbance, they mingled with and succumbed to the influence of the crowd. Police, together with the military, were the first to forcibly enter the building. Policemen pulled Jewish victims from the building and handed them over to the crowd outside. . . . An excited crowd was shouting slogans against the Jews, against the PPR, and against the UB. The crowd was on very good terms with the police, and it enthusiastically cheered the military."[18]

Soldiers entered the building to search for Polish children, and military discipline disintegrated.* The military did not have "official" orders to shoot and kill the Jews. In fact, no order authorizing the use of firearms was ever issued on that day, which was part of the reason the massive assaults against the Jews could not be contained. Once it became manifest that the soldiers were acting against the Jews, the pent-up aggression of the crowd overflowed.[†]

Before breaking ranks, arriving soldiers were taunted by the crowd. An elderly man interviewed by Marcel Łoziński in 1987 wept at the recollection of being slapped on the face and then called "Stalin's flunky" ("pachołki Stalina"*) when his unit was initially deployed to bar the crowd from approaching the building. But it was not clear at what stage of the pogrom his unit was brought to the scene. Edward Jurkowski, sentenced to death in the first Kielce trial for inciting to violence, shouted at a noncommissioned officer standing right next to him "that if he was a hero, he should go and beat the Jews" (Meducki, *Antyżydowskie,* vol. I, pp. 122–23).

†A telling instance of how violence by a uniformed individual was applauded by onlookers can be found in the indictment prepared for the November 18, 1946, trial: "Piotr Szyling, a warden in the Kielce prison, who came to the site [when his shift at work was over]

"I barricaded the door to the office with an armoire and a table. Suddenly I heard screams as they broke into the building. Because until the arrival of the soldiers the crowd did not come inside. After a few moments, they pounded on the door with rifle butts and ordered me to open it immediately or else they would shoot." Chil Alpert was then robbed of 3,000 złoty, forced out of the room into the staircase, and pushed down between a double row of soldiers and civilians who were beating the Jews along the way.* "I got to the very narrow exit door and in the square I saw a looming, black crowd, and empty space in front of it, surrounded by the military. I saw how those who were standing in front of me were thrown into the crowd by the soldiers, including my brother-in-law, Benjamin Fajtel."[19] In the recollection of Ryszard Sałata, a policeman who remained outside, "Jews were brought from the building into the square, where the population cruelly murdered them, and the armed soldiers did not react, they only covered their ears and fled somewhere, and some went back into the building and kept bringing out other Jews."[20] Stanisław Rurarz, who hit one of the Jews "three times with a stone on the chest, in the right leg, and also in the head, but with a very small stone" (*"malutkim kamieniem"*) remembered how four Jews, one after another, were dragged out of the building to be killed in the courtyard.[21] "Two of them were pulling out this Jew, by hands and feet, like a calf."[22]

Albert Grynbaum, a Security Service agent, was on the second floor of Planty 7 when the military detachment arrived around ten A.M. "I assembled about 40 Jews in one room and didn't let the soldiers in. I told them that their task was to restore order in the street, rather than carry out the search. . . . Soldiers went to the 2nd floor [by U.S. usage, the third floor] . . . and a few minutes later two Jews came to tell me that the military were killing the Jews and plundering their possessions. This was when I heard shots."[23]

---

and saw a Jewish woman trying to run away, caught her and started to beat her and kick her until she fell down. The assembled crowd, witnessing this act, proceeded to throw Szyling in the air, shouting *"Niech żyje"* ["Long live"], at which point the woman who had fallen took advantage of the confusion, got up and ran away" (Meducki, *Antyżydowskie,* vol. I, p. 252).

*According to the 1997 investigation, civilians were let into the building by the military commander of Kielce, Major Stanisław Markiewicz. He allowed a group to enter the building, he told interrogators, intending to prove that there were no corpses of Polish children inside, and the crowd rushed in ("Raport głównej komsji badania zbrodni przeciwko Narodowi Polskiemu—IPN o wyniku śledztwa w sprawie wydarzeń kieleckich 4.07.1946" [hereafter GKBZpNP-IPN], p. 20).

Baruch Dorfman was in the kibbutz on the third floor of the building, where

> some 20 people locked themselves in a small room. But they started shooting at us through the door, and they wounded one person, who later died from the injuries. They broke in. These were soldiers in uniform and a few civilians. I was wounded then. They ordered us to go outside. They formed a double row. In the staircase there were already civilians and also women. Soldiers hit us with rifle butts. Civilians, men and women, also beat us. I was wearing a uniformlike vest, perhaps that's why they did not hit me then. We came down to the square. Others who were brought out with me were stabbed with bayonets and shot at. We were pelted with stones. Even then nothing happened to me. I moved across the square to an exit, but I must have had such a facial expression that they recognized that I was a Jew who'd been taken out of the building, because one civilian screamed, "A Jew!" And only then did they attack me. Stones flew at me, I was hit with rifle butts, I fell and lost consciousness. Periodically I regained consciousness; then they hit me again with stones and rifle butts. One wanted to shoot me when I was lying on the ground but I heard somebody else say, "Don't shoot, he'll croak anyway." I fainted again. When I came to, somebody was pulling me by the legs and threw me onto a truck. This was some other military, because I woke up in a hospital in Kielce.[24]

Several Jewish survivors left similar testimony about being delivered into the hands of the crowd by soldiers and then beaten unconscious and robbed in the courtyard by a mixed crowd of men and women. After being struck down by the initial blows, many pretended to be dead, and a few survived as a result.[25] Natan Lapter, after feigning death, was shot in the leg and searched, and his money was stolen by two soldiers. A man named Ferkeltaub had his boots pulled off by soldiers after he had been put on the truck that took him to the hospital. He was also feigning death and "didn't resist since [he] was afraid that they would finish [him] off."[26]

Witnesses remember Jews being flung out of the building directly into the street below. "I saw how policemen threw two Jewish girls off the second-floor [third-floor] balcony and the crowd in the courtyard finished them off," recalled the seamstress Ewa Szuchman, who miraculously escaped injury and was deposed on July 6, two days after the pogrom.[27] Zenon Kukliński, arrested in a bloodstained vest (and later sentenced to death in the first Kielce trial), described how a bleeding Jew, "thrown down from a floor above, . . . brushed against [his] jacket" and how he "pushed the Jew away." Under cross-examination it turned out that two Jews were assaulted in this episode, and that Kukliński stoned and robbed at least one of them: "The Jew was unconscious when he fell on my chest. He was all covered with blood. People took him and threw him away. I didn't hit the Jew with a stone. There were two Jews over there. The second one, I didn't touch at all. I don't know where the coat came from. My wife screamed at me when I was beating the Jew to quit it and to go."[28]

Around eleven o'clock Dr. Kahane was killed by a shot in the back while he was once again phoning for help. The Security Service officer Kwaśniewski was on the other end of the line: "I then heard a loud shot and silence in the receiver."[29]

Several high-ranking officers were milling around in the vicinity of the building—Sobczyński; Gwiazdowicz; the town's military commander, Markiewicz; a Colonel Kupsza, the commanding officer of the 2nd Infantry Division; and a Soviet adviser, Colonel Szpilewoj. None of them took decisive action to suppress the crowd. There was no overall coordination or command over the police, military, and security forces. This was a spectacle of total confusion, with an idle fire truck sitting somewhere in the middle of the square, its hoses cut by the mob.

Sometime between ten-thirty and eleven, Colonel Kuźnicki, the police commander for the Kielce voivodeship, called his superior in Warsaw, General Franciszek Jóźwiak, and asked to be given overall command of the action. Since the Security Service and the military "together with the public" were beating the Jews, argued Kuźnicki, they ought to be withdrawn and the police should be given authority to disperse the crowd. Kuźnicki was rebuffed and told to coordinate his actions with the UB.[30]

Around noon there was a momentary lull in the pogrom, as another detachment of the infantry under Major Konieczny and Captain Bednarz moved in, fired a salvo in the air, pushed the crowd away from the courtyard, and brought trucks to evacuate killed and wounded Jews to a nearby hospital. At this point, prosecutor Jan Wrzeszcz appeared on the scene, intending to start an investigation. "When I asked who was in overall command of the action, I was told that there were several units on the scene and each acted on its own. . . . I turned to officers standing nearby and told them that the crowd had to be dispersed, and the use of firearms had to be considered. I was told in no uncertain terms [*"w formie ostrej"*] that nobody would issue such an order and that the soldiers would not carry it out. . . . I understood that one should not count on energetic action by the military and I said that all the surrounded Jews had to be evacuated on trucks. . . . They didn't agree to this, either."³¹

In frantic telephone calls, meetings, and conversations conducted during the early part of the day by various military, police, and administrative officials, there is constant talk of help being on its way. In the meantime there was nobody to issue orders, take decisive action, or even remove the imperiled Jews from Planty 7. Instead, the building was cordoned off by the soldiers and policemen on the scene, but they proved to be no obstacle to the second wave of attackers already on their way. Within an hour, the Jews who remained inside were assaulted again and scores were killed in the second surge of the pogrom by workers from the Ludwików Foundry who arrived en masse after midday.* They came running, wielding tools, iron bars, and other improvised weapons. Some fifteen to twenty Jews were murdered in the ensuing hour and a half.

The whole area turned into a vast killing field and it was littered with bloody mementos long after the events of the day. S. L. Shneiderman arrived in Kielce with a group of foreign journalists on the following day. He went to the main site of the pogrom, the building at Planty 7. "The immense courtyard was still littered with blood-stained iron pipes, stones and clubs, which had been used to crush the skulls of Jewish men and women. Blackening puddles of blood still remained. . . . Blood-drenched papers were scattered on the ground. . . . I picked up some. . . . These were letters addressed to the victims by their relatives in Palestine, and Canada, and the United States."³² Three days later Helena Majtlis drove across town in a military jeep to the hospital where she would be ensconced for several days nursing the wounded. The city streets, she remembered with horror, were still covered with blood.³³

To sum up the events, then: after the regular police launched their investigation of a child-kidnapping complaint and a restless crowd of onlookers began to assemble to watch the proceedings, the military detach-

---

*In the official log of the industrial guard detachment from the Ludwików Foundry the following entry was recorded at twelve-thirty on July 4: " 'During the lunch break, about 600 workers forced the gate and went in the direction of town, to Planty Street.' . . . According to depositions left by policemen who were present in the square at the time, when the workers arrived nothing could be done any more for the remaining Jews" (Bożena Szaynok, *Pogrom Żydów w Kielcach 4 lipca, 1946*, p. 51).

ment that arrived at Planty 7 around ten o'clock in the morning joined in the ongoing action of the police directed *against the Jews*. When the soldiers arrived, the killing started in earnest, and the mob outside was promptly drawn into the fray. Uniformed representatives of the state and its law enforcement agencies pointed their weapons at the building and used their firearms exclusively against the Jews.

According to autopsy reports from Kielce's hospital describing the condition of eleven of the women and twenty-six of the men killed during the pogrom, five of the men died from gunshot wounds, while the rest of the victims had their skulls crushed by multiple blows. Later it was established that the official autopsy reports for the first Kielce trial were falsified, and in reality more victims died of gunshot wounds.* Bodies were brought to the hospital morgue almost naked, robbed of possessions and clothing. Fifteen remained unidentified.[34]

Medical reports indicate two Poles among the dead. We don't know whether the two Poles were killed "by mistake," or while trying to stop an attack against some Jews.[†] In the sentencing issued on July 11, 1946, during the first trial of Kielce pogrom perpetrators, we read that the two Poles were murdered "while defending the dignity of a Pole's good name" (*"w obronie godności dobrego imienia Polaka"*), but the circumstances of their deaths are not described in the proceedings. The sentencing also specifies that among the dead "there were three Polish soldiers bearing the highest combat decorations."[35] The reference here is, undoubtedly, to Jews who served in the Polish army, as crowds also challenged Jewish-looking soldiers in the streets of Kielce.[‡]

*Szaynok gives a total of seventeen victims who died from gunshot wounds (*Pogrom*, p. 60), while the autopsy report of July 5–6, 1946, quoted in GKBZpNP-IPN (pp. 31, 32), lists eleven victims who died by gunfire. Among thirty-five wounded Jews whose medical examination results were filed at that time, five males had gunshot wounds.

†One Julian Chorążak, in response to a prosecutor's question, explained during his trial: "I was slowly walking over water and stones [a shallow creek, the Silnica, flows near the building at Planty 7]. A man was passing by, and they said he was a Jew, so I hit him. But an officer said that he shouldn't be beaten, that he is not a Jew. If I'd known, I wouldn't have slugged him" (*"Żebym wiedział, to bym nie wlepił"*) (Meducki, *Antyżydowskie*, vol. I, p. 163). Antoni Sałaj, deposed as a witness, gave a more extensive account of a similar episode that took place in the street under his windows. "I saw a group of about 20 people who were beating a Pole with stones and clubs, telling him that he was a Jew. But one person recognized him as a Pole and they stopped beating him. It turned out that this was Citizen Pardoła from Radomska Street. When Citizen Pardoła was released they all went toward Planty Street" (Meducki, *Antyżydowskie*, vol. I, p. 117). Sałaj went along. He later recounts an episode in which a Jew was stoned to death.

‡One such episode, involving Corporal Maks Erlbaum, is particularly well documented and was brought out during the November 18, 1946, trial of fifteen pogrom participants. Erlbaum, who survived the assault, testified during the trial. Another episode of assault against

The shooting death of Regina Fisz and her newborn baby prominently figured in the first trial of the perpetrators, held July 9–11. A Dr. Ocepa, testifying as a medical expert, identified a woman six months pregnant among the dead as well. A Dr. Majewski spoke of a pregnant assault victim who survived, but whose belly and uterus had been pierced, causing her to lose her child. Forty-two corpses were buried in Kielce's Jewish cemetery on July 8. By witnesses' count, as many as eighty others had been wounded during the pogrom, with scores being injured by bullets.[36]

A public appeal for calm, carefully crafted later during the day on July 4 by the Kielce voivode and representatives of the clergy, made a point of the commendable restraint of the police and military personnel: "During the events the authorities maintained complete calm, preventing greater bloodshed," reads the document.* "In a sign of the far-reaching goodwill of the authorities, not a single shot was fired against the people" (*"Do ludzi nie oddano ani jednego strzału"*).[37] Evidently, the two dozen Jews killed and wounded by gunshots did not make the cut as "the people."† The communiqué does not mention at all that Jews had been killed during the day's violence. Indeed, as we shall see later, in a number of statements issued immediately following the pogrom the word "Jew" hardly appears.

In light of what we know about the events, the self-restraint and "goodwill" of the authorities were by virtue of necessity. The officers in the military would not have issued orders to shoot at the crowd, and if they had, the soldiers would not have obeyed them. But the language of the official communiqué inadvertently reveals the state of mind and real concerns of the authorities. The bloody confrontation that took place on July 4 in Kielce had two antagonists. One would be wrong, however, to identify them as pogrom perpetrators and their Jewish victims. Rather,

---

a soldier in uniform was witnessed by Antonina Biskupska, the only woman among the accused in the first Kielce trial, who saw "how the crowd pulled at one soldier's uniform, threw his cap off, and was beating him. People were saying that he was a Jew. I saw that his face was bleeding and I heard how he was screaming, 'I was with the partisans, leave me in peace.' And the crowd screamed 'Give us a stick, hit him hard. Who cares who he was with?' " (*"Niech będzie skąd chce"*) (Meducki, *Antyżydowskie,* vol. I, p. 130).

*The communiqué was not issued in the end, due to the objections of a visiting PPR Politburo member, Zenon Kliszko. Forty years later, in his memoirs, Voivode Wiślicz still held a grudge over Kliszko's dismissal of his successful efforts to draft a joint document on this issue with church representatives in Kielce.

†Or, in a literal translation of the word *ludzi*—"human beings"—"not a single shot was fired against human beings." Jerzy Daniel notes this linguistic peculiarity of the text in his 1996 study: "Apparently," in the minds of the appeal's authors, he writes, two categories needed to be distinguished, as "there were Jews and there were people (human beings)" (Jerzy Daniel, *Żyd w zielonym kapeluszu,* p. 78).

the two sides in the bloody encounter were the people of Kielce and some unspecified objects (as "Jews" were not mentioned in official statements) of their antipathy. And the authorities, understandably, were anxious to project an image of themselves as siding with the people in this gruesome affair.

The Breakdown of Law Enforcement

For the better part of the day, no one was in charge of the effort, such as it was, to restore order and end the pogrom. To begin with, an anti-Jewish riot quickly snowballed into an episode of mass violence unprecedented in postwar Poland as to the numbers of participants and victims. According to a rough estimate by Witold Kula, soon to become a world-famous economic historian, as much as a quarter of the adult population of Kielce was actively involved.[38] Once the moment to nip the riot in the bud was gone, a well-coordinated, disciplined, and ably executed effort by all the law enforcement personnel on the scene would have been necessary to stop the violence. But the two organizations responsible for law and order in the city—the Security Service (UB) and the regular police, the Citizens' Militia (MO)—were barely cooperating even prior to the July 4 debacle. As interrogations of the police commander and of his counterpart from the Kielce Security Service revealed—both men were arrested soon after the pogrom and put on trial jointly in December 1946—the two profoundly disliked each other.

The voivodeship police commander, Colonel Kuźnicki, was stung by the UB's patronizing attitude toward the MO. Even before the altercation in front of Planty 7, policemen had been arrested by the Security Service for various infractions. Kuźnicki did not appreciate that his subordinates were sometimes detained by the UB without a courtesy call informing him beforehand. Major Sobczyński, who headed the local office of the Security Service, complained on the other hand that the militia commander had little sympathy for the current regime and had appointed several former Home Army officers to positions of responsibility in the police.[39] Sobczyński and Kuźnicki fought a continuous turf war. As a general rule all breaches of security with political implications were supposed to be handled by the Security Service. But the division of labor was not sharp in the Kielce voivodeship.*

*A particularly vexing episode took place in December 1945, when the police detained an antiregime nationalist underground group, NSZ, and conducted an investigation of the group and their activities. After his arrest following the Kielce pogrom, Colonel Kuźnicki

This was not at all unusual for the period: the undefined, fluid character of armed groups which engaged in plunder behind a political façade; security police interchangeably using the terms "bandits," "nationalists," and "reactionaries"; local people and local police tangled up in a network of personal and organizational ties dating back to the underground struggle against the Germans; young people in general confused and unsure of their loyalties. But for all its unoriginality, tension between the local police and the Security Service in Kielce contributed mightily to the rapid escalation of anti-Jewish violence on July 4.

On that day, the mob assembled very quickly. Every minute that went by without decisive intervention by law enforcement made the situation less manageable. As early as nine-thirty in the morning, Sobczyński had called Kuźnicki's deputy, Major Gwiazdowicz, who was in charge of the city police. Why was a search of the Jewish Committee building being carried out by a detachment of uniformed police, asked Sobczyński, and did Gwiazdowicz know what was going on? The latter replied that he had been fully apprised of the matter. The police were following up on a complaint that Jews had detained one Polish child in the building and murdered another.

Sobczyński had already been informed by his agent on the scene of the mounting tension and violence, and he rebuked Gwiazdowicz: the complaint was a "political provocation" (ergo, at a minimum, a matter for the Security Service to handle), and he should order the police out of the building. "We will see later whether it is a provocation," Gwiazdowicz retorted. To Sobczyński's urgings that as a political matter this should be handled by the UB, "Gwiazdowicz replied that he knew himself what he had to do, and he didn't need to hear any comments."[40]

Sobczyński and Gwiazdowicz gave diverging accounts of their con-

---

explained that the police proceeded with the investigation because the Security Service refused to take custody of the prisoners when they were turned over without the weapons confiscated at the time of their arrest. Were not the weapons "material proof of the crime which should have been turned over to the Security Service together with the detained?" asked Kuźnicki's interrogator. "I kept the weapons," answered the police colonel, "because my people did not have enough" (Meducki, *Antyżydowskie,* vol. 1, p. 326).

This was a time of shortages, and Kuźnicki's explanation sounds plausible. The police may well have been short of weapons. Mutual trust did not build between the two local law enforcement agencies, however, when soon after their arrest eighteen of the detainees escaped from police custody, while their files and various personal belongings held in deposit were simultaneously lost. Kuźnicki ordered an investigation of the disappearance, he said, "but what happened exactly" he did not remember. "In any case," he explained, "these were not National Armed Forces (NSZ) members, but bandits; seventeen-year-old children. Oh, well," he added, "there were four former Home Army members among them" (ibid., p. 327).

versation on that day (Gwiazdowicz, for instance, insisted that he actually obeyed Sobczyński's orders), but they jointly testified to their mutual dislike. Their telephone conversation on the morning of July 4, as the pogrom unfolded, ended up, Gwiazdowicz complained, with Sobczyński slamming down the receiver.[41]

The disorganization was compounded by Colonel Kuźnicki's firm belief that he "could not come to an agreement with Sobczyński." For this reason, he explained, he disobeyed a direct order from the commanding general of the Citizens' Militia, General Franciszek Jóźwiak, whom he phoned in Warsaw on the morning of July 4. Jóźwiak ordered Kuźnicki to coordinate with the Security Service to quell the developing pogrom, but "I did not carry out the order," Kuźnicki stated under interrogation.[42] For that—i.e., for his profound dislike of Sobczyński—he was later sentenced to one year in prison. In the trial held on December 13, 1946, where the three leading police and security officials on the scene, Kuźnicki, Gwiazdowicz, and Sobczyński, were together accused of incompetence in dealing with the mass disturbances on July 4, he was the only one found guilty.

In addition to the lack of coordination, one may also consider as a factor bearing on the indecisiveness with which they proceeded to restore order that none of the people on the scene with institutional authority were particularly fond of Jews. Sobczyński was known for entertaining anti-Semitic views.* Sobczyński, in turn, denounced Kuźnicki as an anti-Semite. During an afternoon emergency meeting on July 4, the police colonel, according to Sobczyński's testimony, allowed that the Jews might have killed a Polish child, and he had spoken derisively about Jews on earlier occasions.[43] Confronted with this deposition, Kuźnicki explained during interrogation on October 18, 1946, that he had merely advanced a hypothesis "that the events . . . were a provocation which perhaps the Jews themselves had organized."[44] His deputy, Major Gwiazdowicz, when deposed on August 6 (and trying to save his own skin), delivered the goods against Kuźnicki without hesitation: "In his office, in the presence of several people whose names I don't recall now,

---

*One of his officers, Lieutenant Kwasek, confirmed this in a deposition on August 1, 1946. In asking himself why Sobczyński, who was usually very energetic, "was very calm on this day [of the pogrom], as if he didn't care . . . ," Kwasek noted that "During my work I somehow felt that Major Sobczyński was prejudiced against people of Jewish nationality, and I was told about this by a colleague, Captain Kwaśniewski" (Meducki, *Antyżydowskie*, vol. I, pp. 344, 345).

he said that in the Security Service there were only Jews and that Szpilewoj [the Soviet adviser in Kielce] is also Jewish."*

In the meantime, Gwiazdowicz himself had to explain how he felt
about the Jews. Sobczyński testified that he saw him in the crowd on
July 4 (and other security officers on the scene confirmed this testimony) listening to and applauding antiregime and anti-Semitic speech
making. Why did you clap? Gwiazdowicz was asked by his interrogator.
In reply, he spun a convoluted story, which concluded with "someone
screaming 'Long live the Polish army,' [while] the crowd took up this slogan, screaming 'Long live.' And then I said 'Bravo, bravo, long live' and I
made a clap" (*"powiedziałem brawo, brawo, niech żyje i zrobiłem klaśnięcie"*)—an
expression just as awkward in Polish as it is in English.[45] That singular
"clap" was meant, of course, to play down what he had done: he clapped
only once. And when asked why, as some witnesses reported, he shook
the hand of the speaker, Gwiazdowicz replied that he actually took this
man by the hand in order to lead him into Planty 7 to show him that
there were no captive Polish children inside.

Forty years after the events, the then voivode of Kielce, Eugeniusz
Wiślicz-Iwańczyk (who at the time was bedridden after a motorcycle accident, but nevertheless took part in some deliberations during the day
of the pogrom), set forth in his memoirs a host of anti-Semitic stereotypes.[†] The beginning of his memoirs is at once quite telling, with a cari-

---

*Meducki, *Antyżydowskie*, vol. I, p. 336. In broad outline, these stories about Colonel
Kuźnicki were confirmed by the militia's Police Captain Roman Olszański-Przybyłowski,
who was later appointed Kuźnicki's successor (ibid., pp. 346–48). He also added that the
second-ranking police officer on the scene, the said Major Gwiazdowicz, was Kuźnicki's
flunky, and at the same time a drunkard (ibid., p. 349).

†Truly bizarre, also, are his recollections concerning the statements of two soldiers involved in the execution of the perpetrators sentenced to death in the first Kielce murder
trial: "I will never forget a most interesting visit in my apartment from the commander of
the [execution] platoon, a very young and extremely nice lieutenant," writes Wiślicz. After
some small talk, the voivode, "interested in the psychology of this young man," who kept
smiling throughout, asked him: "Why are you so cheerful, Lieutenant . . . ? Should not someone in your situation experience some sort of pangs of conscience? 'Judges and prosecutors
should feel pangs of conscience, I am merely carrying out their will by obeying orders.' . . ."
(Meducki, *Antyżydowskie*, vol. II, p. 92). Later Wiślicz talked to a member of his personal
security detail who had witnessed the execution. When the condemned men were brought
to the execution site, over a ditch dug out in a forest clearing, one of them, the policeman Mazur—the one who killed Mrs. Fisz and her newborn child—managed to free himself
of the manacles and started to run toward the cover of the trees. The platoon commander
ordered all of the condemned men to lie down, and soldiers shot the fleeing Mazur in the
back in an eerie replay of the manner in which he himself had killed Regina Fisz. "I wished
him luck in my heart," said the security policeman to the Kielce voivode, who then described his interlocutor approvingly as a young man whose parents had been killed by the

catured portrayal of the Jewish inhabitants of the building at Planty 7 as
the idle rich, unwilling to go to work, ostentatiously wearing "expensive
suits and golden rings" (which naturally irritated the impoverished Polish population of the city), while the first head of the Security Service in
Kielce, a Jew, Major Kornecki, was "provocatively breaking the law."[46]

But the heart of the matter is that such opinions were those generally prevailing at the time, and that authorities at both local and national
levels (an occasional denunciation of anti-Semitism in official propaganda notwithstanding) were unwilling to confront the population on
this issue. As the pogrom was unfolding and the workers of the Ludwików Foundry had just broken out en masse to join in, the first secretary
of the Polish Workers' Party (that is, the Communist Party) in Kielce,
one Kalinowski, refused to address the crowd in order to quell their aggression because, he said during an emergency meeting at midday with
several officials in his office, "he didn't want people to be saying that the
PPR is a defender of the Jews."[47*]

The breakdown of law enforcement in Kielce on July 4 had thus an
underlying institutional cause. Several people at the summit of political
power knew of the pogrom as it was unfolding. The Politburo member
responsible for security, Jakub Berman, and the minister of public security, Radkiewicz, were in touch with Major Sobczyński. The overall commander of the militia, General Franciszek Jóźwiak, was contacted by
Colonel Kuźnicki. The vice minister of national defense, General Marian Spychalski, was called by the chief of staff of the 2nd Infantry Division, Major Konieczny. The national secretary of the Polish Socialist
Party, Józef Cyrankiewicz, phoned the local secretary of the PPS.[48] And
the response of these various leading figures, as far as we can tell, was
uniform—not because they were in cahoots, but because politically it was
obvious to each of them what had to be done; or rather, it was obvious to
each of them what they had to make sure did not happen.

Jóźwiak did not give any directions to Kuźnicki; he merely ordered
Kuźnicki to coordinate the militia's intervention with the Security Service. Berman and Radkiewicz told Sobczyński "all kinds of nonsense," re-

Germans and who from the tender age of fourteen had fought in the anti-Nazi guerrillas
(ibid., pp. 92, 93).
    *A representative of the Polish Socialist Party reinforced the message during a post-
Kielce pogrom mass meeting in Lublin on July 17: "We don't feel sympathy toward the Jewish nation, and neither does any other nation. We would like to see them [move] somewhere
else" (Szaynok, *Pogrom*, p. 65).

jecting his suggestions to take radical measures against the crowd.[49] Spychalski told Konieczny "not to shoot at the crowd under any circumstances," a position repeated by military officers on the scene to the prosecutor Jan Wrzeszcz.[50] And the Communist Party secretary in Kielce refused to address the second wave of pogromists on the way to the murder scene, so as not to give the impression "that the PPR was a defender of the Jews." A resolution drafted the next day by the bedridden Kielce voivode together with local church representatives stated explicitly—and touting this as a demonstration of responsible statecraft—that "not a single shot was fired at the people" during the events: this, to repeat, after soldiers and the police on the scene killed and wounded by gunshots two dozen Jews.

These discrete episodes and statements add up to a coherent story. Evidently, the political leadership of the regime, as well as its representatives in the city, responded to the news from Kielce by avoiding any action which might indicate that authorities were siding with the Jews against "the people." It was entirely clear to the leading figures of the regime—whether in the Party, in the police, in the Security Service, or in the military—that political expediency allowed no course of action that the general public might construe as benefiting the Jews.* In lieu of rushing to the defense of imperiled citizens—the Jews of Kielce who were being murdered—the guiding concern of the authorities was to persuade the public that they were not unduly preoccupied with safeguarding the Jews.

A Change of Venue

In the early afternoon, as the energy of the assault on Planty 7 spent itself, pogrom activities mutated and spread around the city. "Groups of civilians walked around town searching for Jews and checking people's documents."[51] A saleswoman on the way home for lunch during midday break was stopped by a "man in a uniform, with a shotgun, I don't know whether he was a soldier or a policeman, because when in fear one does not know, and he took me for a Jewess. . . . I was frightened, I couldn't defend myself, I already thought that they would kill me, that I would not live, but he finally let me go."[52] The more conscientious vigilantes might

---

*Not ever, but especially not in the immediate aftermath of the "Three times yes" referendum, which the authorities were publicly claiming to have won.

pull down men's trousers to check whether they were circumcised, which perhaps saved some people from "undeserved" beating or death.*

For once the UB commander, Sobczyński, took preventive measures. In response to rumors that Jewish residents would be assaulted during the night he ordered that "Jews be brought from their private apartments over to the Security Service headquarters. By the evening some fifty people were assembled," he estimated.[53] On the following day, S. L. Shneiderman and a group of foreign journalists met a small crowd of Jewish survivors at the headquarters.

These Jews were sheltered effectively from surrounding violence, but Jews being transported from the pogrom scene to a hospital, or taken into custody by the military, were not necessarily out of harm's way. Sobczyński foresaw that when the wounded were brought to a medical facility the crowd would follow, and he dispatched what turned out to be sufficient manpower to guard against the attempted break-in. But the Jews could not be protected against other patients or medical personnel. Similarly, those who were taken out in trucks by the military and brought to the army barracks were not out of danger. A certain Ferkeltaub, we remember, was robbed of his boots by escorting soldiers while already on the truck, and thought it prudent to pretend he was dead while being transported.

The evidence concerning this aspect of the pogrom is scant; probably no Jews were killed in the custody of the military or in the hospital, but what can be gleaned of their circumstances is not reassuring. During the first Kielce trial, on July 10, Ewa Szuchman was deposed as a witness. She spent the entire day of the pogrom at Planty 7 and, as we already know, escaped unharmed. In reply to an innocuous question by the defense attorney, Chmielewski, about how the violence subsided and in what way the army took control of the situation, she answered that the military evacuated her and the remaining Jews from the building around six P.M., brought them to the barracks in the Stadion section of Kielce,

---

*Corporal Maks Erlbaum, in army uniform bearing a sidearm, was challenged to prove that he was not a Jew. A woman, Jadwiga Manecka, grabbed him by the hand and got him surrounded by the crowd. Erlbaum reached for his documents and then saw a passing lieutenant, to whom he showed his military identification, begging to be saved. Lieutenant Marzecki (he was later put on trial together with Manecka for his behavior) looked at the documents, said that Erlbaum was a Pole, and continued on his way even though Erlbaum was trying to hold on to his belt and asked to be escorted out of danger. There was no rubric stating denomination in the booklet, but a helpful schoolboy looking over the lieutenant's shoulder shouted that Erlbaum had a Jewish name. Manecka then suggested that they pull down his pants. The crowd started to beat him, and he was saved by a Security Service agent who led him to safety (Meducki, *Antyżydowskie,* vol. I, pp. 253, 273, 274, 304).

and then, she continued: "I heard how one military man said while pointing at us: 'Why did you bring them, you should have killed them.' To a soldier's remark that there were children among us, he replied 'You don't know what to do with children, grab by the legs and pull apart in opposite directions.'" At this point the prosecutor interrupted her testimony and admonished defense attorneys not to bring up issues related to the military, because investigation of this matter was still in progress.*

Indeed, the role soldiers played during the pogrom was not addressed at any stage of the trial, even though—actually, perhaps precisely for this reason—among the more than one hundred people arrested on that day were thirty-four soldiers and officers from regular army units and six soldiers and officers from the Internal Security Corps (Korpus Bezpieczeństwa Wewnętrznego, KBW), a uniformed branch of the Security Service.[54] It was in the KBW barracks that Ewa Szuchman heard the words she repeated during the trial, and when she inadvertently opened the subject she was immediately cut off. Similarly, one of the attorneys who asked whether soldiers fired shots in the direction of the building on Planty was compelled by the court to withdraw the question.[55]

As to the city hospital in Kielce, we know that nurses initially mistreated wounded Jews there.† "Patients were afraid to eat in the hospital . . . , they feared that the staff might poison them," recalled Chil Alpert, who after the death of Dr. Kahane remained in charge of what was left of the Kielce Jewish community. Alpert went to Częstochowa to bring Jewish medical personnel to care for the wounded, but he persuaded only one nurse, Helena Majtlis, to come along.[56] Majtlis spent over two weeks in Kielce, from July 8 through July 23, barely sleeping because she was the only nurse assisting a single Jewish doctor in caring for the wounded.‡

*"Attorney Chmielewski explained that he only wanted to clarify circumstances which were brought up in the indictment. Attorney Okińczyc explained that while the defense did not intend to raise controversies during the trial ["*nie ma zamiaru rozdrażniania procesu*"], the proceedings should elucidate the background against which these events took place. Otherwise the defense could not responsibly fulfill its weighty duties" (Meducki, *Antyżydowskie,* vol. I, p. 183).

†One elderly Pole interviewed by Łoziński in 1987 reported being told that when patients in the hospital where his bedridden mother was at the time received news of wounded Jews being brought to the hospital, "a lot of the less sick ones got up to murder them" ("*to się dużo tych lepszych chorych zerwało żeby ich wymordować*"), but he didn't know what actually happened (Łoziński interview).

‡In 1987, when Marcel Łoziński interviewed her for *Witnesses,* she still had a certificate of recognition for her services signed by Alpert. Majtlis spoke very highly of various Polish

Before Helena Majtlis reached town, Yitzhak Zuckerman (better known by his nom de guerre, Antek) arrived in Kielce from Warsaw on July 5. Zuckerman was the last commander of the wartime Jewish Fighting Organization (Żydowska Organizacja Bojowa, ŻOB). When the news of the pogrom reached the Central Committee of Polish Jews in Warsaw, he immediately set out for Kielce with a carload of medical supplies. Despite the heavy military presence in town, Zuckerman concluded that for their own safety Jews should be taken out of the city as soon as possible. The authorities gave him all the assistance he needed to organize the evacuation, as well as a military escort. A special medical train under Zuckerman's command took the bulk of the wounded, as well as any other Jews ready to leave on July 6, to Łódź.

In his long memoirs, Zuckerman rarely loses his composure. But the sight of so many Jews massacred after the war affected him deeply:

> I wanted to remove all the wounded Jews immediately, and this is where things got screwed up: one of the wounded Jews knew me, called me Antek, and started speaking Yiddish to me. I immediately sensed an attitude of sabotage on the part of the doctors, the medics, and the nurses. . . . There was a moment when my nerves gave out and I couldn't maintain my poise. I pulled out a gun and ordered all the patients removed in fifteen minutes. The whole time the ambulances waited outside and the behavior of the staff seemed organized. Now they began running and carrying out orders. The army obeyed my orders, and the patients were quickly loaded onto the ambulances. As the army escorted them from the hospital to the railroad station, I organized the departure of the Jews from the courtyard of the UB and, naturally, I couldn't persuade all the Jews to leave.[57]

The wounded who remained in Kielce must have been too sick to travel. Many of them, suffering from savage blows to the head, were still unconscious when Helena Majtlis arrived. Her first task was to transport the wounded from the city hospital to the military hospital in Kielce, "because of fears that the city hospital might be attacked, and because the staff over there mistreated the patients." As Majtlis did not speak Yiddish, the wounded Jews initially shunned her: "at first, when I ap-

---

specialists—a surgeon and a neurologist—who were called for consultation as needed, and were always available and helpful.

proached them, some tried to hide under the bed." She soon gained their trust, as an old man with a cut to the bone across the right side of his skull and face cried in gratitude for the way she carefully dressed his wound. "Now I understand that you are Jewish," he told her. At the city hospital, a nurse had sharply pulled off his dressing and, when he screamed with pain, had slapped him in the face.[58]

Passionless Killings

Mr. Suszko was a student in Kraków in 1946. Back home in Kielce, he was on the way to the station in the early afternoon of July 4 to catch a train that would take him to the seashore for summer vacation. Suszko had recently spent two weeks in jail following student demonstrations in Kraków on May 3, a prewar national holiday. He prudently tried to stay out of trouble now, taking a circuitous route so as to avoid "excesses" in the city center. But as luck would have it he came upon a crowd in an open meadowlike space by the Silnica creek.

People were already tired. "After several hours of excesses a thin crowd surrounded a Jew, a twenty-some-year-old man, who was bleeding profusely. I remember that he had a vest and a white shirt, and he wasn't screaming or moving anymore. With head hanging low he was just standing in the middle of that creek, in the water, surrounded by a crowd that was stoning him. They were throwing stones in a somehow detached, leisurely manner—a stone would fly, people saw whether the man fell, then somebody else would throw a stone," and in the meantime they were busily carrying on conversations (*"tam był taki nastrój rozgadania"*). "They shared their impressions, observations, how this one caught a Jew here, and that one somewhere else. A young craftsman (butcher?), some thirty years old, wearing a leather apron, was a star of the show," talking animatedly and gesticulating.*

It struck Suszko as "most tragic" in the whole scene "that the crowd was already passionless. . . . After several hours of these events, people were tired but in spite of everything they were lifting stones and throwing them calmly, as if the death of a human being, killing of a person, were not at stake here. This was the most incredible sight. Simultaneously, the

---

Rzemieślnik, "craftsman," and *rzeźnik,* "butcher," sound somewhat similar; Suszko uses *rzemieślnik* first, but later, in an exchange with the interviewer, uses *rzeźnik*—a Freudian slip, I suppose, given the scene that he was describing.

simple everyday quality of these conversations in contrast to this man who was probably killed, . . . it was shocking."[59]

Evoking the picniclike atmosphere of the occasion, and the conversations in which people tried to impress one another by saying that "they saw more than the other person" ("this was very embarrassing . . . as if the events that were discussed did not involve the killing of several people"), Suszko becomes conscious in front of the camera of his own indifference, reproaching himself for saying nothing to anybody at the time and instead going on vacation where he didn't give the matter another thought. Belatedly, he portrays himself as a member of the crowd rather than a mere observer, and instead of "I saw this," the episode now becomes for him, "I was there." Suszko is visibly disturbed and saddened by the realization that he contributed a nonresponse to the day's events, and together with everybody else thus imparted to the killing of Kielce Jews—this radical transgression of norms of coexistence—a kind of normalcy.

Conversations Between Strangers

Regina Fisz and her newborn son were also murdered in an episode of passionless killing. The story is well known because Abram Moszkowicz, taken out together with her to be killed, managed to escape. He then found Regina Fisz's husband and together they went to the police and identified the killers, who were put on trial with the first dozen of the Kielce pogrom perpetrators. From their depositions and Moszkowicz's testimony, we can reconstruct what happened.

Moszkowicz was in Regina Fisz's apartment at number 15 Leonarda Street in the early afternoon on July 4 when three policemen came to search for weapons. They behaved properly, took a drink of water, advised Mrs. Fisz to keep her doors locked, and left. Soon thereafter a Polish cleaning woman rushed in to tell Mrs. Fisz that she overheard some drunkards in a nearby restaurant saying that something untoward might happen to her and that she should leave. But Mrs. Fisz declined. The city streets were dangerous anyway, and she felt safest at home. Some fifteen minutes later a man banged on the door asking to see Mrs. Fisz's husband, but she answered that he was away. Then a group of four men— three civilians accompanied by a policeman—showed up, identifying themselves as police, and she let them inside.[60]

The four men were strangers to one another, though Police Corporal Mazur of the militia and a baker, Kazimierz Nowakowski, whose shop was right across from police headquarters, knew each other by sight. On July 4, Mazur was in charge of the guard detachment at the headquarters. Several of his subordinates, unauthorized, went into town. At some point he set out to find them and, undoubtedly, also to personally find out about the goings-on in the city. While walking through Partyzantów Square, Mazur met Nowakowski, who approached him with a proposition: "I have a little job [*"mam robótkę"*]: Jews are living on Leonarda Street. One needs to close the apartment, take them out, and 'do it.'"[61]

Mazur did not need much persuading. Joined on the way by a "shoemaker [Józef Śliwa] and one more elderly civilian [Antoni Pruszkowski]," they went to the apartment of Regina Fisz where they ordered the Jews to come along.* In the meantime a crowd gathered in the street as the group came down. The abductors, noted Moszkowicz, "didn't know where to go and told us to walk straight along Leonarda Street," while the crowd followed behind.[62]

Moszkowicz read the situation correctly. As they marched their prey along, the four men were trying to figure out how to accomplish what they set out to do. "When we reached Leonarda Square," Mazur continued in his deposition, "Nowakowski said that I should kill the Jews in the park near police headquarters. But I didn't want to, since shots would be heard and everything would come out. So he said we should kill them in the street, but I didn't agree. And while figuring out what to do I saw a truck. So I stopped it. I approached the driver and told him that we had Jews whom we wanted to take out to kill. The driver agreed, he only asked for a thousand złoty, and I said, 'It's a deal.' When we were approaching Leonarda Square the crowd wanted to beat the Jews but the shoemaker and the elderly civilian calmed the crowd down by saying that the Jews would be killed, that 'We ourselves will do them.'"[63] Mazur climbed next to the driver and everybody else got on the truck. They drove to a place in a forest eight kilometers away, near a village called Cedzyna.

During this brief ride, Regina Fisz and Abram Moszkowicz kept

---

*Śliwa, the shoemaker, was married, with no record of prior arrests; Pruszkowski was a homeowner, married, with three children, and also no record of prior arrests. The two younger men who made up the foursome that killed Regina Fisz and her newborn son, Corporal Stefan Mazur and Kazimierz Nowakowski, were bachelors. Nowakowski owned a house and a bakery in Kielce. Altogether these were solid, employed, lower-middle-class and middle-class citizens (Meducki, *Antyżydowskie*, vol. I, pp. 151, 152).

talking to their abductors, begging to spare their lives. Mrs. Fisz offered to pay 150,000 złoty, leave town immediately, and never come back. The four men considered the offer briefly, but decided that it was too risky, as she could identify them later. They took the valuables the Jews had on their persons—a few thousand złoty, seventeen American dollars, two rings, a pin, and a pair of earrings. "We agreed to pretend that we were not paying attention, so that the Jews would try to escape and I would shoot them then," said Mazur to police investigators, and when the Jews took the bait Mazur promptly turned around and shot the fleeing woman dead from behind.[64]* Then they gave chase after Moszkowicz who was carrying the child, but he managed to escape. In his flight he dropped the baby, and Mazur killed the newborn with a bullet in the head.[†]

"At that point, people from the village were already standing in a large group nearby and they saw me shooting. The driver said to one civilian who was riding a bike that they should bury the bodies. Then we returned to Kielce and at the corner of Bodzentyńska Street we got out and went to a restaurant. The driver joined us as well."[65]

The company drank some vodka and had a good meal, which cost them one thousand złoty. Mazur got a two-hundred-złoty advance against anticipated profits from the sale of the victims' valuables, the driver was paid two dollars, and they exchanged addresses and agreed to meet again. Śliwa and Pruszkowski went to a jeweler to sell the loot. Later in the evening, Mazur went to visit Nowakowski for a drink. The baker complained that the price Śliwa and Pruszkowski had fetched at the jeweler's, three thousand złoty in all, was too low, so they returned the money and took back the goods.[66]

No one seemed overly preoccupied with concealing the crime, and there was a lot of coming and going in the aftermath of the murder. On

---

*The shoemaker, Śliwa, trying to persuade the court of his innocence (he explained during the trial that he went along for the ride "in order to protect the murder victims, when civilians tried to harm them after they were released out of town"), said that he motioned the Jews to run away as the four men were (seemingly) absorbed in a conversation (Meducki, *Antyżydowskie,* vol. I, pp. 175, 176). In light of what Mazur revealed about their "plan" to induce the Jews to flee, this only further incriminated Śliwa, of course. In a bizarre twist of fate, as we already know, one week later Mazur would be killed in an analogous scene, while attempting to flee the execution squad.

†Mazur was queried about his actions during the trial and his answers later were repeated in journalistic accounts of the pogrom: "The judge: How could the defendant shoot a little child? Didn't you have pity? The defendant: Of course, but even if one had pity what is there to do when the mother is no more? What can one do, the child would cry" (Daniel, *Żyd w zielonym,* p. 48).

the following day Mazur, accompanied by yet another policeman, went back to Leonarda Street: "I opened the apartment from where, as the super told me, some things had already been stolen during the night. The super was with us, and also somebody from the neighboring apartment. When the super asked who would pay her for all this [the things they were taking] I said, 'All is in order, it's okay to take the stuff, the Jews are not coming back anymore.' "[67]

The Jews did come back, though not without the intervention of two small miracles that kept Moszkowicz alive. In the first place, he managed to escape pursuit by the murderers of Regina Fisz and her child. After running for his life, Moszkowicz crawled on all fours into a field of rye, where he collapsed and lost consciousness. When he recovered, late that afternoon, he decided to report the incident to the police. As he started on foot toward Kielce he noticed some people observing and following him from afar. As he approached town, a man rode by on a bicycle and shouted, "Jew!" In the vicinity of the hospital on Aleksandra Street a group of young men armed with poles, metal rods, and stones awaited Moszkowicz. He was asked to produce identification papers. A man looked over the documents and said briskly to the others, "A Jew, beat him up." Moszkowicz was then pounded unconscious by this vigilante group. When he regained consciousness, a stranger returned his documents and walked him to a police patrol, which took him to the hospital. Two days later, having recuperated somewhat, he went to Leonarda Street and told the story to Regina Fisz's husband. They returned to the crime scene, accompanied by the police. Local children showed them where the bodies were buried.[68]*

The murder of Regina Fisz and her child reminds us that the pogrom in Kielce did not target only individuals who were purported to have killed a Christian child, or Jews who were Communists, or those who occupied positions of power and influence. Regina Fisz and her son fall outside these categories. Similarly, the gang that checked Moszkowicz's papers in front of the hospital needed only to know that he was a Jew before they attempted to kill him. As many Polish citizens of Kielce searched for, tracked down, and then attempted to murder all the Jews within their

---

*Regina Fisz and her child were exhumed from their forest graves and interred at the Jewish cemetery in Kielce, with all the other pogrom victims, during official ceremonies held on July 8.

reach, we come to the realization that the pogrom cannot be narrated as a story about a frenzied mob. What stands out on this gruesome occasion is the widely shared sense in Polish society that getting rid of the Jews, by killing them if necessary, was permissible.

Perhaps the most arresting moment in the story, to my mind at least, comes when the policeman Mazur hails a passing truck in the street, tells the driver that he needs transportation to kill some Jews, and the driver agrees to offer his services for a fee. One does not know what is more startling in this brief encounter—the gall of a policeman in stopping a random stranger to make such a proposition, or the callousness of the stranger who accepts such a proposition on the spot. It does not matter who the protagonists are in this absurdist dialogue. The only thing that matters is that it could have taken place, indeed that it did take place, and that it was a perfectly comprehensible exchange between strangers in Poland in Anno Domini 1946.

Mazur and his murder associates did not know one another to begin with. Barring evidence that they were psychopaths, or otherwise mad, only one reading of binding social norms might allow such a spur-of-the-moment association—and that is a shared understanding that Jews could be killed with impunity. Would the murderers otherwise call on casual bystanders, peasants from Cedzyna, to bury the bodies of a woman and a newborn child killed in their plain view?

A shoemaker, a bakery owner, a police corporal, and the fourth participant in the murder, who owned a house in Kielce and worked as a caretaker in the city hall—law-abiding (none had any record of prior arrests) middle-class citizens—then bonded over their common experience. They treated themselves to an expensive meal in a restaurant, went about settling their affairs, dividing the spoils, selling with profit what they had plundered from the Jews, as if they had just availed themselves of yet another good business opportunity. They publicly consummated their joint endeavor and its proceeds. They didn't feel compelled to conceal their deeds from other strangers. The only thing that made the policeman uncomfortable was that he took the money—"I didn't do it for mercenary reasons," he insisted in court. He was not the only defendant who seemed more embarrassed by accusations of plunder than of beating and murdering Jews.*

---

*Another defendant in the first Kielce trial, Władysław Błachut, who was also a policeman and was also sentenced to death, adamantly denied in court that he ordered the Jew he was caught beating, Mojżesz Cukier, to take off his shoes (Meducki, *Antyżydowskie*, vol. I, pp. 181, 193).

On the Railroad

We already know that Jews were particularly vulnerable to attack on trains in postwar Poland and that the violence of the Kielce pogrom spilled out of town along the railway network. The Kielce train station turned into a death trap for Jews who came to or traveled through town before the military was deployed there in force.

In the morning of July 4 a man named Brunon Piątek and an engineer named Elżanowski went to the Kielce-Herbskie train station to meet Piątek's wife, who was scheduled to arrive from Wrocław. Later Piątek made a statement about events he witnessed and passed it on to the UB office in Kielce, but was never called to make a formal deposition. In 1984 he wrote his recollections again for the Jewish Historical Institute in Warsaw, convinced that a record of these "nightmarish events" should be preserved and that

> nobody else can do it because all present at the time in the Kielce-Herbskie train station actively participated in chasing after or barring escape routes to Jews who were helplessly trying to run away. . . . I know this very well because while facing mortal danger and talking with the surrounding crowd I was constantly scanning the area trying to spot a railroad security guard or some other help. But I didn't see anybody of the sort, and no help ever came. In the distance I only spotted this individual carrying a shotgun, who carefully went around from one corpse to another, checked them over, and even kneeled beside them. Today I realize that he was simply robbing the dead.[69]

This could not be because the label of a thief represented a greater stigma than that of a killer. Indeed, robbery always accompanied the killing of Jews, but its logic was radically different, even opposite. Unlike killing, plunder was egoistic. Killing could be revenge, punishment, retribution, justice, or whatever a Communist, a God-killer, or a child molester rightfully deserved, and a dead Jew represented a collective good—benefiting all in whose interests it was to get rid of the Jewish presence altogether. Killing a Jew reduced the burden of everyone else involved in the cleansing operation, while plundering reduced opportunities for all by taking away what others could have appropriated instead. A plundered Jew benefited only the plunderer and shortchanged the others. While one kind of behavior could be appreciated by fellow citizens, the other generated envy.

We do not know how many trains bearing Jews pulled into the Kielce-Herbskie station before the military established a strong presence there and prevented further killings.*

Such train-station attacks took place in several locations. The episodes were typically brief, lasting not much longer than a scheduled stop.[†] They involved collaboration of passengers traveling on the train with willing individuals already present in the station. The use of heavy iron objects—rail sections or pieces of railroad equipment—to crush people's skulls was reported. Jews had to be identified before being murdered and it appears that boy scouts played a particularly active role in this process.[‡] Men in uniforms with shotguns—railroad guards or traveling soldiers—joined in these rapid assaults and often used firearms.

Both Piątek and Elżanowski were employed in managerial positions, at the Ludwików Foundry. When they arrived at the train station several men were milling around on the platforms. Shortly thereafter a train appeared, and as it was coming to a stop Piątek noticed people being pushed out of railway cars. Those who resisted were pulled out by men already present in the station, who then immediately attacked them. "The manner of killing was to throw stones at Jews, who helplessly ran around platforms and tracks until they fell. Then the fallen prey was finished off with iron weights." Taken aback by the sudden eruption of violence, Piątek and Elżanowski tried to intervene by confronting the persecutors, and found themselves threatened by an angrily screaming crowd: "You Jewish knaves! Jews have killed our children and you dare to defend them!"[70]

"My situation deteriorated further," Piątek continued, "when one of the Jews whom they were killing, a young and strong man, realized that we were trying to help, and while already prostrate on the ground

---

*By noon the troops were already deployed in the Kielce main station. A Mr. Nowak arrived just then on a train from Częstochowa and with all the other passengers was brought into a fenced-off area previously used by the Germans during periodic population roundups. Then, one by one, the passengers' documents were checked and they were slowly released into town (*Witnesses*).

[†]Anszel Pinkuszewicz, in a testimony deposited at Yad Vashem, mentions that the station dispatcher in Piekoszów, some eight kilometers from Kielce, held the train longer in the station to give more time for an impromptu pogrom organized by the passengers (Szaynok, *Pogrom*, p. 59).

[‡]I am somewhat puzzled by this, but their role stands out in the available evidence. Perhaps in early July an unusually high number were traveling to or from their summer camps, for instance. It may also be that on overcrowded trains (at the time people traveled even on rooftops for lack of available space) a slender youth could more easily go up and down a railroad car to look over the passengers.

grabbed me with all his strength by the knees. The tormentors grabbed the Jew, however, and two pulled him away by the legs. I thought that I would not be able to remain standing, and if I fell they would surely finish me off. But the Jew was already bleeding profusely from the head and his grip weakened. Two murderers dragged him a few steps away and then a third man ran up, knelt by the victim, and with a heavy iron weight systematically smashed the Jew's head. The man who finished off the victim was relatively young and weak, and in pounding with the heavy iron weight he bent low over the head of the murdered man. When he stood up, I saw his face spattered with bloody mush from the victim's ruptured head. He must have felt wetness on his face and his mouth as well, for he instinctively wiped it with his arm and licked around the lips. I will never forget this repulsive sight."[71]

Nobody official tried to stop the massacre in the station. There were individuals on the scene wearing uniforms, and some of them carried shotguns, but they joined in the killings. For the most part, Jews were clubbed and stoned to death, though a few shots were fired as well. Altogether Piątek counted seven dead Jews.

It was a close call for Piątek and Elżanowski, especially as the latter froze and stood watching the crowd in a daze. Elżanowski's identification papers were checked by the mob but in the end both men were let go. Piątek went back to work at the Ludwików Foundry, which by then was almost deserted (its crew, as we remember, mounted the second wave of deadly assaults on the building at Planty 7). In the gatehouse, Piątek met a few industrial guards and the beaming secretary of the local labor unions. "To my question 'Where are the workers?' he [the secretary] answered that they went to town, for a demonstration. I told him then about the murders at the train station and that Elżanowski barely escaped alive, to which he replied, 'It serves him right; he shouldn't defend the Jews.' "[72]

That Jews were being murdered did not seem to shock many people in Poland in 1946. It was accepted matter-of-factly by individuals from many walks of life, including those who did not, and probably would not, lend a helping hand to any such endeavors. What foundation of moral economy is necessary to admit such a possibility as a course of normal events?

Piątek's itinerary then took him home. He stopped by Elżanowski's apartment to check whether the engineer had returned safely, and wandered onto a stone bridge over the Silnica some distance away from

Planty 7. A Soviet officer he had met on various official occasions was standing on the bridge, accompanied by his wife. It was evident from the officer's body language and comments that he enjoyed the spectacle.[73] "Unfortunately, most of the people I encountered were in a cheerful mood on account of what was going on [*"Niestety w radosnym nastroju z powodu wydarzeń była większość spotkanych ludzi"*]. In every conceivable place people were getting drunk."[74]

Piątek's testimony—which we find echoed, in two examples: in the narrative by one of Łoziński's interviewees about the leisurely stoning of a Jewish youth; and in the report filed by visiting PPR Central Committee instructors—offers insight into the local people's collective state of mind. The presumed death of innocent Polish children would be a reason for mourning, not for celebration, and if the canard that brought thousands of Kielce inhabitants into the streets were anything but a Pavlovian signal that activated an embedded prejudice, they could not have enjoyed the day.

Three more of Łoziński's interviewees also described the murder of Jews at the train station. A woman who arrived in Kielce from Częstochowa on July 5 remembered a commotion on the train, which made her look out a window. One day after the pogrom, corpses were still strewn along a section of the railroad tracks, and people gawked as the train passed them by. Some Jews were killed and thrown off passing trains, but for the most part, as in the episode at the Kielce-Herbskie station recounted earlier, they were murdered in train stations as news of the pogrom traveled out of Kielce and found a receptive audience keen to emulate the effort.

The Mr. Nowak mentioned earlier tells a characteristic story about trains to and from Kielce meeting at a station along the way. He journeyed from Częstochowa to Kielce on July 4, and in Włoszczowa his train stopped across the platform from one going in the opposite direction. As passengers shouted news of the Kielce pogrom from one train to the other (namely that Jews had murdered Christian children and that inhabitants of Kielce were taking their just revenge), forthwith individuals suspected of being Jewish were pulled from the Częstochowa train and the killings began. "I saw with my own eyes how an elderly Jewess who sold lemonade was killed, she ran into a rye field and was stoned to death." Soldiers on the train positioned themselves in open windows and shot at Jews trying to run away. A Jewish youth fell on the platform and "a railwayman dropped a section of rail on his head, which burst open."[75] The whole episode lasted but fifteen minutes, until the trains departed for their destinations.

Julia Pirotte (née Diament).
SELF-PORTRAIT, MARSEILLE, 1942 (ŻIH, J-22)

Ruins of the Warsaw ghetto, 1946.
PHOTOGRAPH BY JULIA PIROTTE (ŻIH, J-15)

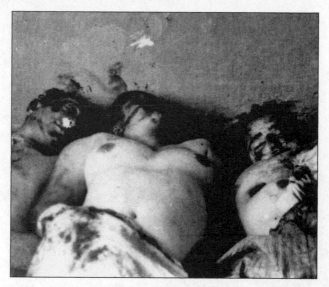

Victims of the Kielce pogrom.
(ŻIH, 1184)

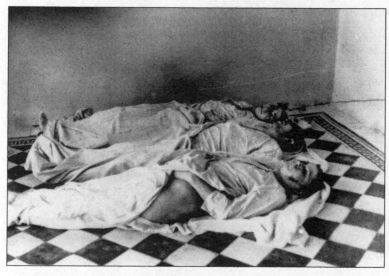

Three male corpses of victims of the Kielce pogrom, in the hospital morgue.
PHOTOGRAPH FROM THE URZĄD OCHRONY PAŃSTWA
(UOP) (OFFICE OF STATE PROTECTION) IN KIELCE (ŻIH, 1181)

Victims of the Kielce pogrom.

*Regina Fisz and her child, murdered during the pogrom in Kielce,
in the hospital morgue.*

Hospitalized Jews, wounded during the pogrom in Kielce.

Yitzhak Zuckerman (Antek),
last commander of the wartime Jewish Fighting Organization (ŻOB),
who organized the evacuation of hospitalized Jews from Kielce after the pogrom.
PHOTOGRAPH BY JULIA PIROTTE (ŻIH, J-14)

Coffins holding the victims of the Kielce pogrom.
(ŻIH, 1171)

Burial ceremony of the Kielce pogrom victims.
(ŻIH, 1172)

Burial ceremony of the Kielce pogrom victims.
(ŻIH, 1176, ŻIH, 1173)

Mosze Russek, Szaja Hirsz Kohn, Jankiel Kohn, Mendel Kohn, and Mejer Markowicz, killed in November 1945 near Zloczów.

PHOTOGRAPH DEPOSITED BY ITZHAK RUSSEK (ŻIH. 13)

Very much like Piątek and Elżanowski, Nowak remembered that he was petrified. He had been told once that he resembled a Jew in physical appearance and he realized that if he were fingered and called a Jew in Włoszczowa station, nothing could save his life. The rapidity and total randomness of the assaults was breathtaking. And if violence subsided while the train was in motion it was held in abeyance only until the next stop. The tension built gradually until the next eruption as excited pogrom participants geared themselves back into action, and as Jewish travelers, if any, hunkered down timidly lest they be found out.

Józef Sztarkman traveled on the night train from Wrocław to Kielce together with his brother-in-law Henryk Gitelis. (This was probably the very train Piątek's wife was supposed to take, if she had not postponed the trip until the following day.) They were deposed on July 8, 1946, and vividly remembered all the events.

For a traveling companion, Sztarkman and Gitelis had a young veteran who must have served in the Polish armed forces abroad. He wore a uniform blouse with foreign insignia and talked most of the way about his exploits during the war. They passed the time pleasantly enough until the train reached Piekoszów. There, as in the Włoszczowa episode recounted by Nowak, while the Wrocław train stopped in the station a train from Kielce pulled in, and the story of Christian children killed by Kielce Jews for matzo immediately spread around. A pogrom ensued in the station right away, with the young man playing a leading role in the events.*

At the next station, Szczukowskie Górki, the veteran disembarked again and people were killed there as well. When the train arrived in Herby, or Kielce-Herbskie, again "he jumped out and went on with the killing, it is a fact that several people were murdered, I don't know how many because I was afraid that I would be recognized [as a Jew]," said Sztarkman in his deposition.[76] This was almost certainly the very same episode that Piątek recounted forty years later; as we follow it through the eyes of passengers on the train it appears as but one link in a chain of events which must have been replicated on several trains traveling this route on July 4.†

---

*Upon hearing the "news" he immediately ran out of the car inciting anti-Jewish violence and went on to kill an elderly Jewish woman as Sztarkman and Gitelis watched from inside the train. Another passenger on the train, Anszel Pinkuszewicz, whose testimony is deposited in Yad Vashem, saw a Jewish-looking army officer shot twice and killed in the same station. He also witnessed the stoning to death of the elderly woman (Szaynok, *Pogrom,* p. 59).

†The Central Committee of Polish Jews estimated that some thirty people were killed on the railroad in Kielce pogrom—related assaults (Szaynok, *Pogrom,* p. 60). If anything, this is a conservative estimate.

Sztarkman and Gitelis were lucky. They must have somehow bonded with the man during an earlier phase of the journey and consequently he couldn't conceive of them as being Jewish. But there were certainly others looking around for suitable victims. A sixteen-year-old boy scout, Kazimierz Redliński, was on a train to Częstochowa on that day. After the word got around that Jews were murdering Polish children in Kielce, Redliński joined in the search for Jews among the passengers, and—we read in the indictment of the November 18, 1946, trial, where he was prosecuted along with fourteen other defendants—"when the train stopped at stations he pushed the Jews out of the cars into the hands of crowds who robbed them and then killed them, most frequently by stoning their victims to death. While the train was in motion Redliński put the strap of his scout cap under his chin, thus emphasizing his pseudo-official status, and walked along railroad cars, searching for Jews among the passengers."*

In view of his youth and membership in the scouts Redliński fetched only a suspended sentence of five years in prison.[77] Evidently by late November the temper of officialdom had cooled. But on July 7, with victims of the pogrom still unburied, a joint meeting of the Kielce voivodeship committees of the Socialist and the Communist Parties issued a strong indictment of young people's behavior. "The mass participation of young scouts on the day of the pogrom [*masowy udział młodzieży harcerskiej w dniu pogromu*] proved that their upbringing is in the hands of irresponsible people, who stoke racial and religious hatred among the young." The third and last recommendation put forth in the joint resolution called for "suspending the local scouting leadership because many scouts were involved as instigators during the pogrom" (*za liczny udział harcerzy w roli podżegaczy do ekscesów*).[78] Apparently, teenagers contributed more than their share to the unseemly sight of *uniformed* individuals taking part in the killings of their fellow citizens. The conspicuous role of boy scouts in these gruesome events is particularly disturbing, for they represent, in a manner of speaking, a secular form of purity: as the "altar boys" of the nation.[79]

---

*Meducki, *Antyżydowskie*, vol. I, pp. 253–54. See also testimony by Michał Klein, a decorated army veteran, who was on a train to Częstochowa on that day and reported witnessing assaults against two Jews by a mob at the Kielce train station. "When the train got in motion some civilians and scouts started walking through passenger cars looking for Jews." At subsequent stations people were repeatedly pulled out of the train and killed (Memorandum of the Jewish Committee in Częstochowa to the CKŻP in Warsaw, July 10, 1946, "Witnesses' Testimonies," in AAN, MAP, 787/22).

Many people approached by Marcel Łoziński for interviews about their recollections of the pogrom refused to talk with the filmmaker. Those who consented were thus a self-selected group. For several, the interview seemed to provide a long-awaited opportunity to try framing their memories in a coherent narrative. One can see on the screen that they are not so much answering the interviewer's questions as letting us eavesdrop on their internal dialogue, a conversation on the subject they were at last engaged in with themselves.

A thoughtful and elegant man introduced in the film as "a historian" is one such interviewee.* A ten-year-old boy at the time, he hadn't seen anything in particular by "objective" standards and only spent a quarter of an hour on July 4 in the Kielce station, sitting politely in a train compartment at his mother's side. But, as he came to realize over the years, the journey had marked him for life. As he slowly articulates answers to the interviewer's questions, he is visibly trying to put into words an internal landscape that has haunted him for decades.

As the train carrying a ten-year-old future historian pulled to a stop in Kielce,

> there was some sort of excitement in the atmosphere which penetrated into the compartment, but without clear information about what was going on. I wouldn't say that one could hear shots, but it is possible. . . . At a certain moment the doors opened and a young boy squeezed in. I felt that he was a bit older than myself, but to the ten-year-old boy I was at the time, he seemed young. I cannot tell at present whether he was wearing a scout uniform, but I was sure that he was a scout; perhaps he was wearing some part of the uniform [a scouting cap with a chin strap, maybe?]. I remember him as a scout. And this boy carefully looked over people who were in his field of vision, and disappeared.
>
> Some time later a few men showed up—more than one; I don't remember the number exactly. I cannot say for sure if they wore uniforms but I know that these were armed railway guards,

---

*At some point he picked up a book from the table and quickly found a passage where Thucydides describes how he used witnesses' testimony in *The Peloponnesian War*.

and they took a man from our compartment.* Today I know that
he was a Jew, a man with Semitic features; I am saying this today,
at the time I couldn't tell. . . . I don't know what happened to this
man. My mother absolutely didn't allow me to even approach
the window. People said that this man was shot by those railroad
guards right there.

What can I add? . . . a flabbergasting reaction of the
people—I mean the absence of any reaction. On the one hand
there was . . . a sense that something bad, not good, was taking
place, but that it could not be helped. It was happening
because it had to be that way. And no attempt to respond, to
defend, nothing of the sort. I remember later that as the
train left and was on its way to Częstochowa people said
that somebody was thrown off the rooftop [because of over-
crowding, people frequently traveled on the rooftops of train
cars]. . . . This would bring discredit to Polish society at any
time, but if something like this takes place one year after the
war, well . . .

Irrespective of the instigators, because I understand that
there had to be some, I think that they are unimportant because
the population participated in this, at least passively, people like
myself who did not react. . . . I am helpless [to explain how such
a pogrom could have taken place one year after the war]. This is
totally incomprehensible to me . . . one can speak about long-
embedded anti-Semitism but this is not enough. . . . This had an
enormous influence on me. If I am not an anti-Semite, having
been brought up in this society, it is for two reasons—because my
father was one, and because of what I witnessed in Kielce.
Awareness that I had been brushed by death, aimlessly capri-
cious death, pointing its finger at completely random people . . .
frightening. And the young boy who took part in this. I don't
know what knowledge he was equipped with to recognize proper
targets. . . . Maybe he was thirteen years old, maybe fourteen,
maybe fifteen, I cannot tell.

Obviously, as a ten-year-old boy, I couldn't have done any-

---

*There existed such a specialized service, the Służba Ochrony Kolei (SOK), and its
members were colloquially called *sokiści,* the word Łoziński's interlocutor uses in the interview.

thing; besides, my mother would not let me. But I know today that I was one of many people—my age is of no importance—who did not react at all to this. The remainder of the trip passed as if nothing happened. . . . The entire society behaved this way. For decades this matter was covered under a veil of silence.[80]

4

THE KIELCE POGROM: REACTIONS

B
Y ALL APPEARANCES, the Kielce pogrom was a complex event, not just a mere inchoate aggression to which the Jews fell victim. In their own minds, people in Kielce were enforcing what was vigilante justice, but justice nevertheless. Scattered uniformed state representatives visibly supported the aroused citizens, who gratefully acknowledged the fact, on occasion shouting "Long live the Polish army!"[1] Their presence on the scene gave an aura of institutional sanction to what was going on. Throughout the day, men in uniform—soldiers, policemen, scouts, railwaymen, a prison guard, an armed watchman from PPS Party headquarters wearing an "American uniform"—were chasing, assaulting, beating up, and killing Jews (as well as people who looked like Jews) all over town.* They applied themselves to this task together with many other concerned citizens. A sense of threat was easily communicated across a vast social spectrum, and a large crowd mobilized quickly to fend off the danger. Why were the people of Poland so threatened by their fellow citizens, the Jews? Was it really because Jews were sucking their children's blood?

---

*A UB agent who arrested Szymkiewicz, one of those sentenced to death in the first Kielce trial, identified him by his "American uniform, and red armband with the letters PPS inscribed on it. . . . The defendant Szymkiewicz seemed especially conspicuous to me because there were only three people in similar uniforms" (Meducki, *Antyżydowskie,* vol. I, pp. 283–84). "American uniform" is probably in reference to a vest that was quite popular at the time, made of cloth used in American or British army uniforms.

On the face of it the claim of ritual murder was taken with utter seriousness by many people. Even distinguished churchmen did not hesitate to express qualified support for this proposition.[2] The Citizens' Militia *was* sent to investigate whether an incident of Christian child kidnapping and murder by the Jews had indeed taken place. In an unpublished appeal to the people of Kielce, the voivode together with a representative of a local bishop stated reassuringly that "on the basis of materials assembled by the investigators, no murder of Polish children by the Jewish population had taken place."[3] When a group of foreign journalists arrived in town the day after the pogrom, they first went to meet with the voivode; "while waiting in the house of the *wojewoda*," writes S. L. Shneiderman, "I asked a soldier who sat in the corridor if he knew what had caused the pogrom. He replied candidly that the massacre had started because 'the Jews had kidnapped Christian children and hid them in their building at Number 7, Planty Street.' "[4]

During the interviews Łoziński filmed in the mid-1980s, forty years after the events, his subjects already knew the politically correct answer to questions about ritual murder, but they did not necessarily agree with it.* So many people, and not just simple people, evidently believed in the accusation "that there had to be something in it," the solidly middle-class widow of a defense attorney said on camera; while a "simple" elderly lady who lived nearby, when asked if the story about ritual murder was true, answered with a noncommittal smile, "It is their secret" (*"To jest ich tajemnica"*).[5]

One of the defense attorneys argued during the first Kielce trial that "the people who went to Planty Street for the purpose of protecting the young were motivated by a paternal feeling. This motive of self-defense should be taken into account by the court in evaluating the psychological condition of the defendants."[6] Shneiderman, who sat in the courtroom and heard the speech, was wrong to view this as an exercise in hypocrisy. As the responses of many people throughout the country to the pogrom in Kielce (and to the summary trial of the first group of perpetrators) were to demonstrate, the attorney's reading of the popular mind was on the mark. Except, of course, that the Jews were not killing Christian children for blood.

---

*Łoziński's collaborator who was doing the interviews did not know how to ask this question properly. She was so convinced of the nonsense she was drawing people to comment about that she repeatedly asked them a leading question—"Do you think that people believed in [or, "What did you, at the time, think of"] *the legend* [emphasis mine] of ritual murder?"

The Kielce pogrom drew an immediate response from the authorities: there was a (kind of) judicial investigation of its circumstances, and there were several trials of the perpetrators. If nothing else, this legal aftermath is a constitutive part of the story, as it additionally serves to establish the historical record of what happened. But response to the pogrom reverberated through various milieus of Polish society, and only by taking these aftershocks into account can we make sense of what happened on July 4 in Kielce.

How the Working Class Reacted to the Kielce Pogrom and What the Communist Party Made of It

The Communist Party always took propaganda very seriously, and in 1946 it was deeply engaged in the struggle for the hearts and minds of the Polish population. Every public event called for ideological spin, and the Kielce pogrom was no exception. The educational and propaganda benefit that the Party initially thought might be derived from the massacre— by drawing "the masses" into protesting against the killings, and then switching the targets of opprobrium from the direct perpetrators to the "real" culprits, that is, "reactionary elements" who presumably "inspired" these events and were the regime's political opponents—backfired: it turned out that "the masses" felt no sympathy for the Jews, even in the face of the horrible crimes to which the Jews fell victim.

A group of the PPR's Central Committee instructors who came to Kielce on July 4 and then fanned out through the region to carry out propaganda work submitted a chilling memorandum a few days after their return to Warsaw. "Attitudes among the masses are for the most part rather negative"—that is, workers are unwilling to publicly condemn perpetrators of the Kielce pogrom—their report begins. "In several localities moral terror had to be used—for example in Pionki, in the State Powder Factory employing some 700 workers...."[7] "Workers in a brewery in Radom opposed an anti-pogrom resolution. Also in a cooperative, and in the Directorate of State Forests, people opposed a resolution condemning the Kielce crime. It is mostly railwaymen who drive anti-Semitic attitudes ... [and] spread anti-Semitic slogans throughout the voivodeship. It is a fact that railway guards identified Jews on the Częstochowa–Kielce line and incited aggressors to beatings. In Radom a number of railwaymen opposed a resolution condemning the pogrom."[8]

The July report of the Radom Department of Information and

Propaganda noted matter-of-factly: "In the current month very strong anti-Jewish opinions manifested themselves, especially among the intelligentsia. The fact of the Jewish pogrom in Kielce met with the moral approval of many groups in our society."*

Padraic Kenney, in his excellent study of the early years of Communism in Poland, drew on local and central Party archives to provide a long description of how the issue played in the industrial center of Łódź:

> Between 8 and 11 July, labor leaders called meetings in many factories to condemn the pogrom. They prepared resolutions and invited workers to sign them. The meetings themselves passed without incident, but few workers cooperated. In the Łódź thread factory "the assembly accepted the proposed resolution indifferently and calmly, but supposedly [only] a small number of workers signed it." Only one shop in Scheibler and Grohman agreed to the resolution, and only some PPR members signed it. The next day, however, the daily newspaper of the

---

*Meducki, Antyżydowskie, vol. II, p. 151. "During a meeting in Ostrowiec," the report of the Central Committee's instructors continues, "Comrade Józef Kasior (PPR) gave a speech against the Jews: 'What is it all about? We are slaving like mad, and Jews in Ostrowiec live as if there was no tomorrow ["żyją sobie jak u Pana Boga za piecem"—literally, "they live as if behind the stove at God Almighty's"], they buy butter and chicken, where were they when we fought in the guerrillas?' This was said by a comrade who studied in a voivodeship and in a central Party school. Another comrade in Ostrowiec turned to a speaker at a meeting: 'Just give Jews a good thrashing and you will draw applause' " (Meducki, Antyżydowskie, vol. II, pp. 139, 140). The Ostrowiec city Department of Information and Propaganda in its July report signaled that condemning the Kielce pogrom perpetrators to death was viewed in the city as "an act that was not entirely just" (ibid., p. 147).

In Skarżysko-Kamienna, 500 people were assembled on July 8 in the Kamienna factory to hear a representative of the PPR's city organization speak on the topic "Pogrom of the Jews in Kielce: Provocation of the Reactionaries." "The atmosphere was rowdy," we read in the report of the local Department of Information and Propaganda. "After the meeting disbanded, workers did not accept a resolution condemning the shameful Kielce crime." Neither did 150 employees of the Polish State Railways, who were addressed on the same day by the first secretary of the PPR's city committee, a Comrade Baran. On subsequent days meetings were held in other factories and institutions in a "good atmosphere" and appropriate resolutions were accepted. We are not told whence the change of mood, but perhaps a dose of "moral terror" was skillfully applied (ibid., pp. 152–54). In Pińczów, the county's Party secretary reproached one of the Central Committee instructors who came there for "defend[ing] Jews too much in his speech." When Comrade Buczyński advised activists in the Pińczów county to organize mass meetings about the Kielce pogrom, one of the comrades from the county committee protested: 'How can one go and defend the Jews in front of peasants if Jewesses get forty thousand złoty for giving birth to a child?' Of course, Comrade Buczyński refuted such lies" (ibid., p. 140). From Sandomierz, the county Department of Information and Propaganda reported on July 10 that "people in the area are saying that Jews really did murder several Polish children and they deserved to be killed in Kielce" (ibid., p. 144).

Łódź PPR reported "in large type" that the workers at these and other factories had approved resolutions and demanded the death penalty for those found guilty of the pogrom. This attempt to propagandize the incident backfired, arousing workers' anti-Semitism and politicizing it by turning it toward the government and the PPR. Workers began to perceive the PPR and the government as "Jewish" in their opposition to the workers. When workers saw this report, strikes broke out at nearly a dozen factories, mostly cotton mills and sewing shops. The strikes' connection to the Kielce tragedy was clear; in one factory, there was even a spurious phone call informing workers that all of Kielce was on strike and asking for Łódź's support.

Although the strikes lasted only an hour or so, PPR observers were taken by surprise at their vehemence. When the PPR secretary in one factory attempted to oppose the strikers, she was beaten by several of them. Warned a Central Committee report: "The situation in Łódź is serious, as evidenced by the mood among strikers, the strikes' swift leaps from factory to factory, and the aggression of striking women in all factories; they clawed and screamed ferociously. Slogans of revenge and terror from the moment of execution [of the convicted killers of Kielce] were heard in the shops. [They] compare the alacrity of the Kielce trial with that of [Arthur] Greiser [Nazi leader of the Warthegau, Polish lands annexed to the Reich], who is still alive, though he is guilty of so many millions of victims. Striking workers use such anti-Semitic arguments as "A pregnant Jew gets a thousand złotys, and what do I have?" . . . [or] "Why don't Jews work in factory shops? Poland is ruled by Jews." Łódź Jews described a "pogrom atmosphere" in the city; there were rumors, for example, that Jews in the Bałuty district (a large worker district and the location of the Jewish ghetto during the war) had murdered a Polish child. While the strikes themselves were easily broken up once the workers had made their demand (usually that a retraction be printed in the newspaper) the hostility lingered long after. The sentencing of the pogrom leaders sparked more protests.[9]

The working class of Łódź had a bellwether quality for the Communists. This is where the wave of strikes began that sparked the 1905 revolution in Russia. The city and its working class—the greater proportion of its garment industry made up of women—figured in Bolshevik lore as a symbolic gateway to the great October. On this occasion, though, the seamstresses and weavers of Łódź did not foreshadow much of anything. They were rather like chorus girls—one voice among many that reverberated throughout the country.* Under the circumstances this made their message particularly significant, and the Party listened carefully.

Some 16,000 workers participated in strikes with anti-Jewish slogans in Łódź alone, and the Communist Party's second highest decision-making body—the Secretariat of the Central Committee—during its first meeting held after the Kielce pogrom, on July 29, 1946, placed on the agenda the issue of workers' *strikes in Łódź, not the Kielce pogrom per se*.[10] The usual self-criticism one finds in Party documents on such occasions—that the quality of Party work and of Party cadres was inadequate and needed to be strengthened in order to counter the influence of "reactionaries"— was refined and sharpened during the discussion by Comrade Witaszew ski. Workers were angry with the regime, he said, because they were exploited by shopkeepers, merchants who sold foodstuffs at bazaars, privately owned eating establishments, and all sorts of individual, private entrepreneurs who did not produce much of anything but acted as middlemen. And when they were angry with the regime, the workers succumbed to reactionary influences, including anti-Semitism.[11] As a countermeasure to overcome anti-Semitism, Witaszewski proposed getting rid of the private sector. The unspoken subtext of this line of argument was that Jews, as paradigmatic middlemen who by and large shirked work and were "unproductive," should be dealt with in the first place.[†]

---

*"A wave of better or less well conceived protests against the Kielce pogrom appeared in various newspapers; in factories, offices, in tramways, on the railroad, among crowds gathering in the street, protests against the sentences passed in the trial of Kielce perpetrators subsided," wrote Witold Kula a month after the Kielce pogrom (Witold Kula, "Nasza w tym rola," in Marcin Kula, *Uparta sprawa,* p. 159).

†This is a very complex theme made up of multiple strands. There was a whole effort, both within the Jewish community and outside it, to bring about "productivization" of the Jews, who presumably did not want to be employed except as middlemen and traders, that is, in jobs that "do not produce" anything. The movement reflects a derogatory outside perception of the Jews as people who live off the work of others, but also an internalized sense of the inferiority and social backwardness of the traditional Jewish community. To fully deconstruct the theme, one would have to concurrently analyze Zionist efforts to teach Eastern European Jews working skills to prepare them for aliyah; Nazi categorizations of Jews in the ghettos according to working ability; *Judenrate* response to those demands during wartime (much was written on the subject in the officially circulated *Gazeta Żydowska*); and also the Communist mythologization of the working class and institutionalized efforts to "productivize" Jews both by the Central Committee of Polish Jews and designated agencies of the Polish government.

This should not be read as an oddball assessment of how to deal with anti-Semitism by a proverbially brainless Communist functionary who in later years would earn the derogatory nickname "General Iron Pipe" ("Generał Gazrurka"). We find this line of argument already in a document submitted by high party officials named Hilary Chełchowski and Władysław Buczyński, who arrived in Kielce at noon on the day of the pogrom and wrote a quick assessment of the situation two days later: "An organizational system where all the Jews are assembled in one place [the reference here is to the building at Planty 7], do not participate in productive work but live very well, and engage in all kinds of wheeling and dealing with impunity and very often to the detriment of the government [*"zajmują się najrozmaitszą kombinacją bezkarnie i bardzo często na niekorzyść Rządu"*], all of which is then exploited by elements inimical to us, should be avoided in the future."[12]*

The July 18 report by the entire visiting delegation of Central Committee instructors takes the matter further: "180 Jews were living in the Jewish building [Planty 7] in Kielce and they did not work; there were only two members of the PPR among them. In Ostrowiec several hundred Jews are also not working. In the majority of state-run spas one finds mostly rich Jews and Polish reactionaries." During a joint meeting of the PPS and the PPR organization in the city on July 11, Central Committee instructors continue, "it was decided to begin arrests among the parasitic elements [presumably those who traded on the free market rather than working "productively" in state enterprises] and to close entertainment establishments. . . . During all mass meetings people transferred their anger *from Jews to parasitic elements in general* [emphasis mine]. The action was very successful as it responded to burning feelings of discontent. A conviction arose that the Party, finally, also seeks out and pun-

---

*Concerning "Jews . . . assembled in one place": A Jewish Committee building in a town with a substantial number of Jewish survivors might typically serve multiple functions. It was often a hostel for Jews returning from camps or hiding places, or for those passing through town or searching for relatives. It might also have a room or two accommodating an impromptu orphanage, or an old people's home, or a school, or a kibbutz where a group of young Zionists was preparing for departure to, eventually, Palestine. Such arrangements stemmed less from an "organizational system" than from the shortage of building stock and the unwillingness of local authorities to accommodate Jewish requests for space beyond some necessary minimum, as well as from the need to provide security for Jews who would be easier targets for assault when dispersed.

There are two documents from Central Committee visitors in Meducki's volume: a longer piece, dated July 18, billed as the report of "Central Committee instructors" (pp. 137–43); and a shorter one, dated July 6, authored by Chełchowski and Buczyński (pp. 98–100). This quotation comes from the shorter report.

ishes those who prey on the people."[13] And while nobody asked specifically for wholesale arrest of the Jews as a well-defined subcategory of "social parasites," at the conclusion of the July 29 Central Committee Secretariat meeting Ostap Dłuski suggested "that an institution be established which would facilitate departure of the Jews from Poland, so that they could join their families."[14]

For the record, the Jewish population in postwar Poland was destitute, emaciated, ruined, sick, and traumatized. If there ever was a group of people suffering from post-traumatic stress disorder before the diagnosis was invented, they were that group. The dire general condition of Jewish survivors is amply documented in the records of the Central Committee of Polish Jews, which for the most part tried to address and remedy the situation. Matters became critical when a rapid influx of Jewish repatriates from the Soviet Union, also impoverished and exhausted, began reaching Poland in large numbers in 1946. In March the CKŻP issued an appeal addressed to world Jewry—"*Tsu Yidn fun der Gancer Welt*"—to send material assistance.[15]

Generalities aside, we can also have a glimpse inside the building at Planty 7 in Kielce as some of Łoziński's interviewees visited the place and remembered it forty years later. We have good testimony by the teacher featured in the opening shots of Łoziński's film, who speaks to the issue briefly in *Witnesses*. She is a good witness because of her intelligence and articulate ease before the camera, but also because of personal circumstances. At the time, she was trying to find people with connections, because her mother had been imprisoned, and she truly hoped that she could get such help among the Jews, who were supposed to be rich, powerful, and well-connected with the authorities.

To her disappointment and dismay she was struck instead by the "bare primitivism" of conditions inside the building where most rooms were furnished only with simple cots and an occasional chair.* "This was a house as if after a funeral." People wrapped in gray blankets sitting on cots "made an incredible impression. They seemed like they were shipwrecked. Among the older ones there must have been some who were

---

*The interview as a whole includes more details about the context of her visit. The family had turned to Jews for help because they had sheltered a Jewish family throughout the war and figured that somebody might return the favor. The woman they saved had written a note, and holding this letter the teacher (at the time still a teenager) went to Planty 7. When the interviewer asked her whether the family thought Jews worked in the secret police or government and therefore could be of assistance, she smiled and uttered an awkward denial, but it was clear that this must have been on the family's minds.

mentally ill. . . . They looked as if they were waiting for something, waiting to go somewhere, find somebody, and start a new life . . . sad, subdued, crushed" ("smutni, przygnębieni, przybici").[16] No one could help her with access to local authorities, but they offered to collect money among themselves so that she could afford to hire a lawyer.

The actual circumstances of this transient, destitute, and sick population did not prevent the circulation of rumors about conspicuous consumption, of Jewish children allegedly bringing delicacies and citrus fruit to school—alongside stories about emaciated and exhausted Jews using captured Polish children for blood transfusions in order to fortify themselves.[17]

The Party Draws Conclusions

The Party lagged in addressing problems confronting the Jews; so did the two law enforcement organizations. At the end of September 1945, several months before the Kielce pogrom, as we may remember, a "strictly secret" memorandum was sent to the Ministry of Public Security, with copies forwarded to the Ministry of Justice and to the Supreme Command of the Citizens' Militia (the MO, or regular police). The head of the political department in the Ministry of Public Administration (MAP) wanted to know what was being done by the Security Service to stem a wave of murders and robberies of Polish citizens of Jewish nationality. We have "numerous complaints and reports" about these crimes, he wrote, and "no information whatsoever" about countermeasures undertaken by state authorities. An addendum was attached to the query listing selected episodes from the preceding six months—unnecessarily, we might add parenthetically, because Jewish Committees from all over the country were continually sending complaints and reports on such matters directly to the UB.*

In August 1945, a few days after the pogrom in Kraków, the Secretariat of the PPR's Central Committee put "the issue of pogroms" on its agenda for the first time. "Attempted pogroms which took place in

---

*AAN, MAP, 786/17, 18; also Meducki, Antyżydowskie, vol. II, pp. 55–61. The Ministry of Public Administration was not the only official forum where assaults against the Jews were documented during this period. In successive sessions of the provisional parliament, the KRN, in May and July 1945, Emil Sommerstein provided statistical and geographical data concerning Jewish casualties and demanded an energetic response from law enforcement organizations and the judiciary (Szaynok, Pogrom, p. 9).

Kraków and in other localities (Radom, Miechów, Chrzanów, Rabka) suggest that they have a general character and that they were planned. That they were planned implies that there was a center issuing orders."[18] Thus the entire problem was framed in the characteristic paradigm of a conspiracy aiming to subvert the rule of the Communist Party.

This was a knee-jerk response by Communist ideologues—any social phenomena not planned by Party organizers must be the result of somebody else's deliberate planning and organization. Especially when a breakdown of public order was at issue—as in strikes, riots, meetings, or, as it were, pogroms—the correct analysis was to suspect a conspiracy, and the right thing to do was to identify those who, hidden from view, were pulling the strings. Apparently the Leninist paradigm of social action was universally applicable. Just as "professional revolutionaries" were necessary to lead the working class to victory, so "professional reactionaries" lurked behind every challenge to the Communist ambition to establish a monopoly of power.*

Yet the really experienced Communists had honed a dual sensibility. While organizational work was supremely important, they believed one also needed to carefully monitor the "pulse of the masses." Party organizers could never sway too far from the concrete interests and ideas held by the people, or else they risked becoming "detached"—and becoming "detached from the masses" was a capital offense under high Stalinism. Over the long run, through propaganda, one could instill the right class consciousness into all subjects. This was, to borrow the title of a canonic novel by Nicolai Ostrovski about forging new Soviet men, "how the steel was tempered."[19] But while forging the new man one had to pay attention to timing. Issues being tackled had to be carefully sequenced, lest the Party risk "losing touch."

In the event, the PPR Central Committee's Secretariat took cognizance of "strong anti-Semitic attitudes in society, as well as an absence of awareness and activity among the democratic parts of society [presumably to counter those attitudes]. The notion of the anti-Jewish pogrom is not yet sufficiently associated among the broad masses *with the activities of the reactionaries aiming to achieve other broader goals* [my emphasis]. Anti-Semitic attitudes can be found even among the leading elements of

---

*One may point out that church sources displayed an exactly identical frame of mind. Thus when Bishop Kaczmarek's commission described how "the authorities," that is, the police and military on the scene, were killing Jews, it asserted that they were acting under orders.

the working class."[20] In the Polish parliament, a left-wing Zionist named Adolf Berman hit the nail on the head during the September 1946 session: "For us, who represent Jewish workers, what happened in several factories in Łódź and in Ostrowiec, after the sentencing in the Kielce trial, came as a great shock. It was the second Kielce pogrom."[21]

Clearly, such treacherous terrain had to be navigated carefully. The Party had "to keep in constant contact with the masses" (*"utrzymać stały kontakt z masami"*) to explain "the core of anti-Semitism as one of the means employed by reactionaries to struggle against us," and in the meantime Jews should be put to work. It was after all, as we remember, their "unproductivity in Poland which fuels anti-Semitic actions." This was a persistent theme, which reemerged as the Party's diagnosis of the Kielce pogrom as well. On July 25, 1946, the Council of Ministers established a new office, that of governmental commissar for the productivization of the Jewish population in Poland.[22] In August 1945, the Secretariat of the Central Committee recommended the enactment of a special decree combating anti-Semitism and putting in place provisions to materially compensate Jewish pogrom victims and their families.[23] A year later, soon after the Kielce pogrom, the initiative was killed in light of the mounting intensity and violence of anti-Semitic assaults. When the Central Committee Secretariat met for the second time to evaluate the issue, in the aftermath of that pogrom, it was primarily, as we know, to discuss working-class reactions to the pogrom rather than anti-Jewish violence itself. The Party did not want, as it were, to be preoccupied with the Jews. It wished that anti-Semitism, and the Jews into the bargain, would go away.[24]

The Response of the Polish Intellectual Elite

Postwar manifestations of hatred toward the Jews—the Kraków and the Kielce pogroms and then the reactions of common people in the aftermath—came as a surprise to the political and intellectual elites in Poland. This is in part, as I will argue in the next chapter, because what had happened between Jews and Poles since 1939 had played itself out on the lower rungs of society and was therefore obscured from the elites' view owing to the highly stratified political culture characteristic of Poland. Whatever the reasons for their surprise, the shock of those who imagined that Nazi occupation had cleared the general public mind of rabid anti-Semitism was overwhelming.

The upper crust of the Polish intelligentsia expressed its despair in the main cultural periodicals. The weekly *Kuźnica* published unsparing details of the Kielce pogrom: the policeman Mazur's statement that he had killed a newborn because the mother was already dead "and the child would cry"; the information that "thousands" participated in the pogrom by stomping, stoning, knifing, and clubbing Jewish victims to death; the specifics of the killings on the railroads; and the involvement of the local police in the day's violence. "Today Kielce is *Judenrein*," wrote Mariusz Margal in this important weekly on July 22, using the German term to drive home the point. "Hitler's plan has been executed in Kielce to perfection and der Generalgouverneur Herr Hans Frank [Hitler's plenipotentiary in occupied Poland and at the time of the Kielce pogrom one of the accused in the Nuremberg Trial] must be very happy in far-away Nuremberg."[25] Given the circumstances and the duration of the pogrom, Margal wrote, "the *entire* [emphasis in the original] Kielce population bears responsibility" for what happened.

But the debate about postwar anti-Semitism had begun in high-brow periodicals a year earlier. Its initial focal point was an article by Mieczysław Jastrun published in the weekly *Odrodzenie* on June 17, 1945, entitled "Potęga ciemnoty," "The Might of Darkness," or dimness rather.[26] The opening paragraph of Jastrun's article articulates precisely what many authors would also find so inexplicable and morally perplexing. "Anti-Semitism in Poland, already deeply rooted before the current war [Germany had only just surrendered], did not abate—even though over three million [Polish] Jews, and presumed Jews, were murdered by the Hitlerite inquisition. In terms of moral evaluation this fact is no less horrifying than the fact of Hitlerite mass murder." One could not be any more direct. And Jastrun continued: "One would expect that this murder, unprecedented in history, and committed by a hated enemy who so mercilessly and brutally repressed the Polish populace, would evoke in Polish society—which had itself been tortured and abused—a collective response of compassion, a sense of brotherhood in suffering. . . . But instead, the Jewish blood spilled so profusely by the barbaric enemy of the Polish nation and free humanity only awakened the mob instincts."

With the passage of time, Jastrun's somber diagnosis gained more adherents who felt moved to speak in a public forum. Kazimierz Wyka wrote three months later (*Odrodzenie*, September 23, 1945) that Jastrun was correct after all, that *"Potęga ciemnoty"* was confirmed. The "last straw" which prompted Wyka to say so came with the Kraków pogrom of August 1945—this "brutal and beastly spectacle which took place in the Kraków district of Kazimierz."

Wyka's article took Jastrun's diagnosis one step further: it was not just "the mob" that was infected with anti-Semitism, he argued, but also the stratum of educated people, the intelligentsia. Poland, said Wyka, coining a brilliant paradox, was now suffering the consequences of not having had a Quisling-like native administration during the Nazi occupation. As a result anti-Semitism was never compromised as a requisite of collaborationism. "It still remained a requisite of patriotism and an attribute of a so-called responsible citizenship syndrome."

A clever insight no doubt, but it did not suffice to bridge the chasm between expectations predicated on common sense and a presumption of simple decency, and the reality of postwar Polish anti-Semitism. Wincenty Bednarczuk, who spent the war abroad, framed this dilemma clearly in an article he wrote following the Kraków pogrom: "The events in Kraków were like a bursting boil, which we had felt filling up since we returned to the fatherland [Poland]. When as émigrés we got the first news about the horrible massacre of Jews perpetrated by the Nazis, still unsure whether the information was exaggerated, we asked with trepidation: how did the Poles respond? . . . We hypothesized that the frightening tragedy of the Polish Jews would cure the Poles of anti-Semitism. It cannot be any other way, we thought, but that the sight of massacred children and old people must evoke a response of compassion and help. The common fate suffered under the occupation must somehow reconcile them. But we didn't know human nature. . . . It turned out that our notions about mankind were naïve. The country surprised us."[27]

One year later, after the Kielce pogrom, the most eminent representative of humanistic sociology in Poland and a public intellectual par excellence, Stanisław Ossowski, wrote a long piece in *Kuźnica,* carefully laying out the multiple aspects and factors that determined shifting Polish attitudes toward the Jews.

> Let us imagine that in 1939 somebody predicted the inconceivable destruction of the Jewish population in Poland during 1940–1944, as well as the political and economic changes that took place in Poland and in Europe after the war. Let us imagine that given those assumptions we were asked to deduce what the attitudes of the Polish population would be toward the remnants of the Jews in 1945 and 1946.
>
> Simple human compassion, in view of the terrible sufferings

of the murdered masses and the horror of the extermination camps; hatred of a common enemy; blood jointly shed on numerous occasions; rejection of the ideology propagated by the defeated occupier; a sense of justice, calling for some satisfaction for the survivors, satisfaction at least in the form of simple human goodwill; and the radical numerical decline of the Jewish population, eliminating the economic bases of prewar anti-Semitism—these would be arguments sufficing, probably, to lead one to conclude that in postwar Poland anti-Semitism as a social phenomenon would be an impossibility.

But someone more insightful, or more cynical, or more disputatious, or better informed about historical precedents could have reminded us even then that compassion is not the only imaginable response to misfortune suffered by other people. That those whom fate has destined for annihilation easily can appear disgusting to others, and be removed beyond the pale of human relations. . . . We could be reminded that if one person's disaster benefits somebody else, an urge appears to persuade oneself and others that that disaster was morally justified, and it could be pointed out that this is exactly the situation of today's proprietors of formerly Jewish shops, or those who felt previously threatened by Jewish competition.

There was a political motive that could be added after the war, writes Ossowski: the well-entrenched habit of associating left-wing politics with Jewish influences. Anti-Semitism could then be imagined as merely an expression of political protest against the current regime. "With foresight one could have predicted postwar anti-Semitism. But only a real cynic or psychopathic misanthrope could have foreseen that in liberated Poland a tendency to continue Hitlerite mass murder would survive. For this murder is something different than barbaric struggle, as it targets not only grown-up men but also the newborn and the elderly."[28]

Intellectuals were flabbergasted by the moral condition of a Polish society that allowed for postwar anti-Semitism. Jerzy Andrzejewski, one of the most eminent epic writers of postwar Poland, published a long essay in *Odrodzenie* (July 7, 1946) entitled "The Question of Polish Anti-Semitism." It must have been written and typeset before the Kielce pogrom as it came out dated only three days afterward and didn't mention the events at all.

"I wish I could honestly say," writes Andrzejewski, "[that] yes, anti-

Semitism in Poland is disappearing. . . . Unfortunately, after many years of thinking about this matter as an open, infected wound festering within our organism, witnessing all that happened in Poland before and during the war, and what is taking place at present; listening to people from various milieus and of different levels of intelligence, noticing their often unconscious gestures and reactions, observing how certain gestures and reactions automatically follow, I am not able to conclude, I cannot conclude, anything else but that the Polish nation in all its strata and across all intellectual levels, from the highest all the way down to the lowest, was and remains after the war anti-Semitic."[29]

Having made this deeply troubling (to themselves, first of all) determination, the nation's most brilliant intellectuals struggled valiantly to explain the phenomenon. One theme recurred in their writings—the presence of an ill-defined stratum of persons who gained material advantages as a result of Jewish catastrophe. Under the pen of marxisant authors, these are portrayed as a residuum of the petty bourgeoisie, stallkeepers in bazaars, worthy only of contempt. The metaphor of the marketplace looms large in characterizations of miscreants—"peddlers and tradesmen"—strangely reminding one of the idiom used before the war for derogatory characterizations of the Jews.

But the matter could not be disposed of so easily, because the shameful sentiment was not limited to a narrow, marginal group in society. Wyka, Andrzejewski, Ossowski, Jastrun, and others said as much in their alarming texts. One reads dramatic warnings: "Anti-Semitism is no longer an economic issue, it is no longer a political issue either . . . it is a moral problem pure and simple. Today it is not a question of saving the Jews from misery and death, it is a problem of saving the Poles from moral misery and spiritual death."[30] Writes Andrzejewski: "Mankind— let us use this big word—fought six years for freedom and justice and for human dignity in the cruelest combats in history, and woe to those nations who are not able to draw appropriate conclusions from that experience. Hatred, contempt, and racial prejudice certainly could not count among such conclusions."[31] He closes his long article, which *Odrodzenie* ran in two consecutive issues, with the following words: "I say this: without respect for a human being, without serious reflection about humanity, without solidarity with the truths for which millions sacrificed their lives—in view of the past few years' experiences, no nation can be worthy of respect."[32]

After Kielce, Polish intellectuals signed dramatic letters of protest and public appeals expressing their sense of the tragedy that had taken place and that should not have done so, if Poland's recent history had been what they thought it was. Several moving texts were published in cultural weeklies signed by dozens upon dozens of eminent intellectuals—writers, actors, journalists, academics, composers. The cause transcended ideological differences: a protest letter by Catholic intellectuals, originally published in *Tygodnik Powszechny* (July 28, 1946), was reprinted in the pages of its fierce ideological opponent *Kuźnica* (August 12, 1946). The Polish Union of Writers put out a powerfully worded statement and members of the organization who had somehow missed the first opportunity to sign—it was midsummer and many were on vacation—kept sending individual letters asking to add their names to the list.[33]

Deeply pained reflections and tough words coming from those who were the country's *maîtres à penser*—every schoolchild in Poland, certainly every student of the humanities, would have been familiar with at least some of their works—make all the difference for Poles today, and can be cherished as a measure of moral sensitivity which has not been dulled among the country's spiritual elite. But at the time they went unheeded, and their calls for vigorously combating anti-Semitism fell on deaf ears, very much like the warnings Jan Karski delivered to the Polish government-in-exile in 1940, when he reported that anti-Jewish measures of the Nazi occupiers resonated well with large segments of the Polish society.[34*]

*An example of spectacular "deafness" and of disregard for the corrupting influence of anti-Semitic violence may be found in the memoirs of none other than Stanisław Mikołajczyk. An eminent personality, the public symbol of Polish freedom trampled on after the war by the Communists, a man who fled the country over a year after the Kielce pogrom and was in a position to inform himself fully in the meantime, wrote a truly outstanding page and a half of nonsense about the day's events in his book *The Rape of Poland,* published in English in 1948. His confabulations are all the more remarkable since at exactly the same time, also in 1948, the former American ambassador to Poland, Arthur Bliss Lane (with whom Mikołajczyk was in frequent contact as leader of the opposition party, whose fate the West monitored as a litmus test of Soviet intentions in Eastern Europe), wrote a balanced and well-informed account of the Kielce pogrom (Bliss Lane, *I Saw Poland,* pp. 246–51).

Mikołajczyk begins his account of the pogrom in Kielce with a little fib about a camel in Częstochowa. "In Częstochowa people were told that a camel—part of the Red Army's livestock—would be displayed in the marketplace. When the people had gathered to view the animal, Security Police raced through the crowd shouting, 'The Jews are killing our people!' A riot was narrowly averted by a quick-thinking priest who stood up and branded the shouting as a provocation.

"In Kielce, Major Sobczyński, the Security Police officer . . . now ordered foundry workers to gather in the marketplace at a certain time, for a meeting. His plan was to point to a Jewish boardinghouse that fronted on the marketplace and to have his operatives shout that Polish children were being killed there. Major Sobczyński hoped to produce a rush on

How the Catholic Clergy Reacted to the Pogrom

Jews had been frightened by persistent anti-Semitism and anti-Jewish
violence in Poland long before Kielce. It was clear to secular and religious
Jewish community leaders that the key, or one of the keys in any case, to
ending the lurking danger was held by the Catholic clergy, who exercised
spiritual authority over the Polish population. Cardinal August Hlond,
the titular head of the Polish episcopate as primate of Poland, was approached at least twice before the Kielce pogrom with a request that he
issue a pastoral letter or a statement condemning anti-Semitism and ex-
plaining that accusations of ritual murder were false. When, one week
after the pogrom, nine foreign journalists appeared at Hlond's residence
for a scheduled interview and asked why he had not earlier published
such a pastoral letter despite urgent pleas from various Jewish personalities, the cardinal answered: "I investigated the facts and did not discover sufficient grounds to publish such a letter. Now the situation has
changed, but I must first consult my bishops."[35]*

---

the building, in which case the army would open fire on the crowd. This would add to the
terror of the times.

"But the Communists had forgotten to remove the telephone from the boardinghouse.
A rabbi, informed that a mob was being provoked to attack the place, phoned the local army
headquarters to appeal for protection. Troops soon arrived under the command of a Russian colonel. The colonel, who was, of course, familiar with the entire plot, was surprised to
see that the crowd on which his men were scheduled to fire had not as yet gathered. He had
to change his plans. Lacking all pity, he sent his men against the boardinghouse, killing forty-
one of its Jewish occupants and wounding forty others. In the hope of arousing the impending crowd to an overt act against the army he ordered the dead thrown into the streets. Any
movement of the crowd would have been his cue to shoot into the gathering. The workers,
however, crossed everybody up by escaping while en route to the scene of their intended
slaughter" (Mikołajczyk, *The Rape of Poland,* p. 167). The most benign interpretation one could
put on this would be that someone had pulled Mikołajczyk's leg and the former prime minister of Poland was so uninterested in the subject that he put the story on paper without
bothering to check any of his facts. One should also note that a 1972 reprint of Mikołajczyk's
book (Westport, Conn.: Greenwood Press) repeats this entire passage verbatim.

*Dr. David Kahane, the chief rabbi of the Polish army, later complained to S. L. Shnei-
derman that one of the attempts was brushed off: "the cardinal returned the memorandum
to us through his secretary and refused to see us." However, Dr. Joseph Tenenbaum, president of the American Federation of Polish Jews, was received by the primate "on June 3,
1946, one month before the Kielce pogrom. Dr. Tenenbaum had made an extensive trip
throughout Poland and informed the cardinal that more than one thousand Jews had been
murdered since the liberation of Poland. As the Polish Jewish leaders had done before him,
Dr. Tenenbaum appealed to the cardinal to publish a pastoral letter dealing with the Jewish

Hlond did consult his bishops, but as a result he did not publish any pastoral letter on the Kielce pogrom, anti-Semitism, or ritual murder. With one notable and very important exception, no Catholic hierarch issued a statement decisively and unequivocally addressing these matters after Kielce. Only the bishop of Częstochowa, Teodor Kubina, spoke forcefully and unambiguously against anti-Semitism and the lie of ritual murder, and he was promptly reprimanded by fellow bishops for having done so.

Direct involvement of Catholic clergy in quelling the Kielce pogrom was insignificant. Sometime between 11 A.M. and noon on July 4, two priests, Jan Danielewicz and the rector of the Kielce cathedral, Roman Zelek, tried to approach the building on Planty 7 but were stopped at a military checkpoint. Upon seeing the crowd, the commotion, and hearing gunfire they nevertheless insisted on talking with a superior officer. A lieutenant showed up, accompanied by two civilians, to tell them that "the situation is under control" and that soldiers were under orders "not to allow civilians into the area."[36] So they turned around and went back where they came from, only to return at 2:30 P.M. in the company of three more clergymen. "It was ascertained on the spot," Meducki quotes from their report, "that there weren't any gatherings on Planty Street,

---

question. The cardinal merely promised to study the reports" (S. L. Shneiderman, *Between Fear and Hope*, p. 111).

In his memoirs, published in Israel in 1981, Dr. Kahane gives a different, milder, and very interesting version of the encounter with Hlond. Before Passover, or Easter, of 1946, leaflets were circulating in many parts of Poland warning the population to watch over the children, because they had lately been disappearing. The Jewish Religious Association got deeply worried, and in the context of increasingly frequent and intense assaults against Jews decided to contact Hlond with a request that he make a calming statement. A secretary of the association, Michał Zylberger, went in the middle of May to Hlond's residence to set up a meeting at which a Jewish delegation could acquaint the cardinal with the situation and present the formal request.

The meeting was unproductive. Hlond procrastinated and did not want to commit to a specific date for the visit, arguing that he was old and indisposed. But he was extremely cordial. As Zylberger later recounted the conversation to Kahane, Hlond expressed his deepest sorrow over murders of Jews committed after the war, adding that those who killed Jews under the pretext that they were fighting Communism were deeply mistaken and wrong. As a Pole and a Catholic, he condemned these acts of thoughtless cruelty, he said. When Kahane compared Hlond's statement during the press conference with the conversation that Zylberger reported, he was very surprised (David Kahane, *Aharei Hamabul*, pp. 60–69).

Conceivably, because of his advanced age and poor health, Hlond was no longer in charge of official business. Younger bishops and his entourage drafted whatever pronouncements he issued to the outside world. Catholic of the old school as he was, this new, ruthless, and aggressive anti-Semitism was probably not much to his taste, but he was no longer running the show.

and that people on Sienkiewicza and Piotrkowska Streets were standing in small groups and were calm."[37]* As we know, for instance from the visit to this place by foreign journalists the next day, the whole area was splattered with blood and littered with pogrom debris, while pogrom activities were continuing all over town.

The earliest statement issued in the aftermath of the pogrom by a church official was drafted jointly one day after the events by Voivode Wiślicz and a priest representing Bishop Kaczmarek of Kielce.† We already know one of its memorable sentences, namely that "people [or "human beings"] were not shot at" in Kielce. In addition, the statement contains a declaration that the Christian ethic does not permit murder and favors religious tolerance, and it summarizes the substance of the day's events in a two-sentence-long hyperbole: "Certain quarters have misled the local population and used it for base purposes, as a result numerous victims fell. Blood stained Kielce's pavements."

Who had killed whom on that day, one cannot tell from this declaration. As for the word "Jew," it appears only once in the text, in the following context: "According to materials already assembled by investigative authorities there was no murder of Polish children by the Jewish population," thus tentatively exonerating the Jews of ritual murder on this particular occasion.[38]

On Saturday, July 6, the first church document was issued by the Kielce diocese. All the priests in Kielce were supposed to read it the next day "without commentary" during mass. On July 4, Kielce was "the site of a bloody drama," the document informs us, with events quickly following one another "like an avalanche." The Kielce diocese declined to comment in the statement on either "the background," the "immediate causes," or "what actually happened" (because it lacked "exact knowledge"), but felt compelled "to state nevertheless that a misfortune took place, especially in that *it* [emphasis mine] all happened in plain sight of youth and underage children. Because of this, no Catholic can refrain from expressing real and sincere regrets at such tragic and deplorable events." The statement ends with an appeal for "calm" addressed to the "Catholic population in the city of Kielce."[39]

*Hlond referred sympathetically to their report; see below.
†It was never published but is part of the record quoted by scholars and invoked by church officials as well as one of its authors in an autobiography written four decades later. I have already quoted some excerpts that were published in the collection edited by Meducki. Cardinal Hlond also mentioned it in his statement of July 11 (see Meducki, *Antyżydowskie*, vol. II, p. 118).

Someone, somewhere, must have concluded that something important was missing from a declaration that did not even acknowledge that
the "deplorable" "it" that took place was murder. So on July 11, a second,
somewhat longer statement was issued by the Kielce diocese, again to be
read during the coming Sunday mass "without commentary." It began
with a preamble condemning murder as such and ended with an appeal
for calm and an admonition that "no Catholic should allow anybody to
deceive and push him toward committing such deeds." The key message
repeated almost verbatim from the previous statement identifies as a
particularly aggravating circumstance that young people had witnessed
what happened.[40]

This may have been rhetorically an improvement over the earlier
formulation, and *Tygodnik Powszechny* duly published the text in its next
issue, even though one still couldn't tell what happened in Kielce—who
killed whom and under what circumstances. As a result of such equivoca-
tions, the only concretely named and identified victims in church-
drafted texts were "youth and underage children" who had witnessed
we-don't-know-what.*

At this point Cardinal Hlond issued his statement during a meeting
with foreign correspondents on July 11. Its content, enumerated in five
points, may be briefly summarized as follows: the Catholic church op-
poses all murder, irrespective of where it takes place or who the perpetrators or the victims are.[†] The primate opined that "the miserable and
deplorable events in Kielce cannot be attributed to racism"—which
probably should be understood as a denial that an anti-Jewish pogrom
had taken place. Whatever the intended meaning of this passage, one
cannot find any indication in the text of the statement that the murder
victims in the day-long violence in Kielce were Jewish. Cardinal Hlond
also stated that "the Catholic clergy in Kielce fulfilled its obligations."[‡]
His fourth and most important point offers an interpretation of the
events cast in a historical rather than theological perspective. "Numerous

---

*Jarring as this is in its awkward insensitivity to the real victims of the pogrom, it was
also misleading. The Kielce clergy knew firsthand that "youth and underage children" did
not just watch what happened, as scouts (and undoubtedly many of their peers not wearing
scout uniforms that day) joined their elders and actively took part in the pogrom.

†A careful reader will note a slightly polemical turn of phrase in Hlond's declaration
that murder is deplorable "also in Poland," and "no matter whether Poles or Jews are being
killed, in Kielce or anywhere else in the Polish Republic."

‡As evidence, the cardinal mentioned two visits by Kielce priests "to where the events
took place" (we know the particulars of these visits already), and statements (with which we
are also already familiar) drafted earlier by Kielce's clergy.

Jews in Poland owe their lives to Poles and Polish priests," Cardinal Hlond begins, truthfully. Then he continues: "and it is Jews, now occupying leading positions within state institutions and bent on imposing a kind of regime which is rejected by the majority of the nation, who are to a large extent responsible for the deterioration of this good relationship. It is a pernicious game, which produces dangerous tensions. In regrettable armed confrontations on the front of political struggles in Poland, some Jews unfortunately perish, but the number of Poles perishing is incomparably greater." In point five of his statement, Cardinal Hlond declared that he was not an anti-Semite.[41]

Even though the cardinal did not state things directly but preferred to put them in oblique generalities, he delivered a blunt and unequivocal opinion about the events of July 4, 1946: whatever happened on that day in Kielce was an episode of "armed . . . political struggle" against a regime that was rejected by a majority of the nation, and to the extent that there were Jewish victims they had only themselves to blame. In any case, the real victims of present-day struggles in Poland were the Poles.

In general outline, this would become the boilerplate position of the Polish Catholic church, and as church dignitaries were approached to address the issue, they followed the line laid down by Cardinal Hlond or remained silent.* Sapieha never broke his silence on the issue of the Kielce pogrom. A French attempt to get him to make a statement condemning the pogrom had failed. Nor did the British ambassador in Poland, Victor Cavendish-Bentinck, succeed in obtaining an interview with Sapieha; he spoke with his chancellor, Stefan Mazanek, instead.[42]

"A meeting of Polish bishops is to be held at Częstochowa on September 5 and thereafter a Pastoral letter will be issued," Cavendish-Bentinck cabled London on August 29.

*When S. L. Shneiderman tried to interview Kraków's metropolitan, Cardinal Adam Sapieha, on the subject of the Kielce pogrom he was received instead by the cardinal's chancellor, Stefan Mazanek. Shneiderman came out of the meeting full of respect for the cardinal, who had maintained dignity and decorum throughout the German occupation. He also appreciated that Sapieha kept under his wing *Tygodnik Powszechny*, a forum for one of Poland's enlightened intellectual milieus. But he heard the same story from Mazanek about the pogrom with which we are already familiar: "express[ing] deep regret over the tragic event, but also repeat[ing] the familiar leitmotif of the excessive number of Jews in the government. But the chancellor couched his remark in a tone of friendly advice to the Jews rather than of reproach, as was the case with Cardinal Hlond. . . . I had left the palace with the feeling that out of this very place might come the just words that would help to appease the flame of blind hatred now raging against the Jews. But the proud and stubborn Sapieha keeps silent" (Shneiderman, *Between Fear and Hope*, pp. 277, 282).

I urged that this letter should contain a condemnation of anti-Semitism or at least of racial hatred, and I understand that the inclusion of some allusion to anti-Semitism has been suggested. However any such allusion will be in a guarded form so that it cannot be interpreted as a repudiation of the interview given by Cardinal Hlond to foreign press correspondents here which is said to have been misinterpreted and twisted. Moreover I was told that owing to deep anti-Semitic feeling in Poland the bishops fear that an open condemnation of anti-Semitism might weaken the Church's influence. This I do not believe, and I regard it as an excuse for evading condemnation of anti-Semitism in strong terms. I fear that the Polish clergy are fundamentally anti-Semitic.[43]

The British were anxious to stem the tide of anti-Semitism in Poland: it was causing panic among the Jews, who were fleeing westward in large numbers, filling Allied DP camps in Germany. For many, the camps were but a brief stopover on the way to Palestine. The resulting illegal Jewish immigration caused enormous difficulties for British mandatory authorities, and in 1946 they were waging a multipronged campaign to ensure that Holocaust survivors from Eastern Europe were repatriated to, and/or stayed put in, their countries of origin. Hence the British ambassador's pleas for a statement condemning anti-Semitism.

But Shneiderman's hope and Cavendish-Bentinck's expectation that Sapieha might publicly condemn anti-Semitism and the hoax of ritual murder were misplaced. Sapieha shared his colleagues' dislike of Jews. A month before the Kielce pogrom, he had received a group of Polish and French Catholic intellectuals and, as writer Tadeusz Breza wrote to Zofia Nałkowska, "the visit with the cardinal turned out to be an awful experience. He seemed a ruthless and evil person, and an anti-Semite (Reverend Glasberg to Sapieha: '60,000 Jews remain in Poland.' Sapieha: 'Well, well, you should add one more zero, father')."* Emmanuel Mounier, whose trip to Poland in 1946 occasioned the Catholic intellectuals' visit

*In late May or early June, a group of French Catholic intellectuals, including Emmanuel Mounier, visited Poland and was received in Kraków by the cardinal. Tadeusz Breza described the meeting to Zofia Nałkowska, a preeminent writer and memoirist of this period. His letter is dated June 10, 1946. In contrast to Sapieha's "ill-disposed and dismissive" attitude, Breza wrote, "the local progressive Catholics were extraordinarily courteous and dignified: Zagórski, Natanson, Turowicz, Morstin-Starowieyska, etc." All the "progressive Catholics" Breza names here were either members of the editorial board or contributors to *Tygodnik Powszechny* (Zofia Nałkowska, *Dzienniki VI*, p. 257).

with Sapieha, was equally baffled by an "anti-Semitism so vivid among
even the highest ranking Catholics, as if extermination of the Jews had
never happened."⁴⁴

While the silence of the Polish Catholic church resounds as an indictment in view of the scope and significance of tragic events in Kielce,
it was worse when churchmen spoke up and openly revealed what they
thought on the matter. "Bishop Bieni[e]k, Auxiliary Bishop of Upper
Silesia, astonished me yesterday," the British ambassador cabled the Foreign Office at the end of August, "by stating that there was some proof
that the child whose alleged maltreatment by Jews had provoked the
Kielce pogrom, had in fact been maltreated, and that the Jews had taken
blood from his arm. If a bishop is prepared to believe this, it is not surprising that the uneducated Poles do so too. I am sending a copy of this
letter to the Holy See."⁴⁵ The Polish clergy was so blatantly anti-Semitic
that the Holy See, Cavendish-Bentinck suggested, should be enlisted to
condemn anti-Semitism with a view to creating "a counterbalance [to]
the innate feeling of the Polish bishops."⁴⁶

It was a rather naïve suggestion on the part of the British diplomat,
for the Vatican was being fed information about the situation in Poland
through church channels and had no reason or intention to speak on behalf of the Jews.* This became evident when Sir Francis D'Arcy Osborne,

*Michael R. Marrus, in his unpublished manuscript, gives an account of another great
French Catholic intellectual, Jacques Maritain, who was then French ambassador to the Holy
See, and his appeal to Pope Pius XII in light of the Kielce pogrom to speak up against anti-
Semitism, pleading

for a solemn declaration denouncing the great scourge of antisemitism in the context of the Nazis' destruction of European Jewry and the widespread complicity of
Catholics in those events. Maritain's interlocutor in the exchange . . . was his old
friend Monsignor Giovanni Battista Montini [the future Pope Paul VI] . . . one of
the very closest aides of Eugenio Pacelli, Pope Pius XII. . . . Some fifteen years
younger than Maritain, Montini considered the French philosopher his teacher. . . .
For many years, the newly installed diplomat reminded Montini, Maritain had been
aware of the most savage hatred directed against "Israel." Nazism had simply carried
the ancient campaign to new levels of atrocity. "During the [recent] war six million
Jews have been *liquidated*," he wrote, "thousands of Jewish children have been massacred, thousands of others torn from their families and stripped of their identity. . . .
Nazism proclaimed the necessity of wiping the Jews off the face of the earth (the
only people that it wanted to exterminate *as a people*)" [emphases in original]. Maritain accepted that during the war, "for reasons of prudence and a higher good, and
in order not to make persecution even worse, and so as not to create insurmount-
able obstacles in the way of the rescue that he was pursuing, the Holy Father ab-
stained from speaking directly to the Jews and from calling the solemn and direct
attention of the whole world to the iniquitous drama that was unfolding. But now
that Nazism has been defeated, and that the circumstances have changed," he asked,

the British ambassador to the Holy See, conveyed to the Foreign Office the content of his conversation with the Vatican's under secretary of state, Domenico Tardini. This high functionary of the Curia informed the British diplomat that "the Russians have recently sent into Poland nearly half a million Bolshevised Jews, many of them Russian, who are expected to promote Bolshevisation of Poland"—a piece of news which Cavendish-Bentinck dismissed with characteristic understatement as a "great exaggeration."[47]*

So, not surprisingly, a long telegram from Ambassador Osborne entitled "Facts about Kielce" and dated September 12, 1946, gave a litany of Jewish mischief as a description of the pogrom. Again we hear about "Russian Jews" and the "mysterious vanishing of Christian children" after these Jews began to arrive in Poland; about the callousness of the authorities who took no steps to search for the missing; and about the population's "tacit suspicions directed towards the large establishment given by the Government to the Russian Jews and situated in the street

---

"could it not be permitted, and that is the reason for this letter, to transmit to His Holiness the appeal of so many anguished souls, and to beg him to make his voice heard." Four days after writing to Montini, on July 16, Maritain had an audience with the Pope. Apparently informed of his [the French] ambassador's request, Pius chose not to act.

[J]ust as Maritain was pursuing his appeal on behalf of the Jews he was learning of new outbursts of antisemitism in Eastern Europe, culminating in the atrocious outburst of communal violence in the Polish town of Kielce, on July 4, 1946. The western press reported these events, together with shocking loss of Jewish life, accusations of ritual murder and the complicity of Polish bishops, immediately before Maritain's letter to Montini on July 12. *Le Monde* relayed the story on July 7 and 8, and *The New York Times* on the 11th. On July 16, the day he saw the Pope, Maritain received an appeal from the Jewish Labor Committee in New York deploring the silence of the Catholic church and appealing to him to denounce the atrocities. Maritain responded sympathetically three days later, on the 19th. That day, with the dreadful events in Poland much on his mind, Maritain saw Montini and once again gave vent to his frustration, as he recorded in his diary: "Visit to Montini. I speak to him of Jews and antisemitism. The Holy Father never even *named* them [emphasis in original]. Catholic conscience is poisoned, something has to be done. Article in the O[sservatore] R[omano] of yesterday on the 'pretext of Kielce' in which the Kielce pogrom is declared to be • *non racial*!!" [*sic*; emphasis in original]

(Michael R. Marrus, "A Plea Unanswered: Jacques Maritain, Pope Pius XII and the Holocaust," unpublished manuscript).

*One may add for good measure that the British ambassador's blunt diagnosis would have been confirmed *in extenso* by the Polish wartime ambassador to the USSR, Professor Stanisław Kot, who in his dispatch to London of January 5, 1942, wrote: "[The Jews'] sense of the humiliation and victimization they suffered, despite their sympathy for Russia, is so great that it has generated resentment, contempt, even hatred for Russia. Their attitude

called Planty." There followed the bloodcurdling story of "Enrico Baslzozyk" and his imprisonment in the nonexistent cellar. And then a description of a literal battle waged against the Jews: "An officer and a group of militiamen arrived at the Centre. They found the doors closed. At orders to open they were greeted with insults by the Jews. The doors were forced and the militia were received with gunfire. The officer was killed and some men wounded. The militia then proceeded to attack the interior of the house. A battle between militia and Jews ensued, the Jews being well-armed even to hand grenades, which caused victims among the militia. . . . How many Jews were killed? How many soldiers fell in the fight against the Jews? The Authorities state that 43 Jews died, but the names of only 11 are given." A lengthy and detailed *laudatio* for the inter-vention of the Kielce clergy is followed by this punch line: "It was thus the clergy and the clergy alone which, in these critical days from the fifth to the tenth of July, managed to maintain calm among the population, which was highly excited and, it would seem, perfidiously stirred by sin-ister agents provocateurs of the U.B. . . . Meanwhile the U.B. has done everything to misrepresent the character and nature of the facts. The Press never tired of repeating that the Jews of Kielce were victims of a lingering racialism in Poland."[48]

Confidential Report from the Bishop of Kielce

All this information was supplied to the Holy See via Polish church chan-nels. And there was more to come, as it is unlikely that by September 12 (the date of Osborne's dispatch) the Vatican had already absorbed a con-fidential report on the Kielce pogrom prepared by a commission set up in secret by Kielce's bishop, Czesław Kaczmarek. A group of priests headed by the Reverend Dr. Mieczysław Żywczyński from Płock (who was later appointed to a chair of history at the Catholic University in Lublin), assisted by some lawyers from Kielce, spent over a month draft-

---

toward Russia today is far sharper and more determined than among ethnic Poles, who had no illusions that Russia would treat them in a friendly manner. So the Polish-Soviet pact and recognition of Polish statehood evoked loud expressions of attachment to the Polish state even among those Jews who were most anti-Polish before. They express allegiance to Polish identity and a desire to return at all costs to Poland and their small towns in the border-lands. . . . Under no condition do the Jews want to remain subjected to Russian rule ["*Po prostu Żydzi za żadną cenę nie chcą być pod rosyjskim panowaniem*"]. Local authorities have a good read-ing of these sentiments and this is, I believe, one of the main reasons for not letting the Jews out of the USSR" (Stanisław Kot, *Listy z Rosji do gen. Sikorskiego*, p. 252).

ing the eighteen-page document, which was handed by Bishop Kaczmarek to the U.S. ambassador in Poland, Arthur Bliss Lane, on September 1, 1946.*

The report of Bishop Kaczmarek's commission was conceived as a
counterweight to the official version of the Kielce events propagated by
the government. It offers, therefore, both a description of what had happened and a polemic. This was an entirely understandable approach to
take for a church engaged in a tough political struggle with Communist
authorities. Official propaganda used the occasion to blame what had
happened on the church and on so-called reactionary political milieus.
The church hierarchy was reproached for its refusal to stem the tide of
anti-Semitism, as it was unwilling to issue an outright condemnation of
anti-Jewish violence or to speak up against the fraudulence of ritual murder claims, which were circulating widely.

Thus, the report issued by Kaczmarek's commission in the first place
takes the government's politicized version of the story to task and shows
that the trial held in the immediate aftermath of the pogrom was a trav-
esty of justice. Not only were the defendants' rights violated, but no examination of how the police, the military, and the Security Service had
acted throughout the day was allowed during judicial proceedings. The
report shows that no proof was offered in support of official claims
blaming the violence in Kielce on underground organizations and on
some alleged conspiracy by the regime's political opponents. In fact, it
was "the authorities," wrote the authors of the report, who had carried
out most of the killings—the police, the military, and workers from a big
enterprise (in the second murder wave at Planty Street), many of whom

---

*The content of Osborne's dispatch follows in almost every detail a long memorandum
describing the events drafted by the rector of the Kielce cathedral. Reverend Zelek was an
eyewitness to the events, participated in conferences with local authorities afterward, and
wrote his account several days later (he mentions the funeral of pogrom victims in the document). He was also a member of the commission that drafted the Kaczmarek report. His
eyewitness memorandum may have been passed along to the Vatican right away.
   Church documents concerning the pogrom, including Zelek's memorandum, were
confiscated by the Security Service on January 12, 1952, during a search of the Kielce cathedral. Bishop Kaczmarek's report of September 1, 1946, was not among these documents. It
surfaced in U.S. diplomatic archives only in the 1990s. For extensive excerpts of Zelek's
memorandum, see Cała and Datner-Śpiewak, eds., *Dzieje Żydów*, pp. 53–57. Kaczmarek's
memorandum has been published by John Micgiel, "Kościół katolicki i pogrom kielecki,"
Niepodległość, XXV (1992), pp. 134–72. On the workings of the commission set up by Bishop
Kaczmarek to draft the report, see Jan Śledzianowski, *Pytania nad pogromem kieleckim*, p. 173.
Osborne's memorandum most likely predates the delivery of Kaczmarek's report to the Vatican (see Micgiel, "Kościół," p. 150).

undoubtedly were Communist Party members. Instead of blaming the regime's opponents, the report points out with sarcasm, the authorities should explain how the "pogrom" could go on for an entire day in the capital of a voivodeship where large detachments of the police, the army, and the Security Service were available on the spot.*

These are all good points and valid questions, which should have been raised; the commission deserves credit for them. Yet in the end, the answers suggested to those well-taken questions, and the description of the day's events in which these answers are grounded, enlighten today's historian more about the mentality of the Catholic hierarchy in Poland at the time than about what actually happened in Kielce on July 4, 1946.

The commission began by raising a very general issue: how was one to account for the extraordinary cruelty of the crowd in Kielce? The answer provided goes to the heart of the commission's argument. Hatred is the self-evident explanation: "There can be only one answer," Bishop Kaczmarek's commission stipulates, "the crowd hated the Jews."[49] But why, since Poles are not particularly sadistically inclined? Furthermore, "after the massive killings of Jews perpetrated by the Nazis in 1943, neither in Poland generally nor in Kielce did people show hostility toward the Jews, or anti-Semitism. Everybody felt compassion for Jews, even their greatest enemies. Many Jews were saved by Poles. After all, without Polish help not even one would have survived. They were saved even though punishment for assisting Jews was harsh, including the penalty of death. It was so in 1944, and in the beginning of 1945."[50]

The seamless mixing of fact and fiction makes it difficult for a casual reader to sort out these claims.† But the false premise being established— of allegedly universal Polish compassion, sympathy, and assistance extended across the board to Jews during the war—is crucial in rendering the rest of the argument plausible. For if Polish attitudes toward the Jews were so friendly and supportive until the end of the German occupation, they must have changed under the impact of what came afterward. The reason for that change is named forthwith and without equivocation: "After Soviet armies entered Poland, and the Lublin government ex-

---

*In the report, the word "pogrom" appears in inverted commas (Micgiel, "Kościół," p. 142).

†Many Jews were indeed saved during the war by the Poles, yet anti-Semitism and hostility toward Jews were widespread in Polish society and made helping Jews such a risky business that righteous Gentiles tried to conceal what they were doing primarily from their own neighbors; and, as we know, Jews were being killed in liberated Poland as early as 1944.

tended its authority over the entire country, the situation radically changed. Enmity toward the Jews began; spreading fast, it engulfed large masses of the Polish society, everywhere, and that means also in Kielce. Jews are disliked, even hated on the entire territory of Poland. This is a phenomenon which cannot be denied." Even those Poles who "belong to the ruling parties" hated the Jews, states the report, for the reason that "Jews are the main propagators of Communism in Poland, while the Polish nation does not want Communism, which is being imposed on it by force."[51]*

Widespread, aggressive anti-Semitism—"Jews are . . . hated"—in postwar Poland was attested to by church authorities, who were certainly competent to make the assertion, and the commission made it plain that the Jews had only themselves to blame for this state of affairs. "Every Jew has a good job or unlimited opportunities and help in industry and commerce. Ministries are full of Jews . . . everywhere they occupy choice, leading, main positions. . . . [T]hey are in charge of security police offices, and carry out arrests." On top of everything else, they were tactless, brutal, and arrogant, and many did not speak good Polish since they came from Russia. "On the basis of the above reasons one can say that Jews are responsible for the lion's share of the hatred that surrounds them."[52]

We have barely reached the fourth of twenty-five pages, but the frame of reference is already firmly established.[53] From here on, the authors merely fill in the blanks. Several of their subsequent arguments are nuanced. Some are unexpected. But, the thrust of the presentation set, it would stay on course to the end.

The commissioners' approach to ritual murder, for instance, shows great dexterity in handling difficult material. They neither confirm nor deny the story directly, but in the end say enough to enable readers to know where the authors stand on the matter.†

---

*The apparent contradiction of the claim that regime supporters hated Jews for introducing Communism into Poland is resolved later in the report, when we are told that the only genuine Communists in Poland were Jewish, while those Poles who supported the regime did so only out of opportunism.

†Children had been disappearing in Kielce for months prior to July and the "general public" (*"szeroki ogół,"* or broad stratum) believed that Jews were using them for ritual murder, states the commission. Even members of the intelligentsia were stirred. "Some, for example, informed this writer that Jews make blood transfusions using the children, and then murder their victims" (Micgiel, "Kościół," p. 146). Those "facts" were reported to the police, who did nothing in the matter, thereby "reinforcing the conviction among the broad masses that Jews can do anything they wish in Poland with impunity" (ibid.). The commissioners do not offer any commentary on these revelations, and they change the subject at this point only to re-

Government propaganda, as well as the indictment in the trial held in Kielce, dismissed the story of the kidnapping as a lie. Why then, asks the commission, did the government not produce the boy at the trial to show that he had been lying? Why wasn't he confronted with the Jew who allegedly sent him to the building on Planty 7 on an errand, only to have him abducted? If the boy was lying, this would have come out. "How did the police establish 'beyond reasonable doubt' that the boy was lying? Was the basement in the building inspected, and had the Jews living in the building been questioned?"[54]*

If what the boy originally said was untrue, "if indeed, the Jews had not tormented him, then someone had to order him to make up that story."[55] Who could have done so? It was established that the so-called reactionary underground did not provoke these events, so—and here comes the pièce de résistance—it must have been the Jews. "This may seem unlikely, even absurd, because it implies that a Jew was the main cause for the murder of Jews in Kielce. But is this indeed so absurd?" the commission's report asks rhetorically.

Given that Jews were pressuring Great Britain for the handover of Palestine, and that they complained of being persecuted in some European countries ("Poland is one of those countries, particularly disliked especially by Russian Jews because it does not want to voluntarily accept the Communist regime being imposed upon it"), "given all the factors here invoked, it is by no means out of the question that some Jew might have persuaded Henryk Błaszczyk to tell the above-mentioned story, expecting that it would incite the crowd, already angry with Jews, to some excesses, which later could be amply exploited [*które będzie można potem obszernie wyzyskać*]. In the light of this hypothesis, the disappearance of Błaszczyk for three days becomes clear (and it does not matter if between July 1 and July 3 he was somewhere in the countryside, or in the basement at Planty 7), and [it also explains] why he was not brought as a witness during the trial. The hypothesis is also strongly confirmed by the fact

---

turn indirectly to ritual murder a few pages later, when they discuss what really happened to Henryk Błaszczyk.

An investigation by the Institute of National Memory revealed only one documented case of a lost child in this period. On June 7, 1946, Maria Bińkowska reported to the police that her eight-year-old son, Jan, had disappeared. He came back home on July 16, claiming that he ran away because of trouble at school (GKBZpNP-IPN, p. 13).

*Inexplicably, commission members didn't seem to know that there was no basement in the building and that several surviving Jews who lived in the building had testified during the trial.

that the police did not try to prevent the crowd from murdering Jews, which could only have happened if it had orders to act in this manner."⁵⁶

The bishop's commission was not constrained by facts or probabilities. It reports as "an indubitable fact" that Jews shot first into the crowd at Planty 7, wounding scores of people. They used, the report implies, automatic weapons—"a series of shots was fired" (*"oddano serię strzałów"*)—a statement repeated twice in consecutive paragraphs; on the second try, the Jews managed also to "kill an officer." "According to witnesses, the Jews inside the house were defending themselves with grenades." "Thus the first victims during the Kielce events were the Poles."⁵⁷*

But the first of two main points I want to draw out of the commission's report is its answer to the question "whether the church refused to condemn the crime in Kielce."⁵⁸ The report goes back over several statements issued by church sources (and discussed earlier in this chapter) following the pogrom and wonders why the official press continues to attack the church for its putative silence about the "excesses in Kielce. The press calls simultaneously for a joint statement of the Polish episcopate condemning anti-Semitism. . . . The vast majority of the Jews in Poland eagerly proselytize Communism, work in the notorious Security Service, make arrests, torture prisoners and kill them, and for this they are disliked by society, which does not like Communism and has had enough of Gestapo-like methods. And here the church, according to the wishes of the government press, is supposed to solemnly declare that this dislike of society is unjustified, that the behavior of Jews is utterly blameless, that only Poles who dislike them are guilty. This is the real meaning of

---

*The report also includes a description of how soldiers and the police killed Jews inside the building ("the military, especially, shared in the hatred of Jews"), and kept bringing Jews out and delivering them to "hysterical individuals" in the "mob" outside ("one could hear in the crowd people screaming: 'Long live the Polish army!' "), who then "massacred" them. There were times, people who had been on the scene reported, when the whole disturbance could have been suppressed "if the security service, the police and the military were willing to really take action" (Micgiel, "Kościół," p. 155). One cannot disagree with this portion of the assessment, which brought a welcome correction to the official version, where the nefarious role of the law-and-order personnel, though mentioned, was downplayed. Having so complimented the commission, however, I would be remiss if I did not reiterate that it was repeatedly carried away by its polemical animus, even in trivial but characteristic matters—as when it noted, for example, that the panel of three judges in the Kielce trial included one "with pronounced mongoloid traits, who did not look Polish, while the other two looked semitic" (Micgiel, "Kościół," p. 157), and when it reproached the authorities for allowing foreign journalists to sit in the audience during the trial ("the Kielce events . . . ," wrote the authors of the report, "were, after all, a crime [*wypadki kieleckie . . . były jednak zbrodnią*], which left a stain on [the reputation of] Polish society)" (Micgiel, "Kościół," p. 160).

what the government press wishes. . . . It seems like a request to have the
church approve the system of terror currently implemented in Poland."⁵⁹

This declaration portrays Jews and Communism as the selfsame
and, conversely, conflates anti-Semitism with anti-Communism. To declare against anti-Semitism is therefore tantamount to supporting the
Communist regime. According to this mental construct, nothing is what
it seems. As the report winds down toward its "conclusions and summary" we are informed that "the analysis of events and of witness' testimonies" demonstrates that "certain Jewish Communist milieus, in
cooperation with the Security Service, which they controlled, [induced]
the pogrom, which could later be trumpeted as proof that Jews should
emigrate to their own country, as proof that anti-Semitism and fascism
predominate in Polish society, and as proof that the church to which the
killers belonged is reactionary."⁶⁰ Jews, in other words, are Communist
and Zionist simultaneously. They support the regime and run away from
it at the same time; in fact, the same Jews do both things at the same
time. Such texts, to paraphrase Cavendish-Bentinck, could not have been
drafted and then passed along by church authorities unless many a "Polish bishop was prepared to believe this."

Finally, it should be pointed out that yet another future grandee of
the Polish church is on record in a similar spirit. In 1946, Stefan Wyszyński was the recently installed bishop of Lublin; following a long and distinguished career, he was hailed after his death as "the primate of the
millennium," and the process of beatification began in Rome. In the files
of the legal department of the Central Committee of Polish Jews we find
a memorandum reporting his conversation with a delegation of Jewish
leaders some two weeks after the Kielce pogrom.

Unlike the old and sickly Cardinal Hlond, who granted only a brief
interview to foreign journalists, Wyszyński gave time generously to his
Jewish interlocutors. He had ample opportunity to explicate his views in
detail, and he directly addressed the issue of ritual murder. The Jewish
delegation left a record of its failed attempt to persuade him to make a
statement condemning anti-Semitism.

"The bishop did not agree with [our] assessment [of the Kielce
events]," wrote the Jewish committee members.

> He argued that the causes are much deeper, that they are rooted
> in the general dislike of Jews who take active part in the current
> political life. The Germans wanted to destroy the Jewish nation

because it was an advocate of Communism. . . . The bishop stresses that the horrors of the Hitlerite camps had their model in Siberian camps. They were the primary school of Hitlerite barbarism, which has its sequel also at the present time. Jews, according to the bishop, should work hard to get a state in Palestine, or some colonies in South America. . . . In Poland, Jews are not the only ones being murdered; Poles, too, suffer that fate. Many are in prisons and in camps. The bishop condemns every kind of murder from the point of view of the Christian ethic. In the specific case of Kielce, the bishop has nothing to add or expressly condemn, because the idea of condemning evil is always spread by the church.

During the discussion of how the crowd was agitated by the myth that Christian blood is necessary to make matzo, the bishop clarified that during the Beilis trial, a lot of old and new Jewish books were assembled, and the matter of blood was not definitively settled.* In the end, the bishop declared that he could not issue an official statement about the Kielce events, but during a soon-to-be-held meeting of priests he would explain this matter in the spirit of calming down the faithful.[61]

This conversation took place almost exactly seven hundred years after Pope Innocent IV issued the first papal bull, in 1247, declaring that accusations of ritual murder against the Jews were fraudulent.[62]

The Response of Bishop Kubina

Among the hierarchs of the Catholic church only the bishop of Częstochowa, Teodor Kubina, spoke with a different voice—direct, informative, and categorical. His proclamation, issued on July 7, was signed jointly with the city and county officials of Częstochowa and carried special weight as it emanated from the most important site of religious pilgrimage in the country. In the very first sentence one reads that Jews had been killed in Kielce, and what a scandal this was, given the horror of the Jewish fate under the German occupation and given that the murder was

*The reference is to the trial of Mendel Beilis, who was accused of ritual murder in Kiev in 1913. The trial was reported on and widely written about at the time as a manifestation of Russia's backwardness and the reactionary politics propagated by the czarist regime. Beilis was acquitted.

perpetrated by people who had also suffered terribly during the war. Those who committed crimes in Kielce were driven by lies and fanaticism, the declaration continues, and into the bargain they also soiled Poland's reputation in the entire world. This crime violated fundamental principles of Christian ethics and simple decency.

> We declare: all statements about ritual murders are lies. Nobody from among the Christian population in Kielce, in Częstochowa, or anywhere else has ever been harmed by Jews for ritual and religious purposes. We do not know of a single case of a Christian child abducted by Jews. All news and stories spread on this topic are either deliberately invented by criminals or come from confused people who do not know any better, and they aim to provoke a crime. Criminals and people who are confused ought to receive a fair trial or merciful pity, but they ought not to be listened to and followed by society at large. We appeal to all . . . to combat with all your strength all the attempts to organize anti-Jewish excesses. We trust that responsible citizens of Częstochowa, attached to principles of Christian morality, will not follow criminal suggestions and will not debase themselves by raising their hands against a fellow citizen only because he is of a different nationality and denomination.[63]

Unlike the other texts we saw earlier with their equivocal "it," mysterious "events," regrettable this and that, or Jews in high office, this was a straightforward statement about ritual murder, anti-Semitism, and the murdering of Jews—all of which had just been fused in an explosion of violence during the Kielce pogrom. How did Kubina's fellow bishops react to his public stand? We can only imagine what was said in personal exchanges, but the written response was not long in coming.

In early September, during its "plenary conference, the episcopate 'obliged individual bishops to refrain from taking individual stands on any and all events ["wobec wszystkich bez wyjątku wydarzeń"] that take place in the country in order not to create a situation similar to that which followed the events in Kielce . . . when a bishop from one diocese . . . collaborated in issuing a statement whose content and intended meaning were unacceptable to bishops from other dioceses on the grounds of fundamental intellectual and canonic principles of the Catholic church.' "[64] This was the "pastoral letter" that the British ambassador hoped would condemn anti-Semitism albeit "in a guarded form." Instead it declared that Bishop Kubina's statement was unacceptable "on the grounds of fundamental intellectual and canonic principles of the Catholic church."

What could Kubina's fellow bishops object to "canonically," except his scathing rejection of the canard of ritual murder? Intellectually, they must have objected to Kubina's identification of Jews as victims rather than as Communists—in any case, those among them who had spoken publicly had consistently done the reverse.

Church historians writing in Poland in the 1990s endorsed the position of the Catholic episcopate criticizing Bishop Kubina's statement. The Catholic church, they argue, which was at the time under political assault by the Communist regime, had to make sure that it spoke with one voice and that Cardinal Hlond's position was not being undermined.* Today's historians remind us that the public rhetoric concerning anti-Semitism was at the time highly politicized, and that the episcopate could not be expected to take a stand that might be misunderstood by the general public as an endorsement for the regime. Using a sentence that could have been lifted from Bishop Kaczmarek's commission report, historian Zenon Wrona wrote in 1991 that calling on the church to issue a condemnation of anti-Semitism was tantamount "to requesting an official endorsement by the church of the entire system of terror that the Communists had introduced in Poland."[65]

As if opposing Communism necessarily requires that one be an anti-Semite! The logic of such a premise hinges on accepting the identification of Communism with Jews. Otherwise, it is not clear why one could not object on moral and doctrinal grounds (rooted in Catholicism, for example) to anti-Semitism and Communism at once. And if there were reasons to fear that the general public did not appreciate the disjunction, one might simply infer that the public had not been properly enlightened on the matter by those whom it trusted to offer spiritual guidance. Bishop Kubina thought so; he tried to remedy the situation and managed to defuse mounting tension in Częstochowa by speaking directly and forcefully against the lie of ritual murder.

Cavendish-Bentinck was shocked that cannibalistic theology held such sway over the minds of the Polish clergy. Likewise, men of letters in Poland were outraged that the worn-out tale of ritual murder could still

---

*It was Kubina who spoke first, on July 7, so that it was Cardinal Hlond who undermined the only public statement by a Catholic bishop about the pogrom when he issued his declaration on July 11.

move people. "If Greiser"—Hitler's plenipotentiary in one area of occupied Poland, who was then on trial for his crimes—"in his last word [at the trial] had justified the extermination of the Jews as the revenge of the German nation for ritual murder, he would have been laughed off by the Germans themselves," mused Jan Rojewski in the July 22, 1946, issue of *Kuźnica.* "In our grandfathers' time one could hear such arguments in the Balkans; today . . . only in Poland."

But, as the British ambassador noted, "uneducated Poles" could hardly be blamed for holding such views if bishops were "prepared to believe this." And so we should not at all be surprised that a medieval prejudice brought people into the streets in postwar Poland on many occasions and in many different towns—in Rzeszów, in Kraków, in Kielce, in Bytom, in Białystok, in Szczecin, in Bielawa, in Otwock, in Legnica.*

This is a history book, not a moral tale, but since the Catholic church's business is with the Ten Commandments, one can evaluate the deeds of its functionaries in the light of moral criteria without being inappropriately judgmental. It behooves us to note that unlike the intellectual elite of the nation, the institutional elite of the Catholic church chose to completely ignore postwar anti-Semitism in Poland.[66] It did not respond even when faced with the breathtaking violence of the Kielce pogrom. Confronted with mass murder committed by people who in their own minds were defending the Catholic religion, all that the shepherds of a flock that had run amok brought themselves to do was to call for calm.

When the people of Kielce lost their way, the hierarchy of Poland's Catholic church abdicated its responsibility to offer spiritual guidance and simply coasted along. Their hands-off attitude reinforced what people had already learned when men in uniforms, bringing a semblance of institutional authority, joined the crowds battering Jews in Kielce: the

---

*The town council of Sopot (or Zoppott), a famous spa on the seashore, took the matter seriously under consideration and passed a resolution ordering the town council's department of culture and art to organize a series of public lectures to demonstrate to the public that ritual murders did not take place. They hoped to organize these lectures in cooperation with the clergy. Then the council took paid advertisements in *Dziennik Bałtycki* (*The Baltic Daily*), *Życie Warszawy* (*The Life of Warsaw*), and *Kuźnica* "in order to encourage town councils elsewhere in Poland to undertake a broad enlightening initiative, aimed at tearing our society away from the mad psychosis of anti-Semitism" (*"mającej na celu wyrwanie naszego społeczeństwa z obłędnej psychozy antysemityzmu"*) (*Kuźnica,* August 19, 1946). I am not sure how well this initiative caught on, but one might still have to characterize such efforts, I am afraid, as a "work in progress."

Jews were somehow at fault. Priests could not and would not condone murder, but Catholic hierarchs said that Jews were Communists and that they brought all their misfortunes upon themselves. The bishops even missed an opportunity simply to keep quiet when one of their ranks made an honorable statement. Their criticism of Bishop Kubina's pronouncement paralleled the indignation of the Łódź and Radom factory workers, who also did not want to be identified with outright protests against the Kielce pogrom. The symbolism of officials "washing their hands" while innocent Jews were tormented to death was lost on this Catholic clergy, blinded by prejudice.*

Not Much Official Ado About the Kielce Pogrom

Two officials from the Central Committee of the Communist Party, the PPR, arrived in Kielce by midday on July 4 and were later joined by several more Central Committee "activists." After a briefing from the bedridden Kielce voivode, the newly arrived Hilary Chełchowski and Władysław Buczyński still had time to mingle with the crowds in the streets; they then wrote a report full of scathing observations about the incompetence of the Kielce Party committee. A day after the event, an important member of the Politburo and Władysław Gomułka's close associate and friend, Zenon Kliszko, arrived in town to assess the situation. All these actions, however, addressed the Kielce pogrom as a breakdown in local public order rather than a major issue of moral or political significance.

In hindsight, one is struck by the inattention, at the highest decision-making levels of the Party and the security apparatus, to pervasive anti-Semitism and continuing assaults on Jews. Political rhetoric and propaganda were turned on immediately after the event, of course, denouncing anti-Semitism and producing, as we saw, considerable embarrassment when workers' meetings refused to condemn the pogrom's perpetrators and occasional strikes broke out venting people's anger against . . . the Jews. "Do you want me to send eighteen million Poles to Siberia?" the minister of public security, Radkiewicz, retorted when fac-

*The faithlessness of Polish Catholic clergy was noted by many an observer, including, recently, an esteemed philosopher and theologian, Reverend Professor Józef Tischner. "In my life," wrote Tischner, "I have not met anyone who has lost faith after reading Marx and Lenin, yet I have met many who have lost faith after meeting with their own parish priest" (quoted from Michał Głowiński, *The Black Seasons*, p. 157).

ing the insistent entreaties by representatives of the Central Committee
of Polish Jews that he counter anti-Semitism after Kielce.[67] But in reality, Poland's leadership had never focused attention on the Kielce
pogrom itself, except in the way described earlier.

If we scrutinized the archives of the leadership of the Ministry of
Public Security or searched the files of the leading bodies of the Polish
Workers' Party, we would hardly be able to tell that the Kielce pogrom
ever took place. We have this on the authority of a scholar who is recognized as a most knowledgeable specialist on matters pertaining to the
history of the security police for this period: "I looked over all the protocols, even though some were incomplete, from the regular meetings of
the leadership of the Ministry of Public Security with chiefs of the
voivodeship security offices," said Professor Andrzej Paczkowski during
a conference about the historiography of the Kielce pogrom. "The issue
of the Kielce pogrom was never addressed in this forum."[68] As Professor
Paczkowski pointed out later in the discussion, this was a busy time for
the Party leadership and the security apparatus: they were hard at work
falsifying the results of the June 30, 1946, referendum.*

Another eminent historian, Professor Jerzy Tomaszewski, suggested
that the absence of Kielce-related documents in government files was
due to lack of interest. The pogrom was not an event bearing on the issue
of holding on to or consolidating power: "Whether five Jews had been
killed, or one hundred, either way the grip on power by the regime was
not threatened by this," Tomaszewski argued. "And therefore this was
not interesting for the authorities. Other things were much more important."[69]

The tragic events in Kielce were described by Bolesław Bierut during
a July 5 meeting of the Presidium of the National Council of the Country (KRN); there followed a report by the minister of public security. But
this is the extent of documented interest in the matter at the highest
echelons of power.[70] Six weeks later, the KRN shelved a project concerning a decree to "combat anti-Semitism." Its chief legal expert, one Itzak

---

*"This was probably the moment when the decision to falsify the results of the referen-
dum was made. Zambrowski, Mazur, Gomułka, Bierut were totally absorbed by the referendum. It is sufficient to peruse the notes left by Bierut: city names, numbers of voting
districts, figures, pluses, minuses, time noted every quarter of an hour. All of this during the
first days of July. A dozen groups of ranking voivodeship Security Service agents plus a large
team of specialists led by Colonel Aron Palkin which came from Moscow, were busily filling
out anew the 'protocols of People's Elections' from eleven thousand electoral commissions"
(Paczkowski, in "O stanie badań," p. 12).

Klajnerman, argued that all the requisite laws were already on the books, and that "it seems unnecessary to issue a new decree specifically devoted to combating anti-Semitism. It is not only unnecessary, but counterproductive, perhaps even harmful, as such a decree would certainly become an excellent pretext for energized agitation against the Jews and against the government. The reactionary underground will offer arguments about the privileged position of the Jews, and the government will be accused of protecting the Jews with special care."[71]

Needless to say Klajnerman was too small, no pun intended, to decide such an issue. During a meeting of the KRN on September 21, 1946, Adolf Berman, the Zionist younger brother of the powerful Communist leader Jakub Berman, gave a speech from which I have already quoted an important portion.[72] Precisely in view of the Kielce pogrom, he called for the passage of a decree aimed expressly at protecting the Jews. "I believe that the moment has arrived when it is necessary to issue a special law or decree to combat anti-Semitism. The current Article 12 of the decree on special courts, in the present situation, after Kielce, is no longer sufficient. It is necessary to state in law, addressing this to the entire nation, that not only murder but also the surreptitious passing around of vicious anti-Semitic propaganda is a punishable crime; that spreading horrible lies about the snatching of children or ritual murder is a punishable crime too. Such a legislation or decree is necessary. I say it in the name of all the Jews in Poland. It is necessary to undertake politico-ideological combat with anti-Semitism among the masses, especially among some parts of the working class."[73] But the legislative initiative, even though already in its final draft, was shelved—one would think inexplicably, given what had just happened in Kielce.[74]

Upon a moment's reflection, however, we realize that the Communists, who were running away from this issue, must have dropped the matter precisely *because* of what happened in Kielce. The vox populi concerning the "Jewish problem" mattered to them, and as the people had spoken loud and clear, the rulers listened. They made a mistake in organizing "spontaneous" protest meetings in the aftermath of the pogrom, but then quickly drew appropriate conclusions. By September, Jakub Berman did not have patience for his Zionist brother's waxing sentimental over the fate of Polish Jews. The Communists would solve all such problems, and more, after they consolidated their grip on power. But in order to do so they needed to sway and cajole the masses into allegiance, not "combat" them at every turn.

The Communists were picking their fights carefully; the defense of Jews against popular anti-Semitism entailed a confrontation they preferred to avoid. The Kielce Communist Party secretary knew it at once, when he refused to address the crowd advancing at midday against the building on Planty 7 because, we remember, he "didn't want people to be saying that the PPR is a defender of the Jews."

The Taste of Matzo

People in Poland were tired and irritated in the early days of July 1946. They had just gone through an intense, rough, and humiliating patch of ideological politics. During the several weeks leading up to the "Three times yes" referendum held on June 30, Poles had been subjected to a barrage of propaganda and intimidation. And in the end they were lied to brazenly when Communist officials falsified the results to show that the people had overwhelmingly supported them.*

Security personnel were also tired. In Kielce the voivodeship police commander, Colonel Kuźnicki, had called in sick that day, and the commanding officer of the Security Service, Major Sobczyński, spent a sleepless night collecting materials while waiting for a plane to take him on the morning of July 4 to Warsaw, where he was to report on his handling of referendum-related assignments. Paradoxically, Communist Parties everywhere always took electoral politics very seriously, not as a mechanism for selection of the leadership, but as a public ritual conferring popular legitimacy upon their own rule. Hence the proverbial 99.9 percent voter turnouts and "yes" votes in elections from Cuba to Vladivostok. The "Three times yes" referendum of June 30 was the first Communist-run electoral experience inflicted on the Poles.[75] If pent-up resentment was to be vented, July 4 was as good a day to act out as any.

A unique negative synergy had been at play in the time span of no more than two morning hours on July 4 in Kielce, transforming an absurd but not unusual complaint into the deadliest peacetime European pogrom of the twentieth century.[†] In the pogrom's opening phase, we

---

*The first secretary of the Communist Party, Gomułka, rhetorically linked, in his inimitable style, the referendum and the Kielce pogrom when he spoke to Party activists in Warsaw on July 7—"The Hitlerite 'nein' [meaning those who did not vote "Three times yes"] spoke immediately after the vote by organizing a Hitlerite pogrom of the Jews" (Daniel, *Żyd w zielonym*, p. 104).
†With the exception of the Kristallnacht, of November 9 and 10, 1938, in Nazi Ger-

witnessed a breakdown of discipline: police agents acting like vigilantes; a crowd rapidly drawn to the scene and energized by the spectacle of official intervention confirming a deeply held and inflammatory prejudice; and small army detachments arriving on the scene without unified command or any clear understanding of what they were supposed to do. Put one way, the choice before policemen and soldiers was not terribly problematic: should Polish children be defended against the Jews, or should Jews be defended against irate Polish mothers and fathers? Those who had a moment to reflect experienced conflicting thoughts, like one man interviewed in 1987 by Łoziński who cringed and cried before the camera at the recollection of the abuse he had suffered from the crowd when he appeared on the scene with his military unit. And so he broke down—then, and forty years later once again, just as many of his colleagues did when the mood of the crowd and the ongoing behavior of the police promptly sucked the soldiers into attacking the Jews.

When the situation got out of hand—and it did so very rapidly—people with institutional authority felt helpless and wanted it to go away. Priests who appeared on the scene simply walked off and declared that everything had returned to normal. Police officials called on the military to intervene. Officers refused to order their soldiers to forcefully suppress the crowd. The Security Service commander, usually an energetic and decisive man, procrastinated and seemed "unusually calm." The Party secretary refused to address the crowd, and the voivode lay incapacitated in bed after a motorcycle accident.

Yet everyone present also knew that there would be a tomorrow. A high-powered investigative team from Warsaw's Ministry of Public Security got to work that very evening. Scores of policemen, soldiers, and security personnel were placed under arrest. Party Secretary Kalinowski was dismissed. The officers responsible for law enforcement, Sobczyński, Gwiazdowicz, and Kuźnicki, were jailed and later put on trial. What amounted to a kangaroo court—given the speed with which it proceeded and how quickly its sentences of death were carried out—dealt immedi-

---

many. But Kristallnacht, where close to one hundred Jews were killed in Nazi-instigated anti-Jewish riots throughout Germany, Austria, and the Sudetenland, was less a "pogrom" than a government action carried out by unorthodox means. Still, if one takes into account also the number of Jews killed all around Kielce on July 4, the total murdered may have topped eighty.

ately with one dozen direct participants of the pogrom, condemning nine of them to execution.*

But the energy of those empowered to assess responsibility for the breach of law and order quickly dissipated. None of the superior military officers present on the scene was ever court-martialed. Of the three main protagonists, Gwiazdowicz, Sobczyński, and Kuźnicki, only the latter received even a slap on the wrist: a one-year sentence.[76] The other two were acquitted and went on to successful careers in the service of the regime. After the first Kielce trial with its nine death sentences, a number of rank-and-file militiamen, soldiers, and junior officers were also tried, as well as a handful of civilians. Many were acquitted, the others given prison terms of varying length; one soldier was sentenced to life in prison. It is difficult to assess the full scale of military trials, as these records were destroyed in 1989. Altogether, perhaps as many as sixty people were tried for their involvement in the Kielce pogrom, and half of them were found guilty.[77]

Coincidence of time, circumstance, incompetence of local officials, and sheer bad luck proved lethal to several dozen Jews in Kielce and the vicinity. But as Krystyna Kersten put it succinctly in her preface to Bożena Szaynok's fine study, we must think about the Kielce pogrom as an episode in collective "behavior involving ordinary people on an ordinary day in an ordinary voivodeship town." This could have happened anywhere in Poland, and at any time during this period.[78]

---

*An official investigation carried out in 1997 (hence with full access to Communist Party and Security Service archives) concluded that the defendants were selected for trial, from among several dozen people detained on the day of the pogrom, on the basis of "unknown criteria" (GKBZpNP-IPN, p. 33). In the immediate aftermath of the pogrom, a Security Service commission—headed by Adam Humer, the deputy head of the Investigative Department of the MBP, who happened to be in town for several days prior to the event in order to supervise the carrying out, or rather the falsification, of the June 30 referendum—tried to assemble all the facts. Humer reported directly to his superior officer, the head of the department, Józef Różański. In 1997 Humer was interviewed by GKBZpNP-IPN investigators preparing their report, and various files of the security police from 1946 to 1947 were declassified for the first time in order to facilitate the investigation.

The authorities wanted a speedy trial of the perpetrators; hence the first group, which was immediately identified by Humer. They may have contemplated some follow-up—the 1997 commission identified several files of forged depositions, for instance—but the effort was apparently abandoned. Several dozen people arrested on the first day were kept in jail without following requisite procedures—for instance, the Błaszczyks, father and son, were held by the Security Service until February 1947—and then were let go for the most part at the end of July 1946, without any follow-up or official disposition of their cases. As Humer told the investigators, no link between the pogrom and any conspiracy by the "reactionary underground" was ever established (see GKBZpNP-IPN, part II, pp. 4, 5).

And this is the essence, it seems to me, that endows the Kielce pogrom with such profound significance. To give an account of the uniqueness of time and place, of specific triggering factors, of the personal relations between actors who controlled organizational resources, is less significant than to understand how thousands of ordinary people could engage in a prolonged murderous assault against their fellow citizens. We can hope to understand this more adequately by following what people actually did during the course of the day and thereafter than by focusing on the initial escalation leading to serial murder or speculating whose *prowokacja* may have triggered the slaughter. One brief recorded exchange between the police corporal Mazur and that anonymous truck driver in the middle of Kielce tells us more about the July 4 events than would a log of telephone conversations held on that day by Major Sobczyński of the UB.

People killed Jews with gusto on that day, and looted their belongings at the same time.* Vast numbers of Kielce residents were involved in the events, young and old, of both sexes and from all walks of life. The assaults on Jews lasted for several hours and took place over an extended area in the city as well as at railway stations along the routes leading to and from Kielce. The scenography of the assaults varied widely, from frenzied mob action near the building on Planty 7 to deliberate, focused, pinpoint attacks on individuals somehow identified as Jewish who were then plucked from the street, a house, or a train compartment and wounded or killed (unless they managed to escape). Complete strangers joined in these endeavors in total openness, unfazed by the blatantly criminal character of the deeds they were embarking upon. Evidently all such concerns were overridden by a widespread social sanction for getting rid of the Jews once and for all.

*Eugeniusz Krawczyk, a messenger employed by the Kielce police, was put on trial with more than a dozen co-defendants on November 18. He came back from a swim on July 4, 1946, we read in his indictment, and quickly "ran to Planty 7, squeezed through the surrounding crowd, and put into a suitcase he found five kilograms of rice, two shirts, two towels, seven packets of tea, one pair of underpants, a blanket, a razor, and some dried apricots and walnuts. He took all this to a store on Sienkiewicza Street, where he sold the rice, tea, and apricots for 1,150 złoty. In the open-air market (*bazar*) he sold one towel to a stall-keeper for 30 złoty and exchanged another for a bottle of lemonade and one cigarette. He took the rest to the [police] barracks, where he sold the razor. He returned to the market, where he saw a Jewish man being led by policemen, and he hit that man with a stone on the elbow. Policemen took the man to the police academy building, on the steps of which Krawczyk hit him several times with a stick found in the street" (Meducki, *Antyżydowskie*, vol. I, p. 250).

Evidently the moral economy of Polish society after the war allowed for the murdering of Jews. The apparent normalcy of this monstrous transgression in the eyes of participants in the Kielce pogrom leaps out of every other document we take in hand, starting with the brief dialogue between policeman Mazur and the anonymous truck driver. This was also the most disturbing realization of Marcel Łoziński's interviewees, with which they visibly struggled before the camera. How could it be that simple, normal people come back from work or a family outing one day, and then take off "to kill them some Jews"? Introductory matter from the November 18, 1946, trial indictment, for instance, reads like *didaskalia* to an *Ubu*-esque play: "Krawczyk Eugeniusz . . . returned on July 4, 1946, from a swim and . . . ; Świtek Zdzisław returned on July 4 from an outing in the countryside with his family around 2:30 PM and . . . ; Franczak Stefan, having finished his shift in the Sanitation Department, dropped by a restaurant with a couple of friends and by 4:30 PM . . . ; Krasowski Mieczysław finished his work for the day at the cooperative 'Społem' and . . ."[79] Only, Alfred Jarry could not have invented the story line. But such is life, always more daring than fiction.

This very same document also shows (and we know this from other sources as well) that the killings in Kielce went on for hours, into the late afternoon, all over town. So much for the reassuring report by five Kielce priests who showed up at Planty 7 around 2:30 P.M. and noted that everything was in order. If what they did was all that needed to be done on that day by Catholic priests, then evidently not much was happening in Kielce on July 4, 1946. In their statement they offered, indirectly, a certificate of quasi normalcy to the day's events. This is where the formula of *prowokacja*—provocation—came in so handy for all concerned.

The conspiratorial frame of reference that put forth *prowokacja* as an interpretive strategy to come to terms with the Kielce pogrom—and which had a very long life in Polish historiography, until Krystyna Kersten shifted the field's perspective in 1981—stemmed from two motives. One was an inability to account for what happened, so well exemplified by the baffled expressions of Łoziński's interviewees when they were asked how such a pogrom was possible in Poland one year after the war. People were helplessly groping for an explanation until the word *prowokacja* was ushered in, and then they latched on to it with a sigh of relief, which in fact was only another way of saying what they already had revealed—that they had no idea how such a thing could have ever come about. And besides their inability to account for what happened, the other reason to invoke *prowokacja* was people's unwillingness to confront the facts.

Instead of studying what had happened during the Kielce pogrom, advocates of the *prowokacja* hypothesis asked *Cui bono?* Who could have benefited from such an act of anti-Jewish violence? And the answer they offered (for the moment, I leave aside Communist propaganda, which also described the pogrom as a "provocation," only by "reactionaries") was "the Communist regime and its Soviet sponsors." By deliberately inducing a Jewish pogrom through *prowokacja,* the Communists (or, more specifically, the Security Service or even the Soviet NKVD) allegedly attempted to divert the world's attention from the referendum vote that they falsified. Simultaneously, they also hoped to reduce Western sympathy for the plight of Polish society as it was being subjected to Sovietization. Or, as in the report of Bishop Kaczmarek's commission, it was the Jews-slash-Communists who tried to accomplish all of the above *plus* induce an exodus of the Jewish masses to Palestine.

Not only is there no material evidence to support such a scenario but also the very fact that the pogrom began, and reached the point of no return, at the level of a police precinct makes the hypothesis untenable.* What NKVD operative would entrust the launch of such an important clandestine operation to policemen Sędek, Zagórski, Zając, a few of their colleagues, an eight-year-old boy, and the boy's semiliterate, alcoholic father?† And if the incompetence and emotional indifference of a slew of higher officers to the day's events—Kuźnicki, Sobczyński, Gwiazdowicz, Szpilewoj, and more—is brought in as supporting evidence of a conspiracy, we would be dealing with a cabal of some two dozen people who, though barely on speaking terms with one another, had managed to coordinate their actions on that day and to keep the secret of their illicit

---

*Save rumors of a sighting in Kielce in 1946 of an NKVD operative, Demin, who in the 1960s allegedly surfaced in Israel and thus, presumably, was a Soviet expert in Jewish affairs who first honed his skills in Kielce. Michał Chęciński puts forth this trope in his book *Poland, Communism, Nationalism, Anti-Semitism.* Chęciński was later interviewed by investigators of the 1997 commission and maintained his version of events. But a detailed search of Soviet archives did not permit an identification of Demin, even though one secret NKVD report from Kielce was signed with that name (GKBZpNP-IPN, op. cit., pp. 29–30). Analysis of dispatches by the Soviet secret police resident in Kielce, Szpilewoj, indicates "that Soviet advisers were surprised by the tragic events in Kielce and there is no basis to link them with the conception that it was a Soviet provocation" (ibid., p. 35).

†See GKBZpNP-IPN, pp. 35–36. There is no record in the secret police files that Walenty Błaszczyk, who was a functionally illiterate alcoholic, was ever a secret collaborator with the UB, as maintained by Chęciński and proponents of the *prowokacja* hypothesis.

collaboration forever, leaving no trace in the archives of the Communist secret police, which have since been opened. This is highly improbable, and there is no need to explore this hypothesis at greater depth except to say that the *Cui bono?* perspective can be turned around and argued against its proponents.

Those who are dissembling often attribute their own motivations to those whom they intend to compromise.* So we may ask instead who benefits from the hypothesis of *prowokacja*? Whose interest does it serve to introduce such a putative explanation of the Kielce pogrom? And the answer is, The interest of those who do not care to find out or dwell on what really happened.

Communists immediately evoked in their propaganda the image of the Kielce pogrom as a conspiracy by "reactionaries," while their opponents in the Catholic-nationalist camp attributed it to a Communist (or Jewish-Communist) conspiracy. Neither side was willing or able to confront anti-Semitism for what it was, and while differing as to the content of the story they agreed about the framing of the narrative.† For if the Kielce pogrom was a *prowokacja,* one needed simply to look for provocateurs. If found, they would be dealt with; if not, then not; and that's where the matter ended.

---

*In the matter of ritual murder accusations, we may identify a directly associated reverse practice, which has never been widely discussed as a contested issue of Catholic-Jewish relations. I have in mind the "ritual murder" of Jewish children by Catholic clergy, which took place, in a manner of speaking, every time a Jewish child was baptized without a specific request or authorization by his or her parents. In January 2005, the international press reported the finding of an instruction from the Holy See to the papal nuncio in France, Angelo Roncalli (the future Pope John XXIII). Roncalli was credited with saving very many Jews from Nazi persecution; the one-page instruction, written in French and dated October 23, 1946, provides guidelines for responding to requests by Jewish institutions reclaiming Jewish children who had been confided during the war to Catholic families and institutions. In the first place, the document stipulates, such requests should never be answered in writing. Second, when it is necessary to respond, it should be stated that the church must investigate each case separately. "Children who have been baptized," we read in point 3 of the instruction, "cannot be surrendered to institutions which could not assure their Christian education." Jewish parents reclaiming children whom they had previously confided to Catholic institutions could get them back (point 5 of the instruction), provided the children had not been baptized. This is a decision that has been approved by the Holy Father, says the last line of the document. (I am grateful to Michael Marrus for providing me with a copy. For press coverage, see, for example, *The New York Times* of January 9, 2005, and an opinion piece by Daniel Goldhagen in *Le Monde*—"Non, Pie XII n'etait pas un saint"—of January 15, 2005.)

†As Ambassador Bliss Lane put it succinctly in his book, "both government and antigovernment sources admitted that it was not spontaneous, but a carefully organized plot" (Bliss Lane, *I Saw Poland,* p. 248).

The crux lay somewhere else, however, and the real challenge—as the Polish intellectual elite knew right away and as some historians, notably Krystyna Kersten, persistently repeated—was to acknowledge and comprehend the mass-scale involvement of Poles from all walks of life in a murderous assault on their Jewish fellow citizens one year after the war. Neither the Communist authorities nor the Catholic church, who rarely agreed on anything in this period, wanted to confront society on this issue.

Nothing on the murderous scale of the Kielce pogrom fit into the repertoire of traditional Polish anti-Semitism, and the customary historiography of the war additionally rendered the episode an emotional enigma. How could one victim assault another, even more cruelly victimized by the Nazis? The question "How could a pogrom like this take place in Poland one year after the war?" was posed by Łoziński's interviewer to every interviewee, and they were all baffled. When asked a leading question some, as I have indicated, readily subscribed to the notion that it was a *prowokacja,* but to the more thoughtful this idea did not bring relief.

Familiar categories are not easily applicable to this story. In the minds of the perpetrators, a sort of justice was administered in Kielce on that day: the Jews got what they deserved. I find the terms "pogrom" and *prowokacja* misleading in denoting episodes of collective behavior such as took place in Kielce.* They relegate the phenomenon to the repertoire of "mob behavior," attributing it implicitly to socially marginal malcontents presumably acting out their frustrations and quite frequently manipulated to do so by unscrupulous agents of the ruling strata, who thus deflect the resolution of mounting social conflicts. But on July 4, 1946, in Kielce, we did not see an unexpected blowup by the lumpen proletariat. Instead, it was Mr. (and Mrs.) Tout-le-Monde, the Mom-and-Pop crowd, deliberate and very much at ease with what they were doing.

One should rather turn to lynching as a useful concept for grappling with such a reality. As to the canard of Jews killing Christian children for blood, which so effectively mobilized people for action, it is perhaps analogous to the imaginary terror of "southern whites, [who] in their belief that black men were preoccupied with having intercourse with white

Pogrom kielecki, or "Kielce pogrom," is by now a proper name denoting the event, and to try to change or substitute it for the sake of conceptual exactitude would result in confusion.

women, were largely battling a monster of their own creation: the long-standing sexual access to black women that white men had enjoyed."[80]

In other words, it was not Jewish violence against Poles (whether innocent children or, for that matter, adults, as put forth in that other canard, which declared Jews responsible for bringing Communism to Poland) that made their continuous presence in Poland unbearable, but the other way around. The conceptual and emotional fog veiling this story lifts somewhat only after we recognize that Jewish survivors were an unbearable sore spot *because they had been victimized* by their Polish neighbors—for centuries, but especially during the Nazi occupation. The wartime historical record, its postwar social consequences, and the findings of experimental psychology all bear this out: people have a propensity to hate those whom they have injured.

This was not an unexpected, spontaneous outburst. Episodes of collective violence that from a distance appear random and elemental are on close scrutiny semantically rich. Virtually every moment is endowed with significance, as people continuously communicate and comment about what they are doing, through symbolic shortcuts and by talking incessantly.[81] As evidenced in depositions from the post-Kielce trials, ongoing conversations during the pogrom were voluminous.

A barber, Tadeusz Szcześniak, who drew a seven-year sentence in the first Kielce trial, thus began his deposition: "I went for a walk and on the corner of Sienkiewicza and Planty I joined some women who were talking and gesticulating wildly, and I heard what sounded like agitation that Poland had three governments [Polish, Russian, and Jewish], that after the present events the newspapers would again surely write, as they did after anti-Jewish riots in Kraków, that they were inspired, provoked, and staged by the National Armed Forces [an anti-Communist conspiratorial organization]. The women then commented ironically that after what happened people should vote 'Three times yes,' and other things like that."[82] The man who witnessed the leisurely stoning of a Jewish youth in the afternoon was struck, as he told the filmmaker, by the sight of a crowd plunged in animated conversation (*"rozgadanie tłumu"*). Abram Moszkowicz and Regina Fisz talked with their would-be murderers while they were being transported outside of Kielce, tried to negotiate terms of release, and argued back and forth. Rachela Finkelsztajn described the intense, long negotiations that preceded the mass murder of Radziłów Jews on July 7, 1941.[83] That same July, near Szczuczyn, a Jewish pastry cook named Magik talked to his murderer, Franek Konopko, all the way to the spot in the Jewish cemetery where he was clubbed to death.

My point is this: the perpetrators involved in collective episodes of anti-Jewish violence gave plenty of thought to what they were doing, and talked about what they were doing as well. Their acts were deliberate, weighed, tested against the arguments of victims, and socially sanctioned in multifaceted exchanges with fellow miscreants.*

The first anniversary of the pogrom was marked by the unveiling of a memorial plaque at the Kielce Jewish cemetery. Afterward, for several decades, the issue sank into oblivion. In Communist Poland, the Kielce pogrom remained a taboo subject. The silence of the authorities, the silence of the Catholic church, and the silence of fellow passengers in a train compartment from among whom a Jew had been plucked for slaughter—all were piercingly resounding statements. And they carried the selfsame profoundly disturbing message, perversely imparting normalcy to what their audiences knew was a monstrous transgression.

The story appropriately ends where it began, with matzo. The building at Planty 7 was sealed at some point that day by security forces. Armed guards were posted there after the events, so the premises of the Jewish Committee would not be completely looted. As the Committee decided to close for business in the aftermath of July 4, a number of Jews returned to the building to collect what remained of their files and other personal items, and move out. In sifting through the debris they found some intact provisions, canned food, and packages of matzo. They couldn't, or wouldn't, take foodstuffs with them, and put everything out for anyone interested to pick up. The Polish woman who lived next door and was interviewed in 1987 for the documentary film *Witnesses* smiled in fond memory of the moment. A lot of people helped themselves to canned food, she said on camera, and "they also took matzo because it tastes good. I liked it too, why not." Łoziński's

---

*Indeed, they kept talking about their misdeeds for years. "Jan Cytrynowicz (Jewish by birth), a harness maker, lived in Wizna before the war and had been baptized there as a child. He lived in Jedwabne after the war and now lives in Łomża: 'I came to Jedwabne after the war and lived with my Polish stepmother. My drinking buddies didn't know about my origins, so after a few drinks they'd start their stories: "I chased that one," "I stabbed that one hard." They were proud if they had killed two or three Jews'" (Anna Bikont, "'We of Jedwabne,'" in *The Neighbors Respond*, p. 276).

assistant, who was conducting the interview, immediately asked a follow-up question: And what about the blood of Christian children that people believed Jews were using to produce matzo? The lady smiled again, shrugged her shoulders, and dismissed the question with a chuckle.

5

BLINDED BY SOCIAL DISTANCE

ONE STRIKING FEATURE in the story of the Kielce pogrom and its aftermath is the response to the pogrom by the elite of Polish intelligentsia. It is not so much that they spoke honorably and without equivocation; one wouldn't expect anything different from individuals who were well educated, sensitive, and intellectually honest. What strikes me as a puzzle is how an entire milieu—precisely a milieu of brilliant intellectuals—could have been so totally unprepared for what had happened. Why did the intensity of Polish anti-Semitism surprise those insightful, sharp, and well-informed observers of Polish society? What made them unable to read the mood of a society that they prided themselves on understanding, shaping, describing, and influencing as its most distinguished writers, poets, and educators? To answer these questions, we need to consider how the wartime Jewish catastrophe was portrayed at the time.

Jews were an elusive subject, and while their fate after the war was rooted in wartime experience, it was not clear what that experience had been and how to describe it. Everybody in Poland knew that Jews were being annihilated as the Holocaust unfolded, but awareness concerning mechanisms of destruction was different in different social strata and it was embedded in historical circumstances and concepts—war, resistance, occupation, uprisings—that were loaded with symbolism. Perspectives shifted and changed, and as a result the destruction of Polish Jewry was never told as an autonomous story. It was always part of something else, refracted through concepts and contexts that sidelined observers and commentators, impeding their ability to name properly what they had actually seen and recorded.

The initial postwar take on the representation of the Jewish fate during the war in Poland conflated it with that of all the rest of Poland's citizens. Politicians and intellectuals spoke alike about wartime devastation. "Poland lost six million victims during the war," ran a standard commentary. The country suffered a harrowing fate at the hands of the German occupiers, and as war losses were totaled at 6 million dead (inflating the real number by roughly 25 percent) the figure was sometimes broken in half by the specification that 3 million of the 6 million victims were Jewish. This established a numerical equivalency of loss between Poles and Jews, further reinforcing the message of a common fate.[1]

We should not attribute this conflated image to deliberate deception. On some level, I think, it carried a very important, noble, and truthful message about the war against Hitler. It pointed out that everybody was in it, so to speak, together. This is exactly what I read, for example, into the meaning conveyed by the first page of the first issue of *Odrodzenie* (*Renaissance*), the flagship literary-political weekly of postwar Poland. It began publication in September 1944 in Lublin, months before Warsaw and Kraków were liberated.

Odrodzenie opened its first issue with an obituary. The first page ever is graphically designed like a death announcement (*klepsydra*) of a type customarily pasted to a church or a cemetery wall. It reads: "For five years so far the Polish nation has suffered under the horror of German oppression. Polish science, literature, and art have incurred enormous, irreplaceable losses." Then, under the rubric "Those Killed by the Germans as well as by Polish and Ukrainian Hitlerites," appears a long list of names, among them Maurycy Allerhand, Marceli Handelsman, Emil Breiter, Tadeusz Hollender, Janusz Korczak, Bruno Schulz, and Ostap Ortwin.[2]

This is a statement made in earnest, with reference to an all-encompassing spiritual category of Polish culture and, by inference, "the Polish nation," where unequivocally Schulz, Ortwin, Handelsman, and Korczak do belong. I detect the same sentiment when Jan Nepomucen Miller, the leading contributor to the center-liberal weekly *Warszawa*, writes on its front page: "In this war with Hitlerism, Polish society suffered proportionally the greatest losses of any nation. As a result of the war, one sixth of the population ceased to exist."[3] One may find the passage conceptually awkward (after all, in multinational prewar Poland the civic and ethnic boundaries of Polishness were not exactly overlapping, and one should not use "nation" and "society" interchangeably), but the message is clear and authentic, and it mourns all the dead equally. As a great scholar of Polish literature, Maria Janion, put it in the title of her recent reflections on Poland's history and its spiritual roots, these were "our dead."[4]

The Rhetoric of Estrangement

But the story of the reception of the Holocaust began in Poland earlier, long before the war ended. Mass killings of Polish Jews, as well as of those Jews who resided east of Poland, took place in situ, not only because the most notorious extermination camps were localized in Poland but also because in countless small towns where a few hundred or a few thousand Jews were confined to their neighborhoods—by no means walled in and out of sight of the Gentile population—a significant proportion, sometimes the majority, were killed right there. In other words, the Holocaust in the East was not confined to the pitch-dark interiors of gas chambers and covered vans. It took place in full daylight and was witnessed by millions of local inhabitants.*

Hence a unique context in which the timing and the process of gaining awareness about the Holocaust needs to be noted with respect to Poland. Polish society had *contemporaneous knowledge* of the Holocaust—it knew about the mass murders of the Jews as they were taking place. Thus, when we investigate what was said about the Holocaust in Poland, and by whom, we must learn how this knowledge was registered and ex-

*I have argued this point at some length with special reference to Dr. Zygmunt Klukowski's extraordinary journal, *Dziennik z lat okupacji zamojszczyzny*. For a more extensive treatment of the subject, see my "Tangled Web: Confronting Stereotypes Concerning Relations Between Poles, Germans, Jews, and Communists," in *The Politics of Retribution in Europe*, especially pp. 87–92. I wrote there the following commentary: "The most revealing information in Klukowski's memoir is two numbers he quotes from a conversation with Szczebrzeszyn's mayor [Klukowski was director of the hospital in Szczebrzeszyn, and his journal covers the wartime history of the town]: that 934 Jews were deported on the first day of the *Aktion* and that 2300 were killed in town over the next two weeks. These proportions may vary from town to town and from ghetto to ghetto. I would guess that from the largest agglomerations a greater proportion of the Jewish population was deported rather than murdered on the spot" (p. 91).

pressed. Unlike in France, Holland, the United States, or even Hungary, in Poland (but also in Russia, the Ukraine, Lithuania, Latvia, and Estonia) there is no mystery as to when and what people knew about the extermination of the Jews: they knew right away, and they knew pretty much everything there was to know.

Likewise, relatively early, already during the war, Polish Jews took cognizance of the unprecedented character of Nazi persecution and proceeded to assemble documentation and historical evidence concerning their own annihilation. The best-known of these initiatives is the Ringelblum Archive, produced in the Warsaw ghetto. But there were more undertakings motivated by similar concerns—in the Białystok ghetto, in the Wilno ghetto (the recently published chronicle by Herman Kruk is a testimony to this undertaking), or in the ghetto in Kovno.[5]

The calamitous fate of Polish Jews is also recorded in non-Jewish Polish sources, such as individual memoirs, the underground press, and official dispatches of underground organizations. And it was a courier of the Polish underground, Jan Karski, who as part of his official mission to the Polish government-in-exile and to the Western Allies brought out the news and evidence of the Nazis' determination to utterly destroy Jewish life in the lands they occupied.[6]

What kind of public record of the treatment of the Jews throughout the occupation appears in contemporaneous Polish sources? By "public record" I mean documents—whether intended as records of actual events or as commentary—that were deliberately produced with an audience in mind, be it made up of readers of the underground press or addressees of organizational reports. The circulation of such statements, their reception, and the discussion they generated established the state of public awareness among Poles concerning the fate of their Jewish fellow citizens.[7]

Nazi policies against the Jews—special discriminatory measures, ghettoization, and then extermination—were written about by wartime underground Polish sources in a timely fashion, but sparingly. They were usually included under a special, separate heading where the treatment of "national minorities" was given coverage. There was nothing unusual in this manner of reporting, as it followed a well-established routine of state bureaucracy where such a distinction was maintained. What made it peculiar, however, given the circumstances of foreign occupation, was the absence of an overarching civic frame of reference. As a result the narrative about Polish and Jewish experiences under the occupation was constructed along two parallel tracks, obviating the common denominator of shared citizenship. The relevance of Jewish fate in the perception of Polish rapporteurs was to exemplify what the Nazis, in some not-too-distant future, were about to do to the Poles.* First they would deal with the Jews, and then they would deal with "us." Whatever they were doing to the Jews now, in other words, they were not doing to "us." Polishness as a civic category was, by and large, missing from the way war experiences were processed, registered, and written about.

I am not passing judgment here. I merely note a striking absence in wartime public discourse about the Jews. Consequently, there is no room in this rhetoric for what we encountered in the immediate postwar period: a matter-of-course conflation of Polish and Jewish losses. Jewish victims had not been counted then as "our" dead. Whatever else was on their minds, underground rapporteurs on matters Jewish did not seem to be writing about the destiny of Polish citizens. In Polish underground press and reports, Polish Jews were portrayed as "other." In some ways they may have even been inimical to the body politic, as their fate threateningly foreshadowed what was meant to happen to "us" next.

Needless to say, Polish Jews understood that their fate was bracketed off in the hearts and minds of their neighbors as the plight of a distant stranger. One needn't even reach for testimonials from "Jewish" Jews to demonstrate the point. The same was clearly perceived and painfully noted by fully assimilated Poles of Jewish origin.

In the first issue of yet another great political-literary weekly of the postwar era, *Kuźnica* (June 1, 1945), we find a beautiful and numbing text by the Polish Jewish writer Adolf Rudnicki entitled "Dzienniki"—"Journals." Rudnicki was in Warsaw, outside the ghetto, when the uprising started on April 19, 1943, and the spectacle of sympathetic onlookers who surrounded SS units shooting at the Jews from the "Aryan" side of the wall etched itself on his mind. He draws a frightening picture of German "artillerymen at Krasińskich and Bonifraterska Streets [who] were loading and firing amid an approving crowd. Children patted enemies on

*Let one reference stand in lieu of many to document the point. A preamble to an order issued by the commander of the Home Army, General Rowecki, on November 10, 1942: "1. Polish society is apprehensive that in the aftermath of the current extermination of the Jews, the Germans may proceed to apply similar methods of extermination against the Poles. I call for restraint and for counteracting these apprehensions with reassurances" (Antony Polonsky, "Beyond Condemnation, Apologetics, and Apologies," in *Studies in Contemporary Jewry*, vol. XIII [1997], p. 218).

the sleeves. Women's eyes followed the audacious runs of SS men up to the walls. One looked at this in disbelief. It hurt too much."*

"This cruel fraternity lasted for one day," wrote Rudnicki. Later, Polish civilians could no longer approach German military positions, as shots were being fired at the SS from surrounding buildings. Crowds of spectators nevertheless assembled outside the walls for the duration of the fighting. At one point Rudnicki came upon a young woman choking with tears. He tried discreetly to calm her down. She was in mortal danger should anyone recognize that she was Jewish, "and in this crowd that surrounded us," he wrote sadly, "just as in the city at large, we had more enemies than friends."[8] Czesław Miłosz's portrayal of the "merry-go-round" under the ghetto walls in his famous poem "Campo di Fiori" captures the same moment, and the same spirit among the onlookers.[9]

Another great Polish Jewish poet, Mieczysław Jastrun, who was teaching in the network of underground Polish schools, described reactions to the Warsaw Ghetto Uprising among high school students in Żolibórz (a neighborhood of progressive Warsaw intelligentsia) and in Praga (a lower-class neighborhood). "The majority of the youth" in Żolibórz, he writes, responded to the "last act of the tragedy of the Polish Jews with understanding and sympathy. But high-school youth from the Praga clandestine school just kept telling each other jokes about what was going on behind the walls" ("bawiła się po prostu dowcipami na temat wypadków za murem").[10] In the article "Potęga ciemnoty," which triggered the first wide-ranging postwar debate about Polish anti-Semitism, Jastrun described another scene he witnessed at the time: "young office girls . . . poured out on a terrace of one of the largest buildings in Żolibórz to watch from there the conflagration of the ghetto—it was during the first days of the Uprising of Warsaw Jews—[and] called out cheerfully in the spring air, shaking with detonations and reeking of smoke, 'Come, look, how cutlets from Jews are frying.' "[11]

---

*Adolf Rudnicki, "Dzienniki," *Kuźnica,* no. 1, June 1, 1945. This fragment was reprinted in Rudnicki's collection of stories *Żywe i martwe morze (The Living and Dead Sea)*, with some significant changes (pp. 301–311). The story is called "Easter" rather than "Journals," the word "crowd" (*tłum*) has been changed to "mob" (*motłoch*), the entire sentence about children ("*Dzieci glaskały wrogów po rękawach*") has been deleted, and the word "some" has been added to make the sentence read "Some women's eyes . . ." (ibid., pp. 303, 304). See also reminiscences by Professor Feliks Tych (at the time of this writing, director of the Jewish Historical Institute in Warsaw), who as a teenager hiding on the "Aryan" side in Warsaw came upon a German artillery piece, surrounded by a group of excited Polish boys acting as spotters, that was firing on the Jews in the ghetto (*Gazeta Wyborcza,* special supplement for the sixtieth anniversary of the Warsaw Ghetto Uprising, April 19, 2003).

That Jews were being made into cutlets must have been a catch-phrase in Warsaw's streets at the time. Fanka Gaerber was interviewed for Yale's Fortunoff Archive Project on April 20, 1983, by coincidence the fortieth anniversary of the Warsaw Ghetto Uprising. In the spring of 1943 she was hiding under an assumed identity in Milanówek, a Warsaw suburb. "I was the one who went into the city to get the food," she told her interviewer, "and when I went into the city I heard [about the uprising] on the bus and the train. I was dressed to look old and inconspicuous. There was a young couple across from me, and he asked if she had heard what was happening. And she said, 'They burned them alive, at least the lice and the bedbugs will burn with them.' I could have killed her. There were other girls saying 'Let's go to the ghetto to see how they make cutlets of Jews.' It was fun for them."*

A similar voice reaches us from England. Ryś Bychowski, a pilot in the Royal Air Force killed in combat during the war, wrote in a letter addressed to his father on December 5, 1943, about the estrangement of Jews from their Polish neighbors. We will find again the same blend of utter despair and surprise in voices emanating from the intelligentsia after the Kielce pogrom in 1946.

"I know that it is difficult in a short time to eradicate twenty years[†] of anti-Semitic propaganda," writes Bychowski,

> but I thought that even if the war against Hitler and common misery wouldn't do it, then this overpowering tragedy of the Jews in the years 1942 and 1943 would produce a revolution in the Polish mindset. Vain hopes . . .
>
> Today, after a year of systematic killings in the capital and in the provinces, the Jewish community in Poland has effectively ceased to exist. What was the reaction of the Polish nation in view of this unprecedented crime committed by a common enemy? My colleagues in the air force and in the army were either uninterested or openly happy about it. For weeks I observed young men contemptuously smirking at the headlines in the

---

*Fortunoff Archive, T-3104. In the reminiscences of assimilated Jews who looked inconspicuous enough to appear in public during the occupation, one often reads about overheard conversations among strangers, or about statements addressed to them directly by acquaintances who did not know that they were Jewish, where such sentiments were expressed. See, for example, Hurwic-Nowakowska, *Żydzi Polscy*, p. 154.

†Interwar Poland, 1918–1939, was colloquially known as *Dwudziestolecie*, "the Twenty Years."

"Polish Daily" [*Dziennik Polski*] that brought the news of the killings of Jews. They didn't want to buy the "Daily" as it constantly spoke about the Jews. . . .

I comforted myself with the thought that it was different in the Homeland. . . . But now I realize that the Jewish people were going to their death surrounded only by callousness, contempt that they were not fighting, and satisfaction that "It is not us." . . . Jews couldn't escape en masse because they had nowhere to go. An alien state was outside the ghetto walls, and an alien population as well—such is, I am afraid, the horrible truth. . . . I am almost sure that I will not return to Poland. I don't want ever again to be a second-class citizen and I don't want my son to face discrimination. But foremost, I am afraid to learn the whole truth about Polish society's reaction to the annihilation of the Jews. I could not live among, talk to, or work with people who took their destruction in stride, moved into their apartments, and blackmailed or denounced surviving remnants. . . .*

This story of wartime estrangement between Jews and Poles—and one could quote numerous other writings to illustrate the point—left a lasting impression on the Polish intelligentsia. I recently found a moving echo in a small essay, "The Evil Shadow of the Wall," published in *Gazeta Wyborcza* on the eve of the sixtieth anniversary of the ghetto uprising, in 2003. "I remember two things," writes Halina Bortnowska,

not from books or recounted stories, but the way one remembers a recurring bad dream. Spring, sunlight, April clouds; dark, im-

*Bychowski entered the history of Polish literature in a rather unorthodox manner: as a result of a high school fistfight. He attended the prestigious King Stefan Batory gymnasium in Warsaw before the war. One day he was insulted with an anti-Semitic slur and together with Krzysztof Kamil Baczyński and Konstanty Jeleński took on a crowd of schoolmates in a big brawl. Baczyński, who would perish at twenty-three as a Home Army soldier in the Warsaw Uprising of August 1944, managed to produce in the intervening years a body of work that secured him a place among the most eminent Polish poets of the twentieth century. Konstanty Jeleński, the only one of the three to survive the war, was among the founders of the Polish literary institute Kultura in Paris. An esthete, a brilliant essayist, and the lifelong companion of the painter Leonor Fini, he became a distinguished public intellectual. Bychowski's mother came from the assimilated Jewish family of the legendary book publisher Mortkowicz, and the letter is quoted in a beautifully written and illustrated family saga by Joanna Olczak-Ronikier, which won Poland's highest literary prize, the Nike award, for 2001 (Joanna Olczak-Ronikier, *W ogrodzie pamięci*, pp. 326–27). The English version of Bychowski's letter was published in *Polin*, vol. XIII (2000), pp. 188–93.

posing, and swirling black snow is falling, flakes of soot. "It's from the ghetto," says my mother, wiping this black snow from the windowsill, from the face, from the eyes. Of course one could hear during the day, and especially at night, explosions and distant shooting. It was not very unusual in Warsaw at that time, but it always brought fear. "It's nothing. It's in the ghetto."

"In the ghetto" then meant—not here; not where we are; this fire will not come here; it will not engulf my street, my courtyard. . . . Does anybody but me still remember that we used to say—"It's nothing, it's in the ghetto"? We used to say it to each other just like that, in a tone of comforting explanation, as soldiers must reassure each other that a particular alarm is for somebody else.

But today I am ashamed of this distance. I see in it the evil shadow of the wall cast over one's soul. It is as if the perpetrators of Warsaw's Holocaust managed to remove the Jews from the realm of human solidarity; and as if they managed to remove us beyond the range where we could experience it. What did I feel when the black snow was falling? Nothing. Nothing, really? [*Czy naprawdę nic?*].[12]

Bortnowska mourns her Jewish fellow citizens and deplores her milieu's insensitivity from the long view of six decades. That a member of the open-minded liberal Catholic intelligentsia would admit such feelings gives ominous credibility to an assessment produced at the time by an underground leader who was among the best informed during the war and in a position to know the state of public opinion in society at large.[13]

The commander of the Home Army, General Stefan Rowecki, in a well-known dispatch to the government-in-exile in London dated September 25, 1941, framed the issue as follows:

I report that all decisions and declarations of the Government [in London] and members of the National Council about Jews in Poland evoke the worst possible impression in the country. They really facilitate unfriendly, indeed inimical, antigovernment propaganda. This applies to the "Day of the Jews" [Dzień Żydostwa, an official seminar held in London and attended by members of the government and the National Council], to the speech by Schwartzbard [a moderate Zionist who was a Jewish representative on the National Council], to the nomination of

Lieberman [a well-known lawyer, a Pole of Jewish origin, appointed minister of justice in London], and to the official greetings [published and broadcast over the radio to occupied
Poland] on the occasion of the Jewish New Year. Please accept it
as a fact that the overwhelming majority of the country is anti-
Semitic. Even the Socialists are not an exception. There are only
differences about tactics. Almost nobody recommends emulating German methods. These methods evoked feelings of compassion, which diminished after the two occupations were
unified [that is, after the Germans invaded Russia] and people
got acquainted with Jewish behavior in the east.[14]

And then Rowecki, who was by no stretch of the imagination an anti-
Semite, writes this concluding sentence: "I don't know the reasons compelling the government to make such moves, but here, in the home
country, they rapidly diminish its popularity."[15]

Rowecki was not a politician, he did not speak on behalf of a party
program, and he did not advocate an ideological point. He was a well
respected, unprejudiced, moderate, very well informed, dedicated public
servant advising his government on a matter of public interest. And it
was his best judgment that the government should stay away from anything that could be construed as advocacy on behalf of the Jews.

A Warning

Thus, by the second year of the war even timid institutional efforts to
cast patriotic propaganda in a civic frame where Poles and Jews as fellow
citizens were treated alike fell on hostile ears. It took no less a man than
Jan Karski to perceive that the Polish Jewish rift in the homeland was
being made use of by the Nazi occupiers, and that this should be viewed
as a matter of the greatest concern by the Polish government-in-exile.
Karski was prescient in his report "The Jewish Problem in Poland Under
the Occupations."[16] He presented his observations to the government-
in-exile while it was still in France, where he arrived as one of the earliest couriers of the Polish underground, during the first winter of the war
(1939–40).

Nazi policies toward the Jews found support in "a broad segment of
Polish society," Karski warned. With all the hatred that the German occupiers evoked in Poland, "this issue constituted a sort of narrow bridge

where the Germans and a large part of Polish society meet in harmony." Such circumstances, Karski continued, could "result in the demoralization of large strata of Polish society, which would create many difficulties for the future authorities of the Polish state undertaking its difficult reconstruction." "To take a neutral attitude toward this state of affairs," he wrote in the concluding section, "might bring the demoralization of Polish society (mostly of its lower strata) and all the dangers following from only partial, perhaps, but in many cases genuine *agreement* [Karski's emphasis; *"szczerej 'zgodności'"*] between the occupier and a large segment of the Poles."[17]

All these passages, and all the conclusions of Karski's report, were suppressed by his superiors. He was ordered to rewrite them in a way that covered up the intensity of Polish Jewish antagonism before the report was translated into English and French, so that Allied governments would not learn the truth.* It is doubtful that the Allies were fooled by this deception, but most certainly Karski's recommendations were ignored by the Polish government. To accept them would have required it to take a series of forceful and forward-looking political steps, which would have to run counter to sentiments prevailing among the Polish public. After all, even gestures as timid as official greetings on the occasion of the Jewish New Year were rebuffed in the homeland.

A consensus of sorts slowly began to emerge concerning Polish *raisons d'état* in matters Jewish. In the "Situational Report" for the period November 15, 1941, through June 1, 1942 (that is, in the middle of the bloodiest phase of Nazi killings of the Jews), the Bureau of Information and Propaganda of the Home Army thus assessed the attitude of Polish society toward "national minorities" (*"Nastroje społeczeństwa. Stosunek do mniejszości narodowych"*): "Bestiality toward the Jews generates compassion and condemnation of Hitlerite methods. Anti-Semitic attitudes are be-

---

*The manuscript of Karski's report can be found in the Hoover Institution archives in California (Stanisław Mikołajczyk Collection, box 12) with handwritten inscription across the cover page: "Attention!! Pages 6+9+10+11 have double pages." Indeed, the doubled pages (6a, 9a, 10a, and 11a) are very carefully prepared. They begin and end exactly in the same place (once including a hyphenated word), for easy substitution. Karski was instructed, as he told me when I queried him about the document, to draft a sanitized version, omitting his description of the anti-Semitism prevailing in Polish society, by Professor Stanisław Kot, a close confidant of then prime minister General Władysław Sikorski. Polish *raisons d'état* vis-à-vis the Allies required that the matter be covered up, he was told. Karski's report was found in the archives by David Engel: see his article "An Early Account of Polish Jewry Under Nazi and Soviet Occupation Presented to the Polish Government-in-Exile, February 1940," *Jewish Social Studies*, vol. XLV, no. 1 (Winter 1983).

coming less violent [*"mniej gwałtowne"*]. But the desire for a quick solution
of the Jewish question after the war—through voluntary or compulsory
emigration of Jewish masses—is universal."[18] It was a matter, the report
continued, among other factors, of leftover Jewish property. We need to
read this statement in a spirit of sociological realism: in consequence
of anti-Jewish measures and the mass killings of Jews, a broad stratum of
Polish society filled the resulting vacuum and experienced upward mobility. This large group of beneficiaries, whose material circumstances
and prospects improved significantly in the process, had no intention of
giving back their newly acquired property or jobs.

So, with a proper caveat in mind—while remembering that there
were people like Jan Karski, or like the entire milieu of Żegota, who
placed assistance to the Jews and a compassionate response to their
tragedy by non-Jewish Poles at the heart of its activities and concerns—
one must recognize that the catastrophe of Polish Jewry was not among
the central preoccupations of the institutions that together made up the
vast and unique phenomenon known as the Polish Underground State
(Polskie Państwo Podziemne).* Whatever the reasons, and there were
many, the fate of Polish Jews did not trigger a special effort and mobilization of resources by the Polish state (in exile or underground) on behalf
of the numerically large category of Polish citizens who were facing a
unique and increasingly catastrophic emergency. Polish society under the
dual Soviet and Nazi occupation had suffered many disastrous blows, and
it needed sustenance from its authorities in London and in the underground, not censure. Accordingly—and also in order to present to the
Allies an image of Polish society unblemished by anti-Semitism—
Karski's warnings went unheeded.

*After the German *Aktion* in the summer of 1942, which resulted in the deportation of
more than 300,000 Jews from the Warsaw ghetto to the extermination camp in Treblinka,
a Committee to Assist the Jews was established in Warsaw. It assembled representatives
from several Polish organizations and political parties and was financed by the office of the
plenipotentiary (*delegatura*) of the Polish government-in-exile. On December 4, 1942, the
committee reconstituted itself into the Council to Bring Assistance to Jews (Rada Pomocy
Żydom), or Żegota, which included also a representative of the Bund and a Zionist representative. The council distributed significant funds provided by the plenipotentiary for assistance to Jews hiding in "Aryan" areas, organized safe houses and forged identity cards, and
lobbied underground organizations to condemn and punish Poles who assisted in the persecution of the Jews and who blackmailed those hiding under assumed identities. It is impossible to gauge the impact of Żegota's work with exactitude, but it certainly saved the lives of
possibly thousands of Jews. The standard reference on Żegota is Teresa Prekerowa's *Konspiracyjna Rada Pomocy Żydom w Warszawie, 1942–45.*

The Forgotten Interface

As I stated earlier, the basic German goal—total eradication of Jewish life—became transparent to Polish witnesses of the Holocaust as soon as the Nazis began its implementation. It was duly recorded in the underground press and in the reports of various organizations. But the rapporteurs paid only scant attention to the manner of *interaction* between Jews and their Polish neighbors at various stages of the process, though this was of crucial importance in the Jewish experience. When the Jewish population was confined to specially designated ghettos, forced changes of residence generated a volume of such interactions, as later did, by definition, life on the so-called Aryan side. The very precise moments of final "resettlement," the *Aktionen,* were accompanied by massive looting of abandoned Jewish property by the surrounding population—again, an interaction. The remarkable memoir of Szczebrzeszyn's hospital director, Dr. Zygmunt Klukowski, leaves an unsparing account of the role played on such an occasion by peasants from this area known as *zamojszczyzna.*[19] There was, finally, the kind of interaction which drew local people into committing acts of murder (as in Jedwabne, for instance), and this was even less visible in public accounts of the Holocaust provided by wartime Polish sources.

The overall fate of Polish Jewry in 1941 and immediately thereafter was sealed, irrespective of attitudes adopted vis-à-vis this group of Polish citizens by their neighbors, or the amount of help extended by underground authorities. But how many Jews survived in each community, and how each successive Jewish community was wiped out, depended very much on local circumstances and the attitudes of the surrounding population. This is not a trivial matter at all—we are talking about hundreds, thousands, tens of thousands, altogether possibly hundreds of thousands of human lives that could have been saved. Christopher Browning's *Ordinary Men* includes a striking passage summarizing the view of German perpetrators about the role played by the Polish population in rounding up and killing local Jews. We can gauge from this one example what a devastating impact the collusion of the local population had on the fate of those Jews who attempted to hide from their Nazi murderers. In Józefów, Browning writes,

Poles helped roust Jews from their dwellings and revealed Jewish hiding places in garden bunkers or behind double walls. Even
after the Germans had finished searching, Poles continued to
bring individual Jews to the marketplace throughout the afternoon. They entered Jewish houses and began to plunder as the
Jews were taken away; they plundered the Jewish corpses when
the shooting was over. . . . Virtually no account of the "Jew hunts"
(*Judenjagd*) omitted the fact that hideouts and bunkers were for
the most part revealed by Polish "agents," "informants," "forest
runners," and angry peasants. But the policemen's word choice
revealed more than just information about Polish behavior.
Time and again they used the word "betrayed." . . . The Jews had
camouflaged themselves very well in the forest, in underground
bunkers or in other hiding places, and would never have been
found if they had not been betrayed by the Polish civilian population.[20]*

Local people joining in searches, or hunts as it were, for hiding Jews
were a ubiquitous phenomenon. Alongside the German policemen, who,
as Browning points out, revealed the fact with self-serving satisfaction,
Polish sources—Dr. Klukowski, for instance—noted it with horror and
abomination, as did numerous Jewish survivors.[21] Polish historiography
of the war period, uninterested in the subject of the Holocaust in
any case, was almost utterly silent about such matters.[†] It sought to
neutralize the issue by portraying similar episodes as the isolated actions
of deviants or socially marginal individuals. But the matter would not
go away and evidence that could not be so circumscribed kept sur-
facing.

One of the outstanding issues in my mind after completing *Neighbors*
was to figure out how historians of the war period could have missed the

*Browning points out that the Germans were very eager to speak about misdeeds by
the Poles, while they were quite restrained and untruthful about themselves and their own
comrades. "Indeed, the greater the share of Polish guilt, the less remained on the German
side. In weighing the testimony that follows, these reservations must be borne in mind"
(Christopher R. Browning, *Ordinary Men*, p. 155).

†According to Ewa Koźminska-Frejlak, publications on the Holocaust in Poland between 1945 and 1947 constitute over 25 percent of all published scholarly production on the
topic between 1945 and 1989. The majority of these books were published under the auspices of the Central Jewish Historical Commission" (Natalia Aleksiun, "Documenting the
Fate of Polish Jewry: The Central Jewish Historical Commission in Poland, 1944–1947,"
p. 15 [in manuscript]).

story of the massacre in Jedwabne for so long. The publication of *Wokół Jedwabnego*, two volumes of essays and documents by the Institute of National Memory resulting from the official investigation of the Jedwabne murder, renders this question moot. It turns out that Jedwabne was but an episode in a two- or three-month-long killing spree during which Polish neighbors kept murdering local Jews in some two dozen villages in the Podlasie region! None of this had entered into the historiography of the period. *Indeed, it has scarcely been noticed by contemporary sources except en passant and in a most general manner.* A more important question arises, then: how was it possible that such a *wave of crimes* against Polish citizens, *committed over an extended period of time* by numerous Polish citizens, *escaped the notice* of the Polish underground authorities dedicated to the task of combating the nefarious and demoralizing effects of the Nazi occupation? This is a more important question because it puts before us an epistemological query: What else is missing? How much can be learned about the fate of Polish Jews during the war from Polish sources in general?

The 1941 summer killing spree in Podlasie offers a good test case to reflect on the matter—it was too bloody, it lasted too long, and it covered too wide a territory to have been missed by coincidence. *And in fact the wave of killings was not missed at all*—it was reported on, and the underground sources where it was covered are conveniently assembled in the *Wokół Jedwabnego* volumes—but the assembled information was immediately ignored and it never entered into the historiography of the period. Let us consider what these sources reveal and how they were produced in order to understand why the subject remained in obscurity for half a century.

In the second volume of *Wokół Jedwabnego*, a section entitled "Documents of the Polish Underground State on the situation in the Białystok region following June 22, 1941" contains reports about the killings of Podlasie Jews by their neighbors.[22] These reports were culled from three institutional sources: the Department of Press and Information of the Government Plenipotentiary's Office (Delegatura Rządu), the Bureau of Information and Propaganda (BIP) of the Supreme Command of the Home Army (AK), and the Military Historical Bureau of the AK.[23] In addition, excerpts from dispatches General Rowecki of the AK sent to London, and from individual AK officers who visited the area and reported to their superiors, appear in the volume. In some cases the officers' identity cannot be ascertained, so we are unable to make an evaluation, but none of the named authors can be suspected of anti-

Jewish bias.* Indeed, exactly the opposite is true. Given the well-deserved reputation of BIP as a liberal, left-leaning, and unprejudiced milieu which put out the *Biuletyn Informacyjny*, we can rest assured that whatever appeared in these texts cannot be attributed to personal or institutional anti-Jewish bias influencing the authors.[†]

This is precisely why their treatment of the subject, and their omissions, are so telling, for they reveal to us something much more interesting than deliberate distortions by anti-Semites would. These were reports by underground units obliged to keep their superiors fully informed, and we know that the people writing these reports did not entertain prejudices that would make them likely to gloss over manifestations of anti-Semitism. We also know that they were very able, judging by the subsequent academic and professional careers of those who survived the war. In short, what we read in these reports is as much as anyone was capable of recording about the unfolding events at the time, and we find in these texts the limits of the ability of underground rapporteurs to assimilate information about local Poles' complicity in the destruction of their Jewish neighbors. We are therefore bound to conclude that what Polish public opinion found so striking sixty years after the war—information about murders of Polish Jews by their Polish Catholic neighbors—was also out of focus during the war, and could not

---

*Stanisław Kauzik, whose Press and Information Department prepared the government plenipotentiary's reports sent to London, was a member of the liberal Labor Party (Stronnictwo Pracy) and a close colleague of the last prewar mayor of Warsaw, Stefan Starzyński. He was a man of moderate views, harboring no anti-Semitic prejudice. General Rowecki, the talented officer who commanded the Home Army at the time, had no right-wing sympathies. Colonel Jan Rzepecki, who was in charge of the BIP, had distinctly left-of-center political views and employed several Jews in his immediate entourage. The head of BIP's Information Department, where periodic summary reports ("Informacja Bieżąca," "Current Information") quoted here were prepared, was Jerzy Makowiecki, one of the founders of Żegota. The editorial committee preparing "Current Information" included Aleksander Gieysztor, Antoni Szymanowski, Stanisław Wertheim, and Stanisław Bronsztajn. Gieysztor, an eminent historian, and Szymanowski, a diplomat, had distinguished careers in postwar Poland; neither had ever shown a trace of anti-Semitic prejudice. Wertheim, killed during the war, was a liberal, brilliant legal scholar from an assimilated Jewish family. Bronsztajn, I think we may safely assume, did not much stray from his colleagues in his views of the Jewish issue. The editors of the "Chronicle of Terror" (another source quoted in the IPN volume) from the Military Historical Bureau, directed by Dr. Stanisław Płoski (again, a man of impeccable credentials as a liberal democrat who, like Gieysztor, would have an eminent academic career as a historian after the war), were Gustaw Kaleński and Adam Próchnik, the latter a prominent left-wing socialist and historian.

[†]The *Biuletyn Informacyjny* was the most important Home Army underground publication; not a single anti-Semitic article appeared in it throughout the occupation.

be sharply captured by honest and intelligent observers striving to report as well as they could the condition of Polish society under occupation.

What Was Recorded About the
Murder of Polish Jews in Podlasie

Immediately after Hitler launched his offensive against the Soviet Union, the Home Army command learned about Polish assaults against the Jews in the areas conquered by the Germans during the summer of 1941. "First reports from the conquered territories," writes Rowecki in a July 4, 1941, dispatch to London, "reveal instinctive sympathy [*"odruchową sympatią"*] to liberators from under the Bolshevik oppression in which the Jews partook to a large extent. In Brześć, Poles liberated from prison organized a pogrom of Jews."[24] In the bi-weekly "Supplement on Terror" for the first half of July (prepared by the Miltary Historical Bureau of the Home Army), the data are more extensive: "In a number of towns (Brześć, Łomża, Białystok, Grodno) the local Polish population carried out pogroms or even massacres of the Jews [*"dokonała pogromów czy nawet rzezi Żydów ludność miejscowa polska"*], unfortunately together with German soldiers."[25]

"The Germans were greeted as saviors," relates the "Supplement on Terror" covering the first half of August.[26] A lengthy report by a Home Army officer who traveled in early September 1941 through Zaręby Kościelne, Czyżew, Wysokie Mazowieckie, Białystok, Sokółka, Grodno, and Druskienniki confirms this diagnosis: "Poles in this area view the Germans as their saviors; everywhere they received the troops almost enthusiastically, with flowers, sometimes with triumphal arches, and volunteered their collaboration. This is true of everybody, irrespective of social class. Germans eagerly avail themselves of the offer. . . . The enmity of Poles toward the Jews is so great [as a result of prior Jewish collaboration with the Soviets, the author has already explained] that the local population does not imagine how normal relations could be reestablished in the future. . . . Let me relate an interesting episode from the road between Czyżew and Zaremby Kościelne," continues this rapporteur. "I saw no Jews in Czyżew, and on my way back I was told that all the Jews were sent to Zaremby Kościelne. On the way to Zaremby I saw a few carts with Jews going toward Czyżew. In Zaremby I also saw only a few local Jews getting ready to report in Czyżew the next morning at eight. The majority had already left a day earlier. There was not a single Czyżew Jew in town. Over a distance of a dozen kilometers separating the two towns, Jews are somehow disappearing [*"Żydzi gdzieś po drodze wsiąkli"*]. There are big ravines and ponds along the way and according to peasants this is where Jews should be found. This translocation is being carried out by Gestapo men from Małkinia."[27]

The mystery of the disappearing Jews is, usefully, dissipated by footnote 6 to this document, which directs a careful reader to pages 370 through 374 of the same volume. One can find there harrowing accounts by Jewish survivors detailing the killing spree that took place in both towns at the end of August and the beginning of September (that is, immediately preceding the said Home Army officer's visit to the area) carried out by the Germans and the local Polish "police."

A Home Army intelligence report from September 12, 1941, stated that "in smaller towns there is only a *Hilfspolizei* ("auxiliary police") composed of former Polish policemen and local Poles and Belorussians. . . . In town halls mainly the Poles are in charge," while a similar report from September 15 reveals that Poles were also being recruited in the Generalgouvernment to serve in police formations in the east.[28] And so it goes.[29] Attacks on Jews are confirmed by situational reports of the government plenipotentiary ("quite big ones took place in Łomża, Szczuczyn, Augustów, and Białystok counties"), as is collaboration on the local level ("at the present time almost all administrative positions, except for the leading slots occupied by the Germans, are in Polish hands").[30] An end-of-September note from the BIP refers to "the vengeance of the local population" on the Jews for their prior collaboration with the Soviets and specifies that while "there were no mass excesses on Polish and Belorussian territory, in the areas inhabited by Ukrainians, and especially those under Lithuanian administration, they were enormous in scale and horrible" (*"przybrały one ogromne rozmiary i potworny charakter"*).[31] In the "Current Information" bulletin dated October 23, 1941 (no. 18), we find a write-up about anti-Jewish terror in Wilno, where "Lithuanians are the butchers. Their cruelty toward the defenseless outdoes the wildest imagination. There is no Pole in Wilno who could speak about these murders without revulsion. . . . Surpassing all Polish animosities toward Lithuanians, feelings of contempt and rejection predominate for their cruelty toward the Jews. People say that there won't be any fraternization with the nation of murderers."[32]

The Limits of Understanding

Two phenomena of major significance are revealed in these reports and dispatches: the local population enthusiastically welcomed and collaborated with the German "liberators"; and it participated in mass killings of Jews. Both facts are mentioned but neither is followed up nor commented upon, even though their significance affects core tasks embraced by the Underground State, namely resistance to the occupier and preservation of societal resources (including human lives and normative order) for as long as the occupation continued.

The killings of Jews by Poles, and Polish collaboration with the German administration, are noted matter-of-factly as isolated, individual episodes. One wonders whether our sensibilities are so different from those of the wartime generation. After all, the story of the Jedwabne massacre created an uproar in Poland in 2000–2001, when it became publicly known. I am sure that the long-neglected story of Polish collaboration with the German "liberators" following Hitler's attack on the Soviet Union—even if that collaboration was on the level of local administration only, within a circumscribed territory, and even if the overt enthusiasm of the population spent itself after a few months—when finally written about will also generate a furious debate among the general public.*

Why did the information about murdered Jews not get proper recognition at the time? Why didn't it raise an alarm among the underground rapporteurs as a symptom of a dramatic breakdown in social solidarity under the dual impact of Nazi and Soviet occupation? In part this was because, as we saw earlier, Jewish experience was bracketed off and removed from consideration when the story of "Polish society under the German occupation" was narrated.† According to the standard ver-

---

*A standard theme in Polish historiography and popular memory concerns the enthusiastic reception that the Red Army received at the beginning of the war, in September 1939, from the Jewish population of eastern Poland when the Soviets occupied the area. It is striking that the similarly enthusiastic reception, as reported in Home Army documents, given the Wehrmacht by the Polish inhabitants of the same territories in 1941 (that is, *two years after Poland's heartland had been occupied by the Germans*) found no echo in Polish historiography at all. One wonders whether the persistent collective memory of alleged Jewish collaboration with the Soviets does not function here as a displacement of the collaboration with the Nazis of Polish peasants and residents of small towns, which is much more troublesome and difficult to square with the dominant narrative of the war.
†I know this firsthand, having contributed to the obfuscation when writing my *Polish*

sion articulated in underground sources, one third of Poland's prewar
citizenry (all the so-called national minorities) were left out of the story.
And for the next fifty years historians pretty much filtered them out.
Likewise, neither the killings of Jews by their Polish neighbors nor, for
that matter, the collusion of the local population with the German administrative apparatus fit into the dominant, heroic narrative about the
experience of Polish society under the German occupation. This also
helped to expunge the Jews from the binding account.

But there was, I believe, still another reason why the killings of Jews
by their Polish neighbors were not given proper recognition at the time
and continued to be neglected in mainstream historiography, why they
were ignored by the Polish intelligentsia. It has to do with myopia resulting from archaic, quasi-feudal residues in the social structure and mental
outlook prevailing in Polish society at the time. An "upstairs-downstairs"
phenomenon, I would call it, in recognition of how very status-conscious
a society it had been, with peasants (or, more generally, the common people) and Jews held in almost equal contempt by the educated strata.

A very important book was published in Poland in 2003, whose title
may be translated as *Broken Flight: The Generation of Postwar Intelligentsia Coming of Age, in the Light of Letters and Diaries from the Years 1945–1948.*[33] Applying
sophisticated and elegant textual analysis, a preeminent Polish sociologist, Hanna Świda-Zięba, sketches in this volume an intellectual and ethical portrait of her own cohort. Teenagers under the German occupation,
this generation of Polish intelligentsia attended the underground school
system and then graduated from high schools in the immediate postwar
years. The author dedicates her volume to her classmates, who received
high school diplomas in Łódź in 1948.

This group represented the last generation of Polish intelligentsia
still steeped in the traditional values and mental outlook of their stratum.
Wartime, Świda-Zięba argues, mainly highlighted the old value system,
and it was only following changes in the organization of schools, as well
as in personnel and teaching programs, after 1948 that "the continuity of
the socialization process broke down. . . . [W]hen I was young," she
writes, "I had the impression that I took life experiences with a sensibility similar to that of my parents rather than to that of my students or the
sister nine years younger than I. Our generation can thus be considered

as 'the last one in a row.' "[34] In Polish, this dramatic phrase, *ostatnia w szeregu*, calls to mind the last link in a long chain. It simultaneously alludes to duty and discipline, for, "the row" evokes an image of soldiers standing at attention, ready to sacrifice their lives, if need be. Indeed, the ethos of the intelligentsia, as Świda-Zięba reminds us, was that of noblesse oblige.

"Young people belonging to the intelligentsia learned quickly that they lived in a hierarchical society. . . . At the top of this hierarchy were situated 'well-brought-up people' [*"ludzie dobrze wychowani"*], in other words the intelligentsia."[35] An *inteligent* was expected to acquire a repertoire of appropriate manners and education and to build personal character suitable to carry on the intelligentsia's most important mission, rooted in the traditional ethos of the gentry and honed by the great Polish romantic literature. He or she was supposed "to be a repository of supreme values, the idea of Poland, and 'the spirit of idealism.' An *inteligent* had a keen sense of belonging to a distinct, better, and superior social milieu, and was supposed to behave in the public and private realm unlike an 'oaf.' "[36]

"Do not behave like an oaf" (*"Nie zachowuj się jak cham"*), "Remember that you are a child from a good family" (*"Pamiętaj, że jesteś dzieckiem z dobrej rodziny"*): these were powerful injunctions carrying the message of noblesse oblige and social stratification at the same time.[37]

"The notion of a 'superior stratum,' " Świda-Zięba points out,

> naturally invokes a concept of an "inferior stratum." . . . The world outside of the intelligentsia was encompassed by a different conceptual category—that of the "common people" [*lud*].*
> The "common people" concept covered those who were not "well brought up." Thus, it included the poor, well-to-do and landless peasants, skilled and unskilled workers, illiterates, the lumpen proletariat, but also uneducated (i.e., ignorant of the intelligentsia's values and manners) merchants and craftsmen. . . . Social reality in Poland was portrayed as divided into the intelligentsia and the common people. . . . Common people were "dumb" [*"Lud był 'ciemny' "*: literally, "dark"], lacking consciousness

---

*Świda-Zięba uses the word *lud,* literally "the people." But the word "people" has such an unambiguously positive connotation in American English that it is very difficult to convey when using it the pejorative and dismissive connotation it carries here in Polish (Świda-Zięba points that the use of *lud* and *cham,* "oafs," were more or less interchangeable in this context). I am translating the expression, therefore, as "common people."

(also in the sense of national consciousness).... Belonging to the intelligentsia—a superior, much wiser, and better mannered stratum—imposed an obligation; an obligation to treat the common people well but in the first place to educate them and to raise their level of consciousness, patriotic, educational, and hygienic.[38]

Needless to say, in all these matters—patriotic, educational, and hygienic—Jews (with the exception of assimilated Jews who belonged to the intelligentsia) fared no better than the "common people." But in any case, as Świda-Zięba points out in a separate section of the book, Polish youth devoted little thought to the Holocaust. The destruction of Polish Jewry was not registered by her generation of young Polish intelligentsia as a subject deserving serious examination. "I can only note this as an astonishing fact today, which I do not comprehend fully, but it was indeed so."[39]

Now we can understand how numerous murders of Jews by Polish peasants, even when recorded and duly noted, had been simultaneously ignored in Polish historiography and collective memory concerning the war. The tragic destiny of the country, forged in the crucible of the Second World War, cast the Polish intelligentsia as the main protagonist. It was the intelligentsia's last grand turn on the historical stage, where it played a hero (as a repository of patriotic ethos and an architect of wartime resistance); a victim (as Soviet and Nazi occupiers targeted elites for particularly severe persecution); a narrator of current events (through penmanship in the unprecedentedly proliferating underground publications); and eventually an interpreter of the experience, a record keeper, and a historian.

Furthermore, the drama of wartime experience was steeped in a rich symbolic brew combining the nineteenth-century *topos* of loss of Poland's statehood, the ensuing series of national uprisings against the partitioning powers, and the great romantic literature that had very effectively worked through these collective traumas to forge a modern national Polish consciousness. In consequence, all that pertained to war, resistance, or sacrifice—a spiritual realm endowed with symbolic significance—was sacred ground, reserved for a happy few, where "oafs" had no admittance and could make no contribution.

In the bifurcated world of "intelligentsia" and "common people," what went on within the latter category was of relatively little significance under any circumstances and became even less consequential when the destiny of the nation and the upholding of its traditional, most sacred values were at stake.* Honor, idealism, supreme values, the so-called imponderables, and sacrifice for the common good delimited a symbolic space where the lower orders, who at their best could be honest, devoted, faithful, and even good—when they were not dumb or "dark," ignorant, lacking in national consciousness or proper hygiene, that is—found no admittance. The collective significance of wartime experience was played in a peculiar key for which the "common people" had no ear. A proletarian, as Lucien Febvre reminded his audience in a lecture series entitled "Honor and Fatherland" delivered at the Collège de France during the first academic year after the war, did not give his word of honor. He might swear on his child's or his mother's head or, as in a colloquial expression in Polish, on his love for his grandma.⁴⁰

It should not come as a surprise, therefore, that what went on between Jews and peasants was noted by underground rapporteurs, but only qua local episodes without a larger significance. Such occurrences did not merit any other evaluation. They did not qualify, they did not deserve, to enter the mainstream myth-producing narrative about Poland's wartime struggles and victims. By definition, what went on "downstairs," between the common people and the Jews, could not have had a larger significance. As a result, even their murderous confrontation was overlooked, since it was confined to a social space of irrelevance.

There was, of course, local knowledge of the events, and it never dissipated, as journalists visiting Jedwabne sixty years after the murder of local Jews discovered.⁴¹ But the larger public, including the professionals whose business it was to register what happened (rapporteurs working for the Underground State and contemporary historians), could not transform this scattered *information about local events* into *knowledge about the epoch.*

Behavior that amounted to murderous assaults against Jews but

---

*I was reminded of the intelligentsia's dismissive attitude to the "human factor" when matters of great historical significance are played out while reading a passage in Marci Shore's brilliant forthcoming study of Polish left-wing intellectuals. She describes a conversation between the poet Władysław Broniewski and Aleksander Wat, sometime in the 1930s, after Broniewski's return from a trip to the Soviet Union. Shore quotes the following passage from Aleksander Wat's memoir, *My Century*: "When he came back I asked him about various things, including the famine in the Ukraine and collectivization, mentioning that the press had reported that five million peasants had lost their lives. And he said, 'Yes, that's right; it's being talked about a lot.' . . . And so I said to Władzio—I remember this exactly; there are moments in life you don't forget—'So, is that the truth?' He whisked his hand disparagingly, dismissing the subject; what did those five million muzhiks mean to him. He didn't say it, but that gesture!" (Aleksander Wat, *My Century,* pp. 85–86).

that took place in urban contexts could not be ignored; and these acts are labeled in the narrative about wartime by a term with an unambiguously powerful negative connotation: *szmalcownictwo*. A *szmalcownik* was an extortionist who blackmailed Jews hiding on the Aryan side, threatening to reveal their whereabouts to the Nazis unless he (or she) was paid off. The concept conveniently marginalized the phenomenon and circumscribed it. "There is scum in every society," a standard commentary on the phenomenon informs us, rendering the story banal and uninteresting.* Killings of village and shtetl Jews by their neighbors, on the other hand, have never made it into the historical consciousness of the epoch at all.

Lucien Febvre, a great French historian whose name I have already invoked, wrote an entire book disputing the attribution of one remark to the author of *Gargantua and Pantagruel*. Rabelais was not the author of the incriminating words, Febvre argued in the conclusion of his *The Problem of Unbelief in the XVIth Century: The Religion of Rabelais*, because one could not be an atheist then.[42] The rules of language usage simply did not allow for articulation of godlessness. Until very recently, it was impossible in public discourse in Poland to attribute collaboration with the Nazis, or murder of the Jews, to anyone except socially marginal, or socially deviant, fringe elements. Since, in addition, from the vantage point of Polish underground sources of the period, the Jews were not counted among "our dead" and yet by the end of the war they were dead, and since the story of their death could not be told as it had happened, eventually Polish and Jewish deaths were conflated into one narrative. Not out of ill will, it seems to me, but because the right words and concepts to tell the story *wie es eigentlich gewesen*, as it had really happened, were missing.

This is why the Polish intelligentsia was so stunned by postwar outbursts of anti-Semitism. It had recorded, but did not process, the deadly wartime violence administered to Jews by Polish neighbors. Consequently, it was taken aback by the center-stage (because urban and including the cultural capital of the nation, Kraków), lynching-like (be-

*This, incidentally, also turns out to be an illusion, as demonstrated in two recent studies—an MA thesis written at Warsaw University by Anita Rodek entitled *Tzw. szmalcownicy: Warszawa i okolice (1940–1944)*, and Professor Jan Grabowski's monograph *"Ja tego Żyda znam!" Szantażowanie Żydów w Warszawie, 1939–1943.*

cause involving mom-and-pop participation) pogroms. If the Nazis had eradicated Jewish life in view of stunned and traumatized (rather than mostly indifferent and partly complicitous) Polish neighbors, postwar anti-Semitic violence would have been a practical and a psychological impossibility.

6

ŻYDOKOMUNA

THE POINT OF CONTACT among three themes that we have followed in this book—Jews, Communism, and Polish anti-Semitism—is conveniently provided by a stereotype conveyed in one word: *żydokomuna*. "Judeo-Communism," *żydokomuna*, is primarily an anti-Semitic slur which informs us about the relationship between Poles and Communism. But since the subject of this book is Polish anti-Semitism after Auschwitz, I take up some of *żydokomuna*'s stereotypical assertions—specifically, that Jews had en masse supported Communism in Poland before the war and made up a vast majority of its adherents, while after the war they enjoyed a privileged position in the regime and benefited from it while imposing it on everybody else. I propose to first examine the stereotype as it emerges in the years prior to the imposition of Communism in Poland, in order to help readers make up their minds "whether the 'Jewish Communism' myth bears any relationship to the actual behaviour of Jews." [1]

The Interwar Context

As a preliminary to this inquiry it may be useful to keep in mind that the universalist and egalitarian impetus of Marxism could be very appealing to anyone confronted by the social inequalities of early twentieth-century Europe. No one was immune to this appeal—neither German workers nor French intellectuals nor East European Jews. National minorities in Eastern Europe were affected after the First World War by economic instability, like everybody else, but they also found themselves battered by the process of nation-state building, carried on at a catch-up pace throughout the successor states of the collapsed empires. As a result, young people who for assorted reasons were peeling off from their traditional communities could be impelled into any of a number of trajectories: assimilating into the dominant majority culture; recasting their ascribed identity into the framework of a modern nationalist movement; or partaking in a project of mankind's universal redemption, such as the one so eloquently argued by Marxism.

"Minority" youth in interwar Poland (a mostly agricultural, poor country, riddled with ethnic conflict and pronounced class distinctions) hardly needed to apologize for being attracted to Communism—except to their own parents, of course, who must have been heartbroken each time they got the shocking news. The whole emotional loading of the term *żydokomuna,* stigmatizing such a life choice as treasonous and opportunistic sycophantism or as a mercenary betrayal of a higher cause, was deeply misleading. The motivation of youthful converts to Communism in this period was selfless and altruistic, and their own life prospects— notwithstanding the promise of a bright, happy future for generations to come—were virtually certain to include imprisonment, material want, and living on the run.*

Much in human life results from contingency and one cannot presume to suggest a binding logic governing the choice of one version of an individual's biography over another. But human beings try to instill some rationality into their lives, and to understand the path people follow and to evaluate their choices, one must consider alternatives not pursued. The three trajectories sketched above, to my mind, seem to be linked in a kind of sequence.

For those who found themselves unable to establish and continue their lives in the confines of traditional communities, assimilation presented the most desirable option. Both for practical and for psychological reasons the dominant culture always carries a fascination for stigmatized minorities. People want to belong, and it is in the embrace of the dominant majority that real opportunities for social advancement can

*True, their lives became full of meaning and camaraderie because of their dedication to a common cause, and the promise of such close-knit bonding offered a powerful incentive to join the movement.

best be found. The assimilation of German Jewry stood as a general example of such successful transition to modernity, and small, assimilated,
prosperous Jewish strata could be found in Poland as well.

But the path to assimilation was narrow, and getting narrower as
time went by. Aggressive nationalism in the 1930s combined with the effects of the Great Depression to set the tone of East European politics.
Inspired by Florian Znaniecki's *The Polish Peasant in Europe and America,* Max
Weinreich of the YIVO Institute for Jewish Research, founded in
Wilno in 1925, organized three contests for autobiographical essays
among Jewish youth in the 1930s. More than six hundred submissions
were received overall in 1932, 1934, and 1939, with about one fourth of
them written in Polish. Almost half of these autobiographies, rescued
from wartime conflagration, surfaced in YIVO's archives in New York.
One may find therein numerous confessions, often in a highly cultured
literary style, of unrequited love by young Jews for their native country.*

Barred from assimilation by ethnic prejudice, restless young Jews
could find homes in a wide spectrum of Zionist organizations functioning at the time in Poland.† Or else, they could embrace leftist political
movements advocating social change. The Polish Socialist Party (PPS)
had a token Jewish representation, predominantly drawn from the assimilated intelligentsia. On the radical left there was the Bund, the oldest Yiddishist Marxist party and the preferred choice of the Jewish
industrial workers, and, finally, the Polish Communist Party with its regional clones and youth organizations.‡ The Communist Party and its
affiliated organizations were illegal.

For the most part, Polish Jews were too busy eking out a meager exis-

---

*A volume including translations of fifteen autobiographies was published as *Awakening
Lives: Autobiographies of Jewish Youth in Poland Before the Holocaust.*
    In a different context, Shlomo Avineri makes the same argument in his beautiful essay
"The Presence of Eastern and Central Europe in the Culture and Politics of Contemporary
Israel" (*East European Politics and Societies,* vol. 10, no. 2 [Spring 1996]). The poem he quotes to
illustrate his point is by Uri Zvi Grinberg, one "of the most radically right-wing and ethno-
centric Israeli poets" (ibid., pp. 169–70): "We had to hate even what we loved, / We loved
the forest, the river, the well, and the mill, / We loved the foliage, the fish, the pail, the bread, /
And secretly, / Very secretly, we loved even the sound of their bells / And the gentile urchins
with their bleached hair."
    †Such as Betar, Dror, Freiheit, Gordonia, Hashomer Hatsair, Hekhaluts, Poalei Zion
Left and Right, Noar Zioni, the Revisionist Party, the United Hitahdut Poalei Zion Party,
and the Zionist-Socialist Party, for instance.
    ‡The Bund was established in 1897 in Wilno as the Algemeyner Yiddisher Arbiter-
bund in Lite, Poyln un Rusland—General Jewish Workers' Union in Lithuania, Poland, and
Russia. "In interwar Poland the Bund was an important political and cultural presence, running candidates in local and national elections, sponsoring Yiddish periodicals, youth move-

tence to contemplate involvement in any kind of politics at all. One needs some social capital, some leisure time, some sense of personal freedom to do as one pleases in order to participate in political life. Jewish youth in Poland did not have much of anything beyond an early necessity to earn a living and/or care for their younger siblings. When they did come out into the wider world—whether by sheer determination, good luck, or pure coincidence—given the choices at their disposal, they did not necessarily embrace Communism as a solution to existential woes.

Between the wars, Communism was but a fringe phenomenon on the Polish political landscape. The Polish-Bolshevik war of 1918–21, threatening the nation's newly regained independence at its dawn, put the Communists outside the boundaries of legitimate political discourse for most of the Polish populace. The Party was made illegal and its adherents were pursued by the police.

Even though the Party could appeal to a potential Jewish recruit by its uncompromising and most vocal stand against anti-Semitism, joining the movement propelled one, paradoxically, into the most radical and unequivocal rejection of Jewish identity. As Jaff Schatz wrote in his fine study of the interwar generation of Polish Communists, "participation in the movement meant . . . denial of specifically Jewish concerns and prospects and of the importance of a specifically Jewish self-assertion."[2] Early in the century the most famous Polish Jewish Communist, Rosa Luxemburg, articulated the sentiment with a literary flair in a letter from prison to her friend Mathilde Wurm: "What do you want with these special Jewish pains? I feel as close to the wretched victims of the rubber plantations in Putumayo and the blacks of Africa. . . . I have no special corner in my heart for the ghetto: I am at home in the entire world, where there are clouds and birds and human tears."[3]

It is safe to assume that not too many young Polish Jews, unhappy

---

ments (*Tsukunft*, SKIF), secular Yiddish schools, and children's camps. Bundists supported the international workers' movement while also championing a secular Jewish diaspora nationalism, in which Yiddish language and culture played a central role. In contrast to Zionists and other Jewish political movements that advocated Jewish emigration from Eastern Europe, the *Bund* fought for the rights of Jews to live in Poland" (*Awakening Lives*, pp. 430–31). The Polish Communist Party (KPP, initially KPRP) was founded in 1918 and joined the Comintern a year later. The quasi-autonomous Communist Party of Western Ukraine (KPZU) and CP of Western Belorussia (KPZB), subject to leadership by the same Politburo, were affiliated with it. The Party also fielded a youth organization (KZMP), a number of publications addressed to different social milieus, and a host of front organizations. Even though it had been made illegal, it presented lists of candidates for parliamentary seats and participated in electoral politics. In 1938, the Party was dissolved by the Comintern. Most of its leaders were arrested in the Soviet Union and perished in the Gulag.

and torn away from their traditional communities, were keen to em-
pathize in equal measure with the victims of the rubber plantations.
Communism was a means of psychological emancipation for young Jews,
on condition that they push the ghetto out of the "special corner of their
hearts" and sever familiar relationships with other Jews. "It could be argued that it was precisely the desire to be part of a united society with the
Poles that played a role in drawing some part of Polish Jewry to Communism. The Jews who became communists wanted a more just society for
everyone and believed in the Marxist promise of equality. They were
never out to get the Poles as a nation and they always stood in solidarity
with their non-Jewish comrades."[4]

A 1974 official Polish encyclopedia puts the combined total of KPP,
KPZU, and KPZB membership (in the peak year of the movement's
popularity, 1933) at 16,000.[5] Jaff Schatz, also culling his data from various
official Polish sources, gives combined membership totals for the three
parties *and* their youth organizations that are twice as high, at 33,000.
And then he adds, apparently omitted in the calculation, close to 7,000
imprisoned Communists for a combined new total of "approximately
40,000 committed Polish Communists."[6]

This is an unreasonably high evaluation. If one were to take a mid-
point between the Polish encyclopedia's estimate and Schatz's, one
would end up with a figure of 28,000. Say, to play it safe, that the total
number of Communists in Poland before the war oscillated somewhere
in the bracket of 25,000 to 30,000.

It is very difficult to make sense of such rough numbers, and they
lend themselves to interpretation either in the "glass half-full" or "glass
half-empty" spirit, depending on what larger argument one might wish
to make. In a country of 35 million, with several mass parties and a robust
political life (albeit conducted, since 1926, within the confines of the
limited authoritarianism of the ruling Sanacja regime), one might wish
to filter any membership figures through the prism of electoral results, as
the Communist Party and pro-Communist organizations regularly fielded
electoral lists in elections. In 1922, as the Union of the Proletariat of
Town and Country, the Communists received 1.5 percent of the total
vote and two seats in the parliament. In the 1928 elections, they polled
4.1 percent of the vote, their greatest electoral success in interwar Poland,
yielding 19 deputies in the parliament (of a total of 444) and 1 senator
(out of 111). In 1930 they got 2.5 percent of the vote and 5 parliamentary
seats.[7] All in all this was not enough to make the transition from "police
problem" into "political problem" in the life of a country.

As to the number of Jews in the movement, again we do not have reliable data. Figures fluctuated from year to year and differed from one organizational component to another. "All in all," writes Schatz after reviewing multiple sources, "most estimates put the proportion of Jews in the KPP at an average of from 22 to 26 percent throughout the 1930s"—say 25 percent overall. This would mean that at the moment of the Communist Party's greatest popularity, some 7,000 to 7,500 Jews—one fifth of one percent of the total Jewish population at the time—were involved.* Membership of the Bund alone, together with its youth organization, in 1931, can be estimated at circa 15,000.[8] Surely, the likelihood that an average Pole meeting a Jew would also be stumbling upon a Communist was truly remote.

To assess the validity of the nationalist-patriotic mantra of *żydokomuna* and Jewish malfeasance *after the war*, one must additionally consider how many Polish Jewish Communist cadres were likely to survive the combined assault of Hitler's Holocaust and the Stalinist gulags. Jewish Communists predominated among the interwar leadership cadres of the Party, on account of higher literacy rates among Jews and their better educational background (the KPZU and KPZB drew much of their membership from Belorussian and Ukrainian peasants and agricultural laborers). Most of the seats on the Central Committee, the field leadership positions in the Party, and "the party's *technika*, the apparatus for production and distribution of propaganda materials," were held by Jewish Communists.[9] The total number of Jews involved in these capacities could amount to several hundred, perhaps a thousand or so. But at the end of the era this very fact had a devastating effect on Jewish Communists, for when the dissolution of the KPP took place in 1938, scores of Jewish Communists perished in the Stalinist Great Purge. "This was a fate met by the entire leadership of the KPP and all those minor functionaries who fell into Soviet custody," writes Schatz. "The exact number of victims is unknown; estimates run from 'several hundred' to 'some five thousand.' In the opinion of the respondents [for his project, Schatz interviewed in depth forty-three Jewish former Communists], the truth lies somewhere in between. *The proportion of Jews among the victims of this purge was very high* [my emphasis]."[10]

All the talk about *żydokomuna* notwithstanding, far from being a "sub-

---

*Revisiting the subject in 2004, Schatz offers the following estimate: "Although interwar Polish Jewry was overwhelmingly non- or even anti-Communist, there were between 5,000 and 10,000 Communists of Polish Jewish descent" (Jaff Schatz, "Jews and the Communist Movement in Interwar Poland," *Studies in Contemporary Jewry*, vol. XX [2004], p. 24).

versive element," the Jewish masses actually constituted the most consistently law-abiding and pro-regime portion of the public during the interwar years. Without going into more details about the politics of the time than this presentation can sustain, let me simply note that Jews were often among the most reliable supporters of the Sanacja regime established in Poland after the May 1926 coup by Józef Piłsudski.* If one were to predict voter behavior in the elections held in 1928, the percentage of Jews in an electoral district would be the best indicator of support for the ruling regime.

Thus, in the pregnant language of the day (given that reestablishment of statehood in 1918 had been the ever elusive goal of Polish patriots throughout the nineteenth century), Jews in their overall political behavior embodied a *"państwowotwórczy element,"* a "state-supporting public," if you will. As two American sociologists concluded in the summary of their analysis of Jewish voting patterns in the 1922 and 1928 Polish elections, "the bulk of Jews drifted into establishment politics, disproportionately supporting the pro-government Bloc. Contrary to the myth of the 'Jewish Communist,' Jews provided only a small fraction of the electoral support for the communist parties. The evidence shows that not only were the overwhelming number of Jews not communist supporters but the vast majority of communist voters were not Jews."[†]

*The name "Sanacja" was derived from the Latin root *sanus* and signified Piłsudski's commitment to restore "health" and clean up Polish political life which, he believed, had deteriorated in the contentious and corrupt climate of parliamentarism. Under the Sanacja regime a limited political pluralism was tolerated in Poland, and only after Piłsudski's death in 1935 was a more rigid authoritarianism imposed. In the 1928 elections, Sanacja fielded an ad hoc political organization characteristically called a Non-Party Bloc of Cooperation with the Government (best known by its initials, BBWR) with which the conservative party of religious Jews, Agudas Yisroel (the party of "rabbis and Jewish businessmen"), entered in electoral alliance. "The alliance between Agudah and the Piłsudski camp was based on common values and ideologies, optimism and wishful thinking. As a fairly conservative, business-backed, non-partisan Jewish political movement, Agudah did not find it hard to identify in principle with a regime that preached non-partisan competent government for the whole country" (Gershon C. Bacon, "The Politics of Tradition: Agudat Israel in Polish Politics, 1916–1939," in *Studies in Contemporary Jewry*, vol. II, p. 158).

†Jeffrey S. Kopstein and Jason Wittenberg, "Who Voted Communist? Reconsidering the Social Bases of Radicalism in Interwar Poland," *The Slavic Review*, vol. 62, no. 1 (2003), pp. 87–109.

The best-calibrated instrument to measure the relative preferences of Jewish voters may be obtained by scrutinizing the municipal, rather than national, election results. "In December 1938 municipal elections were held in Warsaw, Łódź, Kraków, Poznań and 492 other cities and towns. This electoral period, which lasted until May 1939, brought great success for the Bund. The party made significant gains in Warsaw and Łódź and in 1939 in Vilna, Lublin, and Białystok. Joseph Marcus [a historian of the period] estimated that in seven

Pace the empirical evidence, the myth of *żydokomuna* was never intended "as a description, but as an epithet."[11] That is probably why it has had such a long life in Poland. After Communism collapsed and the Jews were long gone, the idea morphed into the familiar archetype of an all-pervasive Jewish conspiracy. As the popular weekly *Wprost* reported on January 18, 2004, in a nationwide survey of public opinion, 40 percent of the respondents declared that the country is still being governed by Jews.

Wartime and Postwar Official Soviet Attitudes Toward the Jews

The framework for the actual encounter between Polish Jews and Communism *after the war* is provided by developments taking place in the Soviet Union. It should be traced to the imprisonment and execution in the USSR of Polish-Jewish Communist cadres following the 1938 Comintern-ordered dissolution of the KPP. Soon thereafter an Old Bolshevik, and a Jew, Maxim Litvinov, was replaced as commissar of foreign affairs by Vyacheslav Molotov, whom Stalin ordered "to get rid of the Jews" in the foreign service. These preliminaries, as we know, were followed by a Boundary and Friendship Treaty between Stalin and Hitler. But perhaps the first truly defining moment for the relationship between Polish Jews and Communism in postwar Poland came during a December 3, 1941, meeting in the Kremlin.

The USSR had by then already joined the Allied cause. Polish-Soviet diplomatic relations were restored in the late summer of 1941, and Prime Minister Władysław Sikorski had arrived in Moscow for important discussions. His first order of business was to visit Polish citizens just released from captivity in the Soviet interior, and to speed up their recruitment into the Polish army in the East, which General Władysław Anders was organizing. The December 3, 1941, conversation between Polish and Soviet statesmen—Prime Minister Sikorski, General Anders, the Polish ambassador in the USSR, Professor Stanisław Kot, Vyacheslav Molotov, and Stalin—has a permanent place in history books if only

---

major cities, with a total population of approximately 840,000 Jews (Warsaw, Łódź, Lublin, Vilna, Białystok, Kraków, and Lwów), some 40 percent of the Jewish voters voted for the Bund. In the twenty-six cities with Jewish populations of less than 10,000 approximately 20 percent of the Jewish residents voted for the Bund, and some 45 percent for the Zionist lists. All in all, Marcus estimated, the breakdown was as follows: Bund 38 percent, Zionist lists 36 percent, middle-class group and Agudas Yisroel 23 percent, others 3 percent" (Daniel Blatman, "The Bund in Poland, 1935–1939," in *Polin: Studies in Polish Jewry*, vol. IX, p. 79).

because of the cruel cynicism with which Stalin responded to General Sikorski's repeated inquiries about the thousands of missing Polish POWs. The brief exchange of particular interest for our subject came up later during the same meeting. It was a throwaway, really, no more than a casual remark, and can be fully appreciated only in hindsight.

At a certain moment in the conversation, General Anders proceeded to describe in detail the supply and manpower problems he encountered while organizing the Polish army. He could put up eight full divisions, he said, as 150,000 men were available for service. "*Anders:* Perhaps there are even more of our people, but that includes a substantial Jewish element [*sporo elementu żydowskiego*] which does not want to serve in the army. *Stalin:* Jews make poor soldiers. *Anders:* Many among the Jews joining the army are speculators or convicted smugglers; they will never make good soldiers. The Polish army does not need them. 250 Jews deserted from Buzuluk after a false alarm about the bombardment of Kuibyshev. Sixty deserted from the 5th Division one day before an announced distribution of weapons. *Stalin:* Yes, Jews make poor soldiers."*

In the Soviet Union (and after the war, likewise, in the satellite countries of the Soviet Union), Stalin's word was law. "Jews make poor soldiers." This is arguably an offhand remark, but also a giveaway concerning budding official anti-Semitism in the USSR.

The Great Patriotic War—*Velikaya Otechestvennaya Voyna*—as Soviet official rhetoric would dub the Second World War, quickly acquired a mythical status in the Soviet Union equal to that of the October Revolution. From the 1940s onward, it was invoked as a foundational event by Soviet ideologists to legitimize Communist Party rule in the USSR as well as Soviet domination over its Eastern European empire. To be labeled collectively as poor soldiers, or as people shirking their patriotic duty, cast the Jews to the bottom of the emerging Soviet status hierarchy. As Amir Weiner wrote in his important book about the meaning of war,

---

*Kot, *Listy z Rosji*, p. 204. It is hard to second-guess a general on the subject of desertions from an army under his command, but I have not seen anywhere else any mention of desertion from the Polish army in the East *while it was still in the USSR*. To join the ranks was a prize most coveted by Poles and Jews alike, and it was systematically denied to the Jews, to their great chagrin. By joining the Anders army, Polish citizens escaped, to some degree, from the grip of the Soviet state, gained access to regular food supplies and medical care, and acquired a realistic hope of leaving the USSR after all. Jewish recruits did desert from the Polish army in the East, but later—when it was garrisoned by the British in Palestine. Among those who then left the ranks was Menachem Begin, and several others who formed the core of the Irgun and the Hagana; as their enemies on the battlefield were soon to find out, they turned out in fact to be rather good soldiers.

"in a polity that identified military service with local, national, and supra-national Soviet identities, and sacrifice on the battlefield as a sign of true patriotism, exclusion from the myth of the war amounted to exclusion from the Soviet family."*

One month after the conversation with Stalin, Ambassador Kot filed a dispatch informing the Soviet Foreign Ministry that "the NKVD was a source of suggestions that Jews are the worst element in the military, cowardly, always complaining, and that it would be desirable to get rid of this element."[12] Constantly attuned to what Stalin desired, Soviet insti-tutions immediately picked up on his moods, and proceeded—if one may borrow a brilliant phrase from Ian Kershaw's study of the Nazi regime— "to work towards the Führer."

In the meantime, Soviet Jews were spoiling to join in the fight against Hitler. As Soviet citizens they naturally deferred to higher au-thority during the hiatus of the Ribbentrop-Molotov Pact. As soon as the spell was broken and the Soviet-Nazi alliance fell apart, "a group of Jew-ish intelligentsia" asked permission to organize a meeting in Moscow to call on Jewish public opinion in the entire world, including the United States (Pearl Harbor was still several months away), to join in the anti-fascist struggle. Solomon Lozovsky, the head of the Sovinform Bureau— an agency created on June 24, 1941, to disseminate news abroad about the Soviet war effort as well as Soviet propaganda—passed the idea with a positive recommendation to his superior, a powerful secretary of the Central Committee, Aleksander Shcherbakov. One week later, on Au-gust 24, 1941, the meeting was held in Moscow.

The driving force behind this effort was a theater director and a legendary actor of the Yiddish theater, a towering figure of the Soviet-Yiddish cultural establishment and "a national artist of the USSR," Solomon Mikhoels. The meeting was broadcast live over the radio and

---

*Amir Weiner, *Making Sense of War: The Second World War and the Fate of the Bolshevik Revolution*, p. 231. Weiner elaborates, noting that "a barrage of popular novels" published in the imme-diate postwar years "portrayed Jewish characters as draft dodgers who lived the war years in the safety of the rear—and on the blood—of their Soviet compatriots. It was a short step from the exclusion of Jews from the Soviet fighting family to their isolation from the Soviet family at large. The wartime stereotype of the Jew as evader of the front occupied a central place in the anticosmopolitan campaign as it assumed an increasingly anti-Semitic character. This rootless cosmopolitanism was embodied by the worst antipatriotic act of all, the delib-erate evasion of the front when the motherland needed the ultimate sacrifice of each and every of its sons. The sons responded, except for the rootless cosmopolitans. They had lived the war in the safety of the Soviet rear, which did not prevent them from seeking medals for their 'sacrifice' when the war ended" (Weiner, *Making Sense*, pp. 229–30; see also pp. 216–22).

Pravda printed a dispatch about it on the following day.[13] Such were the origins of the Jewish Antifascist Committee (JAFC), an important wartime initiative headed by Mikhoels.

It took another six months for the committee to come into being.* By February 1942, Mikhoels and Shakhno Epstein worked out a specific program for future JAFC activities. In March, Shcherbakov signed off on a detailed blueprint, and in April, Lozovsky informed foreign correspondents that several antifascist committees, including the JAFC, had been established under the auspices of the Sovinform Bureau. In May 1942, during its first plenary meeting, the JAFC set "mobilization of material assistance in the West" for the Soviet war effort as one of its principal tasks.[14]

Stalin's Russia had to backpedal a distance in order to forge a positive image in Western eyes. Its ideological stance and the only recently discarded friendly relationship with Nazi Germany (terminated by Hitler, not Stalin, as those who cared to remember knew well) seemed like formidable obstacles to overcome. The initial success of the Nazi attack threatened the very survival of the Soviet regime: the USSR needed as much goodwill from the West as it could muster, and needed it right away. Without massive material assistance from abroad, the regime might have collapsed under the German onslaught.

But six months into the war, in addition to propaganda addressed to an audience abroad, Soviet national-patriotic propaganda designed for internal consumption was already taking a clear shape as well. It was implemented under the supervision of the very same official, Shcherbakov, who had approved the establishment of the JAFC. An important Party magazine, *The Bolshevik,* in January 1942 published an article describing the contribution of various "Soviet peoples" to the defense of the fatherland. The author was a vice chairman of the Presidium of the Supreme Soviet of the USSR, A. Ye. Badayev. He "gave statistical data on the nationalities of those rewarded with military orders and medals. First, he separately listed the numbers of Russians, Ukrainians, Belorussians, and so forth. At the end of this long list he then mentioned in a jumble and

---

*The JAFC had an important Polish Jewish component at its inception. The two most important leaders of the Bund, Henryk Erlich and Wiktor Alter, whom the Soviets had arrested in 1939 and had already sentenced to death, volunteered to play a significant role in mobilizing Western public opinion on behalf of the USSR after Hitler attacked the Soviet Union. They were released from jail following the Sikorski-Majski agreement, the NKVD head, Lavrenty Beria, personally received them, and they were tapped for leading positions in the JAFC. But in December 1941 Soviet security police had a change of heart and the men were rearrested. Sometime later Erlich committed suicide in jail and Alter was executed.

without reference to numerical data all other nationalities that were rewarded for their half-year participation in the war, with Jews coming after Buryats, Circassians, Khazakhs, Avars, Kumyks, and Jakuts."*

In actuality Jews fought the Nazi onslaught with at least as much stamina as any other "Soviet" nationality. In numbers of medals awarded for bravery in January 1943, the Jews were in fourth place (6,767), after Russians (187,178), Ukrainians (44,344), and Belorussians (7,210); half a year later, by June 1, 1943, they had taken third place from Belorussians.[15] Given that the total number of Jews was but a fraction of either Slavic nationality, and that no Jews in occupied territories collaborated with the Nazis (while Russians, Belorussians, and Ukrainians in large numbers joined various auxiliary military and police organizations set up by the Germans), the net Jewish contribution to the defense of the Soviet fatherland (as compared with the net Russian, Ukrainian, or Belorussian contribution) was nothing short of outstanding.[†]

Mikhoels and Epstein, leaders of the Jewish Antifascist Committee, took early note of xenophobic undertones in wartime propaganda. They sent a note to Shcherbakov on April 2, 1942, alerting him that "such distorted information could be taken up 'by Hitler's agents, who spread the malicious slander that the Jews did not fight.' "[16] But the omission, and then the denial, of the Jewish contribution to the war effort in public pronouncements became, in time, part of official routine. Ilya Ehrenburg, the most popular and widely read Soviet war correspondent, recalls in his memoirs how an official from the Sovinform Bureau rebuffed his

---

*Gennadi Kostyrchenko, *Out of the Red Shadows: Anti-Semitism in Soviet Russia,* p. 23. What Stalin and General Anders were earlier in full agreement about—the image of the Jew as a draft dodger—functioned in Russia as part of a long established stereotype. See, for example, Sheila Fitzpatrick's "The World of Ostap Bender: Soviet Confidence Men in the Stalin Period," *Slavic Review,* no. 3, (Fall 2000), esp. pp. 551, 552.

†Due to the shortage of German personnel, the Nazi police structure in the east relied heavily on local manpower to carry out its various tasks. For patrolling the countryside, the German gendarmerie established a network of small posts in each of the various towns. The ratio of gendarmes to local police (*Schutzmannschaft*), however, was initially at least one to five and worsened from the summer of 1942. . . . The strength of *Schutzmannschaft* increased dramatically during the course of 1942 from 33,000 to some 300,000 men. . . . Given the limited degree of supervision by the gendarmes, the local police held considerable arbitrary power within these rural communities, which they often abused" (Martin Dean, *Collaboration in the Holocaust: Crimes of the Local Police in Belorussia and Ukraine, 1941–1944,* pp. 60, 70). To take the full measure of the involvement of former Soviet citizens on the Nazi side, one would also have to factor in all the combatants who joined the so-called Vlasov army, as well as SS detachments (the Ukrainian division SS *Galizien* may be the prime example). Collaboration of Soviet citizens with the Nazis was a mass-scale phenomenon—except among Jews. "There were by 1944 over 250,000 Cossacks serving on the German side. In total an estimated one million Soviet soldiers ended up fighting against their country" (Richard Overy, *Russia's War,* p. 264).

efforts in the summer of 1944 to publish a book describing the bravery of Jewish soldiers and partisans: "There is no need to mention the heroism of Jewish soldiers in the Red Army; this is bragging," Ehrenburg was told.[17]

"As the war drew to a close, Jews were no longer marked as a separate group in either public presentations of war heroism or in confidential reports," Amir Weiner concludes in his exhaustive investigation. "Statistics of military awards bestowed on partisans in Ukraine by 1 January 1945 singled out a variety of nationalities, including non-Soviet ones. Jews were not among them. They were incorporated into the category of 'other nationalities.' Seven years later Jews were omitted altogether from the public celebration of combat heroism. In a mass-circulation book from 1952, which specified the ethnic breakdown of recipients of military awards in general and Heroes of the Soviet Union in particular, Jews were dropped from the list."[18]

Ignoring their contribution to the war against Hitler was only one component of the newly emerging Soviet policy toward the Jews. More significantly, a comprehensive "campaign to cleanse the Soviet elite of ethnic Jews" was put in place while the war was still going on. "[It] began as early as May 1939, . . . gathered speed during the Nazi-Soviet alliance, [and] became a part of government policy during the Great Patriotic War."[19] The Agitprop Department of the Central Committee of the CPSU spearheaded the campaign. The selfsame secretary Shcherbakov also supervised the Agitprop Department, which was headed by one of his closest colleagues, the leading Marxist philosopher G. F. Aleksandrov.

At the time when the outcome of the war on Germany's eastern front was still uncertain, Aleksandrov produced a report entitled "Selection and Promotion of Personnel in the Arts." It must have been considered urgent business, since while the Battle of Stalingrad was in full swing, in August 1942, he put it in the hands of three secretaries of the Central Committee, Comrades Georgy Malenkov, Aleksander Shcherbakov, and Andrei Andreyev. As a result, while the future of the Soviet Union hung in the balance, the most powerful men in the USSR were reading about how the Bolshoi Theater, the Moscow State Conservatory, the Leningrad State Conservatory, and the Moscow Philharmonic Society were guilty of "glaring distortions of national policy" in promoting Jews to leadership positions on their staffs.* "The Agitprop authors

*Kostyrchenko, *Out of the Red Shadows*, p. 15. In language devoid of any equivocation, the Agitprop report noted that in the Moscow Philharmonic "all affairs are run by a business-

concluded with a request 'to impose upon the Arts Affairs Committee of the USSR CPC [Council of People's Commissars—that is, the Soviet government] the duty of pursuing, consistently and steadily, the correct national policy in the field of art,' and for this reason they proposed that 'measures aimed at training and promoting Russian personnel' be taken immediately 'to partially renew the guiding staff in a number of art establishments.' " [20]

Soon the entire cultural establishment was busy eradicating those pernicious Jewish influences—in literary criticism, theater, and cinematography as much as in the fields of music or the ballet. Among eighty-seven Soviet circus directors and administrators, forty-four Jews were tracked down, while no less a figure than G. M. Malenkov, who supervised personnel matters on behalf of the Central Committee, ordered the dismissal of twelve Jewish journalists from the main Soviet sports newspapers. [21] In October 1942, the head of the Film Affairs Committee in the Council of People's Commissars, a certain Bolshakov, sent a report to the Central Committee's secretary Shcherbakov informing this powerful watchdog of Soviet ideological orthodoxy how he, Bolshakov, turned down Sergei Eisenstein's request to cast the actress Ranevskaya in "the role of the Russian princess Yefrosinya Stavitskaya in his new film *Ivan the Terrible* because 'Ranevskaya's Semitic features are clearly visible, especially in close-ups.' " To make sure that his diligence was appreciated Bolshakov sent along "several portraits and profile snapshots of her try-outs." [22]

With the passage of time the whole thing got messier. "Dear Leader and Teacher I. V. Stalin," wrote a certain Ya. Grinberg in May of 1943.*

---

man, who has nothing to do with music, a non–Party member, Lokhohin, a Jew, and a group of his close administrators, also Jews: Ginzburg, Veksler, Arkanov, and others. . . . As a result . . . almost all Russians have been dismissed from the Philharmonic Society staff: gifted performers and vocalists Sakharov, Korolyov, Vyspreva, Yaroslavtsev, Yelkhaninova, and others. And almost only Jews remained on the staff: Fikhtengolts, Lisa Gilels, Goldshtein, Fliyer, Emil Gilels, Tamarkina, Zak, M. Grinberg, Yampolski, and others" (ibid., p. 17). All of this could come about, the Agitprop report continued, because the cultural and literary editors of the main newspapers were Jewish. And there followed a list, beginning with the main Soviet newspapers, *Pravda* and *Izvestia*, with the names of the cultural sections' editors marked "a Jew" (or "a Jewess") where appropriate.

*There was a special routine in the Soviet Union which produced a distinct literary genre: letters addressed to Joseph Stalin. He was a wise, good, just, and distant presence in the lives of the Soviet people—a *khazyain*, a lord of the manor. Surely if only his subordinates kept him well informed he would set things straight, whenever they were out of kilter. People wrote about various things in their correspondence: they sought advice, complained about powerful local bosses, or communicated their personal loyalty and devotion even on the eve of being marched to the gallows. Anyway, in the topsy-turvy turmoil of Soviet life, it felt good to pour one's heart out to the leader once in a while. And so, understandably upset by the rising tide of anti-Semitism, Ya. Grinberg wrote to Stalin as well.

How can one explain that at such a grim time for the Soviet country a muddy wave of disgusting anti-Semitism has risen again and penetrated some Soviet institutions and even Party organizations? . . . There are rumors and conjectures that a directive might have been given from above to develop Russian national culture, perhaps even to promote national regulations for personnel. In bodies that manage art organizations this is mentioned with a secretive look and a whisper in one's ear. . . . Today Jews of any qualifications cannot count on getting an independent job, even of a modest rank. This policy has loosened the tongue of many ignorant and unstable elements. . . . It has already come about that some Communists (Russians) and even secretaries of local Party organizations . . . in a perfectly official way raise the question about official bodies being "choked up" apparently with Jews.[23]

From the point of view of our inquiry, what matters most in the events just described is the timing of Stalin's increasingly aggressive anti-Semitic campaign. While the earlier purge of the Jews from the Commissariat of Foreign Affairs (1939–1941) could be "explained" by tactical considerations and a desire to appease Hitler, after June 22, 1941, the argument could no longer hold water. The anti-Semitism of Soviet officialdom predates by several years the postwar conquest of Eastern Europe, and we must take cognizance that, as Yuri Slezkine put it in his important new book, "the creation of the new Stalinist regimes [in East Central Europe] had coincided with Stalin's discovery of Jewish untrustworthiness."[24]

The Jewish Antifascist Committee and "The Black Book of Russian Jewry"

In the meantime Jews, like everybody else (only a little bit more so), were busy defending their socialist fatherland against the Nazi invasion. The Jewish Antifascist Committee, launched in the spring of 1942, was very effective in mobilizing support abroad on behalf of the USSR. It spawned various associations in England, the United States, and also in Palestine, which collected substantial amounts of money to aid the Soviet war effort.[25] Solomon Mikhoels and Itsik Feffer traveled to the United States, Canada, Mexico, and England in the summer and autumn of 1943 and were enthusiastically received. Fifty thousand people came to an open-air meeting at the Polo Grounds in New York to hear them speak. At the suggestion of Albert Einstein and the American Committee of Jewish Writers, Artists, and Scientists, the JAFC decided to document the fate of Russian Jews under Nazi occupation. This project became known as "The Black Book of Russian Jewry." How the publication of the book was scuttled by Soviet officialdom provided yet another ominous signal of what awaited Jews in the Soviet Union itself.

The idea was discussed for many months, both in the Committee, with higher Party authorities, and with outsiders, notably the writer Ilya Ehrenburg. In his capacity as a frontline journalist, Ehrenburg was already collecting testimonies about Nazi atrocities from his readers. Many described Jewish suffering at the hands of the Germans, but also revealed the anti-Semitism of the surrounding local population. In the spring of 1944, the JAFC engaged him to lead the "literary commission" preparing the composition of the volume. Another great writer, Vassili Grossman, was drawn to the project as well.[26]

The initial idea was to have the volume translated and published simultaneously in several foreign languages, but not in Russian. In August 1944, at Ehrenburg's insistence, the JAFC sent a request to the Central Committee of the Communist Party to do a Russian-language version of the book too. Between August 1944 and March 1945, when Ehrenburg finally resigned in a huff from the editorial committee, a complicated contredanse took place, while parts of the manuscript were dispatched to the United States in anticipation of the forthcoming English-language edition. In May the Sovinform Bureau put together a new editorial board, which reviewed all the materials once again, solicited more outside reviews, and decided in the light of forthcoming criticism to eliminate from the testimonies all mention of how the local population aided the Germans and collaborated in the persecution of the Jews.[27]

The consensus view at the October 1945 meeting of the JAFC Presidium was that the book's amended version would soon be published in Russian. The new agreed-upon draft of the manuscript was sent abroad for translation and it came out—after yet another last-minute correction by Soviet editors—in New York in the spring of 1946.* The Russian-language publication of the volume seemed imminent.

---

*At the last moment Albert Einstein's introduction to the volume was suppressed because he wrote in it of the Jewish people as the nation that had suffered the most during the war and that afterward deserved an unfettered opportunity to emigrate to Palestine. "We consider this formulation about the history and the future of our people unnecessary," concluded the letter signed jointly by three Soviet editorial board members, Mikhoels, Gross-

But the political atmosphere in the USSR was rapidly changing for the worse. After a period of relative fluidity and openness during the war, the ideological orthodoxy known as "zhdanovism" was already creeping in. Frustrated by the continuing procrastination of the powers that be, on November 28, 1946, the writer Vassily Grossman, Mikhoels, Feffer, and Ehrenburg jointly sent a letter to the man who decided cultural and ideological matters on Stalin's behalf, the very Andrei Zhdanov whose name later served to characterize the period, begging for help in the speedy publication of the book. Somehow, they refused to read the writing on the wall: three months earlier, the JAFC offices had been visited by the secret police, who trucked all the committee's files over to the Ministry of State Security headquarters at the Lubyanka for inspection.

At the end of September a politically devastating report about the JAFC was forwarded to Mikhail Suslov. The JAFC had become " 'an ideological captive' of Jewish nationalism and Zionism," the reviewing commission concluded. " 'The JAFC employees . . . had not only joined the aggregate orchestra of the world's Zionism, but also found themselves siding with the policy of American Baruchs who strive for implanting in Palestine a mass intelligence service of American imperialism by means of a mass migration of Jews.' "[28]

More inflammatory language can hardly be imagined, and it clearly spelled an imminent criminal indictment. In October the report was circulated at the highest government levels with an attached recommendation from Mikhail Suslov, to disband the JAFC. Finally, on November 26, 1946—two days before the Mikhoels-Grossman-Feffer-Ehrenburg letter to Zhdanov—it was sent to Stalin. And there, at the summit of the Soviet pyramid, the final blow against the committee was held in abeyance.

Stalin often acted to keep his foes and allies off balance and guessing. In this case, he chose to pounce on the Jewish Antifascist Committee a year later, in January 1948, when he ordered his minister of state security, Viktor Abakumov, to kill Mikhoels. A car accident was staged in Minsk when Mikhoels visited the city, and his body was dropped on a deserted street. Abakumov, arrested by Stalin in a 1951 purge of the Ministry of State Security, later described the affair in detail.* The rest of the com-

man, and Feffer (Shimon Redlich, ed., *Yevreyskii Antifashistovskii Komitet v SSSR, 1941–1948,* pp. 243–44).

*"As far as I can remember in 1948 the head of the Soviet government, I. V. Stalin, gave me instructions to carry out an urgent task for the officers of the MGB [Ministry of State

mittee would die by judicial murder, sentenced to death after a trial in camera in May 1952, and executed in August. Of fifteen accused, thirteen were condemned to death and one died in prison.

Not surprisingly, "The Black Book of Russian Jewry" would not see the light of day in Stalin's Russia. In November 1946, Zhdanov called on the head of Agitprop, Aleksandrov, to deliver the coup de grâce to the project, and the philosopher-apparatchik promptly obliged. The authors of "The Black Book," he opined,

> advanced a particularistic and inaccurate representation of suffering. "The preface written by Grossman," Aleksandrov wrote to Zhdanov, "alleges that the destruction of the Jews was a particularistic provocative policy and that the Germans established some kind of hierarchy in their destruction of the peoples of the Soviet Union. In fact, the idea of some imaginary hierarchy is in itself incorrect. The documents of the Extraordinary State Committee [for the study of German-fascist atrocities] convincingly demonstrate that the Hitlerites destroyed, at one and the same time, Russians, Jews, Belorussians, Ukrainians, Latvians, Lithuanians, and other peoples of the Soviet Union."[*]

Once again, it is the timing of these events which is most significant for proper understanding of the Communist subjugation of Eastern Europe. Apparently, by 1947 the political scorecard that the Jews received in the USSR was already marked. In the words of the former head of the Department to Investigate Cases of Special Importance, M. D. Ryumin: "From late 1947 the tendency to consider persons of Jewish nationality as enemies of the Soviet state ... became clearly noticeable in the works of the Department to Investigate Cases of Special Importance. This directive led to the unreasonable arrest of persons of Jewish nationality ac-

---

Security] of the USSR—to organize Mikhoels's liquidation. He entrusted this matter to special persons. Then it was learned that Mikhoels had arrived in Minsk with his friend, whose last name I do not recall [a Jewish theater critic and police informer, V. I. Golubov-Potapov, who was also murdered on this occasion]. When Stalin was informed about this he immediately gave orders to carry out the liquidation right in Minsk" (Kostyrchenko, *Out of the Red Shadows,* p. 90).

[*]The incriminating fragment of Grossman's preface reads as follows: "The German race was declared to form the apex of this [racial] pyramid—a master race. They were followed by the Anglo-Saxon races, which were recognized as inferior, and then by the Latin races, which were considered still lower. The foundation of the pyramid was formed by Slavs—a race of slaves. [Then] the Fascists placed the Jew in opposition to all peoples inhabiting the world" (Weiner, *Making Sense,* p. 216).

cused of anti-Soviet nationalist activity and of American espionage."[29] The situation got progressively worse, until "on December 1, 1952, at the dramatic meeting of the Presidium of the Central Committee, Stalin declared that 'every Jew is a potential spy for the United States.' " However, as Jonathan Brent and Vladimir Naumov explain in a footnote referencing this quote, "*Stalin had spoken in this fashion since 1947* [my emphasis]. Ryumin admitted that everyone was guided by this dictum of Stalin. Stalin was said to have repeated this to several people who then repeated it until it became common knowledge of an opinion attributed to Stalin."[30]

I am at a loss to account for the anti-Semitism that so clearly emanated from the center of Soviet power. One of the great attractions of Communism, after all—for lower-class minorities and highbrow intellectuals alike—was an explicit and unequivocal rejection of ethnic definitions at a time when nationalist rhetoric dominated political discourse. But Communists in power also proved to be opportunistic *Realpolitiker,* adjusting to circumstances as they presented themselves. The fragility of the Soviet regime's legitimacy in the early phases of war may have induced Stalin, as Amir Weiner suggests, not to allow the myth of the Great Patriotic War to become "Judaicized" as had happened with the myth of the October Revolution.[31] Such "contamination" would have been almost inevitable, however, if the official Soviet history of Nazi occupation depicted the Holocaust and factored it into the binding narrative of wartime suffering visited upon the peoples of the USSR.

Anti-Semitism may also have been a lingering personal idiosyncrasy of Stalin. After all, many of the Old Bolsheviks whom he destroyed in the Great Terror of the 1930s were of Jewish origin.* Later, during the Great Patriotic War, he certainly appreciated the legitimizing force of the national-patriotic costume that the regime donned to shore up the fighting spirit of Soviet citizens against the Nazi invasion, and may have decided to stick in peacetime to what had worked for the Soviet power when it was truly endangered. Furthermore, it would not have been easy to find some other common denominator for perpetuating the national-patriotic message in a multiethnic empire-state. Naturally, the project brought out a familiar echo from Russia's imperial past—"*Bii zhidov i spasai*

*Weiner refers to Svetlana Alliluyeva on this point and then goes on to quote Goebbels's diaries of January 25, 1937: "Again a show trial in Moscow. This time once again exclusively against Jews. Radek, etc. The Führer still in doubt whether there isn't after all a hidden anti-Semitic tendency. Maybe Stalin does want to smoke the Jews out" (Weiner, *Making Sense,* p. 235).

Rassiyu" ("Beat/kill the kikes and save Russia")—an association that en-
hanced the nationalist credentials of the Soviet regime, perhaps, but had
to be disguised behind a suitable vocabulary that squared with Marxism-
Leninism.* Last but not least, Stalin was also preparing to unleash
another period of "great terror," and the banner of "rootless cosmopolitanism" offered a broadly appealing screen behind which a pulverization
of Soviet officialdom could be carried out one more time.†

In the end, at the conclusion of World War II, "Soviet society would
recognize neither unique Jewish suffering at the hands of the Nazis nor
the distinct contribution of Jews in the war against the invaders. With
the emergence of the war as the core legitimizing myth of the polity, Jews
were separated as *a group* [Weiner's emphasis] from the Soviet family. . . .
Whereas the various nations of the Soviet Union were ranked in a
pyramid-like order based on their alleged contribution to the war effort,
their suffering was undifferentiated. . . . Jewish participation in the trials
of combat service [was] ignored in public and denied in private. By
the time Stalin addressed the commanders of the Red Army, Jews had
disappeared from public representation of the war. The Holocaust was
incorporated into the epic suffering of the entire Soviet population, its
uniqueness for the Jews was ignored."³² Such was the official blueprint
for "the meaning of war" disseminated by Soviet propaganda.

The project of tracking down and weeding out the Jews from Soviet
institutions conformed to the regime's characteristic modus operandi
from the mid-1940s through the mid-1950s. "The Party's relentless will
to purge and its routine 'personnel policy,' " writes Yuri Slezkine, thus
"merged to become an exercise in investigative genealogy."³³ At the same
time, it was unlike anything that had ever happened in the Soviet Union.

> The anti-Jewish campaign was both public and relatively clear
> about its objectives. It was directed at some of the most vital
> and articulate elements of the Soviet state—and it contra-
> dicted some of the state's most fundamental official values. . . .

---

*This could be (and was) easily accomplished, as the regime was supremely skilled in
symbolic manipulation and propaganda—more so, probably, than widely recognized masters
of political propaganda such as the Nazis. Unlike the SS, surely the NKVD troops, who
guarded prisoners in the Soviet gulags and were responsible for the death of millions, would
never have adorned their uniforms with skulls.

†Jews tended to have more extensive family and organizational connections in the
West, which rendered them especially suspect in the climate of international paranoia that
prevailed by 1946 on both sides of the Iron Curtain.

For the first time since the revolution, the ethnically Jewish members of the Soviet elite were being attacked directly and unequivocally—not because of some "alien elements" in their midst, as in 1937–1938, but because they were ethnically Jewish. . . . The result was a rapid spread of anti-Semitic rumors, insults, leaflets, threats, and assaults culminating in the hysterical unmasking of "murderer physicians."[34]

Political cartoons in Soviet newspapers and satirical magazines from the period could just as well have been published in that Nazi rag the *Volkischer Beobachter.* A taboo of Soviet revolutionary etiquette—that pseudonyms or adopted names of Communists were never "decoded" in print—was broken. Jewish family names that had not been used by their bearers in decades were given in brackets, as incriminating evidence presumably, alongside the actual names of people who were being denounced in the press. Ever seeking comic relief, Soviet Jews fancied a little rhyme capturing the idiocy and relentlessness of the purge: *"Mark Avrelijj, nye Evrey-li?"* ("Isn't Marcus Aurelius a Jew?")[35]

To Aleksander Werth, who knew the USSR very well after a stint as a war correspondent in Moscow, it appeared that "in Russia cosmopolitanism ha[d] now become a philosophical concept and ha[d] been given a place of honour in the vocabulary of Soviet polemical writing, along with formalism, bourgeois nationalism, anti-patriotism, anti-Sovietism, comparativism, Hegel-mongering, and toadying to the West."[36] Given this evolution of the political climate in the Soviet Union throughout the 1940s, and the very close scrutiny, monitoring, and consultation that went on between East European Communists and their Moscow-based "elder brothers," the thought of Jews, or Jewish Communists, receiving preferential treatment anywhere in the region must be classified as political science fiction.*

*We should also be reminded that the Communist cadres were deeply suspicious of one another (see, for example, Teresa Torańska, *Oni,* p. 113), as the logic of internal power play in the Stalinist era (show trials and purges) set one against another. Thus, it is fair to assume that any putative Jewish cabal within the Communist Party—if such a thing were suggested by a conspiracy-theory buff—would have been promptly denounced in the exercise of routine "revolutionary vigilance."

Jews in the PPR

An eminent Jewish Communist and wartime guerrilla leader, Hersh Smolar, stumbled upon an interesting document before his return to Poland from Moscow in 1946. In the offices of the Association of Polish Patriots (ZPP), he was given a transcript of a conversation between Władysław Gomułka and Joseph Stalin soon after the pogrom in Kraków. The first secretary of the PPR pleaded during the meeting with the Soviet leader for a ban on the repatriation of a quarter million Polish Jews who would soon be eligible to return to Poland. Stalin was noncommittal and in the end did not oblige, but he commiserated with his Polish colleague about how each Jew taken separately was such a wonderful fellow, but as a group, taken altogether, Jews were a problem.[37]

Polish Communists were always preoccupied with, or self-conscious about, the Jewish origins of Communist Party members. During a crucial moment in the postwar history of the regime (and also a critical time for him personally), after the August 31–September 3, 1948, plenary meeting of the Central Committee, which removed him from the post of Party first secretary because of his "nationalist deviation," Gomułka wrote a letter to Stalin. Dated December 14, 1948, it apparently followed up on a conversation they had some time earlier—"I must have expressed myself incoherently and didn't make everything clear because I do not know Russian well enough." The stakes were high—Gomułka knew the rules of the game when a Party purge was in motion, and he was simply trying to save his head.

One of the three main points of clarification he offers in the letter concerns the Jews. Too many Jewish Communists had been appointed to responsible positions in Poland, writes Gomułka, and as the first secretary, he says, he opposed this practice because it thwarted the Party's appeal to the masses. Other highly placed Jewish comrades, the letter continues, did not follow his call. True, there was a shortage of Polish-born Party cadres, but still his former colleagues in the Politburo had allowed too many Jews to be appointed to the administration and Party apparatus.[38]

So Communists in Poland—including the very important one who held the post of first secretary from November 1943 to September 1948—like everybody else were of the opinion that too many Jews occupied positions of responsibility. This was a situation which, in their judgment, did not serve the interests of the Communist Party well. Additionally, Gomułka cleverly used the occasion to denounce the "low vigilance" of unnamed highly placed Jewish-born Party comrades who did not see as sharply as they should have, because of their "national nihilism," as he put it, what needed to be done to win the allegiance of the Polish working class.[39]

Terms such as "national nihilists," "rootless cosmopolitans," and "Zionists" (always pejoratively loaded when used by Party officials) were but the *Salonfähig* ideological jargon by which Communist functionaries expressed their impatience with the Jews whose existence, within the Party and outside it, evidently complicated the imposition of Soviet rule in East Central Europe. As Józef Adelson put it in his fine study, the postwar Jewish community in Poland appeared as a kind of "ballast for the PPR."*

Gomułka's was not some esoteric knowledge, and he was not reputed to nurse a personal anti-Jewish animus. Indeed, he had a Jewish wife. Ethnic background, generally, did not matter in the private lives of Party comrades. But in politics, as a matter of good politics especially, Jewishness in Polish Communists was frowned upon and tolerated by their comrades only *faute de mieux*. Jewish Communists were, for instance, routinely ordered to polonize their names. A commission that took care of this matter for higher Party cadres was run by Gomułka's very wife, Zofia, who was rather homely looking and, as just pointed out, Jewish. Turning around a phrase she apparently often used in exasperation when assigning people new names—"*Wygląd w porządku, ale co za nazwisko*" ("The looks— i.e., external appearance—are okay, but what a name")—Party members said of her, "*Nazwisko w porządku, ale co za wygląd*" ("The name's okay, but those looks . . . !"). Hersh Smolar draws on a contemptuous Yiddish word customarily used to describe religious converts, *shmad,* and calls the practice a *shmad protzedur.*[40] An ironic, derisive phrase was coined among older Jewish Communists to describe this state of affairs, and comrades who

---

*"Responding to manifestations of anti-Semitism, sending special teams to cool down public excitement after pogroms, the need for constant propaganda on this issue, having to answer the interpellations of Jewish parliamentarians, the stigma of Judeo-Communism with which the Party was branded, international opinion, which had to be persuaded that the regime wants to address the problem—all of this put a heavy burden on the team, which had a lot of problems to attend to already" (Józef Adelson, "W Polsce zwanej ludową," p. 405).

had their names changed on Party orders were called "acting Poles"—as in "acting director": *pełniący obowiązki Polaka,* or POP for short.*

Not surprisingly, POP Party functionaries suspected that their place in the apparatus was precarious and only temporary. The head of the regional Office of Press Control in Olsztyn could read the fine print already in October 1945, when he wrote this letter to Adolf Berman:

> It is becoming ever clearer to me that there is no future for us on this path, and that I am here only by accident, as an unwanted and alien intruder. Please do not misunderstand me: I did not have the slightest problems on account of my ethnic background; my views derive from more general reflections.... [A member of the] Jewish intelligentsia employed in high positions is an intruder, an undesirable phenomenon, tolerated even in the most democratic milieus only with deep regret because this is against proper "tactics." We know how closely our comrades investigate the sound of people's names, their facial features, etc., from the point of view of "Aryan" characteristics before they decide to appoint someone to an important assignment. How often they advise people to hide nationality, or even to change or polonize their names. This is everyday stuff.

Jews would be left in their positions only for as long as it would take to find a Polish-born substitute, concluded Aleksander Masiewicki, adding at the end that this was how the situation had evolved in the Soviet Union itself.[41] Since the very earliest moment of their postwar power grab— their *Machtergreifung*—the Communists in Poland had been running away from any putative association between Jews and Communism, which was hurting the Party and which they knew was on the public's mind.[†]

---

*Old-time Jewish Communists could be offended by this practice. An eminent Yiddish-language poet, David Sfard, spoke on the issue forcefully during a conference organized in August 1945 in Moscow by the Organizational Committee of Polish Jews at the ZPP, the Association of Polish Patriots. He described the dropping of Jewish names by Party activists in Poland as an affront to "national dignity" and to the "dignity of being a Communist" as well. It reflected an attitude, he said, that verged on adopting "a racist point of view." Also, the Party should not condone such behavior "because it opens the door to careerists who have the same attitude toward the Party as they do toward their nationality" (August Grabski, *Działalność komunistów wśród Żydów w Polsce, 1944–1949,* p. 86). Sfard, obviously, was a better writer than politician.

†A small but telling detail of this careful distancing may be found in the minutes of the August 11, 1945, meeting of the second highest executive body of the Communist Party: the Central Committee's Secretariat. The entire meeting was devoted to the discussion of

In postwar Eastern Europe, Jewish Communist officials were a liability impeding the task of Sovietization, yet several dedicated and talented Communists in Eastern Europe happened to be Jewish. "In Hungary, Romania, and Poland, a high proportion of the most sensitive positions in the Party apparatus, state administration, and especially the Agitprop, foreign service, and secret police were held by ethnic Jews, who had moved up the ranks because of their loyalty and now had to be squeezed out because of their nationality."[42] "In his memoirs Khrushchev comments on how Jakub Berman and Hilary Minc 'were far ahead of other members of the Politburo with their organizational talent, education, Marxist-Leninist knowledge' . . . [Yet] soon after the war [Khrushchev] cautioned Bierut about his choice of advisers, pointing to rumors of dissatisfaction with the ethnic composition of the Party leadership. . . . Bierut looked at him with his particular smile and appealed for understanding. He was aware that the presence of Jews in such high-profile positions could provoke resentment, but he needed Jakub Berman."[43]

Brilliant or not, Minc and Berman were certainly smart enough to know it all. "I was a cosmopolite soon to be discarded," Jakub Berman told journalist Teresa Torańska. After Stalin's crimes were denounced by Khrushchev at the Twentieth Congress of the Communist Party of the Soviet Union, Berman explained tearfully to a younger comrade that during Stalinism he had lived "with a noose around his neck."[44] Ironically, as Masiewicki confided in the just-quoted letter to Jakub Berman's brother, Adolf—and he was speaking, I think, for his entire cohort when he put these words on paper—"I do not like Jews. Specifically, I find Jewish mannerisms reprehensible; Jewish ways of behavior offend me tremendously. Often I'm ashamed of Jews. Yet I am one of them!" How

---

the peasant cooperative movement, Związek Samopomocy Społecznej (Peasant Self-help Association), which had been established to monopolize credit, retail trade, and grassroots economic activity in the countryside. The Communists were working together with the left-wing Peasant Party, the Stronnictwo Ludowe (SL), which they favored as political ally and counterweight to Mikołajczyk's PSL in the peasant milieu. It was pointed out during the meeting that Peasant Party activists entertained anti-Semitic views and, in particular, strongly objected to the presence of Jews in the apparatus of the Samopomoc cooperative. "To bring up the Jewish issue in the context of Samopomoc," concluded Comrade Zambrowski, a Jew and an influential member of the Politburo, "is reactionary. After all there are only 3 Jews among the 74 employees of the Main Administration of the Samopomoc. Still, it must be recognized, that Jews cannot be in Samopomoc because unlike in the workers' milieu, they have no tradition of working among the peasants" (Aleksander Kochański, ed., *Protokoły Posiedzeń Sekretariatu KC PPR, 1945–1946,* pp. 89, 91). Four comrades were designated to draft an appropriate resolution.

strange and demoralizing it must have been for Jewish Communists who did not feel Jewish at all (and who often joined the movement precisely because it was ethnically blind) to realize that they remained Jewish in the eyes of their comrades after all.

Frakcja PPR in the CKŻP

Jewish Communists more aware of their Jewishness, on the other hand, were concerned with matters Jewish and focused their Party work primarily on the Jewish constituency.* Before the war there was a Jewish Bureau in the Polish Communist Party (Komunistyczna Partia Polski, KPP), and some of the same people now set up an entity informally called Fraction (Frakcja) comprising Party members who were also active in the Central Committee of Polish Jews (CKŻP). Their main preoccupation—to win people over to the cause of Communism and to solidify the rule of the Communist Party in Poland—did not differ, in principle, from what all the other Communists were doing. It differed only in one important detail, that the primary audience of their effort was the Jews.

Again, like pretty much every other constituency in Poland in those days, Jews were giving the Communists a hard time. And as the regime did not care to be associated with Jews in the eyes of the general public anyway, the Party leadership ended up declining to deal with the Jews at all. Hence the annoyance of Jewish Communists in the CKŻP, who felt abandoned by the Party leadership and unable to check the spreading influence "of all the other Jewish associations inimical to us."

On May 15, 1945, the Frakcja sent a reproachful letter to the Central Committee of the Communist Party:

> Since the CKŻP moved to Warsaw [from Lublin] we have approached the Central Committee of the Party several times already asking for guidance in various matters, and we have never

---

*The sense of personal identity differed from individual to individual. One of the key figures involved after the war in this work, Michał Mirski, emigrated from Poland after the outburst of official anti-Semitism in 1968 to Denmark (not to Israel). From there he corresponded with Adolf Berman, and in a letter dated September 16, 1970, wrote as follows: "Who am I? Which country is my homeland? In this matter I have a clear view: I am a political emigrant and my homeland is Poland" (Goldstein-Goren Diaspora Research Center in Tel Aviv, Adolf Berman Archive, p-70/63; quoted by Marci Shore in her forthcoming book *Caviar and Ashes: A Warsaw Generation's Life and Death in Marxism, 1918–1968*).

gotten any answers. A circular we suggested concerning Communist cells attached to Jewish committees was never sent out. For a group of PPR members in the CKŻP, it is clear that we cannot leave the Jewish constituency to various Zionist and Bundist organizations. . . . Our group at the CKŻP has not yet received any instructions from the Central Committee of the Party; we feel detached and left to make our own decisions in matters of the greatest significance on occasion. . . . As a result of this state of affairs, Jewish survivors are not encompassed within the work and organizational influences of our Party, and they fall under the influence of all the other Jewish associations inimical to us. Those comrades who work with provincial Jewish committees are not assisted by local Communist Party committees either, and they are also left to their own devices.

They end their *lettre de doléance* with a clever disclaimer: "Our group at the CKŻP cannot give them any instructions because we have not been empowered to do so by the Central Committee of the Party."[45]

It does not seem that such entreaties were ever answered to the satisfaction of Jewish Communists, who continually worried that the Party was losing its battle for hearts and minds among the Jewish population. They were additionally thrown off balance by the ideological shift concerning Jews that they detected in the decision-making bodies of the PPR.

Jewish Marxists—whether Bundists or Communists by party affiliation—had a clear position concerning Jewish emigration from Poland before the war. They were squarely opposed to it. They argued for the Jewish working class to stay put, believing that improvement in the collective condition of the Jews could come only through class struggle, not through emigration. They argued with equal zeal against the Zionists and against "reactionary and anti-Semitic" local ruling establishments. The noninterference of Communist Polish authorities with Jewish flight from Poland after the war, the official green light and de facto encouragement given to this mass exodus, was shocking and ideologically unpalatable to Jewish Communists. When Prime Minister Edward Osóbka-Morawski asserted on July 21, 1945, during a meeting of the National Council for the Country (KRN), that the authorities would "not oppose emigration of those citizens of Jewish nationality who desire[d] to emigrate," a leading member of the Frakcja in the CKŻP, Zelicki, simply called his statement "anti-Jewish." The Frakcja viewed this attitude on the part of the authorities as an indication that they "lack[ed] concern for Jewish survivors of the Holocaust," and that "the government, instead of providing assistance and work, wanted to offer the Jews open borders."⁴⁶

The Frakcja queried higher-ups for clarification in May 1945 and then, disciplined Party members that they were, accepted the new policy under a face-saving formula—yes to emigration (for humanitarian reasons, in view of the Holocaust and the desire of survivors to join family members still living abroad) and no to "emigrationism" (that is, to Brikha, the illegal emigration organized by the Zionists, and to overt Zionist propaganda⁴⁷). Try as they might, *Jewish Communists could not get the leadership of the Polish Communist Party interested in the special circumstances of Polish Jews.* The Party leadership simply wanted the "Jewish problem" to go away, and sooner rather than later. So the flight of Jews from Poland, organized by Brikha and facilitated by the authorities, continued and gathered speed as time went by, while physical assaults against Jews went on and culminated in the Kielce pogrom.

In September 1946, Hersh Smolar, who would take over the leadership of the CKŻP after the Stalinist *Gleichschaltung* in 1949, sent an alarming letter to a friend in the Jewish Antifascist Committee in Moscow, Itsik Feffer. In the propaganda war that the PPR was now conducting in Poland, Smolar wrote, the Party successfully portrayed the USSR as a guarantor of Poland's territorial integrity. It also demonstrated persuasively that the Soviet Union each day extended to Poland significant assistance of every sort. "We are thereby delivering deathly blows to the agents of Anglo-Saxon reaction in Poland. *The only milieu where this propaganda does not work is that of the Jews* [my emphasis]."⁴⁸

The reason for this failure, Smolar explained, was that all the organizations working in the Jewish milieu—the Joint Distribution Committee, Zionists of all kinds, and the Bund—drew assistance from the United States. This was well known; they "make our community life dependent on Jewish agents of Byrnes [the U.S. Secretary of State at the time], and they flood us with anti-Soviet publications." Smolar concluded with a plea for immediate help "to fight against Jewish agents of Anglo-Saxon reactionaries." He then proceeded to enumerate publications and magazines coming out under the auspices of the JAFC that he wanted Feffer to provide for the CKŻP. He also requested that a delegation headed by Mikhoels be sent to Poland for an extended tour of Jewish communities.⁴⁹

Feffer dutifully passed Smolar's letter to Mikhail Suslov in the Department of Foreign Affairs of the CPSU's Central Committee, by then supervising all matters pertinent to the JAFC. Suslov's answer is missing from the volume of published documents. But in the autumn of 1946, we remember, Suslov recommended that the Jewish Antifascist Committee be closed down.*

To bundle the Jews together with Anglo-Saxons and reactionaries may seem an exaggeration, but it evidently carried a grain of political truth. Hersh Smolar's assessment soon prevailed, and when the Communist Party finally took off its gloves and imposed full-steam-ahead Stalinization on Polish society, he was appointed chairman of the Central Committee of Polish Jews. The organization was defanged for good measure, and had its name changed as well, when it was fused with the Jewish Cultural Association and became the Jewish Socio-Cultural Association (TSKŻ) in October 1950.†

In the end, instead of Jews qua instruments of Communist power carrying out the subjugation of the Polish masses, we encounter Jewish Communists trying to sway a Jewish audience to the cause of Communism, and failing. They clearly failed to persuade a vast majority of Polish Jews to their cause after the war; otherwise, the latter would not have fled the country en masse. And the bottom line, presented here by multiple voices of worried Jewish Communists, is that neither was the Party in postwar Poland interested in Jews nor were the Jews interested in Communism. The Frakcja people say it *à contre-coeur.* They would have preferred that the very opposite were true.

Jews and the Postwar Regime

While thinking through this material we should be mindful of an important distinction between, on the one hand, Jewish attitudes toward the postwar regime (or government) in Poland and, on the other hand, their

---

*What his missing answer may have been may be gauged by another exchange of letters soon thereafter. In late November, Feffer and Mikhoels jointly wrote to the big boss of Soviet culture, Andrei Zhdanov. They were invited to a conference about Jewish culture in Poland and their participation, they ventured, "would strengthen the position of progressive elements in their struggle against reactionary Jewish circles." A week later, on December 6, 1946, we find a document under Suslov's signature again, denying their request (Redlich, *Yevreyskii,* pp. 221–22).

†Could it be that the words "Central Committee" had to be protected from any untoward association in the public mind? Something similar had already happened once, during the war, when a Jewish welfare organization, Żydowska Samopomoc Społeczna (ŻSS), was ordered by the Judenrat to use only its German name and initials (JUS) in official correspondence, because the Polish abbreviation included the two letters "SS," and the Germans apparently found this offensive.

attitudes toward Communism. These are two separate issues which called for making very different choices between different sets of alternatives. Jews were a state-supporting and pro-government—oriented constituency in postwar Poland, just as they had been in Poland before the war. To some extent they were pro-regime in both (very different) periods for the very same reasons—because the alternatives were so unattractive, because Jews were generally excluded from buying into them anyway, and because only state authority could provide relative security to the Jews in a society where anti-Semitism was widespread and occasionally violent.

Many decent people (including some Jews) were skeptical of, critical toward, or frankly hostile to the postwar regime, but the church-sustained rank-and-file Catholics who opposed the regime, and the mass base of the legal opposition (Stanisław Mikołajczyk's Polish Peasant Party), not to speak of the illegal underground organizations, wanted nothing to do with the Jews, to put it mildly. Jews, in toto, had no workable option on the Polish political spectrum but to ally themselves with "the forces of people's democracy and progress," as the then current expression would have it. Furthermore, they had no doubt who their friends were and to whom they owed a debt of gratitude: it was the Red Army, after all, that defeated the German occupiers in the area and saved Jewish remnants from a certain death.

But this demonstrably pro-state and pro-regime inclination of the Jews in postwar Poland did not turn them into Communists. "Sympathy for Communism, and especially for the kind of Communism represented in 1948 by the PPR, was, against all appearances, minimal among the Jews."[50] When they were not confronted with the necessity of making an actual choice between alternatives exclusive to Polish politics, Jews, for the most part, turned somewhere else. To begin with, a majority simply fled the country. And as long as they remained in Poland and while there was still limited freedom of choice, they cast about for different options. In July 1946 the Frakcja PPR membership hovered around 2,500 (mostly concentrated in Lower Silesia), while the numerically strongest Zionist party (of seven then legally in existence), Ichud, had almost 11,000 members.[51] To grasp how deeply Jews, in comparison with everybody else, were invested in Communism in the immediate postwar years, the following general numbers might be worth keeping in mind: in July 1944, the PPR had 20,000 members; in December 1945, 235,000; in the beginning of 1947, 555,000. Frakcja PPR (that is, Jewish Communists) numbered 4,000 at the end of 1946, and by May 1947 its strength had increased to about 7,000.*

The regime could count on Jews as loyal citizens who would rather resort to exit than to protest when fed up with and frightened by the conditions prevailing in Poland.[52] At a time when there were shortages of qualified personnel, when the population was uprooted and documents and employment records had been lost, when people had to fill out detailed biographical questionnaires which were then scrutinized for signs of potential disloyalty, this should have made a Jew, in a blind draw, less of a security risk than a random Pole. But local and lower-level administration personnel, as we know, were often anti-Semitic. On the upper level of state and party bureaucracies, on the other hand, Jews often served in "POP" capacity for reasons of political expediency, and in the end everybody was dissatisfied. For while the population and anxious Party comrades (including Władysław Gomułka) felt that too many Jews held important positions, Jewish incumbents feared that they were serving in office only under temporary reprieve.

Of course there were Jews in the Polish Communist Party, and some of them were dedicated, and very talented, and lucky, and shrewd, and cunning—endowed, in a word, with all the skills that make a successful politician. A number of such individuals rose high in the Party ranks. But no matter how far they ascended, they could always be reminded, by friend and foe alike, and they could never forget, no matter how emotionally and intellectually distant they may have been from their family background, that they were Jewish.[†] Their ethnic background was a colossal liability and an impediment to their careers, from every point of view.

The Co-optation of Radical Nationalists

Anti-Semitism, of course, was not a part of Communist ideology.[‡] In an ideal world, with Communists safely in power, there wouldn't be any

---

*Grabski, *Działalność*, p. 26. Of course, there were also scores of Jews in the Communist Party who had never registered with the CKŻP for a variety of reasons, primarily because they felt totally assimilated. So the actual numbers are higher, but this would not change the overall meaning of the quoted statistics.

†Hilary Minc and Jakub Berman, who rose as near as any Communist in Eastern Europe to the pinnacle of power, were occasionally mocked by Stalin for their Jewish origins—he would speak to them, whenever he felt like it, with a distorted pronunciation meant to emulate Yiddish-inflected speech (interview with Berman in Torańska, *Oni*, p. 325).

‡Lest I be misunderstood, given what has been described in the preceding pages, let me quote from a highly respected historian of Soviet Russia: "Official anti-Semitism was a more

anti-Semitism. But in the ideal world envisaged by Communism there wouldn't be any Jews, either. Ethnic identification was an epiphenomenon, to use Marxist vocabulary: a thing of the past that was bound to go away. If it found a political articulation and congealed into an organized movement, then it would be promptly denounced as "nationalism" and destroyed; the anti-Zionist campaign that Stalin launched in his last years is a case in point.

Communists (this was deeply ingrained already in Lenin's contribution to the Bolshevik tradition) were also paramount pragmatists of power. Since the wartime experiences of the USSR they understood that patriotic, indeed nationalist, popular sentiment must be tapped to safeguard the rule of the Communist Party. If such sentiments—among the Russians, the Ukrainians, the Romanians, or the Poles—came with a mixture of xenophobia or anti-Semitism, so be it. There seems little doubt that Stalin catered to and instrumentalized anti-Semitism in his last years. The underlying anti-Semitic impetus of Ana Pauker's imprisonment in Romania, the Rajk trial in Hungary, and especially the Slansky trial in Czechoslovakia were unmistakable. One could point out that these episodes came in the late 1940s and early 1950s, but even as far back as the earliest phase of the Communist reach for power in Eastern Europe, the Party had made a clear choice between Jews and their local enemies.

---

ambiguous phenomenon. On the one hand, the regime's nationalities policies, predicated on equality of ethnic and national groups, forbade discrimination on national and ethnic grounds including (and often particularly) anti-Semitism. This remained in force in the late Stalin period: indeed, the party's Control Commission was still reprimanding communists for blaming Jews as a group for the offenses of individuals at a time when official anti-Jewish policies implied that this was just what they should be doing. Official anti-Semitism was always expressed obliquely, never in the form of a statement that Jews were harmful or inferior as a group or that Jewish nationality gave grounds for suspicion. On the other hand the regime's own actions in the past (for example, the deportation of 'traitor nations' during the war) had appeared to contradict this principled stance against ethnic discrimination, as a number of policy decisions involving Jews did in the 1940s" (Sheila Fitzpatrick, "The World of Ostap Bender: Soviet Confidence Men in the Stalin Period," *Slavic Review*, no. 3 [Fall 2002], pp. 551–52).

Stalin himself was brilliantly elusive on this issue. In February 1947, he had a conversation with Gheorghiu Dej, a Romanian Communist leader, about conflicts within the leadership of the Party. "Stalin pressed on, asking Dej 'whether there was any truth to the rumors reaching him that there exists a current in the RCP that wants only Romanians to be in the party; that is, in concrete terms, that Ana Pauker and Luca, not being of Romanian nationality, should not hold leadership positions in the party.' If that was the case, Stalin emphasized, then the RCP was being transformed 'from a social and a class party to a race party' " (Robert Levy, *Ana Pauker: The Rise and Fall of a Jewish Communist*, p. 80). This was at the time when Stalin already described the Jews, in toto, as potential American spies.

Immediately after the war ended, Communist parties all over Eastern Europe began to court former members of prewar fascist movements. "I, the undersigned, herewith declare that I was a member of the Arrow Cross Party from . . . to . . .* I now realize that my activities were directed against the interests of the people and that my conduct was faulty. I am resolved to atone for what I have done. I promise to support the fight for a people's democracy with everything in my power and to devote my entire energy to the achievement of this task. I herewith solemnly pledge myself to be a faithful fighting member of the . . . branch of the Hungarian Communist Party."

To an American journalist who traveled all over liberated Europe in 1945, the Hungarian Communist Party leader, Mátyás Rákosi, explained the matter thus: "Look, these little fascists aren't bad fellows, really. They were forced into fascism, see. They were never active in it. All they have to do is sign a pledge, and we take them in."[53] In Romania, Ana Pauker, the proverbial symbolic Jewish Communist of Eastern Europe, struck a deal with the Legionnaires (as former members of the fascist Iron Guard were customarily called) immediately after her return to Bucharest ("influenced by the fact that there were more of them, and especially workers, than I'd imagined"), and the rank-and-file Iron Guardists were admitted en masse into the ranks of the Party.[54] At the same time in Poland, the leader of the prewar fascist ONR-Falanga, Bolesław Piasecki, was released from jail on the orders of the top NKVD operative in the region, Ivan Serov, and allowed to set up an organization of "progressive" Catholics, PAX, to neutralize the influence of the Catholic church. Two days after he was freed, Piasecki was received by none other than Władysław Gomułka.[55]

Serge Moscovici, one of a cohort of brilliant Romanian self-exiled intellectuals who settled in Paris after the war, noted the complementary predicaments of radical right and radical left in East European politics. The rightists had ample social backing before the war, but did not have power and were reaching out for it. The leftists, on the other hand, had power in the immediate postwar years, but no social base to speak of, and

---

*The "arrow cross" was a symbol of the fascist Hungarian Arrow Cross Party, founded by Ferenc Szalasi in 1935. It controlled the Hungarian government during the last phase of the war, from October 1944 to April 1945, and was responsible for massacres of Hungarian Jews.
    The Legion of the Archangel Michael (whence the shorthand designation "Legionnaires"), known also as the Iron Guard, was the principal fascist movement in Romania during the interwar period. Led by the charismatic Corneliu Codreanu, who was killed in 1938, it also reached the height of its power during World War II.

had to mobilize one in order to acquire legitimacy.[56] Hence the carefully orchestrated fusion between Communists and fascists in postwar Eastern Europe, in a literal exemplification of the principle that *les extrêmes se touchent*. We can appreciate now how a man convicted in the Jedwabne murder trial, who was a rabid nationalist before the war and who managed to join the Communist Party immediately after the war, could write in his clemency plea from jail without being completely ridiculous: "I believe that on shoulders like mine our workers' regime may safely rest."[57]

Let us be careful here: the central authorities in Warsaw (or Prague, Bucharest, or Budapest, as the case may be) were not happy about this state of affairs. They gave vent to their disapproval: the Ministry of Public Administration sent memos, as we remember, to its subordinates, imploring them to give Jews equal treatment; the Ministry of Justice in Warsaw set the Jedwabne murder investigation in motion; and so on. But then, one has to observe—as subordinates both in the bureaucracy and in the judiciary must have known very well—that Warsaw did not press the issue.

Communists in Eastern Europe had their hands full. They had to pick their fights. Making sure that Jews were treated fairly was not a priority. Hal Lehrman published a long piece on Hungary in the January 1946 issue of *Commentary*, where he reported that "neo anti-Semitism is not the Jews' chief complaint here. Its existence is obscene, to be sure, after the price paid in lives but it could have been expected. . . . What is startling and, in the opinion of Hungarian Jews, the most shocking element in their present position is the cool indifference [to the resurgence of anti-Semitism] of the new anti-fascist regime."[58] In a few paragraphs tinged with sadness, Moscovici similarly assessed the circumstances of postwar Romania: "This renaissance of anti-Semitism in national life—which was neither dead nor dormant—was embarrassing. Not much could be done about it, however, since it was so useful to everybody. Of all popular passions this was the only one that remained intact. Liberal parties discreetly let it spread around. The Communist party declined to fight against it in order not to irritate the people."[59]

Communists in Poland were confronted with overwhelming popular sentiment on the "Jewish issue," and they could ignore it, or fight it, only at their own peril. On August 19, 1945, in the cinema Raj ("Heaven") in Bochnia, one thousand delegates assembled for a county meeting of the Peasant Party. The gathering, by invitation only (*"za zaproszeniami imiennymi"*), brought together local activists, the elite of Stanisław Mikołajczyk's political opposition (he had, we remember, given up the prime ministership of the government-in-exile in London, and returned to Poland). An anonymous rapporteur submitted an account of the meeting to the Kraków voivodeship office, writing as follows: "In turn the third speaker took the rostrum (his name unknown), and by analogy to a thesis from [Minister of Public Administration] Kiernik's speech that Poland must be a mono-ethnic state [this was apropos of expulsions of the German population from newly incorporated territories], put out a resolution that Jews should also be expelled from Poland, and he also remarked that Hitler ought to be thanked for destroying the Jews (tumultuous ovation and applause)."[60]

Jews in the Apparatus of Repression

Just as all roads lead to Rome, there is a node in the postwar *żydokomuna* argument where all the threads converge: Jews in the Communist apparatus of repression. What about these Jews?—and a slew of names of the most notorious, top-ranked, UB functionaries will follow—we are bound to be asked, sooner or later. Frankly, there is not much to say in direct reply except that these were bad people, for sure. But what about them, indeed? If Jews were, by definition, an alien group of people, unpatriotic, ill disposed toward the Poles and naturally inclined toward Communism, then one would expect to see them acting in roles that fit the stereotype. Their presence in the Communist apparatus of repression should not raise an eyebrow. But what about Poles in the Security Service—were they not the real traitors to patriotic avocation? Ask a nationalist-patriot for names of Polish operatives in the Security Service and you will most likely draw a blank. I doubt there is much heuristic value to such an endeavor, but since some names and numbers are repeatedly invoked in discussions of this period, let us examine the ethnic makeup of the enforcers of Communist rule in Poland to see if we can gain any better insight into the subject of our inquiry.

The state exercised coercion over Polish society by means of the Ministry of Public Security (MBP) and the military. To recapitulate from chapter 1, the MBP's most politicized and feared instrument was the Security Service, colloquially called the *bezpieka* or UB, deployed all over the country through a network of Public Security Offices (Urzędy Bezpieczeństwa Publicznego). Then, twice as numerous as the UB, there was the ubiquitous regular police force, or Citizens' Militia (Milicja

Obywatelska, MO), also subsumed under the Ministry of Public Security. A uniformed quasi-military branch of the Security Service, the Internal Security Corps (Korpus Bezpieczeństwa Wewnętrznego, KBW), and an auxiliary police force, the so-called ORMO (Ochotnicze Rezerwy Milicji Obywatelskiej, Voluntary Reserves of the Citizens' Militia), were also available. As needed, regular army units were deployed to quell disturbances (as in Kielce), or to assist in large-scale cleansing operations (primarily by the KBW) against the armed anti-Communist underground and/or the Ukrainian nationalist insurgency, the UPA.

Understandably, the top-echelon Security Service personnel had to be thoroughly vetted by Polish Communist Party leadership, as well as the NKVD, which provided training, the blueprint, and advisers to establish the organization. In retrospect, scholars note that several key appointments went almost exclusively to former members of the KPP (and affiliated organizations) who had spent the war period in the USSR.[61] Since most of the KPP activists were killed by Stalin in the Gulag, they were as a rule younger people, a third or fourth tier of the old cadres who somehow slipped through the net. Many Communists who met those criteria were Jewish, though this was not an ironclad rule.

Any history buff in Poland can name a half-dozen high-ranking Jewish functionaries in the Ministry of Public Security from that period—Józef Różański and his deputy Adam Humer from the Department of Investigations; two vice ministers, Roman Romkowski and Mieczysław Mietkowski; Julia Brystygierowa, who headed a department monitoring the Catholic church and also kept tabs on intellectuals; and Anatol Fejgin and his deputy Józef Światło, from a super-secret department that watched over the political orthodoxy of top Communist Party cadres. The Ministry of Public Security had many more Jewish employees, especially in its Counterintelligence Department (Marcel Reich-Ranicki, whose memoirs I quote in the introduction, was employed there briefly as a young man), in the Censorship Office, and in its various "technical" departments.

But the MBP did not look specifically for Jews to fill the available positions. There was an overall shortage of qualified personnel; people were being pulled every which way to take jobs all over the new administration, and what one ended up doing was very often a matter of pure coincidence. In any case, a closer look at the available records offers a complex picture and no good data from which to draw firm conclusions about the ethnic composition of the MBP's personnel.

Three weeks after the July Manifesto was proclaimed in Lublin, 217 men arrived in town, eagerly awaited by Stanisław Radkiewicz, the official in charge of organizing the *resort,* later called Ministry, of Public Security for the new regime.* They had just finished a three-month intensive course at an NKVD school in Kuibyshev. The Kuibysheviaks, as they were soon to be known in the security establishment, "became the main organizers of the *bezpieka* and its core personnel at the level of the ministry, in voivodeship and in county offices."[62] The career paths of several dozen men from this group that can be documented today indeed show them in leadership positions of the security apparatus all over Poland. A right-wing historian who published a well-documented article on the subject in a right-wing periodical took care to point out the Jewish origins of his protagonists. He was able to identify by name fifty-one men who received training in Kuibyshev, and four of them were Jewish.[63]

The most concise and thorough compendium of available numerical information on Jews in the UB was put together by professor Andrzej Paczkowski in an article published in 2001.[64] Information bearing on the subject is scattered and sources are occasionally difficult to reconcile, but this is what the best effort to put them all together has yielded.

The first source providing a general overview of the ethnic composition of the Security Service is a report by Nicolai Seliwanowski, the top NKVD adviser in Poland, sent to Lavrenty Beria on October 20, 1945. Seliwanowski writes that overall 18.7 percent of employees in the Ministry of Public Security are Jewish, as are half, 50 percent, of its "leading personnel." He gives a handful of percentages for Jews in various departments of the ministry, including one for "the Radom office," where, according to Seliwanowski, 82.3 percent of the functionaries were Jewish.[65] From the same period there is another source, also originating at "the top," dated November 25, 1945. A note prepared by Bolesław Bierut on the basis of information provided by Stanisław Radkiewicz puts the overall proportion of Jews among MBP employees at 1.7 percent (438 of the total staff of 25,600), and their ratio among the "leading personnel" at 13 percent (67 of 500). It is not possible wholly to reconcile Seliwanowski's and Bierut's numbers, but it seems likely that Seliwanowski was writing exclusively about the personnel in the ministry in Warsaw,

*The designation *resort,* used in the original bureaucratese when the Polish Committee of National Liberation (PKWN) was established, and before *resorty* were turned into ministries, stuck long after the official name was changed. He or she works in the *resort,* one might say, and it was immediately understood that the interlocutor had the *bezpieka* in mind.

while Bierut had in mind the entire security apparatus, including its voivodeship and county offices.

A 1978 internal publication of the Ministry of the Interior, MSW (as the MBP was known by then) gives information on 447 people who in the years 1944–1956 occupied leading positions in the central apparatus of the ministry (that is, excluding those who made it to the top in the territorial network but never worked in the *"centrala"* in Warsaw). Of that number, 29.6 percent, or 131 individuals, are identified as being of "Jewish nationality." In 1944–1945 the proportion of Jews among the leading personnel in the ministry, according to this document, was 24.7 percent— "thus it amounts to half of the number quoted by Seliwanowski" (who was also reporting on the leading personnel in the ministry).[66] For the most part, concludes Paczkowski, except in 1944–1945, Jews made up about 30 percent of the "leading personnel" in the central security apparatus.

Data on the ethnic composition of the territorial network of the UB is even more spotty. Two monographs put together detailed and reliable information about the Lublin voivodeship and the Rzeszów voivodeship Security Service. On February 1, 1946, there were 19 Jews among the total of 1,122 Security Service employees in the Lublin WUPB (Voivodeship Office of Public Security), 1.7 percent overall. Fourteen among them held "higher ranks," and worked in the voivodeship office in Lublin itself, while among the 102 people who occupied "leadership positions" in the Rzeszów voivodeship Security Service during the five-year period 1944–1949, there were altogether 4 Jews. As a result of regional variations, Paczkowski points out, many more Jews could have served in the Security Service in Silesia, for instance, but that half of the Łódź UB was Jewish (as one report from 1945 indicates), or that 82.3 percent of the staff at the Radom UB office was Jewish, as stated by Seliwanowski, "seems much less probable," concludes Paczkowski.* "And this is more or less everything I was able to find in the sources and reliable monographs making it possible to present the issue in a statistical form."[67]

Careful scrutiny of bad data may not yield informative insights, but the range of numbers that are significant here, it seems to me—Jews in leading positions at the MBP—is somewhere between 67 (from Bierut's

---

*Mieczysław Moczar, a well-known anti-Semite then and later, was in charge of the WUPB office in Łódź at the time, so Paczkowski's skepticism is well founded.

note) and 131 (from the 1978 report by the MSW). Or, if we want to really cast our net wide, we might take as an upper limit 438 Jewish employees in the whole MBP in 1945 (from Bierut's note again). The mesmerizing "50 percent" from Seliwanowski's note has to be considered carefully, as we don't know what exactly he had in mind—most likely the top five or ten *really* leading positions at the ministry, "half" of which were occupied by Jews.

But this "numbers game," fundamentally, is meaningless. For what does it mean that there were 67 Jews in the MBP, or 131, or 438? What would have changed if the corresponding figures were 50 or 380, for example? There were 3½ million Jews in Poland before the war, and a quarter million Jews passed through Poland or lived there for some time in the immediate postwar period; can one draw statistically grounded inferences about the general characteristics of such a population by following the life trajectories of 67, 131, or even 438 individuals? People served in the Security Service, or any other branch of the administration, as individuals, or as Communists called by Party comrades to fulfill their duty, or as opportunists, but not as Jews—or as Poles for that matter. The functioning of the Communist secret police had nothing to do with Jews (or Poles)—it operated just as smoothly and followed a similar blueprint in Albania, East Germany, Cuba, China, and North Korea. If one wanted an explanation of the aggregate Jewish presence in the Communist apparatus, there was a familiar story about Marxism and the labor movement it inspired as powerful venues of modernization in twentieth-century Europe, and about the anti-Semitism of the surrounding society, which compounded the effect of early capitalism's social inequalities on ethnic minorities. This is how a sliver of restless Jewish minority urban youth was funneled into the Communist movement. And it was perverse for anti-Semites to latch onto the sociological effects of their forebears' prejudice as an alleged justification for their own.

If there were a reason to count Jews in the UB it would be just as good to count all of its personnel according to ethnic background. Then we would have to note that "63.5 percent" of MBP's "leading personnel," employed in the central administration, were ethnic Poles and that thousands upon thousands of the regime enforcers were Polish peasants, for the day-to-day coercive apparatus of the state—the Security Service and the Citizens' Militia combined—was roughly 80,000 people strong.[68] And as two young Polish scholars specializing in the subject remind us, "One should beware of thinking that the Militia was a more noble formation than the security forces."[69] In fact, the UB and the militia worked hand in hand, their tasks and responsibilities overlapping and providing ample opportunity for turf wars, as they also traded "leading personnel" on occasion. And as we reconstruct in broad outline how the strong arm of the regime was put together we gain a more intimate insight into the "human factor" behind the Communist-sponsored coercion to which Polish citizens were subjected at the time.

In addition to former members of the KPP who spent the war years in Russia, people who during the war were in the Communist Party–sponsored guerrilla movement in Poland (the Gwardia Ludowa [GL; the People's Guard] and the Armia Ludowa [AL; the People's Army]) also commanded voivodeship offices in the Security Service. Especially important were Mieczysław Moczar and Grzegorz Korczyński.* The top ranks of the Citizens' Militia were recruited from a similar pool of candidates, with a tilt toward former anti-Nazi guerrillas of the GL/AL.† The latter moved en masse into the lower ranks of the regular police, the MO, as did in this early period young men who had been in non-Communist guerrilla formations, such as the Peasant Battalions (BCh) and/or the Home Army.‡ The former chief of staff of the

---

*Moczar moved back and forth between the area under Nazi occupation and the USSR, and also went to an NKVD school, but in Gorki. Immediately after the war, Korczyński held high-level posts both in the police and in the Security Service. Both men were known to hold anti-Semitic views. Moczar and his acolytes from the Security Service as well as from the Association of Wartime Combatants, ZBOWiD, engineered the anti-Zionist campaign in Poland in 1968. He was minister of the interior (earlier, public security) at the time.

†At the end of his meticulously documented monograph about the MO, Zenon Jakubowski included an appendix with forty-two short CVs of the "organizers of the militia," who worked in the central command, in voivodeship offices, and in some instances on the county level. We can put together a collective profile of the group on the basis of the information he provides.

Twenty people on Jakubowski's list (including one woman) held membership in the KPP or an affiliated organization; fifteen spent the wartime in the USSR; ten had been both in the KPP and in the USSR during the war; five were Jewish (one of the five had also been in the KPP and in Russia); eighteen were in the GL/AL during the war; five had been in the AK/BCh or in the prewar police; and five, including one Jew, moved at some point laterally from the MO apparatus to the UB (Zenon Jakubowski, *Milicja obywatelska, 1944–1948*, pp. 491–510).

‡See, for example, Jakubowski, *Milicja,* pp. 189–92, 204–206; Tomasz Miller, "Jak się rodziła przewodnia siła," in *Biuletyn IPN,* no. 5 (2002). "Frequently militia detachments were simply established by underground units. Of course, later the militia was 'cleansed' of people who couldn't be trusted, including members of the armed underground and sympathizers of the PSL [Mikołajczyk's Peasant Party]" (see "O aparacie bezpieczeństwa— z Krzysztofem Lesiakowskim i Grzegorzem Majchrzakiem rozmawia Barbara Polak," in *Biuletyn IPN,* no. 6 (2002), p. 9).

People's Army, Franciszek Jóźwiak (he used his wartime pseudonym, Witold, to sign official orders after the war as well), was in charge of the MO. Jóźwiak's strong personal position in the Party leadership gave the police a certain degree of autonomy, even though organizationally they were subordinated to the minister of public security.

The coercive apparatus of the state was independent of the state bureaucracy—the police and the Security Service were not subsumed under the authority of the Ministry of Public Administration (MAP) or its country-wide personnel.[70] Instead, they answered directly to the MBP in Warsaw, just as, for example, the courts were directly subordinated to the Ministry of Justice. The apparatus of coercion and the local administration were supposed to work in concert, but especially at the time of a simmering civil war, local commanders of the police and the UB acted very much as they pleased.[71]

Take one well-documented episode as an example of what was going on without, I am sure, usually leaving any paper trail. During the first conference of "heads of non-unified offices and authorities" ("*naczelników władz i urzędów niezespolonych*": that is, the police, the Security Service, the judiciary, and the fiscal authorities) on September 8, 1945, the Warsaw voivodeship commander of the police, a Captain Dowkan, "attacked the courts for allegedly passing sentences incompatible with the spirit of the July Manifesto. He pointed out that the Citizens' Militia, entrusted with enforcement of democracy, faced a dilemma whether to enforce court sentences ordering workers to vacate apartments they had been assigned and thereby commit an injustice, or to disregard those court rulings. He said in the end that he ordered his men to inform him about all instances when they were ordered to enforce court rulings that were unjust or contrary to the spirit of democracy, and he would then make a decision whether to act on them or not."[72]

We would probably be on safe ground in assuming that at least some of those cases were brought by Jews trying to recover their property. But irrespective of the parties in the disputes, Dowkan publicly displayed such blatant disregard for the law that the president of the Court of Appeals from Łódź, who was present at the meeting, angrily retorted that "the usurpation by the Citizens' Militia of the right to decide whether to enforce court rulings would lead to anarchy." The follow-up discussion must have been contentious, and when the deputy voivode of Warsaw, one Żrałek, finally wrapped up the discussion he also said, somewhat ominously, that "the statement of the commander of the Voivodeship

Citizens' Militia will be taken up in a different place, and by different authorities."[73]*

Captain Dowkan's career, however, did not suffer as a result of his excessive candor. He must have realized that his statement did not go over too well, for he tried to placate the audience, inadvertently further implicating the police: "As multiple complaints were voiced during today's meeting against the Militia . . . one has first to take stock of its moral condition" (*"w pierwszym rzędzie należy poznać stan moralny Milicji"*), he pleaded. "In this respect one may use as a good illustration that in the period so far, ten thousand persons were dismissed from the force, as unfit to serve in the ranks of the Militia."[74]

He did not follow in their footsteps, though he could have, for the total number of dismissals from the service in 1944–1946 reached 20,000. By 1948, the number of dismissals from the militia had doubled once again, to 40,000. By October 1949, in the entire *resort* of Public Security the "fluidity" of personnel reached a staggering 90,000. During a single "verification" ordered following the Kielce pogrom, after a countrywide four-month-long screening process, 4,600 militiamen were let go from the service.†

Before their dismissal, militiamen and Security Service functionaries who would be later found wanting might serve in the ranks for weeks or sometimes months. And how some of them fulfilled their responsibilities as guardians of law and order we have been able to follow in the preceding chapters. Dowkan, in the meantime, made a lateral move to Wrocław where he soon took over command of the Security Service office, and then moved up again to take a position among the "leading personnel" of the MBP in Warsaw.[75]

As early as November 1944 the Politburo of the Polish Workers' Party passed a resolution condemning drunkenness, thievery, and general demoralization of the militia personnel, as well as infiltration of the ranks of the MO by former Home Army members.[76] The initial process of recruitment into the force was often spontaneous. Numerous units of the MO on the local level were formed through local citizens' initia-

---

*"Other speakers limited themselves to mutual recriminations," reads the transcript.

†See Jakubowski, *Milicja*, pp. 178, 179, 185, 186; "O aparacie bezpieczeństwa," p. 10. These are very high numbers given that the total strength of the police during 1945–1947 was about 55,000 men (in constant rotation, as we know now), and of the UB about 25,000. By January 1949, the manpower of the militia got reduced to 40,000 (Jakubowski, *Milicja*, p. 186).

tives.[77] "It is difficult to say precisely how many former Home Army
members served in the Militia in 1944–1945. On the basis of fragmen-
tary data from certain units it follows that these were rather substantial
numbers."[78] As a result the post–Home Army underground was able to
penetrate the ranks of the militia, which therefore often proved ineffec-
tive in combating local anti-regime organizations. In one spectacular security breach a county militia commander in Jędrzejów took his entire
outpost, thirty-two men strong, with all the weapons and went "into the
forest."[79] A similar walkout was staged by a onetime UB county commander in Nowy Targ, who under the nickname Ogień, "Fire," later became a legendary outlaw in the mountainous region of Podhale, where he
battled the regime by killing Jews who were fleeing Poland by one of the
Brikha exit routes.*

In general, one wouldn't expect the most idealistic members of the
Home Army to change sides so radically right away and join the militia.
Rather, the strong-arm organizations of the regime took in local toughs
who sided with whoever momentarily had the upper hand—the NKVD,
German gendarmerie, the underground guerrilla, and finally the PPR—
and gave their sycophants a chance to live off the land and other people.[†]

One year after the aforementioned Politburo resolution, during a
two-day conference of all the heads of the Voivodeship Security Service
offices at the headquarters of the MBP, Minister Radkiewicz chastised his
top subordinates for similar failures. But there were limits, he was told,
to what could be accomplished with the manpower at hand. In the Białystok voivodeship Security Service office "forty people are employed,"
explained Major Piątkowski; "they are dedicated to the cause of democracy but frequently they are illiterate. The only operational agents who
can be relied upon are Kokoń and Kaczorowski."[80]

Four years later, in 1949, the quality of available operatives still left
much to be desired. Out of eight investigators from the UB office in
Łomża who compiled dossiers of the twenty-two accused brought to trial
for participation in the killing of the Jews from Jedwabne, one had a high

*The real name of this folk hero was Józef Kuraś. He duly recorded various exploits in
a personal diary, including the multiple murder of twelve Jews who were traveling toward
the border on the night of May 3, 1946, near Krościenko.
†See *Neighbors,* esp. the chapter "Intimate biographies"; also, Anna Bikont, "My z Jedwabnego," *Gazeta Wyborcza,* March 10–11, 2001. On local anti-Semites who joined the ranks
of law enforcement after the liberation, see Turkov, *Noch der befrajung,* pp. 179–81, 272; on
wartime signatories of the *Volksliste* and an SS man doing likewise in Silesia, see Antoni
Dziurok, "Początki milicji na Górnym Śląsku," in *Biuletyn IPN,* no. 6 (2002), p. 47.

school diploma, four had finished primary school, and three had not completed primary school.[81]

In the security apparatus, as two researchers of the IPN recently put it, the employees were "mainly young people, often very young indeed. They came from the countryside and small towns, and usually had almost no education."[82]

In an unrelated communication one month after the previously mentioned meeting between Radkiewicz and the top UB leadership, Władysław Gomułka complained to the minister of public security about a continuing string of abuses and outright robberies that the police and the UB were responsible for in the newly incorporated territories. Gomułka held the post of minister of recovered territories in addition to his other functions, and on that account was well informed about goings-on during resettlement in and out of the area.[83] A county *starosta* from Bytom, speaking around the same time, sarcastically described militia detachments "not as guarantors of security of the Polish population but, quite the opposite, as guarantors of insecurity."[84]

"In the immediate postwar years, functionaries of the *resort* were trying to establish themselves materially [*"byli ludźmi na dorobku"*]. Breaking the law for profit was therefore very common."[85] One such character, whose greed and nepotism have been described in an internal document of the Security Service personnel department, was someone already familiar to us, Major Sobczyński. Prior to taking command in Kielce, where we met him during the pogrom, he was in charge of the Rzeszów voivodeship Security Service office, where he employed a slew of family members and freely took from the commissary more than his share of various rationed provisions.[86]

On a local level—and this is where contact between society and the state apparatus of coercion took place daily—agents of the state were hardly more than uniformed thugs (or plainclothes thugs, as the case may be). Official impunity notwithstanding, they were living dangerously, for this was a time of civil war and social disorganization. In the 1944–1948 period, 1,618 Security Service men, 4,018 militiamen, and 495 members of the auxiliary militia, the ORMO, lost their lives in the line of duty.[87] And since they gave as well as they took, the brutalization of law enforcement, if one may use this expression, was widespread.

So the bottom-line story about the imposition of Communist rule in Poland is that the strong-arm enforcers for the new regime—who fought against the post–Home Army underground, who terrorized the countryside and supporters of Stanisław Mikołajczyk's Polish Peasant Party, who flaunted their status as government agents as if they were above the law—were for the most part local boys, and not the brightest ones, either. Not strangers with sharp, pointed features driven by alien ideology, but men with familiar faces whose literacy level (as anyone who has ever read the protocols of interrogations compiled by them can readily attest) could be vastly improved. Highly placed Jews in the Security Services— Humer, Fejgin, Różański, Światło, and others—were second to none in cruelly abusing their prisoners, but they interrogated primarily a thin sliver of the elite of the regime's opponents, and as loyal Communists totally subservient to the current Party line, were ready to torture confessions out of Communists who had fallen from favor, and/or out of Jews, with as much vigor as they applied to beating Peasant Party leaders or former Home Army officers.*

One may point out that this does not matter, for as long as they had done what they had done they were instrumental in imposing Communism on Polish society after the war—a fine proposition, provided that "they" signifies "zealous Communist apparatchiks," not "Jews," and that ethnicity does not factor into the equation. The imposition of Stalinism on Poland, after all, did not hinge on the consent of a few dozen (or 67, or 131, or even 438) Jews to act as Stalin's stooges. For if Churchill and Roosevelt could not save Poland from Communist subjugation, a couple of hundred Jews (if only they had said no to Stalin) could not have saved Poland, either.

Whether they acted qua Communists or not does not really matter, some may retort in a final rebuttal, as long as they fit into a stereotype. They were Jewish, after all, and in the public perception this sufficed to feed the image of a Jewish conspiracy. But then, if Berman, Mietkowski, Romkowski, Światło, Fejgin, Różański, Humer, Brystygierowa, and the few dozen others who played most nefarious roles during the Stalinist

---

*That Jews serving in the Secret Service were involved in the persecution of Jews (or anybody else who had been targeted for persecution at a given moment) is well illustrated by the Soviet example, where "N. I. Eitington, who had organized the murder of Trotsky (among many others), was accused of planning to murder the soviet leaders; L. F. Raikhman, who had run the secret surveillance of the Jewish Anti-Fascist Committee, was arrested as a Jewish nationalist; Lieutenant Colonel Kopeliansky, who had interrogated the savior of the Budapest Jews, Raoul Wallenberg, was fired as a Jew; and M. I. Belkin, who had staged the Rajk trial in Hungary, confessed to having spied for the Zionists and recruited, among others, the head of the Hungarian secret police and his fellow Jew Gabor Peter" (Yuri Slezkine, *The Jewish Century*, p. 304).

period had never existed, would the national-Catholic public believe any less strongly that the introduction of Communism into Poland was the result of a Judeo-Bolshevik conspiracy?*

The police frequently mishandled Jews in the line of duty. They eagerly investigated phony complaints about Jews abducting Christian children, looking not for the authors of incendiary rumors but for Jews and their nonexistent prey.† In his memoirs from Lublin, Jonas Turkov refers to several episodes in which Jews were killed by policemen in the months immediately following the proclamation of the July Manifesto. "It got to the point," he writes, "that one could not distinguish between a real militiaman and a bandit."[88] Jewish Committees all over the country complained about the anti-Semitism of the regular police. This fact was well known to the commander of the force, Franciszek Jóźwiak.[89] On occasion people perceived the Citizens' Militia as their natural ally in the persecution of Jews. A Jewish woman fleeing Kielce two days after the pogrom was pulled off a train by fellow passengers. Failing in an attempt to lynch her, they delivered her into the hands of the militia—"to be shot."‡ The archives of the Jewish Committee from Tarnów describe re-

---

*Emmanuel Mounier, as we already know, was shocked by the persistence and spread of anti-Semitism in Poland in 1946. He confronted his interlocutors on this subject and was told that Jewish prominence in government structures caused the enmity. He mused in his piece on the lack of alternatives for Jews in an anti-Semitic society, on how they have to rely on government bureaucracy for employment and a guarantee of relative security, and then concluded his reflections with a rhetorical question: *"Mais l'antisemitisme se nourrit-il de raison?"* ("Does anti-Semitism feed off rational arguments?")

†On occasion the whole matter was treated, one is tempted to say, with a disarming simplicity: On October 19, 1946, a few tipsy fellows were looking for a lost child in a building where Jewish returnees lived in Kraków, at no. 10 Stradom Street. A small crowd began to assemble in the street, and when guards of the building proceeded to disperse it "the head of the militia patrol [which in the meantime had been called by alarmed residents] told one of our guards that 'if your child got lost, citizen, you would also be searching around' " (*"gdyby obywatelowi zginęło dziecko, to obywatel też by szukał"*) (ŻIH, CKŻP, Żydowski Instytut Historyczny, box 1-2, folder 1, p. 114, memo dated 6.11.1946).

‡"I noticed on the train that I was being observed. One of the women pointed at me: 'This is a filthy kike, throw her under the train!' Another said: 'We'll turn her over to the police at the next station, let them shoot her.' When we reached the next station, women grabbed me by the feet and by the head and pulled me onto the tracks to throw me under the train. I begged them to spare my life, but they said that I was Jewish and so I must die. Children started to throw stones at me. I begged a railwayman to shoot me, because I could not suffer any longer, but he answered: 'You would like to die an easy death; slowly, you can suffer a little longer.' Fortunately a policeman was passing across the tracks, he ordered them to let me go, and said that he will take care of me. They let me go, and the policeman asked that I give him something. I gave him my last 500 złoty. He let me go. I boarded a train once again, and again women recognized me and turned me over to the police, screaming 'Kill the kike' " (Ida Gertsman, "Zajścia w Kielcach," *Biuletyn Żydowskiego Instytutu Historycznego*, pp. 23–24).

peated assaults by uniformed soldiers against local Jews, and the futility of lodging complaints with the authorities.[90] "Local units of the Militia and the Security Service did not intervene [to quell anti-Jewish violence] and their functionaries were occasionally involved in murdering and otherwise abusing [the Jews]."[91] Soldiers and policemen were in the forefront of the two most notorious and deadly episodes, in Kraków and in Kielce, where scores of them were arrested.

On the whole the Security Service was kept on a tighter leash. But we should not have any illusions about what kind of sentiment toward the Jews prevailed in the ranks of the UB. Certainly the leadership was oblivious to the threats and violence that Jews were being subjected to. It is worth repeating what has already been said in a previous chapter: during all the periodic top-level conferences held at the Ministry of Public Security, where voivodeship office commanders were brought together with the ministry's "leading personnel," *not once* was the failure to provide security for the Jewish population in Poland discussed.[92]

On occasion the most politicized organ of coercion, the UB, made local Jews uneasy. In Oświęcim, for example, a theatrical "revue" was put on by the Sports Club "Force." "The themes and content of this show," staged on January 24 and 25, 1947, "was to make fun of the Jews in various sketches and songs. We want to stress that the main part in these anti-Jewish japes was played by the commander of the Security Service in Oświęcim."[93] Seliwanowski's report to Beria, mentioned earlier, includes an item about anti-Semitic rumors spread among employees in the headquarters of the Ministry of Public Security in Warsaw.[94]

Anecdotal evidence notwithstanding, we should note that since 1956, when the internal politics of the regime became more transparent, the Security Service emerged as a consistent repository of hard-line anti-intellectual and anti-Semitic xenophobia. It was then the same organization as before, minus a few dozen Jews who had been replaced among the "leading personnel." "From this time anti-Semitism took firm root in the *bezpieka* and persisted until its end," writes Paczkowski in the concluding paragraph of his essay. "The problem of 'Jews in the UB' went away and the problem of anti-Semitism in the Security Service came up."[95] The most outlandish episode of official anti-Semitism was staged in Communist Poland in 1968 by the minister of the interior, Mieczysław Moczar (who until 1948 commanded the Voivodeship Public Security Office [Wojewódzki Urząd Bezpieczeństwa Publicznego, WUPB] in Łódź), and was assisted for good measure by the Veterans' Association,

ZBOWiD, in which former partisans from the People's Guard and the People's Army formations played leading roles.

The apparatus of enforcement in postwar, Communist Poland—the regular police (MO), the Security Service (UB), and the military—was made up overwhelmingly of ethnic Poles. Recruited more or less at random, or through self-selection (drawing on young men who knew little else besides toting a gun, or who liked to bully people), it brought together a bunch of lower-class youth who in their personal views could not but reflect the anti-Semitism widespread in their social milieus.[96]

A Pragmatic Approach to the "Jewish Question" in Eastern Europe

In the process of postwar *Machtergreifung,* Eastern European Communists wanted to authenticate themselves as the only organizational embodiment of true national interest in the societies where they were politically active.* To reach this goal they did not shy away from playing on xenophobia and ethnic prejudice. On the occasion of the "Three times yes" referendum, Władysław Gomułka, who as we have seen was eventually shunted aside for "nationalist deviation," labeled the legal anti-Communist political opposition the camp of *drei mal nein.* Just like that, in German, and a lie to boot: the opposition called for only one "no" vote.

The patriotic rhetoric deployed in the immediate postwar years by Polish Communists replicated the message of right-wing nationalists in many important respects. Virulent anti-Germanism and mellow pan-Slavism blended into familiar calls promising "national unity" and invoking "national will." "Nation," in all its forms and linguistic variations, "nation" as a noun and as an adjective, was the word most frequently used in public speeches and party documents of this period.[97] An integral verbal nationalism—using organic metaphors of *Blut und Boden,* or rather of *z krwi i kości,* "blood and bones"—when sketching the purported lineage of the movement (as part and parcel of struggles for national liberation by Polish patriots of earlier centuries)—replaced class analysis and Marxist arguments for historical inevitability. The word "Communism"

---

*After Khrushchev was reinstated as the first secretary of the Communist Party in the Ukraine, he said to a Jewish veteran who wondered why the destruction of Ukrainian Jewry was not properly commemorated: "Here is the Ukraine and it is not in our interest that the Ukrainians should associate the return of Soviet power with the return of the Jews" (Weiner, *Making Sense,* p. 212).

was nowhere to be seen, frankly, to the discomfort of some older comrades. They also must have frowned at the spectacle of a seasoned Party operative—Comrade Tomasz, to those who knew him from the organization—who, as Bolesław Bierut, identified himself as a man without party affiliation (*bezpartyjny*), and concluded with a formulaic "so help me God" when he took the oath of office as the country's first chairman of the National Council.

The Polish Communist Party (KPP), dissolved by the Comintern on Stalin's orders in 1938, was reconstituted after the Communists belatedly joined the anti-Nazi underground struggle in 1941, but as the Polish Workers' Party (PPR). It kept that name until the "unification congress," when it absorbed the Polish Socialist Party in December 1948 and reappeared as the Polish United Workers' Party (PZPR), again without the word "Communist" in its name. All these disguises notwithstanding, the public was not fooled, as a popular reading of the abbreviation "PPR"—"Płatne Pachołki Rosji," or "Russia's Mercenary Knaves"—showed plainly.

But the Communists were unfazed. Knowing the corrosive power of persistence—repetition as the cornerstone of successful propaganda—they went after a whole range of their political opponents' traditional vocabulary. At Stalin's insistence, a core of Communist activists, being groomed in the Soviet Union to play leading roles in postwar Poland, formed an organization called the Association of Polish Patriots (ZPP). Wanda Wasilewska, an éminence grise of this association, was initially somewhat put off by its name.[98] The word "patriot," she pointed out to Stalin, had a "compromised" connotation to Polish Communists. To this he replied, "Every word can be given a new meaning, and it is up to you what meaning it will be endowed with."*

Behind this screen of "Polish patriotism," "national unity," "national will," "blood and bones," *"raisons d'état,"* "so help me God," and mellow pan-Slavism, the Sovietization of Polish society was energetically pursued. To quote Jakub Berman, a symbol of *żydokomuna* for the regime's opponents and one of the most influential Politburo members at the time, "The history of the workers' movement acquires blood and a body [*"nabiera krwi i*

---

*Marcin Zaremba, *Komunizm, legitymizacja, nacjonalizm,* p. 131. In the realm where Soviet Communists established themselves in power, infusing language with new meaning was a most effective mechanism of social control, second only to the direct application of police terror. In this case—a pretty daring one even by the standards of the time—the term "Polish patriots" was proposed as a label designating an organization of individuals ready to serve as proxies of the Soviet power.

ciała"] when we manage to place it in the wholeness of national history. It is time to tie together, to organically unify the history of our party and of the workers' movement with the history of the nation."[99] Given that efforts to legitimize the Communist Party were taking this tenor, it is no wonder the Party had so little room (even if it had any will) to simultaneously champion Jewish interests, however construed.

Recapitulation

Already during the interwar years, there was an intimate relationship between Jews and Communism in Poland. Jews who desired to cast off their Jewish identity and emancipate themselves from the restrictions it imposed—and who were endowed with a political temperament, to boot—had no alternative *in Polish politics* but to join the Communist (or the Socialist) movement: anywhere else *on the Polish political spectrum* they would be unwelcome. In that sense, there was a very direct relationship between Jews and Communism, but contrary to the repeated mantra it did not reside in Jews bringing Communism to Poland. If anything, the relationship was in the opposite direction: it was Poland—or, to be more precise, the limited tolerance for Jews and outright anti-Semitism that were widespread in Polish society—that helped to bring Jews over to Communism.

Between the Bund, the whole rainbow of Zionist parties, and the conservative religious Agudas Yisroel, becoming Communist was a marginal option among politically active Jews. Communism was a fringe phenomenon in Poland, anyway. Due to this double marginality (and to some extent because of it) the few Jews who did become Communists—no more than 7,500 altogether in a country of 35 million—were a significant proportion of all Communist Party members. But if we take into consideration that Communism was an urban phenomenon and that Jews were predominantly an urban population, the ethnic composition of the movement becomes much less of a statistical oddity.

Furthermore, in evaluating the putative affinity between Jews and Communism we should also consider the sectarian character of the Communist movement, which made Jewish Communists "un-Jewish" not simply on account of the Communist ideology's incompatibility with traditional Judaism. Joining a Party cell before the war was like joining a sect today. One didn't merely have to continuously repeat certain stock ideas; one also changed one's milieu, companions, readings, everyday routines, residence, and everything in between. All was determined by

FEAR

this commitment, one's entire daily life, the choice of friends and lovers as much as that of enemies. Frankly, the word "different" does not adequately convey the radicalism of opting for Communism. Jewish converts were not merely estranged from their ascriptive identity (or their bourgeois identity, if they came from a prosperous family background, or from both), but felt for it outright contempt.*

Neither subversive agents of Soviet domination, nor godless contaminants of Polish organic unity, but urban minority youth who cast off their national identity, who wanted to assimilate, who felt scandalized by the social inequalities of early capitalism, and who were pushed by the dominant majority population's ethnic intolerance into radical left-wing politics—this, in a nutshell, is the social history, such as it is, of "Judeo-Communism" in Poland. As to the reported enthusiasm of Jewish converts to Communism, one need only consult the intellectual history of the Communist movement to discover the seductive force of Marxist ideology. Communist zealots in Poland, whatever their social or national background, were in very good company, judging by the distinguished roster of scholars and public intellectuals from all over Europe who in their memoirs have mused on their youthful infatuation with the same.[100] Last but not least, as I already noted, Polish Jews were the most law-abiding and state-supporting community in interwar Poland, and sociological analysis of voting patterns demonstrates that they supported the ruling Sanacja regime from the mid-1920s onward more consistently than did any other category of citizens.

After the war, for better or worse, the Communist organizers of public order in Poland adopted an attitude of not very benign neglect with respect to the "Jewish problem." They decided to let matters take their course; if anything, from time to time they even attempted to ride the tiger. When Stalin's increasingly aggressive anti-Semitism was factored in, the implicit contract between Communist authorities and the newly subjugated Polish society—that they mutually benefited from con-

---

*Admittedly this is no more than anecdotal evidence, but the chief propagandist of the postwar Polish Communist regime, Roman Werfel (born into a well-to-do, partly secularized Jewish family from Lwów), who as a teenager was already involved with the movement, to spite his Jewish schoolmates made a point of bringing matzo sandwiches with ham to class as the High Holidays were approaching (Torańska, *Oni*, p. 74); or, as Aleksander Masiewicki put it in the already quoted letter to Adolf Berman, "I do not like Jews . . . I find Jewish mannerisms reprehensible . . . often I'm ashamed of Jews"; or, as Rosa Luxemburg wrote, "What do you want with these special Jewish pains. . . . I have no special corner in my heart for the ghetto."

sidering the wartime fate of Polish Jews a nonissue, would not scrutinize what exactly happened to the Jews during the war, and would encourage and facilitate the departure of the remnants of Polish Jewry—became a given. My sense is that this was an implicit "give" for the "take" of power.*

The proof of the pudding is in the eating, and one way or another, we must recognize that in the brief span of five years following the end of the war—while Communist rule in Poland was being consolidated and, if my argument stands, *as a constitutive part of the process*—Poland was rendered *Judenrein.* The last cleansing touches were applied during two subsequent waves of Jewish emigration, both permitted and induced by the Communist authorities: in 1956–57 and in 1968–69. Thus, quite appropriately, under the stewardship of the same man who had been accused of "nationalist deviation" in 1948 and came back to power in 1956 as a patriotic Communist, what began as the proudly advertised "national road to socialism" ended twenty years later, in 1968, *toute proportion gardée,* in a variation of National Socialism plain and simple.

Rather than bringing Communism to Poland, as facile historiography of this period maintains, after a millennial presence in these lands, Jews as a matter of political expediency were finally driven out of Poland under the Communist regime. In the words of the Nobel Prize–winning poet Czesław Miłosz—"Let it be stated here clearly: the Party / Descends directly from the fascist Right"—Poland's Communist rulers fulfilled the dream of Polish nationalists by bringing into existence an ethnically pure state.[101]

---

*Thus, the new rulers' neglect of the Holocaust of Polish Jewry, their putting the issue aside with other unmentionables, did not necessarily exemplify bad faith, but flowed naturally from the essence of the leading ideology and practicalities of the moment. That is why, also, in the Auschwitz museum, dedicated to the commemoration of the international antifascist struggle and martyrology, the word "Jew" could hardly be found at all throughout the period of Communist rule in Poland.

As to the persistence of the *żydokomuna* myth in popular memory, one may attribute it, among other reasons, to an attempt by complicitous Poles to deflect their own guilt over having contributed to the triumph of Communism.

CONCLUSIONS

W HILE JEWS were literally running away from Communism, the Communists were politically running away from the Jews. What of the "Judeo-Communism" conflation then, a myth that had many lives, and that, to judge by the opinions of various historians and public personalities in Poland, has currency even today? Its epistemological status, it seems to me, is about the same as that of a proposition which identifies Jews as vampires. That many people believed in both (many of the same people, one might add), and that many people acted on these beliefs, unfortunately does make them "real in their consequences," but does not make them true.[1] *Jews were not* drinking Christian blood, just as *they were not* using it in their religious rituals, and *Jews were not* responsible for bringing Communism to Poland. In other words, that Jews were Communist, or that Jews were vampires, could not have been the reason they were perceived as a threat by their neighbors—because they were neither.*

To blame the Jews for Communism, or for killing Christian children to make matzo, was but to give excuses; these were pretexts, to which people latched on with passionate intensity.† This was not because they

---

*Neither of these ideas taken separately could withstand an empirical test, but entertained simultaneously they were indeed a mind-boggling concoction, offering proof that once a narrative breaches the boundary of nonsense and can no longer be tamed by reasoned argument, anything goes.

†When all is said and done, we may as well recognize that the relationship between Polish Jews and Communism has been subjected to a sort of crude *experimentum crucis*. We know the degree of affinity between the two due to a historical happenstance. It was in the

hated Communism so fiercely that they wanted to wipe all its potential carriers from the face of the earth; nor was theirs a passionate manifestation of parental love and despair in the face of mortal danger threatening their children. Such explanations of anti-Semitism would not be grounded in real experience.

Nobody ever saw a Christian child murdered "for blood" by the Jews and, indeed, Polish inhabitants of Kielce appreciated "the taste of matzo." Assaulting Jews did not visibly promote one's children's welfare. Likewise, assaulting Jews was not an effective way to undermine the Communist regime in Poland, and for the most part, people reconciled themselves to the new rulers, went on with their lives as well as they could, and did not nurture a combustible hatred for Communism ready to explode into destructive fury at the slightest opportunity. *One could not explain the nearly universal presence and the intensity of anti-Jewish prejudice in Polish society on the grounds of anti-Communism and belief in ritual murder unless one allowed for a complete disjunction between actual experience, on the one hand, and social action (as well as collective mentalities), on the other.* This would be a radical assumption, undermining vast areas of the sociology of knowledge and organization, the psychology of learning, the economics of market behavior, and a few other scholarly disciplines to boot.

Neither could one explain postwar anti-Semitism by pointing to the historical roots of Polish anti-Semitism, which was not exterminatory in the first place. Besides, the Holocaust should have defanged traditional Polish anti-Semitism by taking care, in a manner of speaking, of its historical demands. Poland's Jewish population was shrunk to insignificance as a result of war, removing the perceived threat of Jewish social ascendancy over ethnic Poles.*

Thus, *we must seek the reasons for the novel, virulent quality of postwar anti-Semitism in Poland not in collective hallucinations nor in prewar attitudes, but in actual experiences acquired during the war years.* At the same time, we must guard against the easy insight that Nazi policies simply rubbed off onto the Poles, who grew to emulate the occupiers and became "demoralized."

Polish language that some of the early debates in the first parliament of the first Jewish state of the modern era were conducted. Polish Jews were the core and bulk of the Ashkenazi ruling elite in Israel in the year 1948. At exactly the same time as the Soviet Union was subjugating Eastern Europe, Polish Jews—even though it was entirely up to them—were decidedly *not* introducing Communism in Israel.

*One may adduce in evidence the remark overheard by many a memoirist to the effect that despite all his malfeasance a monument should be built to Hitler for having rid Poland of most of the Jews.

Given the ruthlessly exploitative character of the Nazi occupation, the occupiers' universally displayed contempt for the Poles, and the ferocious resistance their measures engendered in all milieus of Polish society, anything the Nazis did was only a recommendation for the Poles to do the opposite.

Nazi attitudes and behavior could not be passed on to Polish society through any sort of contagion or socialization. When Jan Karski noted early during the occupation a "genuine *agreement* [Karski's emphasis] between the occupier and a large segment of the Poles," he pointed to their common interest in dispossessing the Jews. He knew at once that this could lead to disastrous consequences and must be strenuously opposed by the Polish government-in-exile and the underground authorities in Poland, but his warning was in vain.

I see no other plausible explanation of the virulent postwar anti-Semitism in Poland but that it was embedded in the society's opportunistic wartime behavior. Jews were perceived as a threat to the material status quo, security, and peaceful conscience of their Christian fellow citizens after the war because they had been plundered and because what remained of Jewish property, as well as Jews' social roles, had been assumed by Polish neighbors in tacit and often directly opportunistic complicity with Nazi-instigated institutional mass murder. Consequently, when attacking Jews in order to get rid of them once and for all, people were not acting out their vampire fantasies or their Judeo-Communist fantasies, nor were they acting on beliefs and attitudes inculcated by the Nazis; they were defending their real interests, quite often premised on murky deals or outright criminal behavior.

The postwar hatred of the Jews in Poland was too lethal, too widespread, too untamed to be grounded in anything else but concrete, palpable fear. It would have mellowed, subsided, or ossified had Jews not represented an existential threat to the Poles. Such hatred could not have sustained itself on figments of people's imagination, unsupported by evidence or everyday experience. There had to be real reasons for it or else it would have paled, if only out of pity for the boundless suffering that the Jews had experienced. How could Polish society's "inability to mourn," or, less ambitiously, the absence of compassion among the Poles for their Jewish fellow citizens, be accounted for when the Holocaust had been directly witnessed by millions of bystanders?

Until someone offers an alternative explanation, we must consider that it was ordinary Poles' widespread collusion with the Nazi-driven extermination of the Jews which alone could produce such callousness. Living Jews embodied the massive failure of character and reason on the part of their Polish neighbors and constituted by mere presence both a reminder and a threat that they might need to account for themselves. A live Jew converted *mienie pożydowskie,* "formerly Jewish property," into property that belonged to somebody else, and various strata of Polish society could not bear any examination of the books documenting how it acquired, in an infinite multitude of transactions, what went under the *pożydowskie* label.* Each village in Poland has its own contentious microeconomic history of the redistribution of Jewish wealth, which cannot be told without mutual recriminations even by Polish beneficiaries alone. Imagine the likelihood of a narrative reconciling Polish and Jewish claims—and such a narrative would have to be produced, unless the Jews were gotten rid of for good.

In *Nazi Germany and the Jews,* Saul Friedlander describes a scene from Witlich, a small town in the Moselle Valley, on the morning following the Kristallnacht: "Jewish businesses were vandalized, Jewish men beaten up and taken away: Herr Marx, who owned the butcher shop down the street, was one of the half dozen Jewish men already on the truck. . . . The SA men were laughing at Frau Marx who stood in front of her smashed plate-glass window [with] both hands raised in bewildered despair. 'Why are you people doing this to us?' she wailed at the circle of silent faces in the windows, her lifelong neighbors. 'What have we ever done to you?' "[2]

Decades later, after Friedlander gave a public lecture in Hamburg, a young man came up to him passing on greetings from his grandmother from Witlich. To Friedlander's uncomprehending stare, he answered that his grandmother was a neighbor of Frau Marx. When looted Jewish belongings were sold at bargain prices to local residents, she acquired a pillow from Frau Marx's household, and it now weighed heavily on her

---

*This bizarre linguistic innovation exists only in two variations—denoting formerly Jewish and formerly German property, *mienie pożydowskie* and *poniemieckie.* Thus the phenomenon of massive expropriation of Jews and Germans that took place, in effect, outside the law, is brought out into the open by being coded into language. The words *pożydowski* and *poniemiecki* are immediately understandable to a native speaker of Polish as signifying "formerly" Jewish (or German) "leftover" property. If, on the other hand, by analogy the expression *poangielski* or *pofrancuski* was used, a native speaker would assume that whoever uttered these words had made a mistake—a Russianism, to be exact—and should have used *po angielsku* and *po francusku* instead, in order to say "in the English [or "in the French"] language." To put it simply, owing to historical happenstance only Jewish and German property were ever massively plundered in Poland, never property belonging to the French or the British.

conscience. She now kept the pillow buried deep in a closet at home and would very much have liked Friedlander to tell her how she should dispose of it (Saul Friedlander recounted the story during his public lectures at the Remarque Institute in New York City, on October 12 and 13, 1999).

"You could have killed ten Jews and you would have gotten a house," replied a man in Radziłów to a woman's request for a "formerly Jewish" house where she intended to put her in-laws. In an attempt to establish proper credentials, the woman's mother-in-law explained that her grandson was the one who climbed on the barn in which the Jews were burned and doused its roof with gasoline. However, in point of fact, killing Jews does not establish title to anything at all, and only destroys the moral fabric of those who believe in an ethics founded on the Ten Commandments.

The Holocaust of the Jews constituted a truly radical breakdown of European civilization, and we do not know how to face up to it. We did not know then, and we are still at a loss at present. Survivors' guilt might serve as a good measure of the difficulties of coming to terms with the Shoah. Those who were lined up as victims and whose turn simply did not come feel overburdened with the pangs of conscience. Is there another group of Europeans imaginable who were objectively less implicated in the crime? If Holocaust survivors could not reconcile themselves to their role (or fate?) in this man-made catastrophe, who else can, or could ever be expected to?

Opportunistic complicity with anti-Jewish Nazi policies was a universal phenomenon in occupied Europe—as much an experience of Jews and their neighbors in Paris, Amsterdam, Vienna, and Salonika as it was in Warsaw, Wilno, Riga, Minsk, Tarnopil, and Lwów. However, there were more Jews in Poland before the war than anywhere else; they were dispersed, and a multitude was killed in situ. As a result, many people became complicit in their exploitation and, as it transpired, in their death.

We must also remember, on the other hand, that while the crimes of Polish neighbors were opportunistic, Poles did not seek the opportunity to commit them. Those crimes would not have taken place but for the circumstances created under Nazi occupation. Poles did not want the Nazis to occupy their country, and they did everything possible, with commendable bravery, to stave them off. In retrospect, however, with the sad irony that history so generously bestows on human subjects, this unexpected and uninvited opportunity to prey on their neighbors may

prove the most significant and lasting consequence of the Second World
War. "They," said Hannah Arendt, "who were the Nazis' first accom-
plices and their best aides truly did not know what they were doing nor
with whom they were dealing."[3*]

Poles who found a "genuine agreement" with German occupiers in
the exploitation of the Jews, a phenomenon that so deeply disturbed Jan
Karski at the beginning of the occupation, did not initially contemplate
that massive killings of their Jewish compatriots would take place. In the
westernmost and central parts of Poland, the local population was drawn
into complicity step by step. Only in the territories conquered from the
Soviets after June 22, 1941, was brutalization swift. By the summer of
1941, the Nazis were much more advanced in their thinking and exterminatory practices than in the fall of 1939. Likewise, the local population
was already unhinged from the moorings provided by community institutions, which were devastated after two years of Sovietization. This was
the context of the Jedwabne mass murder on July 10, and of the well-
documented sweeping wave of mass murders of Jews by their neighbors
throughout the Podlasie region.

In each case the experience was intimate, violent, and profitable. It
took place at the interface of Polish Jewish relations, on the lower rungs
of society, and it was insular. Each community followed its own dynamic
and structure of opportunities, and the memory of those events remains
sharp, distinct, and localized. Who got what of the "formerly Jewish
property" is very well known in each little town and hamlet even today.

How is it that this story has not already been clearly outlined in Polish historiography? For one thing, the dominant heroic narrative of the
war left no room to tell the story. Also, the complicity of the Poles in
wartime assaults on their Jewish fellow citizens was really obscured by
the stratification of prewar society, as a result of which social elites, especially in larger cities, remained basically unaware of what happened between Jews and peasants or small-town dwellers except in episodic,
anecdotal forms, recounted as isolated incidents.

This compartmentalization of knowledge was predicated on social

---

*To quote another brilliant twentieth-century philosopher and a witness to these
events, Jean-Paul Sartre: *"D'un bout à l'autre de la guerre* nous n'avons pas reconnu [author's em-
phasis] *nos actes, nous n'avons pas pu revendiquer leurs consequences"* (Jean-Paul Sartre, "Paris sous l'occupation," in *Situations III*, p. 37). In English: "From the beginning to the end of the war, *we did
not understand* what we were doing, and we could not take responsibility for the consequences
of our behavior."

distance and the archaic, quasi-feudal, vertical structure of Polish society. We must also recognize that during collective stress, revolution, and rapid social change, people acquire tunnel vision. They seem less capable of following, or being interested in, the experience of others. Their own social class, their town, their city block, their own family, become the exclusive foci of all the energies and resources they can muster. Social interaction contracts as individuals retreat into the familiar intimacy of primary groups. If in addition the organizers of public order, those who are engineering social change, deliberately prevent social communication, denying freedom of speech and political liberties to all concerned, it is exceedingly difficult and rare to be informed about the fate of others.

The obfuscation of violence meted out against the Jews went even deeper. Why don't you give me your possessions—we recall a good, friendly neighbor suggesting to Chaja Finkelsztajn—otherwise, those who are about to harm you are going to get it all. A young Polish historian, Dariusz Libionka, quotes a characteristic sentence from an official underground report informing Polish authorities in London about current events in Poland for the period of October 15 through November 20, 1940. Jews were being confined into a designated neighborhood, the ghetto, in Warsaw at the time, and the rapporteur writes in annoyance that: "Frequently Jews prefer to have their goods confiscated by the Germans rather than to give them to Poles for use for some time." Libionka comments on this passage: "Without pausing to consider the absurdity of such a perception of reality, there is little doubt that a large segment of Polish society, and not exclusively the uneducated ones, could think in those categories."[4]

Thus the Jewish victim is confronted with a choice framed as a potential violation of a neighborly norm of friendly consideration. And we discover that deadly interactions between Jews and their neighbors were not driven by Nazi coercion, but rather by a perverted logic of self-interest and mutual obligation: Are you still my friend? Well, in any case, if I don't plunder the Jews somebody else will, and either the Germans or my neighbors will be enriched . . . at my expense. Instead of obeying a distant, superior Nazi authority, people act effectively compelled to do what they are doing by a mechanism of indigenous social control. And so, understandably, those who do not conform become social outcasts.

A brilliant interpreter of Polish society's wartime experience, the lit-

erary scholar Kazimierz Wyka, observed that it was Poland's misfortune
not to have had a Quisling-like government during the occupation. Consequently, Wyka quipped, anti-Semitism was never compromised in
public opinion as an attribute of servile collaborationism with the Nazis.
Likewise, he might have noted, the spoliation of Jewish neighbors could
not be attributed to people's following the orders of some higher authority or institution. Those who killed in Jedwabne, those who plundered in
Szczebrzeszyn, those who took advantage of their Jewish neighbors *in periculo mortis* anywhere and in any manner whatsoever, *could have refrained from
doing so.*

Many did refrain, and some even chose to extend assistance to their
Jewish neighbors, only too frequently to become outcasts in their own
communities. How else to explain this startling phenomenon from
which I began my inquiry—that people who brought assistance to Jews
had to conceal their actions from neighbors—but that spoliation of the
Jews became a community-accepted norm?* Otherwise, would those
who helped the Jews remain shunned or imperiled as outcasts after the
war? Otherwise, would Jewish survivors returning from the dead be
killed or compelled to run away from their hometowns? On the available
evidence, we must also conclude that the moral economy of Polish society after the war made allowances for murdering Jews. As Alina Cała observed after three surveys of Polish peasants' attitudes toward Jews, from
the mid-1970s to mid-1980s, "Even those who had severely condemned
the Nazi persecutions judged the postwar murders very tolerantly or
even justified them."†

We read a description of a murder scene near Szczuczyn in the
files of a court case brought after the war against a certain Franciszek
Konopko. Two witnesses left similar independent accounts.

*" 'Everyone was called to hunt the enemy,' said Theodore Nyilinkwaya, a survivor of
the massacres in his home village of Kimbogo, in the southwestern province of Cyangugu.
'But let's say someone is reluctant. Say that guy comes with a stick. They tell him, "No, get a
masu." So, OK, he does, and he runs along with the rest, but he doesn't kill. They say, "Hey, he
might denounce us later. He must kill. Everyone must help to kill at least one person." So this
person who is not a killer is made to do it. And the next day it's become a game for him. You
don't need to keep pushing him' " (Philip Gourevitch, *We Wish to Inform You That Tomorrow We
Will Be Killed with Our Families*, p. 24).
†Cała, *The Image of the Jew*, p. 218. Let me make clear, however, in explicit terms, that I do
not equate this tolerance for murdering Jews in the moral economy of postwar Polish society with the exterminatory anti-Semitism of the Germans. This was a moral economy that
no longer recoiled from the idea of killing *some* Jews, *pour encourager les autres* to make themselves scarce and leave once and for all.

In the fall of 1941 I was returning to Szczuczyn with my mother . . . on the road from the Skaje hamlet I saw exactly how Franciszek Konopko . . . holding a birch cudgel thick as an arm, together with a Szczuczyn inhabitant, Aleksander Domiziak . . . also holding in hand a similar birch club, chased in front of them toward the Jewish cemetery . . . a Jew I knew, whose name was Magik, and who had made candy in Szczuczyn until 1939. When those men leading the Jew passed by us I heard how Magik was pleading with Domiziak: "Let me go, Olek, was I not feeding your children? Didn't I give you a lot of sugar on credit? I have a gold watch that I will give you." I saw how Konopko kicked the Jew Magik with the tip of his boot in the rear part of the body and said "Go fuck yourself, Jew."

"I heard screams"—a second witness thus began to describe the scene— "and I got off my bike and I saw Franciszek Konopko standing with an arm-thick club over the Jewish pastry cook Magik . . . I heard how the Jew Magik begged Konopko . . . 'Franek, where are you taking me?' "[5]

A person being taken off to be killed tries to figure out till the very last moment why she has been singled out for imminent death. Regina Fisz argued with her soon-to-be murderers on the truck from Kielce, as did the Jewish pastry cook Magik on a country road near Szczuczyn. People *in periculo mortis* keep asking questions. The most dramatic occasionally pops up in the form of the first-name diminutive with which prospective victims address their murderers—the bloodcurdling "Jurek" Laudański or "Jerzyk" Tarnaczek in Szmul Wasersztajn's original testimony about the Jedwabne murders, or "Olek" and "Franek" in Magik's last words near Szczuczyn.[6]

Intimacy between murderers and victims affects a distant observer across time and cultural divides. It imparts distrust in our own experience. If living side by side, playing in adjacent courtyards, passing each other in the street, meeting in a marketplace, looking over one another's Sunday best during an evening stroll—if all of this does not presume mutual recognition and some degree of reciprocal obligation, then we cannot trust our own senses, and the experience of everyday life is profoundly misleading. Or else, we must assume that a radical breach may suddenly open up between human beings, so that people engaged in a murderous encounter belong in effect to a different species. On deeper reflection it is not the victims who are relegated to nonhuman status as a result of that rupture, only the men holding cudgels, since it is they who lose the genus-specific ability of speech, and all they can answer when queried about what they are doing is "Go fuck yourself, Jew," or a *kein warum.**

"One of the most significant facts established about human behavior, as it relates to warfare and other acts of violence against conspecifics, is the following: cultural evolution permits the development of *pseudospeciation*" (emphasis in source).[7] Jane Goodall, who revolutionized human knowledge of primates, wrote these remarks in order to explain some disturbing behavior of chimpanzees that she observed in Africa.

> Pseudospeciation (or cultural speciation as I prefer) in humans means, among other things, that the members of one group (the in-group) may not only see themselves as different from members of another group (the out-group), but also behave in different ways to group and non-group individuals. In its extreme form, cultural speciation leads to the dehumanizing of out-group members, so that they may come to be regarded almost as members of a different species. This frees group members from the inhibitions and social sanctions that operate within the group, and enables them to direct acts toward "those others" which would not be tolerated within the group.[†]

But "human beings, obviously, are of a common species. That is a simple fact of the natural world."[8] In that sense "pseudospeciation" is inherently arbitrary.

---

*In one of his stories, Primo Levi quotes an SS man he overheard in Auschwitz saying that people should forget here about the question "Why?," that Auschwitz was a realm of *"kein warum."* This observation was not revealing a truth about Auschwitz, but about butchers from Auschwitz, because victims, always, until the last moment, kept asking that very question—"Why?" What better proof can one garner than the only sentence that has reached us from the abyss of the gas chambers in Bełżec—"But Mommy, I was a good boy, it's dark, it's dark . . ." (*"Mamusiu, przecież ja byłem grzeczny, ciemno, ciemno . . ."*) (Rudolf Reder, *Bełżec,* p. 66).

†Jane Goodall (with Phillip Berman), *Reason for Hope: A Spiritual Journey,* p. 129. I am grateful to Stephanie Steiker for drawing my attention to Jane Goodall's work on this subject. In what follows, Goodall vividly describes the consequences of "pseudospeciation" among the chimpanzees. Here is what happens when primates, in a manner of speaking, adopt a common pattern of human behavior: "The Gombe chimpanzees quite clearly show the precursors to cultural speciation. Their sense of group identity is strong . . . far more sophisticated than mere xenophobia. The members of the Kahama community had, before the split, enjoyed close and friendly relations with their aggressors; in some cases they had grown up with them and had traveled, fed, played, groomed, and slept together. By separating

255

255

255

Unfolding over generations, and self-limited by recognition of similar rights held by others, we know "cultural or social speciation" as a process of acquiring national consciousness. It is an artifice, a construct, that may unfold on occasion with lightning speed.* Here lies the crux of the injury self-inflicted by communities that aided and abetted the extermination of the Jews and the source of the pervasive fear of Jews in Polish society after the war: once a community has condoned arbitrary killings (that is, the kind aimed at some general category of fellow human beings who were thereby arbitrarily removed beyond the boundaries of the species) it has no ground to stand on in principle when some other agency, armed with another criterion of "pseudospeciation," shows up at its doorstep ready to kill somebody else. Those who accept or legitimize (by their behavior or in their hearts) the ultimate violence against fellow humans thereby renounce their own prospective claim to victimhood. Even simple folk know such simple truths.†

---

themselves, it was as though the Kahamans had forfeited their 'right' to be treated as group members—instead, they were treated as strangers. And, just as civil wars in our own species can be the most shocking, so it was with the assaults on these onetime friends. All those attacks were brutal, but the worst, for me, was the attack on my old friend Goliath, who had inexplicably cast his lot with the southerners [i.e., the group from Kahama]. He was so ancient, thin, and frail and utterly harmless. He was trying desperately to hide, crouching under some thick undergrowth, when they found him. He was dragged out, screaming. Five adult males, his former grooming partners, took part in this assault. And an adolescent seized every opportunity to rush in and contribute his own small blows, screaming in excitement. For eighteen minutes they attacked, hitting and biting and dragging, twisting one leg round and round. When they left, wild with excitement, the old male tried to sit up, but fell back, shivering. . . .

"Time and again the Kasakela males, when attacking Kahama chimps, showed aggressive patterns not seen during fights with members of their own community yet seen regularly when chimpanzees are trying to incapacitate and dismember a large prey animal. So that in addition to being hit and kicked and pounded on, the unfortunate Kahama victims had their bones broken, strips of skin torn off, and, as we saw with Goliath, their limbs twisted round. They were dragged and flailed in the gang assaults. One aggressor even drank his victims' blood. The Kahama chimps were indeed treated as though they were prey animals—they were thoroughly 'de-chimpized.' Unfortunately, cultural speciation has become very highly developed in human societies around the world" (pp. 129–31).

*The writer Brian Hall was told by a Muslim man from Bosnia: "Five years ago I never even thought about who was who. Croat? Serb? Muslim? Why would I care about something like that? I didn't even know what some of my friends were. What really frightens me—and even more than that, what *amazes* me—is how quickly the tribal feelings have arisen" (quoted in Kai Erikson, "Drawing Ethnic Boundaries," p. 22).

†Local people knew that a fundamental transgression had taken place in their community, and the foreboding sense of a curse hanging over their town informed conversations in Jedwabne long after the war (see Marta Kurkowska-Budzan, "My Jedwabne," in Antony Polonsky and Joanna B. Michlic, eds., *The Neighbors Respond: The Controversy over the Jedwabne Massacre in Poland*, pp. 204–206). It probably was no different in other communities where local Jews had been killed by local people.

Because Jews were part of the human species, widespread involvement in their annihilation rendered members of the society that gave them up vulnerable and exposed. For if people marked by their Jewishness could be dealt with inhumanly, then any other marker could be used with just as much justification to single out some social group for "repression." People know that they cannot credibly claim rights that they have withheld from others, and communities that assisted in the annihilation of their Jewish neighbors thereby morally surrendered to a new organizer of public order poised to carry out comprehensive social engineering. Those who had helped the Nazis were unwittingly among the most effective instruments of postwar Sovietization.

Invoking what was apparently in his days already an ancient wisdom, Tacitus writes in "The Life of Cnaeus Julius Agricola," "It is, indeed, human nature to hate the man whom you have injured."[9] Jews were so frightening and dangerous, in other words, not because of what they had done or could do to the Poles, but because of what Poles had done to the Jews.* Widespread involvement in the murder and plunder of the Jews revealed—in each community where assaults and plunder took place—a propensity for internecine violence from which, in principle, nobody was immune. The Jews who survived the war were not threatening just because they reminded those who had availed themselves of Jewish property that its rightful owners might come back to reclaim it. They also induced fear in people by reminding them of the fragility of *their own* existence, of the propensity for violence residing in *their own* communities, and of *their own* helplessness vis-à-vis the agents of pseudospeciation who now invoked class criteria for elimination from public life.

Finally, people could not bear the Jewish presence after the war because it called forth their own feeling of shame and of contempt in which they were held by their victims. A humble carpenter, beloved by his people for putting into words their feelings as only a few ever could, wrote a song in Kraków in February 1940:

> . . . It hurts!
> It hurts terribly!

---

*In point of fact, Jews had not done much of anything—as we know, Jews did not use Christian blood for matzo, they fled Communism, and even if all the surviving Jews had succeeded in reclaiming their property, since 90 percent of Polish Jews had been murdered, almost all Jewish property would have remained in the hands of the new proprietors anyway.

When it isn't a foreign foe,
But they—
Poland's sons and daughters,
Whose land will some day
Be ashamed of them,
But who now chuckle, gasp with laughter,
Seeing down in the street
How our common enemy
Ridicules the Jews,
Strikes and torments the old,
Then plunders them undisturbed,
Cutting off the beards of Jews
Like they were slices of bread . . .
And they,
Who are left like us
Without a land,
Who feel now like us
The crazed enemy's hand—
How can they heckle, laugh, rejoice
At such a time ·
When Poland's pride and honour
Are so disgraced,
When Poland's white eagle
Is dragged on the ground,
Between the beards,
The grey and black hair
Of Jewish beards—
Is this not eternal shame
For all of them?
Isn't it like spitting
Right in their own faces?
It hurts!
How terribly it hurts!

Mordecai Gebirtig had a gift for words, but he only expressed what many others who observed the wrongdoing had noticed.[10]

   In the midst of the slowly unfolding murderous assaults on the Jewish community in Radziłów, Chaja Finkelsztajn pleaded with the town's Catholic priest "to tell his parishioners that war does not last forever and that they should not soil the Poles' reputation with their evil deeds against the Jews. And that parents should tell the children not to help the Germans."¹¹* In the last stanza of his terse poem "A Poor Christian Looks at the Ghetto," written in Warsaw in 1943, Czesław Miłosz laid out the consequences of breaking the bond with fellow human beings: "I am afraid, so afraid of the guardian mole. / He has swollen eyelids, like a Patriarch / Who has sat much in the light of candles / Reading the great book of the species. / What will I tell him, I, a Jew of the New Testament, / Waiting two thousand years for the second coming of Jesus? / My broken body will deliver me to his sight / And he will count me among the helpers of death: / The uncircumcised."¹²

The only retaliation available to helpless victims is to hold their tormentors in contempt. Wherever Jews had been plundered, denounced, betrayed, or killed by their neighbors, their reappearance after the war evoked this dual sense of shame and contempt, which could be overcome only by mourning. And as long as Polish society was unable to mourn its Jewish neighbors' deaths, it had either to purge them or to live in infamy.

What happened to Jews in Poland after the war may not be, intrinsically, much of a story. That a quarter million people were no longer welcome by the majority population in a country their ancestors had lived in for centuries was not very unusual by the standards of the epoch. As ethnic cleansing goes, the murder of some 500 or 1,500 people should not have raised many eyebrows, either. As to flight into exile, those Jews who ran away from Poland for the most part successfully resumed their lives in Israel, Canada, the United States, Australia, and various countries in Western Europe and South America—certainly a lucky denouement by twentieth-century criteria. And yet, half a century later we ask ourselves with dismay, How could there be anti-Semitism in Poland, of all places, after Auschwitz?

What makes the story of postwar anti-Semitism in Poland so rich in

*The Radziłów parson declined to address his parishioners and he used the same argument that Bishop Juliusz Bieniek invoked when asked by the British ambassador to Poland to condemn anti-Semitism after the Kielce pogrom. "Do you think I can speak from the pulpit on behalf of the Jews?" Chaja Finkelsztajn writes in her memoir, "As big as I am (and he raised a hand over his head and he was really so tall and well fed that he could not fit into a regular door, and then he lowered his hand to the ground), I would become so small in their eyes. . . . So great is their hatred against the Jews. . . . All Jews are communists, from twelve to sixty years old" (*Wokół Jedwabnego*, vol. II, p. 299).

significance lies, in a manner of speaking, outside of the period, or, more precisely, in the framing of the issue. First, by following what happened we acquire an unexpected insight into the nature of the mutual relationship between Jews and Communism in Eastern Europe. Much as they were an ideological alternative to nationalism in the region, Communist parties were first of all committed to *Machtergreifung*, the power grab, in East Central Europe. They accomplished that goal at the bidding of the growing national-patriotic Soviet Union and in the context of Stalin's increasingly unabashed anti-Semitism, and they willingly put on a national costume in order to succeed.

In Poland, broad segments of society desired immunity for sometimes willful and sometimes unwitting involvement in the spoliation of their Jewish neighbors, and the Communist Party was ready to provide it. Restitution of private property to rightful owners was nowhere on the Communists' agenda anyway, as they gradually implemented their program of "socialization of the means of production and collectivization of agriculture." And in their desire to portray themselves as an indigenous political movement rooted in the "blood and body . . . of national history," they deliberately turned a blind eye to problems confronting the Jewish population and tried to insulate themselves from any association with "the Jews."

Thus, the Communist authorities acquiesced in society's violently expressed desire to render the country *Judenrein*, and the "Jewish question" was, so to speak, taken off the agenda, along with the investigation of, and accounting for, what happened to Jews at the hands of their fellow citizens during the German occupation. Together with the social mobility ensured by Soviet-type forced industrialization, this may have been the most important positive incentive (an indispensable addition to police terror) ensuring acceptance of the new regime and the political disenfranchisement by the general populace.

And second, we come to the realization that the subject is so compelling because it reveals a wartime horror story. Polish society's allergic reaction to Jewish survivors makes no sense unless Polish neighbors had harmed the Jews during the war, so as to be unable to examine that chapter of their mutual relations. In order to make sure that the subject remained suppressed once and for all, Jews had to be removed from the scene for good. The tale of ritual murder and the mantra of *żydokomuna* were but themes that could be conflated with actual events and then substituted, in the collective consciousness of the Poles, for what really happened. We know in hindsight that this turned out to be a successful and long-lasting strategy of dissimulation.

In the end, the postwar treatment of Jews in Poland (the whole complex story of society's aggressiveness and the regime's institutional inertia in counteracting it, except by facilitating Jewish flight from Poland) appears as the smoking gun that reveals the true character of wartime Polish Jewish relations. If all evidence about what took place between Poles and Jews during the war had disappeared, and if we knew only the particulars of Nazi crimes, we would still be able to tell that broad strata of Polish society took advantage of Nazi policies and joined in the spoliation of their Jewish neighbors. We would know it on the strength of virulent postwar anti-Semitism and from the social ostracism of the Righteous Among Nations who, at enormous personal risk, had helped some Jews to survive. Given the character of the Holocaust, which had been witnessed by the surrounding population, and the human misery it inflicted, I cannot think of any other explanation for the persistence of these attitudes among the Polish population.*

People don't avail themselves of every opportunity that comes their way. That Polish society proved vulnerable to totalitarian temptation and that numerous Poles joined in Nazi-organized victimization of their Jewish fellow citizens was facilitated by indigenous anti-Semitism. Poland's anti-Semitism was the standard brand, widespread in the countries of Christian Europe and the United States at the time. The only difference was that three and a half million Jews lived in Poland on the eve of

---

*One of the most accomplished historians of twentieth-century Poland, Dariusz Stola, reaches out, albeit halfway, in the same direction. In the November 2005 special issue of I P N's *Bulletin* devoted to "Jews in People's Poland," Stola says the following: "For me one of the greatest mysteries of our twentieth-century history is Polish attitudes toward the Jews after the Holocaust. Specifically in the 1940s (1944–48), when very few Jews remained, but manifestations of hatred toward them—both in verbal form and as actual deeds—were many. This is when the medieval myth about Jews snatching Christian children, which seemed long dead, gets resurrected. True, Jews were overrepresented in the apparatus of power, there were conflicts concerning Jewish property taken over during the war, but this is not enough to explain the phenomenon. . . . A new approach enlightens us a bit concerning this mystery . . . the psychology of post-traumatic syndrome. . . . What are the consequences of witnessing something horrible? . . .

"Poland is the very European country where the largest number of people directly witnessed the Holocaust. The German population saw Jews being taken away, as did the French, or the Dutch . . . but it was different in Poland (and also in Ukraine, in Lithuania, etc.). Here hundreds of thousands, if not millions, saw the death of Jews, heard the dying, smelled the horrible sweetish smell of death. . . . Psychological reaction to such an experience is complex and irrational . . . and it often evokes feelings which are not necessarily those of pity or sympathy" ("Wszyscy krawcy wyjechali," pp. 11, 12).

the war (far more than in any other country occupied by the Germans) and the Nazis proceeded to murder them right there. In the process, "bystanders" were incrementally drawn into complicity, as Poland's "fundamentally anti-Semitic clergy" (Ambassador Cavendish-Bentinck's diagnosis) proved unwilling to step in and prevent their flock from getting involved.* Deep religiosity compelled individual Catholics to shelter and help human beings facing mortal peril and save many a Jewish life. But rescuers represented a small minority, ostracized in their own milieus, while the religious veneer of the Polish clergy was thin, easily chipped away at by the prejudice and greed they shared with the common folk.

"Anti-Semitism," Hannah Arendt wrote in 1945, "is one of the most important political movements of our time," and even though "the whole world, including the Jews, has . . . learned to put up with it, so that today anyone who concerns himself with it seriously seems slightly ridiculous . . . the fight against it is one of the most vital duties of the democracies, and its survival is one of the most important indications of future perils."[13] Her call ought to especially ring true to the inhabitants of *Polín,*† Poland, where Jews made their home for close to a thousand years. Catholic mobs acting during and after the war on their anti-Semitic fantasies were breaking with Poland's romantic tradition of nurturing the weak and defending the persecuted, and they were equally thrashing the ennobling belief in Poland's destiny as "the Christ of Nations." Since the spiritual heritage these myths embody provided sustenance to the nation during the time of its greatest peril for more than a century of lost independence, the Poles can ill afford ever to discard it.

---

*Catholic priests could have invoked the fundamentals of Christian ethics and categorically forbidden their parishioners to partake in the killings of Jews. They could have done this—indeed some did and with very good effect—in every community, without grandstanding, through the grapevine, without endangering their own lives. In this sense, in each district where the voice of its representatives was not heard on this issue, the Church became complicitous in murderous assaults by Polish Catholics against their Jewish neighbors. Albert Camus's remark in the September 26, 1944, issue of *Combat*—"During these four dreadful years all Frenchmen [and ipso facto all Poles as well] were witnesses to a crime not foreseen by any law (and in saying this we are weighing our words carefully): the crime of not doing enough"—applies here with full force (Levi-Valensi, *Camus at Combat*, p. 48).

†The word *Polín,* Poland, carries an unequivocally positive connotation for Jews. The false etymology used by the Jews (of course, *Polín* is merely a version of *Polen*) was Po—"here," and *lín*—"find a haven"; and *Polanya,* a version of *Polonia,* was explained etymologically as Po—"here," *lan*—"found a haven," *ya*—"God" (*Yahwe*); i.e., "Here God found a haven."

ACKNOWLEDGMENTS

I owe a debt of gratitude to several people and institutions for their help and encouragement. I wish to thank good friends and colleagues Omer Bartov, Anna Bikont, Daniel Blatman, Peter Brown, David Engel, Kai Erikson, Roman Frydman, Irena Grudzińska-Gross, Henryk Kowalski, Martin Krygier, Arno Meyer, Norman Naimark, Alicia Pittard, Antony Polonsky, Julia Przyboś, Brigitta van Rheinberg, Marci Shore, Timothy Snyder, Nicholas Stargardt, Amir Weiner, and Klaudiusz Weiss, who read the manuscript and offered comments and advice. I am particularly indebted to Natalia Aleksiun for translating Hebrew and Yiddish texts and for sharing her considerable knowledge of archival sources pertinent to the subject; to the filmmaker Marcel Lozinski, who made a documentary film about the Kielce pogrom entitled *Świadkowie* (*Witnesses*), for copies of complete interviews that he recorded in 1987–88; to my son, Tomek Gross, for editing the first version of the manuscript and proofreading galleys of the book; and to Sarah Chalfant, for skillfully chaperoning the manuscript into print.

I am grateful for being able to use as illustrations photographs by Julia Pirotte (1908–2000), née Diament in Końskowola to a poor Jewish family. Her estate was donated to the Jewish Historical Institute in Warsaw, which kindly gave me permission to reprint photographs from its collections. Upon returning after the war to her native Poland, Pirotte organized the Military Photographic Agency (Wojskowa Agencja Fotograficzna, WAF) and produced many iconic images of the period.

Some of her work captured the life and death of the Jewish community during the postwar years.

The staff at Random House—Will Murphy, Fleetwood Robbins, and Janet Wygal—handled production of the book with professional skill. My heartfelt thanks go to Jolanta Benal for her exquisite copyediting.

I completed the research for this book during a Senior Fulbright Research Fellowship and an IREX Fellowship in Poland. The writing of *Fear* was facilitated by a faculty fellowship at the Remarque Institute of New York University and a grant from the University Committee on Research in the Humanities and Social Sciences at Princeton University. I am grateful for this support.

I dedicate *Fear* to the memory of Felek Scharf.

Princeton, January 2006

BIBLIOGRAPHY

ARCHIVES AND COLLECTIONS

Archiwum Akt Nowych (AAN), Ministerstwo Administracji Publicznej (MAP)
Archiwum Państwowe w Krakowie (APK)
Archiwum Państwowe w Lublinie (APL)
Goldstein-Goren Diaspora Research Center in Tel Aviv
Instytut Pamięci Narodowej (IPN)
United States Holocaust Memorial Museum Archives
Yad Vashem (YV)
Yale University, Fortunoff Video Archive for Holocaust Testimonies (Fortunoff Archive)
Żydowski Instytut Historyczny (ŻIH), Centralny Komitet Żydów w Polsce (CKŻP)

DOCUMENTS, DOCUMENT COLLECTIONS, AND ENCYCLOPEDIAS

Altman, Ilya, ed. *Neizvestnaya chernaya kniga. Svidelstva ochevidsev o katastrofe sovetskikh evreev (1941–1944)*. Moscow/Jerusalem: Tekst, 1993.

Bordiugov, Gennadi, and Gennadi Matveev, et al., eds. *SSSR-Polsha: Mekhanizmi podchinyenya 1944–1949, Sbornik dokumentov*. Moscow: Airo-XX, 1995.

Cała, Alina, and Helena Datner-Śpiewak, eds. *Dzieje Żydów w Polsce 1944–1968. Teksty źródłowe*. Warszawa: Żydowski Instytut Historyczny, 1997.

Churchill, Winston S. *His Complete Speeches, 1897–1963*. New York and London: Chelsea House Publishers, 1974, vol. 7.

Encyclopedia Judaica. Jerusalem, 1972.

Encyklopedia Powszechna. Warszawa: Państwowe Wydawnictwo Naukowe, 1974.

Grynberg, Michał, and Maria Kotowska, eds. *Życie i zagłada Żydów polskich 1939–1945: Relacje świadków*. Warszawa: Oficyna Naukowa, 2003.

Heymont, Irving. *Among the Survivors of the Holocaust, 1945: The Landsberg DP Camp Letters of Major Irving Heymont, United States Army.* Cincinnati: American Jewish Archives, 1982.

Informator o nielegalnych antypaństwowych organizacjach i bandach zybrojnych działających w Polsce Ludowej w latach 1944–1956. Warszawa: Ministerstwo Spraw Wewnętrznych biuro "c," 1964. Published by Wydawnichtwo RETRO, Lublin, 1993.

Katyń—Dokumenty ludobójstwa. Dokumenty i materiały archiwalne przekazane Polsce 14 października 1992r. Warszawa: Instytut Nauk Politycznych PAN, 1992.

Klukowski, Zygmunt. *Dziennik z lat okupacji zamojszczyzny.* Lublin: Ludowa Spółdzielnia Wydawnicza, 1958.

Kochanowski, Jerzy, ed. *Protokoły posiedzeń Prezydium Krajowej Rady Narodowej, 1944–1947.* Warszawa: Wydawnictwo Sejmowe, 1995.

Kochański, Aleksander, ed. *Protokoły posiedzeń Sekretariatu KC PPR, 1945–1946.* Warszawa: Instytut Studiów Politycznych Polskiej Akademii Nauk, 2001.

Kochavi, Aryeh Josef. "The Catholic Church and Anti-Semitism in Poland Following World War II as Reflected in British Diplomatic Documents." *Gal-Ed on the History of the Jews in Poland,* no. 11, 1989.

Kruk, Herman. *The Last Days of the Jerusalem of Lithuania: Chronicles from the Vilna Ghetto and the Camps, 1939–1944.* New Haven and London: Yale University Press, 2002.

Księga Żydów Ostrołęckich. Ostrołęka–Tel Aviv, 2001. (Translation of *Sefer Kehilat Ostrolenk: Buch fun Ostrolenker Kehila, Book of Kehilath Ostrolenka.* Tel Aviv, 1963.)

Meducki, Stanisław, and Zenon Wrona, eds. *Antyżydowskie wydarzenia kieleckie 4 lipca 1946 roku. Dokumenty i materiały.* Kielce: Urząd Miasta Kielce i Kieleckie Towarzystwo Naukowe, 1992, vols. 1 and 2.

Paczkowski, Andrzej, ed. *Aparat bezpieczeństwa w latach 1944–1956, taktyka, strategia, metody. Część I. Lata 1945–1947.* Warszawa: Instytut Studiów Politycznych Polskiej Akademii Nauk, 1994.

———, and Tatiana Cariewskaja, et al., eds. *Teczka specjalna J.W. Stalina. Raporty NKWD z Polski 1944–1946.* Warszawa: Oficyna Wydawnicza RYTM, 1998.

"Raport głównej komisji badania zbrodni przeciwko Narodowi Polskiemu—IPN o wyniku śledztwa w sprawie wydarzeń kieleckich 4.07.1946" [GKBZpNP-IPN] (in manuscript, 1997).

Redlich, Shimon, ed. *Yevreyskii Antifashistovskii Komitet v SSSR, 1941–1948: Dokumentirovannaya Istoria.* Moscow: Mezhdunarodnoe Otnoshenya, 1996.

Shandler, Jeffrey, ed. *Awakening Lives: Autobiographies of Jewish Youth in Poland Before the Holocaust.* New Haven and London: Yale University Press, 2002.

NEWSPAPERS AND MAGAZINES

L'Ésprit
Gazeta Wyborcza
Kuźnica
Le Monde
Mówią Wieki
The New York Review of Books
The New York Times

Odrodzenie
Tygodnik Powszechny
Warszawa
Wprost

BOOKS AND ARTICLES

Adelson, Józef. "W Polsce zwanej ludową," in Jerzy Tomaszewski, ed. *Najnowsze dzieje Żydów w Polsce.* Warszawa: Wydawnictwo Naukowe PWN, 1993.

Aleksiun, Natalia. "Documenting the Fate of Polish Jewry: The Central Jewish Historical Commission in Poland, 1944–1947" (in manuscript).

———. *Dokąd dalej? Ruch syjonistyczny w Polsce (1944–1950).* Warszawa: Wydawnictwo TRIO, 2002.

———. "The Situation of the Jews in Poland as Seen by the Soviet Security Forces in 1945," in *Jews in Eastern Europe,* 3(37), 1998.

Andrzejewski, Jerzy. "Zagadnienie polskiego antysemityzmu," in *Odrodzenie,* July 7, 1946, and July 14, 1946 (parts 1 and 2).

Arendt, Hannah. "Organized Guilt and Universal Responsibility," in *Essays in Understanding, 1930–1954.* New York: Schocken Books, 1994.

———. "The Seeds of a Fascist International," in *Essays in Understanding, 1930–1954.* New York: Schocken Books, 1994.

Auerbach, Rachela. *Oif die felder fun Treblinka.* Warszawa-Lodz-Kraków: Żydowska Komisja Historyczna, 1947.

Avineri, Shlomo. "The Presence of Eastern and Central Europe in the Culture and Politics of Contemporary Israel," in *East European Politics and Societies,* vol. 10, no. 2, Spring 1996.

Bacon, Gershon C. "The Politics of Tradition: Agudat Israel in Polish Politics, 1916–1939," in *Studies in Contemporary Jewry,* vol. 2, 1986.

Bak, Samuel. *Painted in Words: A Memoir.* Bloomington: Indiana University Press, 2001.

Banning, Joop van SJ. "Watykan i mord rytualny," in *Mord rytualny: Legenda w historii europejskiej.* Stanisław Musiał SJ and Susanna Buttaroni, eds. Kraków-Norymberga-Frankfurt: 2003.

Bednarczuk, Wincenty. "Dwie ważne sprawy," in *Odrodzenie,* September 9, 1945.

Bielawski, Shraga Feivel. *The Last Jew from Wegrów.* New York: Praeger, 1991.

Bikont, Anna. *My z Jedwabnego.* Warszawa: Prószyński i S-ka, 2004.

———. " 'We of Jedwabne,' *Gazeta Wyborcza,* March 23, 2001," in Antony Polonsky and Joanna Michlic, eds. *The Neighbors Respond: The Controversy over the Jedwabne Massacre in Poland.* Princeton and Oxford: Princeton University Press, 2004.

Blatman, Daniel. "The Bund in Poland, 1935–1939," in *Polin: Studies in Polish Jewry,* vol. 9, 1996.

Bliss Lane, Arthur. *I Saw Poland Betrayed: An American Ambassador Reports to the American People.* Indianapolis and New York: The Bobbs-Merrill Co., 1948.

Bohlen, Charles E. *Witness to History, 1929–1969.* New York: W. W. Norton and Co., 1973.

Brent, Jonathan, and Vladimir P. Naumov. *Stalin's Last Crime: The Plot Against the Jewish Doctors, 1948–1953.* New York: HarperCollins Publishers, 2003.

Browning, Christopher R. *Ordinary Men: Reserve Police Battalion 101 and the Final Solution in Poland.* Harper Perennial, 1998.

Cała, Alina. *The Image of the Jew in Polish Folk Culture.* Jerusalem: The Magnes Press, The Hebrew University, 1995.

Chęciński, Michał. *Poland, Communism, Nationalism, Anti-Semitism.* New York: Karz-Cohl Publishers, 1982.

Chmieleńska, Irena. "Wartime Children" ("Dzieci wojenne"), in *Kuźnica,* December 9, 1945.

Chruszczow, Nikita S. "Fragmenty wspomnień N.S. Chruszczowa," in *Zeszyty Historyczne,* Paris, no. 132 (2000).

Churchill, Winston S. *Triumph and Tragedy.* Boston: Houghton Mifflin Company, 1953.

Cichopek, Anna. *Pogrom Żydów w Krakowie 11 sierpnia 1945.* Warszawa: Żydowski Instytut Historyczny, 2000.

Cohen, Yohanan. *Operation "Brikha"—Poland, 1945–1946.* Tel Aviv: Massna, 1995.

Daniel, Jerzy. *Żyd w zielonym kapeluszu. Rzecz o kieleckim pogromie 4 lipca 1946.* Kielce: Scriptum, 1996.

Deak, Istvan, Tony Judt, and Jan Gross, eds. *The Politics of Retribution in Europe: World War II and Its Aftermath.* Princeton and Oxford: Princeton University Press, 2000.

Dean, Martin. *Collaboration in the Holocaust: Crimes of the Local Police in Belorussia and Ukraine, 1941–1944.* New York: St. Martin's Press, 2000.

Djilas, Milovan. *Conversations with Stalin.* New York: Harcourt, Brace and World, 1962.

Dobroszycki, Lucjan. "The Jewish Community in Poland, 1944–1947: A Discussion of Postwar Restitution," in Yisrael Gutman and Avital Saf, eds. *She'erit Hapletah, 1944–1948, Rehabilitation and Political Struggle.* Jerusalem: Yad Vashem, 1990.

Dray, Philip. *At the Hands of Persons Unknown.* New York: The Modern Library, 2003.

Dudek, Antoni, and Grzegorz Pytel. *Bolesław Piasecki. Próba biografii politycznej.* London: Aneks, 1990.

Dziurok, Antoni. "Początki milicji na Górnym Śląsku," in *Biuletyn IPN,* no. 6, 2002.

Eden, Anthony. *The Memoirs of Anthony Eden, Earl of Avon: The Reckoning.* Boston: Houghton Mifflin Co., 1965.

Egit, Jacob. *Grand Illusion.* Toronto: Lugus, 1991.

Elon, Amos. *The Pity of It All: A History of Jews in Germany, 1743–1933.* New York: Henry Holt and Company, 2002.

Engel, David. *Beyn Shichrur le'Bricha: Nitzolei ha-Shoah be'Polin ve'hamaavak al hanhagatam, 1944–1946 (Between Liberation and Flight: Holocaust Survivors in Poland and the Struggle for Leadership, 1944–1946).* Tel Aviv: Am Oved Publishers, 1996.

———. "An Early Account of Polish Jewry Under Nazi and Soviet Occupation Presented to the Polish Government-in-Exile, February 1940," *Jewish Social Studies,* vol. 45, no. 1 (Winter 1983).

———. "Patterns of Anti-Jewish Violence in Poland, 1944, 1946," in *Yad Vashem Studies* 26, 1998.

Erikson, Erik H. "Ontogeny of Ritualization in Man," *Philosophical Transactions of the Royal Society of London,* vol. 251, 1966.

Erikson, Kai. "Drawing Ethnic Boundaries" (in manuscript).

Febvre, Lucien. *"Honneur et patrie": Une enquête sur le sentiment d'honneur et l'attachement à la patrie.* Librairie Academique Perrin, 1996.

Fitzpatrick, Sheila. "The World of Ostap Bender: Soviet Confidence Men in the Stalin Period," in *Slavic Review,* Fall 2000, no. 3.

Friedlander, Saul. *Nazi Germany and the Jews* (vol. 1). New York: Harper Perennial, 1998.

Friszke, Andrzej. *Polska. Losy państwa i narodu, 1939–1989.* Warszawa: Wydawnictwo Iskry, 2003.

Furet, François. *The Passing of an Illusion: The Idea of Communism in the Twentieth Century.* Chicago: Chicago University Press, 1999.

Garlicki, Andrzej. *Bolesław Bierut.* Warszawa: Wydawnictwa Szkolne i Pedagogiczne, 1994.

Garton Ash, Timothy. *The Polish Revolution: Solidarity.* London: Penguin Books, 1999.

Gay, Ruth. *Safe Among the Germans. Liberated Jews After World War II.* New Haven and London: Yale University Press, 2002.

Gebirtig, Mordecai. *The Song That Never Died: The Poetry of Mordecai Gebirtig.* Niagra Falls, NY: Mosaic Press, 2001.

Gechtman, Roni. *Yidisher Sotsializm: The Origin and Contexts of the Jewish Labor Bund's National Program.* Ph.D. dissertation, NYU, 2005.

Gerrits, André. "Anti-Semitism and Anti-Communism: The Myth of 'Judeo-Communism' in Eastern Europe," *East European Jewish Affairs,* vol. 25, no. 1 (1995).

Gertsman, Ida. "Zajścia w Kielcach," *Biuletyn Żydowskiego Instytutu Historycznego,* no. 4, 1996.

Głowiński, Michał. *The Black Seasons.* Evanston, Illinois: Northwestern University Press, 2005.

Goldhagen, Daniel. "Non, Pie XII n'était pas un saint," in *Le Monde,* January 15, 2005.

Goodall, Jane (with Phillip Berman). *Reason for Hope: A Spiritual Journey.* New York: Warner Books, 1999.

Gourevitch, Philip. *We Wish to Inform You That Tomorrow We Will Be Killed with Our Families.* New York: Farrar, Straus and Giroux, 1998.

Grabowski, Jan. *"Ja tego Żyda znam!" Szantażowanie Żydów w Warszawie, 1939–1943.* Warszawa: Wydawnictwo IFiS PAN, 2004.

Grabski, August. *Działalność komunistów wśród Żydów w Polsce, 1944–1949.* Warszawa: Wydawnictwo Trio, Żydowski Instytut Historyczny, 2004.

Gross, Jan T. *Neighbors: The Destruction of the Jewish Community in Jedwabne, Poland.* Princeton: Princeton University Press, 2001.

———. *Polish Society Under the German Occupation—Generalgouvernement, 1939–1944.* Princeton: Princeton University Press, 1979.

———. *Revolution from Abroad: The Soviet Conquest of Poland's Western Ukraine and Western Belorussia.* Princeton: Princeton University Press, 1988.

———. *Sąsiedzi, historia zagłady żydowskiego miasteczka.* Sejny: Pogranicze, 2000.

———. "Tangled Web: Confronting Stereotypes Concerning Relations Between Poles, Germans, Jews, and Communists," in *The Politics of Retribution in Europe: World War II and Its Aftermath,* Istvan Deak, Tony Judt, and Jan T. Gross, eds. Princeton: Princeton University Press, 2000.

———. *Wokół Sąsiadów. Polemiki i wyjaśnienia.* Sejny: Pogranicze, 2003.

Gryz, Ryszard. "Stanowisko Kościoła katolickiego wobec pogromu Żydów w Kielcach. Stan badań," in *Nasza Przeszłość,* vol. 93 (2000).

Halévy, Élie. *L'Ère des tyrannies: Études sur le socialisme et la guerre.* Paris: Gallimard, 1938.

Hall, Brian. *The Impossible Country: A Journey Through the Last Days of Yugoslavia.* Penguin, 1994.

Hartman, Stanisław. *Wspomnienia (lwowskie i inne).* Wrocław: Oficyna "Leopoldium," 1994.

Hirschman, Albert O. *Exit, Voice, and Loyalty: Responses to Decline in Firms, Organizations, and States.* Cambridge, Mass.: Harvard University Press, 1970.

Hobsbawm, Eric. *Interesting Times: A Twentieth Century Life.* London: Allen Lane, 2002.

Hochberg-Mariańska, Maria, and Noe Gruss. *Dzieci oskarżają.* Kraków-Łódź-Warszawa: Centralna Żydowska Komisja Historyczna w Polsce, 1947.

Hurwic-Nowakowska, Irena. *Żydzi Polscy (1947–1950). Analiza więzi społecznej ludności żydowskiej.* Warszawa: Wydawnictwo IFiS PAN, 1996.

Jakubowski, Zenon. *Milicja obywatelska, 1944–1948.* Warszawa: Państwowe Wydawnictwo Naukowe, 1988.

Janion, Maria. *Do Europy—tak, ale razem z naszymi umarłymi.* Warszawa: Sic!, 2000.

Jastrun, Mieczysław. "Potęga ciemnoty," in *Odrodzenie,* June 17, 1945.

Jedlicki, Witold. "Chamy i Żydzi," *Kultura,* no. 12, 1962.

Jowitt, Ken. "Moscow 'Centre,' " in *East European Politics and Societies,* 1987, no. 3.

Kahane, David. *Aharei Hamabul.* Jerusalem: Mossad Harav Kook, 1981.

Kennan, George F. *Memoirs, 1925–1950.* Boston, Toronto: Little, Brown and Company, 1967.

Kenney, Padraic. *Rebuilding Poland: Workers and Communists, 1945–1950.* Ithaca: Cornell University Press, 1997.

Kershaw, Ian. *Hitler, 1936–1945: Nemesis.* New York: W. W. Norton, 2000.

Kersten, Krystyna. *Rok pierwszy.* Warszawa: Wydawnictwa Szkolne i Pedagogiczne, 1993.

Kopstein, Jeffrey S., and Jason Wittenberg. "Who Voted Communist? Reconsidering the Social Bases of Radicalism in Interwar Poland," *The Slavic Review,* vol. 62, no. 1, 2003.

Korkuć, Maciej. " 'Kujbyszewiacy'—awangarda UB," in *Arcana,* no. 46–47 (4–5, 2002).

Kostyrchenko, Gennadi. *Out of the Red Shadows: Anti-Semitism in Soviet Russia.* Amherst, New York: Prometheus Books, 1995.

Kot, Stanisław. *Listy z Rosji do gen. Sikorskiego.* London, 1955.

Kott, Jan. "Droga do realizmu," in *Kuźnica,* March 4, 1946.

Kovaly, Heda Margolius. *Under a Cruel Star: A Life in Prague, 1941–1968.* New York: Penguin Books, 1986.

Koźminska-Frejlak, Ewa. "Polska jako ojczyzna Żydów—żydowskie strategie zadomowienia się w powojennej Polsce (1944–1949)," in *Kultura i Społeczeństwo,* vol. 43, 1999 (1).

Kula, Witold. "Nasza w tym rola: Głos pesymisty," in Marcin Kula, *Uparta sprawa: Żydowska? Polska? Ludzka?* Kraków: Universitas, 2004.

Kurkowska-Budzan, Marta. "My Jedwabne," in Antony Polonsky and Joanna Michlic, eds. *The Neighbors Respond: The Controversy over the Jedwabne Massacre in Poland.* Princeton and Oxford: Princeton University Press, 2004.

Lagrou, Pieter. *Legacy of Nazi Occupation: Patriotic Memory and National Recovery in Western Europe, 1945–1965.* Cambridge and New York: Cambridge University Press, 2000.

Lehrman, Hal. "Hungary: Liberation's Bitter Fruit," *Commentary,* January 1946.

———. *Russia's Europe.* New York and London: D. Appleton Century Co., 1947.

Lendvai, Paul. *Anti-Semitism Without Jews; Communist Eastern Europe.* Garden City, NY: Doubleday, 1971.

Levi-Valensi, Jacqueline. *Camus at Combat. Writing 1944–1947.* Princeton and Oxford: Princeton University Press, 2006.

Levy, Robert. *Ana Pauker: The Rise and Fall of a Jewish Communist.* Los Angeles: University of California Press, 2001.

Libionka, Dariusz. " 'Kwestia żydowska' w Polsce w ocenie Delegatury Rządu RP i KG ZWZ-AK w latach 1942–1944." Paper presented at the conference "Les Juifs et la Pologne, 1939–2004," January 13–15, 2005, Bibliothèque Nationale de France, Paris.

———. "Polska ludność chrześcijańska wobec eksterminacji Żydów—dystrykt lubelski," in *Akcja Reinhardt. Zagłada Żydów w generalnym gubernatorstwie.* Dariusz Libionka, ed. Warszawa: Instytut Pamięci Narodowej, 2004.

Lizak, Wojciech. " 'Niepamięć zbiorowa'—z perspektywy ludu." *Tygodnik Powszechny,* November 7, 2004.

Łuczak, Czesław. "Szanse i trudności bilansu demograficznego Polski w latach 1939–1945," in *Dzieje Najnowsze,* 1994 (2), pp. 9–14.

Machcewicz, Paweł, and Krzysztof Persak, eds. *Wokół Jedwabnego.* Warszawa: Instytut Pamięci Narodowej, 2002, vol. 1 and 2.

Majer, Piotr. *Milicja obywatelska w systemie organów władzy PRL.* Toruń: Wydawnictwo Adam Marszałek, 2003.

Margal, Mariusz. "Podczas procesu Greisera," in *Kuźnica,* July 22, 1946.

Marrus, Michael R. "A Plea Unanswered: Jacques Maritain, Pope Pius XII and the Holocaust" (in manuscript).

Micgiel, John. "Kościół katolicki i pogrom kielecki." *Niepodległość,* 25 (1992).

Michel, Henri. *The Shadow War: European Resistance 1939–1945.* New York: Harper and Row, 1972.

Michlic-Coren, Joanna. "Polish Jews During and After the Kielce Pogrom: Reports from the Communist Archives," in *Polin,* V.XIII (2000), pp. 253–67.

Mikołajczyk, Stanisław. *The Rape of Poland: Pattern of Soviet Aggression.* New York: Whittlesey House, 1948.

Milewski, Jan J. "Wybrane akta procesów karnych z lat 1945–1958 w sprawach o udział w zbrodni na ludności żydowskiej w Radziłowie," in *Wokół Jedwabnego,* vol. 2.

———. "Zagłada Żydów w Wąsoszu w świetle akt sprawy karnej Mariana Rydzewskiego," in *Biuletyn Historii Pogranicza,* no. 3 (2002).

Miller, Tomasz. "Jak się rodziła przewodnia siła," in *Biuletyn IPN,* no. 5, 2002.

Miłosz, Czesław. "The Rescue" ("Ocalenie"), in *New and Collected Poems, 1931–2001.* New York: Ecco, HarperCollins Publishers, 2001.

Moscovici, Serge, *Chronique des années egarées.* Paris: Editions Stock, 1997.

Mounier, Emmanuel. "L'ordre regne-t-il à Varsowie?," *L'Ésprit,* June 1946.

Nałkowska, Zofia. *Dzienniki VI.* Part 1 (1945–1948), Warszawa: Czytelnik, 2000.

"O aparacie bezpieczeństwa—z Krzysztofem Lesiakowskim i Grzegorzem Majchrzakiem rozmawia Barbara Polak," in *Biuletyn IPN,* no. 6, 2002.

Olczak-Ronikier, Joanna. *W ogrodzie pamięci.* Kraków: Znak, 2001.

Ossowski, Stanisław. "Na tle wydarzeń kieleckich," in *Kuźnica,* September 30, 1946.

"O stanie badań nad pogromem kieleckim. Dyskusja w Żydowskim Instytucie

Historycznym (12. III. 1996) z referatem wprowadzającym prof. Krystyny Kersten," *Biuletyn Żydowskiego Instytutu Historycznego,* no. 4/1996.

Overy, Richard. *Russia's War.* New York: Penguin Books, 1998.

Oz, Amos. *A Tale of Love and Darkness.* New York: Harcourt, Inc., 2004.

Paczkowski, Andrzej. *Zdobycie władzy, 1945–1947.* Warszawa: Wydawnictwa Szkolne i Pedagogiczne, 1993.

——. "Żydzi w UB, próba weryfikacji stereotypu," in Tomasz Szarota, ed., *Komunizm: Ideologia, system, ludzie.* Warszawa: Wydawnictwo Neriton Instytut Historii PAN, 2001.

Peleg-Mariańska, Miriam, and Mordecai Peleg. *Witness: Life in Occupied Krakow.* London and New York: Routledge, 1991.

Perechodnik, Całek. *Spowiedź.* Warszawa: Ośrodek Karta, 2004.

Piątek, Brunon. "Wypisy z moich wspomnień: Pogrom," in *Biuletyn Żydowskiego Instytutu Historycznego,* no. 4/96.

Polonsky, Antony, "Beyond Condemnation, Apologetics, and Apologies: On the Complexity of Polish Behavior Toward the Jews During the Second World War," in *Studies in Contemporary Jewry,* vol. 13, Oxford University Press, 1997.

——. *Politics in Independent Poland, 1921–1939.* Oxford: Clarendon Press, 1972.

——, ed. *"My Brother's Keeper": Recent Polish Debates on the Holocaust.* London and New York: Routledge (for Institute for Polish Studies), 1990.

——, and Joanna Michlic, eds. *The Neighbors Respond: The Controversy over the Jedwabne Massacre in Poland.* Princeton: Princeton University Press, 2004.

Prekerowa, Teresa. *Konspiracyjna Rada Pomocy Żydom w Warszawie, 1942–45.* Warszawa: Państwowy Instytut Wydawniczy, 1982.

Putrament, Jerzy. "Odbudowa psychiczna," in *Odrodzenie,* October 1, 1945.

Rakowski, Mieczysław. *Dzienniki polityczne, 1967–1968.* Warszawa: Iskry, 1999.

Reder, Rudolf. *Bełżec,* Kraków: Fundacja Judaica i Państwowe Muzeum Oświęcim–Brzezinka, 1999.

Reich-Ranicki, Marcel. *The Author of Himself: The Life of Marcel Reich-Ranicki.* Princeton: Princeton University Press, 2001.

Rodek, Anita. *Tzw. szmalcownicy: Warszawa i okolice (1940–1944),* MA thesis, Warsaw University, 2002.

Rojewski, Jan. "Siedem dni," in *Kuźnica,* July 22, 1946.

Rudawski, Michał. *Mój obcy kraj?* Warszawa: Agencja Wydawnicza Tu, 1996.

Rudnicki, Adolf. "Dzienniki," in *Kuźnica,* June 1, 1945.

——. *Żywe i martwe morze.* Warszawa: Ksiazka i Wiedza, 1952.

Rzepecki, Jan. "Organizacja i działanie Biura Informacji i Propagandy (BIP) Komendy Głównej AK," in *Wojskowy Przegląd Historyczny,* vol. 16, no. 4.

Rzepliński, Andrzej. "Ten jest z ojczyzny mojej? Sprawy karne oskarżonych o wymordowanie Żydów w Jedwabnym w świetle zasady rzetelnego procesu," in Paweł Machcewicz and Krzysztof Persak, eds., *Wokół Jedwabnego,* vol. 1.

Sartre, Jean-Paul. "Paris sous l'occupation," in *Situations III,* Paris: Gallimard, 1949.

Schatz, Jaff. *The Generation. The Rise and Fall of the Jewish Communists of Poland.* Los Angeles: University of California Press, 1991.

——. "Jews and the Communist Movement in Interwar Poland," in *Studies in Contemporary Jewry,* vol. 20, 2004.

Shneiderman, S. L. *Between Fear and Hope.* New York: ARCO Publishing Co., 1947.

Shore, Marci. *Caviar and Ashes: A Warsaw Generation's Life and Death in Marxism, 1918–1968.* New Haven: Yale University Press, 2006.

———. "Children of the Revolution: A Warsaw Family Story" (in manuscript).

Shtokfish, David. *About Our House Which Was Devastated (Sefer Kielce).* Tel Aviv: Kielce Societies in Israel and in the Diaspora, 1981.

Śledzianowski, Jan. *Pytania nad pogromem kieleckim.* Kielce: Wydawnictwo "Jedność," 1998.

Slezkine, Yuri. *The Jewish Century.* Princeton and Oxford: Princeton University Press, 2004.

Smolar, Hersh. *Oif der letzter pozitzye mit der letzter hofenung.* Tel Aviv: I. Peretz Verlag, 1982.

Świda-Zięba, Hanna. *Urwany lot: Pokolenie inteligenckiej młodzieży powojennej w świetle listów i pamiętników z lat 1945–1948.* Kraków: Wydawnictwo Literackie, 2003.

Szaynok, Bożena. *Ludność żydowska na Dolnym Śląsku, 1945–1950.* Wrocław: Wydawnictwo Uniwersytetu Wrocławskiego, 2000.

———. *Pogrom Żydów w Kielcach 4 lipca, 1946.* Wydawnictwo Bellona, 1992.

Tacitus. "The Life of Cnaeus Julius Agricola," in *Complete Works of Tacitus.* New York: Random House, The Modern Library, 1942.

Torańska, Teresa. *Oni.* London: Aneks Publishers, 1985.

Turkov, Jonas. *Noch der befrajung—zichroines.* Buenos Aires: Central Farband fir Pojlishe Yidin in Argentina, 1959.

Wat, Aleksander. *My Century: The Odyssey of a Polish Intellectual.* Berkeley: University of California Press, 1988.

Weiner, Amir. *Making Sense of War: The Second World War and the Fate of the Bolshevik Revolution.* Princeton and Oxford: Princeton University Press, 2001.

———. "When Memory Counts: War, Genocide, and Postwar Soviety Jewry," in Omer Bartov, Atina Grossman, and Mary Nolan, eds., *Crimes of War: Guilt and Denial in the Twentieth Century.* New York: The New Press, 2002.

Wood, E. Thomas, and Stanisław Jankowski. *Karski: How One Man Tried to Stop the Genocide.* New York: John Wiley and Sons, 1994.

Wrona, Zenon. "Kościół wobec pogromu Żydów w Kielcach w 1946 roku," in Longin Kaczanowski, et al., eds. *Pamiętnik Świętokrzyski. Studia z dziejów kultury chrześcijańskiej.* Kielce: KTN, 1991.

"Wszyscy krawcy wyjechali. O Żydach w PRL—z Natalią Aleksium i Dariuszem Stolą rozmawia Barbara Polak," in *Biuletyn Instytutu Pamięci Narodowej,* no. 11 (2005), pp. 4–25.

Wyka, Kazimierz. "Potęga ciemnoty potwierdzona," in *Odrodzenie,* September 23, 1945.

Zaremba, Marcin. *Komunizm, legitymizacja, nacjonalizm: Nacjonalistyczna legitymizacja władzy komunistycznej w Polsce.* Warszawa: Instytut Studiów Politycznych PAN, Wydawnictwo Trio, 2001.

Zuckerman, Yitzhak ("Antek"). *A Surplus of Memory: Chronicle of the Warsaw Ghetto Uprising.* Los Angeles and Oxford: University of California Press, 1993.

Żbikowski, Andrzej. "Pogromy i mordy ludności żydowskiej w Łomżyńskim i na Białóstoczyźnie latem 1941 roku w świetle relacji ocalałych Żydów i dokumentów sądowych," in *Wokół Jedwabnego,* vol. 1.

NOTES

INTRODUCTION

1   For her wartime story, see Miriam Peleg-Mariańska and Mordecai Peleg, *Witness: Life in Occupied Kraków*.
2   Maria Hochberg-Mariańska and Noe Gruess, *Dzieci oskarżają*.
3   Ibid., p. XXXII.
4   Marcel Reich-Ranicki, *The Author of Himself: The Life of Marcel Reich-Ranicki*, pp. 204–205. Neal Ascherson makes a reference to this very episode in his review of Ranicki's memoir, *The New York Review of Books* (April 11, 2002, p. 56).
5   Żydowski Instytut Historyczny (ŻIH), 301/445.
6   ŻIH, 301/681.
7   *Księga Żydów ostrolęckich*, p. 388. This is the Polish translation of *Sefer Kehilat Ostrolenk: Buch fun Ostrolenker Kehila, Book of Kehilath Ostrolenka*.
8   Alina Cała, *The Image of the Jew in Polish Folk Culture*, pp. 209–210.

CHAPTER 1

1   The point was made by Élie Halévy, a great French historian, in a lecture delivered at Oxford in 1929, "Une interpretation de la crise mondiale, 1914–1918," in *L'Ère des tyrannies: Études sur le socialisme et la guerre*, p. 173.
2   See my essay "Themes for a Social History of War Experience and Collaboration" in *The Politics of Retribution in Europe: World War II and Its Aftermath*, Istvan Deak, Tony Judt, and Jan T. Gross, eds., pp. 15–36.
3   See, especially, chapter 2, pp. 58–73, and Conclusions.
4   Just imagine the organizational wherewithal necessary to regularly obtain such amounts of paper, which couldn't be purchased legally, and then transporting it in

and out of carefully hidden secret printing presses (Jan Rzepecki, "Organizacja i dzialanie biura informacji i propagandy (BIP) komendy głównej AK," in *Wojskowy Przegląd Historyczny*.

5   Henri Michel, *The Shadow War: European Resistance 1939–1945*.

6   E. Thomas Wood and Stanisław Jankowski, *Karski: How One Man Tried to Stop the Genocide*, pp. 223–38.

7   Stanisław Kot, *Listy z Rosji do gen. Sikorskiego*, p. 194.

8   See *Katyń—Dokumenty ludobójstwa. Dokumenty i materiały archiwalne przekazane Polsce 14 października 1992r*, pp. 34–46.

9   Winston S. Churchill, *Triumph and Tragedy*, pp. 132, 133.

10   Andrzej Friszke, *Polska, Losy państwa i narodu, 1939–1989*, p. 109.

11   Anthony Eden, *The Memoirs of Anthony Eden, Earl of Avon: The Reckoning*, p. 597.

12   Milovan Djilas, *Conversations with Stalin*, p. 114.

13   Winston S. Churchill, *His Complete Speeches, 1897–1963*, vol. 7, p. 7117.

14   Timothy Garton Ash, *The Polish Revolution: Solidarity*, p. 3.

15   Andrzej Paczkowski, *Zdobycie władzy, 1945–1947*, p. 5; also Andrzej Garlicki, *Bolesław Bierut*, p. 43.

16   Friszke, *Polska*, p. 151.

17   Primarily the National Armed Forces (Narodowe Siły Zbrojne, NSZ), the National Military Unification (Narodowe Zjednoczenie Wojskowe, NZW), and the National Military Organization (Narodowa Organizacja Wojskowa, NOW).

18   A very interesting, and "politically correct" for the period, artistic portrayal of these dilemmas can be found in Jerzy Andrzejewski's novella *Ashes and Diamonds*, which was later turned into an internationally successful movie under the same title by Andrzej Wajda.

19   See *Informator o nielegalnych antypaństwowych organizacjach i bandach zybrojnych działających w Polsce Ludowej w latach 1944–1956*, pp. 23–26 and 45–46. For an alphabetical index listing all the organizations, see pp. 205–217.

20   Mikołajczyk, *The Rape of Poland*, pp. 161–62.

21   Bliss Lane, *I Saw Poland*, p. 232.

22   Friszke, *Polska*, p. 125.

23   For an assessment of the theory that Communist provocation was at the source of the pogrom see chapter 4, especially pp. 160–163.

24   Mikołajczyk, *The Rape of Poland*, pp. 240–42.

25   Churchill, *Triumph and Tragedy*, pp. 496–97.

26   On the novelty of the strategy of social control which underlaid Communist takeovers see my *Revolution from Abroad*, especially "Epilogue: The Spoiler State."

27   For an extensive discussion of the intelligentsia's take on the subject of wartime and postwar anti-Semitism, see pp. 128–133.

CHAPTER 2

1   Centralny Komitet Żydów w Polsce (CKŻP), Wydział Organizacyjny, 304/3. To fully identify the source, one needs to know the date of the document. If it appears in the text I don't give it again in the footnotes.

2   Ibid.

3   Ibid.

4   Jonas Turkov, *Noch der befrajung—zichroines*, pp. 12, 13.

5   David Engel makes this argument in his *Beyn Shichrur le'Bricha: Nitzolei ha-Shoah be'Polin ve'hamaavak al hanhagatam, 1944–1946 (Between Liberation and Flight: Holocaust Survivors in Poland and the Struggle for Leadership, 1944–1946).*

6   The most comprehensive study of Jewish community life in Lower Silesia is by Bożena Szaynok (*Ludność żydowska na Dolnym Śląsku, 1945–1950*). In the English language, most informative is the memoir of the chairman of the Lower Silesia Jewish Committee, Jacob Egit, *Grand Illusion*. See the discussion later in this chapter of conflicts arising from property claims by returning Jewish survivors.

7   Turkov, *Noch der befrajung*, p. 12.

8   Archiwum Państwowe w Krakowie (APK), Jewish Voivodeship Committee, file 14, p. 87.

9   Mounier was the founder of personalism and of the important Catholic periodical *L'Ésprit*. He wrote this one month before the Kielce pogrom (Emmanuel Mounier, "L'ordre regne-t-il à Varsowie?," pp. 999–1000).

10 Archiwum Akt Nowych (AAN), Minsterstwo Administracji Publicznej (MAP), 786, 29.IX.1945.

11 Ruth Gay, *Safe Among the Germans. Liberated Jews After World War II*, p. 183. For the incorrect "generic" invocation of the "AK," or Home Army, as a source of such threats, see chapter 1 of this book.

12 Cała, *The Image of the Jew*, pp. 214–17, 218.

13 Wincenty Bednarczuk, "Dwie ważne sprawy," *Odrodzenie*. The same point is made by Jerzy Putrament ("Odbudowa psychiczna," *Odrodzenie*), Kazimierz Wyka ("Potęga ciemnoty potwierdzona," *Odrodzenie*), and other authors.

14 Zygmunt Klukowski, *Dziennik z lat okupacji zamojszczyzny*, entry of April 13, 1942. This is in spite of the fact that several entries of Klukowski's *Journal* were "edited" before publication to tone down the degree of Polish participation in the persecution of the Jews (see Dariusz Libionka, "Polska ludność chrześcijanska wobec eksterminacji Żydów—dystrykt lubelski," in *Akcja Reinhardt. Zaglada Żydów w Generalnym Gubernatorstwie*, Dariusz Libionka, ed., pp. 310, 311). For plunder of the Otwock ghetto by local Poles in the days immediately following the *Aktion* there, see the memoir of Calek Perechodnik (*Spowiedź*, pp. 74, 75). The most recent Polish historiography is finally beginning to come to grips with this matter; see, for instance, Jan Grabowski, *"Ja tego Żyda znam!" Szantażowanie Żydów w Warszawie, 1939–1943*, p. 130. Grabowski is a professor of history at the University of Ottawa, but his book was published in Poland in October 2004. A dramatic text on this issue was published by another Polish historian, Wojciech Lizak, in the influential Catholic weekly *Tygodnik Powszechny* of November 7, 2004: " 'Niepamięć zbiorowa'—z perspektywy ludu."

15 Paweł Machcewicz and Krzysztof Persak, eds., *Wokół Jedwabnego*, vol. 2, p. 358.

16 Yad Vashem, 033/730, September 24, 1945.

17 Rachela Auerbach, *Oif die felder fun Treblinka*, p. 101.

18 Anna Bikont, *My z Jedwabnego*, p. 150. In a testimony from June 1946, deposited at the Jewish Historical Institute in Warsaw, Menachem Finkelsztajn confirms that

the peasants from Wąsosz, who came to town after they murdered their "own" Jews on July 5, left Radziłów before the mass murder of July 7.

19 ŻIH, CKŻP, Wydział Organizacyjny 304/5, 2.V.45.

20 Gay, *Safe Among the Germans.*

21 Two numbers—54,594 for the total who returned from "western republics of the USSR" between 1944 and 1948, and then the total of 136,579 Jews returning to Poland in 203 repatriation transports between February 8 and July 31, 1946—are quoted by Adelson (op. cit., pp. 388, 397). To some extent, these groups overlap. According to David Engel, the total number of repatriates from the Soviet Union can best be estimated as falling somewhere between 150,000 and 175,000 (personal communication).

22 Heda Margolius Kovaly, *Under a Cruel Star: A Life in Prague, 1941–1968,* pp. 46–47.

23 See, for example, *Wokół Jedwabnego,* vol. 2, pp. 379–80.

24 Ibid., vol. 2, p. 305.

25 Shraga Feivel Bielawski, *The Last Jew from Węgrów,* p. 72.

26 The exchange has a linguistic flavor indicating a class difference between the two women that I cannot render in English: "*Buty to mogłaby mi paniusia już zostawić!— Józefowo, ja jescze żyję!—Ojejku, odyć nic nie mówiłam, ino że buty fajne!*" (David Shtokfish, *About Our House Which Was Devastated [Sefer Kielce],* p. 200).

27 It is not clear from the transcript how persuasive her protestations were to Godlewski and whether the women got the apartment they were seeking (see *Wokół Jedwabnego,* vol. 1, pp. 41, 246; vol. 2, pp. 932, 954). See also my book *Neighbors,* pp. 106–107.

28 Irving Heymont, *Among the Survivors of the Holocaust, 1945: The Landsberg DP Camp Letters of Major Irving Heymont, United States Army,* pp. 49–50.

29 Quoted from Dariusz Libionka, " 'Kwestia żydowska' w Polsce w ocenie delegatury rządu RP i KG ZWZ-AK w latach 1942–1944."

30 Ibid.

31 Lizak, " 'Niepamięć zbiorowa.' "

32 Most but not all of the files are to be found on two microfilm series, B-2612 and B-2613, in the MAP collection at the Archiwum Akt Nowych (AAN).

33 AAN, MAP, B-2612, pp. 152–56.

34 AAN, MAP, B-2612, pp. 16–19.

35 AAN, MAP, B-2612, p. 15.

36 AAN, MAP, B-2612, pp. 149–56.

37 ŻIH, 301/1184, Sala Ungerman. Sala Ungerman remarked about the source of her story in her deposition: "In 1944 the sister of my sister-in-law (Malcia—during the war she was in Warsaw with forged Polish identity papers) got a letter from my sister-in-law that she remained the only aunt of their child. She must have felt already that they wanted to kill her."

38 See Paweł Machcewicz's introduction to the *Wokół Jedwabnego* volumes; Dariusz Libionka is currently working on the Lublin court district files (personal communication).

39 For his extensive legal expertise on the Jedwabne trials, see Andrzej Rzepliński, *Wokół Jedwabnego,* vol. 1, pp. 353–459.

40   I have provided my own translation of Rzepliński's interview. For a complete English-language translation, see Antony Polonsky and Joanna Michlic, eds., *The Neighbors Respond*, pp. 137–44.

41   Paweł Machcewicz, "Wokół Jedwabnego," in *Wokół Jedwabnego*, vol. 1, pp. 21–22. See, especially, Andrzej Żbikowski, *Wokół Jedwabnego*, vol. 1, pp. 159–271; Jan J. Milewski, ibid., vol. 2, pp. 863–983; and Jan J. Milewski, *Biuletyn Historii Pogranicza*, no. 3, pp. 87–112.

42   Archiwum Państwowe w Krakowie (APK), Urząd Wojewódzki (UW) 2, File 1073.

43   Ibid., memo from the County Jewish Committee in Chrzanów to the Sociopolitical Department of the Kraków voivodeship, dated 11 July 1945.

44   ŻIH, CKŻP, Wydział Organizacyjny, 304/5, 1.III.1945.

45   Ewa Koźminska-Frejlak, "Polska jako ojczyzna żydów—Żydowskie strategie zadomowienia się w powojennej Polsce (1944–1949)," in *Kultura i Społeczeństwo*, p. 131.

46   AAN, MAP, 787, 30.X.1945, p. 12.

47   Józef Adelson, "W Polsce zwanej ludową," in Jerzy Tomaszewski, ed., *Najnowsze dzieje Żydów w Polsce*, p. 402.

48   ŻIH, CKŻP, Wydział Opieki Społecznej, 303/VIII/24. Referat dla spraw pomocy ludności żydowskiej przy Prezydium Rady Ministrów. Ósme sprawozdanie z działalności (za miesiąc luty 1945). Despite its serious and long-winded name, the office was essentially a one-man operation and Herszenhorn, a well-respected physician and community activist from Lublin, was it.

49   ŻIH, CKŻP, Wydział Organizacyjny, 304/21, "Memoriał w sprawie bezpieczeństwa życia i imienia Żydostwa Lubelskiego," 25.III.1946.

50   Archiwum Państwowe w Lublinie (APL), UW, Wydział Społeczno-Polityczny, 50, 21.III.1945.

51   Turkov, *Noch der befrajung*, pp. 275–77.

52   ŻIH, CKŻP, Prezydium, 303/1, 24.VII.1945.

53   Hersh Smolar, *Oif der Letzter Pozitsye mit der Letzter Hofenung*, p. 53.

54   ŻIH, CKŻP, Prezydium, 303/1.

55   ŻIH, CKŻP, Wydział Produktywizacji, 303/XII/6, 25.IV.1945.

56   Ibid., "Wydział dla Spraw Produktywizacji. Sprawozdanie z Działalności."

57   ŻIH, CKŻP, Wydział Produktywizacji, 303/XII/18, VI–VII, 46.

58   APK, UW 2, File 1073.

59   *Kuźnica*, October 14, 1946.

60   Zofia Nałkowska, *Dzienniki VI*, part 1 (1945–1948), p. 112.

61   See CKŻP, Wydział Organizacyjny, 304/3, 29.V.45; see also, 304/5, 18.IV.45; 304/5, 2.V.45. An illegibly signed penciled note can be found in the files as well: "Receipt, Ostrowiec, May 5, 1945. I acknowledge receiving the original of a warning letter to citizen Mejer Cytrynbaum, together with six shotgun bullets which were included with the letter" (CKŻP, Wydział Organizacyjny, 304/5, 5.V.45).

62   Michał Głowiński, *The Black Seasons*, pp. 147, 148, 162.

63   Miriam Hochberg-Mariańska and Noe Gruss, eds., *Dzieci oskarżają*, pp. XXIX, XXX.

64   For an extensive description and analysis of the Kielce pogrom, see chapters 3 and

4. The citation is from *Antyżydowskie wydarzenia kieleckie 4 lipca 1946 roku. Dokumenty i materiały,* Stanisław Meducki and Zenon Wrona, eds., vol. II, p. 118.

65 Michał Głowiński, *The Black Seasons,* p. 118.

66 Such efforts "to protect the children," however, were often in vain. "The child frequently learned that he or she was Jewish from unfriendly strangers, who made the revelation punctuating it with derogatory epithets" (Hurwic-Nowakowska, op. cit., pp. 141, 142). Often children learned about their Jewish identity from playmates, or other children at school.

67 Zofia Nałkowska, *Dzienniki VI, 1945–1954,* pp. 69–70. The editors of Nałkowska's journals quote in a footnote materials found in her personal archives concerning the Rzeszów pogrom. See, also, the report of the Jewish Historical Commission (ŻIH, 301/1320).

68 The last two items are listed in Captain Siatko's report (IPN-Rz-062/5). Other details of the arrest are from Landesmann's account given to the Jewish Historical Commission in Kraków on October 5, 1945 (ŻIH, 301/1581).

69 ŻIH, 301/1581.

70 The railroad police actually sent word to put Jews fleeing from Rzeszów under arrest. Responding to the call the Security Service arrested a group of Jews in Tarnów with consequences I have earlier described.

71 "To odprowadzanie przez miasto odbywało się przy bojowej postawie naszych milicjantów, jako też przechodników katolickich, którzy obrzucali kamieniami Żydów odprowadzanych" (ŻIH, 301/1320).

72 ŻIH, 301/1320, 1581; Fortunoff Archive, T-1014.

73 ŻIH, 301/1320.

74 IPN-Rz-062/5, 1.IX.1945.

75 This must have been the person who wrote a long memorandum on September 1 to the Ministry of Justice in Warsaw, as a result of which Landesmann was freed twelve days later.

76 ŻIH, 301/1581.

77 IPN-Rz-005/16, vol. II, "Raporty sytuacyjne KWMO Rzeszów, 1945 Rok"; IPN-Rz-04/251.

CHAPTER 3

1 Anna Cichopek, *Pogrom Żydów w Krakowie 11 sierpnia 1945,* aneks no. 52, pp. 200–214. The top Soviet NKVD operative in Poland, Nicolai Selivanovskii, reported to his boss Lavrenty Beria that "40 policemen" were arrested in connection with the pogrom in Kraków (Natalia Aleksiun, "The Situation of the Jews in Poland as Seen by the Soviet Security Forces in 1945," in *Jews in Eastern Europe,* vol. 3, no. 37, p. 63).

2 Hartman, *Wspomnienia,* pp. 96–97.

3 ŻIH, 301/1582

4 Hartman, *Wspomnienia,* p. 96.

5 I am basing this account primarily on three reconstructions of the July 4 events: the "Chronicle of the Tragedy" from volume 1 of the documents published as *An-*

tyżydowskie wydarzenia kieleckie 4 lipca 1946 roku. Dokumenty i materiały, Stanisław Meducki and Zenon Wrona, eds., vol. I, pp. 57–70, hereinafter cited as Meducki, *Antyży-dowskie*; Bożena Szaynok's study of the Kielce pogrom, especially the chapter "Rekonstrukcja Wydarzeń," (*Pogrom Żydów w Kielcach 4 lipca, 1946,* pp. 31–57); and the mimeographed report "On the results of the investigation concerning the Kielce events of July 4, 1946" prepared by the Main Commission for Investigation of Crimes Against the Polish Nation of the Institute of National Memory ("Raport głównej komisji badania zbrodni przeciwko narodowi polskiemu—IPN o wyniku śledztwa w sprawie wydarzeń Kieleckich 4.07.1946" [GKBZpNP-IPN]), for which various security police files were declassified for the first time. This report also made use of previously inaccessible military archives as well as files obtained from the Russian State Archives (GKBZpNP-IPN, pp. 2, 3). Its conclusions, written in 1997, are based on the most thorough documentary foundation that may ever be assembled about the Kielce pogrom.

I used testimonies collected in 1987 by Marcel Łoziński for his award-winning documentary film *Świadkowie (Witnesses)*. I am deeply grateful to Mr. Łoziński for giving me transcripts of his interviews *in extenso*. Whenever I draw on material that has been included in his film I will reference it to *Witnesses*; otherwise I will indicate the source by referencing "Łoziński interview."

Błaszczyk, as Jerzy Daniel, who interviewed him repeatedly at a later time, maintains, was wrongly identified as a nine-year-old at the time (*Żyd w zielonym kapeluszu. Rzecz o Kieleckim pogromie 4 lipca 1946,* p. 18).

6   He mentioned the cherries to a group of visiting journalists who interviewed him one day after the pogrom (see S. L. Shneiderman, *Between Fear and Hope,* pp. 93, 94). See also the interrogation of Jan Bartosiński, whose farm young Błaszczyk visited. Błaszczyk was friends with two sons of Bartosiński, Józek and Czesiek (Meducki, *Antyżydowskie,* vol. I, p. 109; Daniel, *Żyd w zielonym,* p. 26). I will evaluate Błaszczyk's role in light of the claim that the Kielce pogrom was a provocation.

7   GKBZpNP-IPN, p. 11.

8   Meducki, *Antyżydowskie,* vol. I, pp. 226, 275; also GKBZpNP-IPN, pp. 14–15. There is no paperwork preserved in the archives documenting the arrest and interrogation of Singer, but the commission found a complaint filed by a military prosecutor that a Kalman Singer was beaten up in the police precinct by a policeman named Zając (GKBZpNP-IPN, p. 14).

9   GKBZpNP-IPN, p. 15.

10   Meducki, *Antyżydowskie,* vol. I, p. 110.

11   Ibid., p. 320.

12   GKBZpNP-IPN, p. 16.

13   Meducki, *Antyżydowskie,* vol. I, p. 350.

14   GKBZpNP-IPN, p. 17; also Szaynok, *Pogrom,* pp. 38–39.

15   David Shtokfish, *About Our House Which Was Devastated (Sefer Kielce),* p. 202.

16   Meducki, *Antyżydowskie,* vol. I, p. 62.

17   Shtokfish, *About Our House,* p. 201.

18   Meducki, *Antyżydowskie,* vol. II, p. 137.

19   Shtokfish, *About Our House,* pp. 201–202.

20 Meducki, *Antyżydowskie,* vol. I, p. 62.

21 He fetched a five-year sentence, but as a result of a general amnesty, walked out of jail in March 1947 (ibid., p. 222).

22 Ibid., p. 126.

23 Szaynok, *Pogrom,* p. 41.

24 Shtokfish, *About Our House,* p. 198.

25 A nurse who cared afterwards for wounded Jews, Helena Majtlis, was also told this by her wards (Łoziński interview).

26 Meducki, *Antyżydowskie,* vol. I, pp. 244–46.

27 Ibid., p. 112.

28 Ibid., pp. 168, 169.

29 Szaynok, *Pogrom,* p. 45.

30 Meducki, *Antyżydowskie,* vol. I, p. 324.

31 Ibid., p. 64, and Szaynok, *Pogrom,* p. 51. The 1995 report identifies the two officers who spoke to Wrzeszcz as Police Colonel Kuźnicki and an unnamed lieutenant-colonel in army uniform (GKBZpNP-IPN, p. 25).

32 Shneiderman, *Between Fear and Hope,* p. 92.

33 *Witnesses.*

34 Meducki, *Antyżydowskie,* vol. I, pp. 103–105; see also Szaynok, *Pogrom,* pp. 55, 56, 60; GKBZpNP-IPN, pp. 31, 32.

35 Meducki, *Antyżydowskie,* vol. I, p. 201.

36 Ibid., p. 187; Shtokfish, *About Our House,* pp. 199, 204.

37 Meducki, *Antyżydowskie,* vol. II, p. 87; see also Szaynok, *Pogrom,* p. 113.

38 *"Nie przesadzimy chyba gdy przyjmiemy, że co czwarty mieszkaniec Kielc wziął czynny udział w pogromie,"* wrote Kula one month after the events, in an article rejected by the editorial board of the weekly *Kuźnica.* Kula's son, an eminent social historian in his own right, included the piece recently in his own collection of essays on the subject of Polish Jewish relations (Witold Kula, "Nasza w tym rola: Głos pesymisty," in Marcin Kula, *Uparta sprawa: Żydowska? Polska? Ludzka?,* p. 161).

39 See the interrogation protocols of Sobczyński and Kuźnicki, as well as testimony by Gwiazdowicz, especially in Meducki, *Antyżydowskie,* vol. I, p. 336.

40 Ibid., pp. 314–15.

41 Ibid., p. 333.

42 Ibid., p. 329.

43 Ibid., pp. 322, 323.

44 Ibid., p. 330.

45 Ibid., pp. 317, 335.

46 Meducki, *Antyżydowskie,* vol. II, p. 81.

47 Meducki, *Antyżydowskie,* vol. I, pp. 316–17.

48 See GKBZpNP-IPN, pp. 19, 28, 29.

49 Ibid., p. 28.

50 Ibid., pp. 25, 29.

51 Meducki, *Antyżydowskie,* vol. I, p. 317.

52 *Witnesses,* Łoziński interview.

53 Meducki, *Antyżydowskie,* vol. I, p. 317.

54 GKBZpNP-IPN, p. 33.

55 Łoziński interview; also GKBZpNP-IPN, p. 30.

56 Shtokfish, *About Our House*, pp. 197–98; *Witnesses*.

57 Yitzhak Zuckerman ("Antek"), *A Surplus of Memory: Chronicle of the Warsaw Ghetto Uprising*, p. 663.

58 Łoziński interview.

59 *Witnesses*, Łoziński interview.

60 Meducki, *Antyżydowskie*, vol. I, p. 118.

61 Ibid., p. 132.

62 Ibid., p. 119.

63 Ibid., pp. 132–33.

64 Ibid., p. 133.

65 Ibid., pp. 133–34.

66 Ibid., pp. 173–74.

67 Ibid., pp. 133–34.

68 Ibid., pp. 119, 120, 186.

69 Brunon Piątek, "Wypisy z moich wspomnień: Pogrom," in *Biuletyn Żydowskiego Instytutu Historycznego*, no. 4, p. 21.

70 Ibid., p. 19.

71 Ibid.

72 Ibid., p. 20.

73 He was later transferred and Piątek never saw him again.

74 Piątek, *Wypisy*, p. 21.

75 *Witnesses*.

76 Meducki, *Antyżydowskie*, vol. I, p. 136; for both testimonies, see pp. 135–38.

77 Ibid., pp. 300, 308.

78 Meducki, *Antyżydowskie*, vol. II, p. 119.

79 I am grateful to my colleague Peter Brown for this insight and phrasing.

80 *Witnesses* and Łoziński interview.

CHAPTER 4

1 See, for example, the report of Bishop Kaczmarek's commission on the events in Kielce, in John Micgiel, "Kościół katolicki i pogrom kielecki," *Niepodległość*, XXV, p. 155.

2 See below for the Catholic church's response to the pogrom.

3 Meducki, *Antyżydowskie*, vol. II, p. 87.

4 Shneiderman, *Between Fear and Hope*, p. 87.

5 *Witnesses*.

6 Shneiderman, *Between Fear and Hope*, p. 106.

7 Meducki, *Antyżydowskie*, vol. II, pp. 142, 143.

8 Ibid., p. 139. For full English translation of this, and four other reports, see Joanna Michlic-Coren, "Polish Jews During and After the Kielce Pogrom: Reports from the Communist Archives."

9 Padraic Kenney, *Rebuilding Poland: Workers and Communists, 1945–1950*, pp. 114, 115.

10   Aleksander Kochański, ed., *Protokoły posiedzeń Sekretariatu KC PPR, 1945–1946,* p. 273.

11   Ibid., p. 276.

12   Meducki, *Antyżydowskie,* vol. II, p. 100.

13   Ibid., pp. 138, 142.

14   Kochański, *Protokoły,* p. 280.

15   For a brief summary of Jews' dramatic material circumstances and needs all over Poland immediately after the war, see David Engel, *Beyn Shichrur,* pp. 55–60. CKŻP's appeal was published in *Dos Naye Leben* on March 23, 1946 (see August Grabski, *Działalność komunistów wśród Żydów w Polsce, 1944–1949,* p. 121).

16   *Witnesses,* Łoziński interview.

17   Ibid.

18   Meducki, *Antyżydowskie,* vol. II, p. 53.

19   A prototypical bildungsroman of the Soviet era was Nicolai Ostrovski's *How the Steel was Tempered* (Moscow: Foreign Languages Publishing House, 1952).

20   Meducki, *Antyżydowskie,* vol. II, p. 54.

21   Ibid., vol. II, pp. 164, 165.

22   AAN, MAP, 786/72.

23   Meducki, *Antyżydowskie,* vol. II, p. 54.

24   Twenty years later, in 1968, it would find itself haunted by "anti-Semitism without the Jews," when a major intraparty crisis was choreographed as a campaign to cleanse the Party ranks, and the country to boot, of "Zionists." See Paul Lendvai, *Anti-Semitism Without Jews; Communist Eastern Europe.* The best two Polish-language sources on the political use of anti-Semitism by the Communist regime in Poland in 1967–68 are Dariusz Stola's *Kampania Antysyjonistyczna w Polsce, 1967–1968* (Warsaw: Instytut Studiów Politycznych Akademii Nauk, 2000), and the third volume of memoirs by Mieczysław Rakowski (*Dzienniki polityczne, 1967–1968*).

25   *Kuźnica,* July 22, 1946.

26   *Ciemny* means "dark" in Polish, but also "uneducated, primitive, and uncouth," especially in the variation *ciemnota.*

27   *Odrodzenie,* September 9, 1945.

28   *Kuźnica,* September 30, 1946.

29   *Odrodzenie,* July 7, 1946.

30   *Odrodzenie,* September 9, 1945.

31   *Odrodzenie,* July 7, 1946.

32   *Odrodzenie,* July 14, 1946.

33   *Warszawa,* August 11, 1946.

34   For an extensive discussion of Karski's report, see chapter 5, especially pp. 176–178.

35   Shneiderman, *Between Fear and Hope,* p. 114.

36   Meducki, *Antyżydowskie,* vol. I, p. 64; Szaynok, *Pogrom,* p. 50; GKBZpNP-IPN, p. 24.

37   Meducki, *Antyżydowskie,* vol. I, p. 65.

38   Szaynok, *Pogrom,* p. 113.

39   Meducki, *Antyżydowskie,* vol. II, pp. 110–11.

40   Ibid., pp. 111–12.

41   Ibid., pp. 117–18.

42   Aryeh Josef Kochavi, "The Catholic Church and Antisemitism in Poland Follow-

ing World War II as Reflected in British Diplomatic Documents," *Gal-Ed on the History of the Jews in Poland,* no. XI, p. 119, n. 13: "Cardinal Sapieha was absent from Cracow, but I spoke to his principal coadjutor and also to the auxiliary Bishop of Upper Silesia."

43 Ibid., p. 124.

44 Emmanuel Mounier, "L'ordre regne-t-il à Varsowie?," p. 999. "And we know," wrote Kula upon reading Mounier's article about Poland, "whom the delegation of the French intellectuals visited here" (Kula, "Nasza w tym rola," p. 164).

45 Kochavi, "The Catholic Church," p. 123.

46 Ibid., p. 124.

47 Ibid., pp. 121, 125.

48 Ibid., pp. 125–28.

49 Micgiel, "Kościół," p. 144.

50 Ibid.

51 Ibid., pp. 144, 145.

52 Ibid., p. 145.

53 In the original version, the report was eighteen pages long; I am referring to the version published by Micgiel in *Niepodległość.*

54 Micgiel, "Kościół," p. 153.

55 Ibid., p. 152.

56 Ibid., pp. 152, 153.

57 Ibid., pp. 154, 155.

58 Ibid., p. 164.

59 Ibid., pp. 164, 165.

60 Ibid., p. 167.

61 CKŻP, Wydział Prawny, 303/XVI/408.

62 Joop van Banning, SJ, "Watykan i mord rytualny," in *Mord rytualny: Legenda w historii europejskiej,* pp. 61–67.

63 Meducki, *Antyżydowskie,* vol. II, pp. 112–14.

64 Szaynok, *Pogrom,* p. 97.

65 Zenon Wrona, "Kościół wobec pogromu Żydów w Kielcach w 1946 roku," p. 298. Wrona did know of the report by Kaczmarek's commission, but he had not read it when he wrote his article (see ibid., p. 295). See also Ryszard Gryz, "Stanowisko Kościoła katolickiego wobec pogromu Żydów w Kielcach. Stan badań," in *Nasza Przeszłość,* vol. 93, pp. 421–22. A biographer of Bishop Kaczmarek, a church historian by the name of Jan Śledzianowski, in his monograph *Pytania nad pogromem kieleckim* published in 1998, was familiar with Kaczmarek's commission report and essentially fully endorsed its content.

66 The silence of the clergy was noted at the time, and vigorously denounced in cultural periodicals. See, for example, Juliusz Żuławski, "Do redakcji Kuźnicy," *Kuźnica,* August 5, 1946.

67 Szaynok, *Pogrom,* p. 10.

68 "O stanie badań nad pogromem kieleckim. Dyskusja w Żydowskim Instytucie Historycznym (12.III.1996) z referatem wprowadzającym prof. Krystyny Kersten," *Biuletyn Żydowskiego Instytutu Historycznego,* p. 11. The reports were subsequently published in a volume edited by Paczkowski.

69 "O stanie badań," p. 12.

70 *Protokoły posiedzeń Prezydium Krajowej Rady Narodowej, 1944–1947,* Jerzy Kochanowski, ed., p. 200.

71 Klajnerman's official title was "*Naczelnik Wydziału Prawnego Biura Prezydialnego KRN*" ("Head of the Legal Bureau of the Presidium of the KRN"). See ibid., p. 302.

72 Adolf Berman was a member of Left Poalei Zion, a Marxist party that supported Jewish settlement in Palestine but opposed the idea of a monoethnic Jewish national state.

73 Meducki, *Antyżydowskie,* vol. II, p. 164.

74 The full text of the decree "to combat anti-Semitism" was ready for passage and signing, and it is reprinted in the second volume of documents published by Meducki (*Antyżydowskie,* pp. 167–69). Grabski notes in his monograph that the project of the special decree was discussed in the KRN for about a year—the idea was first broached after the pogrom in Kraków, then was tabled after the Kielce pogrom (August Grabski, *Działalność komunistów wśród Żydów w Polsce, 1944–1949,* p. 165).

75 With the exception of the October 22, 1939, "plebiscite" for unification of the so-called Western Ukraine and Western Belorussia with the USSR, held in the Red Army–occupied eastern half of Poland at the beginning of the Second World War (see my *Revolution from Abroad,* the chapter entitled "Elections").

76 Kuźnicki was punished—we read in the sentencing of the military court in Warsaw—for disobeying the order of his superior officer, General Franciszek Jóźwiak (to coordinate the actions of the militia with the Security Service), because of his "unfriendliness" toward Major Sobczyński (*Wyrok w imieniu Rzeczypospolitej Polskiej, dnia 16 grudnia 1946,* Wojskowy Sąd Rejonowy w Warszawie, nr. akt R. 871/46. I am grateful to Dr. Zbigniew Nawrocki for sharing this document with me.).

77 I am basing this estimate on a careful survey by Bożena Szaynok (*Pogrom,* pp. 84–93). Zenon Wrona gives forty-eight for the total number of people who were tried for participation in the Kielce pogrom (op. cit., p. 282).

78 Szaynok, *Pogrom,* pp. 7–8; see also Kula, "Nasza w tym rola," p. 162.

79 Meducki, *Antyżydowskie,* vol. I, pp. 250, 252.

80 Philip Dray, *At the Hands of Persons Unknown,* p. 70.

81 When a military officer during the pogrom ordered some people to clear out, a certain Stępnik who had used a stick to stab a Jewish woman lying on the ground opened his shirt in a theatrical gesture and said, "Shoot, mister" (Meducki, *Antyżydowskie,* vol. I, p. 252).

82 Ibid., p. 167.

83 See *Wokół Jedwabnego,* vol. II, pp. 296–305.

CHAPTER 5

1 I am grateful to David Engel for pointing out that this is not all that different from perceptions in other countries at the time. The notion that the systematic mass murder of Jews could not be subsumed under the general rubric of suffering and

losses inflicted by a brutal regime did not sink into public consciousness anywhere until the late 1950s.

2   *Odrodzenie,* September 3, 1944.

3   *Warszawa,* no. 2, June 16, 1946.

4   Maria Janion, *Do Europy—Tak, ale razem z naszymi umarłymi.*

5   The Jewish Historical Institute in Warsaw is in the process of publishing the Ringelblum Archive in a careful edition reproducing original documents. So far three volumes, some 2,500 pages, have been published. Herman Kruk's monumental chronicle of 700 pages was recently published in English translation by the Yale University Press in collaboration with the YIVO Institute for Jewish Research, *The Last Days of the Jerusalem of Lithuania: Chronicles from the Vilna Ghetto and the Camps, 1939–1944.*

6   For Karski's biography, consult E. Thomas Wood and Stanislaw M. Jankowski, *Karski: How One Man Tried to Stop the Holocaust.* I shall discuss Karski's mission later in this chapter.

    I am not aware, though, of any systematic effort to document the destruction of Polish Jewry by non-Jewish Polish civic initiatives. To the best of my knowledge there were no underground groups of historians, civil servants, or concerned citizens who focused their efforts on such a task.

7   As distinct from "private" knowledge, which has also been recorded, but in memoirs and diaries rather than underground papers and reports. It was a different knowledge, and frequently revealed a discrepancy between attitudes and opinions visible in public and the private sensibilities of the authors. In addition to individual idiosyncrasies of the authors, these differences also captured the stratified character of knowledge and attitudes concerning the Holocaust in Polish society.

8   Adolf Rudnicki, *Żywe i martwe morze,* p. 309.

9   Published in 1946 by Czytelnik in Warsaw, in a powerful volume of Miłosz's wartime poetry, *Ocalenie (The Rescue).* After the war Czesław Miłosz settled in the United States, where he taught Slavic literature at U.C. Berkeley, and in 1980 he received the Nobel Prize for literature.

10 Mieczysław Jastrun, "Potęga ciemnoty," *Odrodzenie.*

11 Ibid.

12 *Gazeta Wyborcza,* April 18, 2003.

13 Bortnowska is a regular contributor to the distinguished Catholic weekly *Tygodnik Powszechny.*

14 *Wokół Jedwabnego,* vol. II, p. 141.

15 Ibid.

16 *Mówią wieki,* November 1992, pp. 2–9.

17 Ibid.

18 *Wokół Jedwabnego,* vol. II, p. 153.

19 Zygmunt Klukowski, *Dziennik z lat okupacji zamojszczyzny.* See especially the journal entry of April 13, 1942.

20 Browning, *Ordinary Men,* pp. 155, 156.

21 Klukowski, op. cit., journal entries for August 8, October 26, and November 26,

1942; Michał Grynberg and Maria Kotowska, eds., *Życie i zagłada Żydów polskich 1939–1945: Relacje świadków,* pp. 104, 408, 409.

22 *Wokół Jedwabnego,* vol. II, pp. 123–54.

23 I assume that this is an exhaustive set as it results from the teamwork of a half-dozen historians who spent almost two years researching the subject as part of the IPN investigation.

24 *Wokół Jedwabnego,* vol. II, p. 130.

25 Ibid., p. 132.

26 Ibid., p. 135.

27 Ibid., p. 138.

28 Ibid., p. 139.

29 Ibid., p. 140.

30 "Raport sytuacyjny delegatury rządu RP na kraj za okres 15 sierpnia—15 listopada 1941," ibid., p. 147.

31 *Wokół Jedwabnego,* vol. II, p. 142.

32 Ibid., p. 144.

33 Hanna Świda-Zięba, *Urwany lot: Pokolenie inteligenckiej młodzieży powojennej w świetle listów i pamiętników z lat 1945–1948.*

34 Ibid., p. 7.

35 Ibid., p. 42.

36 Ibid., p. 43 .

37 Ibid., p. 44.

38 Ibid., pp. 44–45.

39 Ibid., p. 94.

40 Lucien Febvre, *"Honneur et patrie": Une enquête sur le sentiment d'honneur et l'attachement à la patrie,* pp. 70–71.

41 See, for example, a newspaper article published on May 5, 2000, in the daily *Rzeczpospolita* just as the Jedwabne story was breaking out in Poland. The journalist Andrzej Kaczyński went to Jedwabne to check what the local people knew about the alleged murder of Jedwabne Jews by their neighbors during the war and discovered that his interlocutors were familiar with the event and confirmed the story (Andrzej Kaczyński, " 'Burnt Offering,' *Rzeczpospolita,* 5 May 2000," *The Neighbors Respond,* pp. 50–59).

42 English translation published by Harvard University Press.

CHAPTER 6

1 As a scholar of modern Jewish history put it succinctly: "Judeo-Communism is a 'xenophobic assertion,' . . . indeed a myth, a delusion, [which] has never existed" (André Gerrits, "Anti-Semitism and Anti-Communism: The Myth of 'Judeo-Communism' in Eastern Europe," *East European Jewish Affairs,* vol. 25, no. 1, pp. 50, 51).

2 Jaff Schatz, *The Generation: The Rise and Fall of the Jewish Communists of Poland,* p. 115.

3 Quoted from Amos Elon, *The Pity of It All: A History of Jews in Germany, 1743–1933,* p. 346. Rosa Luxemburg (1871–1919) was one of the leading theoreticians and po-

litical activists of the international (but especially Polish and German) social democratic workers' movement. Independent minded, she was involved in fierce polemics with Eduard Bernstein and V. I. Lenin alike. Co-founder of the German Communist Party, she was murdered with another CP leader, Karl Liebknecht, by a right-wing officers' conspiracy.

4 I owe this formulation to Marci Shore (personal communication).

5 *Encyklopedia powszechna,* vol. 2, p. 526.

6 Schatz, *The Generation,* p. 84.

7 Antony Polonsky, *Politics in Independent Poland, 1921–1939,* pp. 77, 249, 322.

8 I am grateful to Roni Gechtman, for putting together the figure from various unpublished sources. One should add that the Bund's electorate, especially in municipal elections in the late 1930s, amounted to hundreds of thousands—in such cities as Warsaw and Łódź, the majority of Jewish voters supported the Bund (see Roni Gechtman, *Yidisher Sotsializm: The Origin and Contexts of the Jewish Labor Bund's National Program*).

9 Schatz, *The Generation,* p. 97.

10 Ibid., p. 102.

11 I am borrowing the phrase from Kai Erikson's reflections on the instrumentalization of ethnic hatred during the decomposition of Yugoslavia in the 1990s (in manuscript).

12 "To the Minister of Foreign Affairs, Kuibyshev, January 5, 1942," in Kot, *Listy z rosji,* p. 249.

13 Shimon Redlich, ed., *Yevreyskii Antifashistovskii Komitet v SSSR, 1941–1948: Dokumentirovannaya Istoria,* pp. 35–49.

14 Ibid., pp. 32, 33.

15 Kostyrchenko, *Out of the Red Shadows,* p. 23.

16 Ibid.

17 Quoted from Amir Weiner, *Making Sense,* p. 225.

18 Ibid., pp. 219–20.

19 Yuri Slezkine, *The Jewish Century,* p. 301.

20 Kostyrchenko, *Out of the Red Shadows,* p. 18.

21 I take these examples from Yuri Slezkine's book, where many other interesting and bizarre cases are discussed (*The Jewish Century,* pp. 303, 304).

22 Kostyrchenko, *Out of the Red Shadows,* p. 19.

23 Ibid., pp. 19–20.

24 Slezkine, *The Jewish Century,* p. 314.

25 "During World War II the Soviet state received around $45 million from various Jewish organizations, most of them US-based" (Slezkine, *The Jewish Century,* p. 454).

26 Redlich, *Yevreyskii,* pp. 238–39.

27 Recently a book containing materials which were censored from the original manuscript of the Black Book has been published. Its focus, therefore, is on the complicity of the local population in the destruction of Russian Jewry. Ilya Altman, ed., *Neizvestnaya chernaya kniga. Svidelstva ochevidsev o katastrofe sovetskikh evreev (1941–1944).*

28 Kostyrchenko, *Out of the Red Shadows,* pp. 61, 62.

29 Ibid., p. 88.

30 Jonathan Brent and Vladimir P. Naumov, *Stalin's Last Crime: The Plot Against the Jewish Doctors, 1948–1953,* pp. 184, 362.

31 See Kostyrchenko, *Out of the Red Shadows,* p. 23, on the massive collaboration of Soviet citizens with Nazi occupation authorities. For Weiner, see *Making Sense,* p. 235.

32 Amir Weiner, "When Memory Counts: War, Genocide, and Postwar Soviet Jewry," in Omer Bartov, Atina Grossman, and Mary Nolan, eds., *Crimes of War: Guilt and Denial in the Twentieth Century,* pp. 202–203.

33 Slezkine, *The Jewish Century,* p. 301.

34 Ibid., pp. 309–310.

35 Wacław Bartczak, "W paszczy krokodyla," *Gazeta Wyborcza,* August 23, 2002.

36 *Manchester Guardian,* April 25, 1949; quoted in Kostyrchenko, *Out of the Red Shadows,* p. 153.

37 Hersh Smolar, *Oif der letzter pozitzye mit der letzter hofenung,* p. 25.

38 Gennadi Bordiugov and Gennadi Matveev, et al., eds., *SSSR-Polsha: Mekhanizm podchinyenya, 1944–1949,* p. 274.

39 Ibid., p. 275.

40 Hersh Smolar describes his encounter with Gomułka in his memoirs (Smolar, *Oif der letzter,* pp. 30, 31; see, also, August Grabski, *Działalność komunistów wśród Żydów w Polsce, 1944–1949,* p. 36).

41 Goldstein-Goren Diaspora Research Center in Tel Aviv, Adolf Berman Archives, P-70/51, letter from Aleksander Masiewicki, October 12, 1945.

42 Slezkine, *The Jewish Century,* p. 314.

43 Nikita S. Chruszczow [Khrushchev], "Fragmenty wspomnień N. S. Chruszczowa," in *Zeszyty Historyczne,* no. 132, pp. 170, 172; quoted from Marci Shore, "Children of the Revolution: A Warsaw Family Story," in manuscript, pp. 20, 21.

44 His interlocutor, who was also Jewish, replied that they had all had a noose wrapped around their necks but added that this did not exculpate Berman for what he had done as the Politburo member supervising the security apparatus (Torańska, *Oni,* interview with Stefan Staszewski, p. 138. See also the interview with Jakub Berman, p. 324).

45 Goldstein-Goren Diaspora Research Center, in Tel Aviv, Adolf Berman Archives, P-70/126.

46 Grabski, *Działalność,* p. 79.

47 Engel, op. cit., pp. 97–101. See, especially, the October 9, 1945, resolution of the "First national conference of Jewish activists of the PPR," ibid., p. 98. An extensive discussion of the conference is provided in Grabski (*Działalność,* pp. 88–97).

48 Redlich, *Yevreyskii,* pp. 218–19.

49 Smolar, *Oif der letzter,* pp. 219–20.

50 Adelson, "W Polsce zwanej," p. 394.

51 Grabski, *Działalność,* p. 109.

52 The reference here is to the influential political essay by Albert Hirschman, *Exit, Voice, and Loyalty.*

53 Hal Lehrman, *Russia's Europe,* p. 187.

54 Robert Levy, *Ana Pauker,* p. 76.

55 See Antoni Dudek and Grzegorz Pytel, *Bolesław Piasecki. Próba biografii politycznej,* pp. 156–62, and Levy, *Ana Pauker,* pp. 75–77.

56 "The essential difference between the two civil wars arose from the fact that the Iron Guard was founded on a popular base of peasants, young people, soldiers, and priests, and that they used terror as a means of political action. With respect to the Communist Party, one should not have any illusions: it lacked support, even among the oppressed classes and the poor. If civil war was, for the Iron Guard, a means of seizing power, for the Communists it was a means of creating for themselves that support among peasants and workers, so as to legitimize the power that was, in a way, assured" (Serge Moscovici, *Chronique des années egarées,* p. 360).

57 Jan T. Gross, *Neighbors: The Destruction of the Jewish Community in Jedwabne, Poland,* p. 116. For the full text of Zygmunt Laudański's petition, see *Wokół Jedwabnego,* vol. 2, pp. 607–609.

58 Hal Lehrman, "Hungary: Liberation's Bitter Fruit," *Commentary,* p. 30.

59 Moscovici, *Chronique,* p. 359.

60 APK, UW 2, file 91, "Sprawozdanie z powiatu bocheńskiego," dated 21.08.1945.

61 See, for example, "Introduction" to *Aparat bezpieczeństwa w latach 1944–1956, taktyka, strategia, metody. Część I. Lata 1945–1947,* Andrzej Paczkowski, ed., p. 17.

62 Maciej Korkuć, " 'Kujbyszewiacy'—awangarda UB," in *Arcana,* no. 46–47, pp. 81, 82.

63 Ibid., pp. 84, 86, 87, 91, 92.

64 Andrzej Paczkowski, "Żydzi w UB, próba weryfikacji stereotypu," in Tomasz Szarota, ed., *Komunizm: Idelogia, system, ludzie,* esp. pp. 196–98.

65 For a full English-language text of Seliwanowski's report, see Natalia Aleksiun, "The Situation of the Jews in Poland as Seen by the Soviet Security Forces in 1945," in *Jews in Eastern Europe,* pp. 52–68. The Polish-language version of the text referenced by Paczkowski (Tatiana Cariewskaja et al., eds., *Teczka specjalna J. W. Stalina. Raporty NKWD z Polski 1944–1946,* pp. 419–22) contains only excerpts from the document.

66 Paczkowski, "Żydzi w UB," p. 197.

67 Ibid., p. 198.

68 Ibid., p. 197.

69 "O aparacie bezpieczeństwa—z Krzysztofem Lesiakowskim i Grzegorzem Majchrzakiem rozmawia Barbara Polak," *Biuletyn IPN,* no. 6 (2002), p. 15.

70 Or, to use the expression current at the time, it was "not unified [*"niezespolony"*] with the general administration."

71 This, of course, had a bearing on the kind of people attracted to service in the security apparatus (see, for example, "O aparacie bezpieczeństwa," p. 9).

72 AAN, MAP, B-876, pp. 1, 2.

73 Ibid., p. 2.

74 Ibid., p. 31.

75 Jakubowski, *Milicja,* p. 493.

76 Piotr Majer, *Milicja obywatelska w systemie organów władzy PRL,* p. 124.

77 Jakubowski, *Milicja,* pp. 56–59, 99–100.

78 Ibid., p. 204.

79 Ibid., pp. 207–208.

80 "Sprawozdanie z odprawy kierowników wojewódzkich urzędów bezpieczeństwa publicznego 30 listopada i 1 grudnia 1945 r.," in Andrzej Paczkowski, ed., *Aparat bezpieczeństwa w latach 1944–1956. Taktyka, strategia, metody. Część I. Lata 1945–1947,* pp. 26, 40, 41.

81 See Andrzej Rzepliński, op. cit., p. 374.

82 "O aparacie bezpieczeństwa," p. 8.

83 Majer, *Milicja obywatelska,* p. 49.

84 Antoni Dziurok, "Początki milicji," p. 46.

85 "O aparacie bezpieczeństwa," p. 19.

86 *Do kierownika wydziału personalnego MBP, raport o panujących stosunkach służbowych w woj. rzeszowskim,* Władysław Sobczyński, *akta osobowe,* IPN, 0193/7009. (I am grateful to Dr. Zbigniew Nawrocki for sharing this document with me.)

87 Jakubowski, *Milicja,* p. 433.

88 Turkov, *Noch der befrajung,* pp. 29, 178–80, 272.

89 ŻIH, CKŻP, Prezydium, 303/3.

90 ŻIH, CKŻP, Wydział Organizacyjny, 304/35, 29.VI.46.

91 Adelson, "W Polsce zwanej," p. 402.

92 For transcripts of these conferences through November 1947, see Paczkowski, *Aparat bezpieczeństwa.*

93 ŻIH, CKŻP, Central Special Commission, box 1-2, "Komisja specjalna w Krakowie, Oświęcim," 27.01.1947.

94 See Aleksiun, op. cit., pp. 63, 64.

95 Paczkowski, "Żydzi w UB," p. 204.

96 As manpower needs arose, army recruits might be offered the option of serving in the police instead.

97 A young Polish historian, Marcin Zaremba, gives an excellent analysis of this phenomenon in a recent study: Marcin Zaremba, *Komunizm, legitymizacja, nacjonalizm: Nacjonalistyczna legitymizacja władzy komunistycznej w Polsce,* esp. chapters 4 and 5.

98 A fascinating political biography of Wasilewska still remains to be written. She was the daughter of Leon Wasilewski, Piłsudski's close friend and interwar Poland's first minister of foreign affairs. She was a writer and an activist of the Polish Socialist Party until she met Stalin during the 1939–1941 Soviet occupation of eastern Poland and promptly gained his confidence and friendship. She was possibly the only woman who wielded political influence with the Soviet ruler. Wasilewska later married a prominent Ukrainian Communist Party activist and writer, Alexander Korneichuk, and remained in the Soviet Union after the war. Marci Shore, in her forthcoming monograph *Caviar and Ashes,* puts together what is so far the most interesting and comprehensive intellectual portrait of Wanda Wasilewska.

99 Berman's speech of September 15, 1946, quoted from Zaremba, *Komunizm,* p. 168.

100 For illustrious examples among historians it may be enough to mention François Furet in France (*The Passing of an Illusion: The Idea of Communism in the Twentieth Century*) and Eric Hobsbawm in England (*Interesting Times: A Twentieth Century Life*).

101 Czesław Miłosz, *New and Collected Poems, 1931–2001,* p. 122.

CONCLUSIONS

1   The allusion here is to the famous proposition of the sociologist W. I. Thomas: "If people define a situation as real, it is real in its consequences."

2   Saul Friedlander, *Nazi Germany and the Jews,* p. 278.

3   Hannah Arendt, "Organized Guilt and Universal Responsibility," in *Essays in Understanding, 1930–1954,* p. 126.

4   Libionka, " 'Kwestia żydowska' w Polsce."

5   Jan T. Gross, *Wokół Sąsiadów: Polemiki i wyjaśnienia,* p. 118. I owe this quote to an extended manuscript version of Dr. Andrzej Żbikowski's contribution to the volume *Wokół Jedwabnego.*

6   See my *Neighbors,* pp. 18, 37, 38.

7   The term "pseudospeciation" was introduced by Erik H. Erikson in "Ontogeny of Ritualization in Man." I am grateful for this information to Erik Erikson's son, the sociologist Kai Erikson.

8   I am quoting here from the work of the sociologist Kai Erikson, who also uses the terms "pseudospeciation" and, synonymously, "social speciation" in his study of war-torn Yugoslavia ("Drawing Ethnic Boundaries," unpublished manuscript, p. 16).

9   Tacitus, "The Life of Cnaeus Julius Agricola," p. 703.

10   Mordecai Gebirtig, *The Song That Never Died,* pp. 130–131.

11   *Wokół Jedwabnego,* vol. 2, p. 299.

12   From the cycle "Voices of Poor People," originally published in Warsaw in 1945 in the volume entitled *Ocalenie (The Rescue)*: Czesław Miłosz, *New and Collected Poems, 1931–2001,* pp. 63–64. The poem would serve in 1987 as a take-off point for Jan Błoński's important article, "The Poor Poles Look at the Ghetto," in *Tygodnik Powszechny* (January 11, 1987). He raised in it the question of Polish responsibility for the manner of witnessing the Holocaust. The article as well as the wide-ranging public debate that followed are presented in an English-language volume edited by Antony Polonsky: *"My Brother's Keeper": Recent Polish Debates on the Holocaust.* See, especially, pp. 34–48.

13   Hannah Arendt, "The Seeds of a Fascist International," in *Essays in Understanding, 1930–1954,* pp. 140, 141.

INDEX

Page locators that include an "n" indicate information that will be found only in the footnote on that page.

TSKŻ (Jewish Socio-Cultural
  Association), 220
Turbota, Michał, 45n
Turkov, Jonas, 33–34, 237

UB (Security Service), 14n
  see also Security Service (Bezpieka or UB)
Ukraine, 22, 189n, 204, 239n
UN Relief and Rehabilitation
  Administration, 36
Underground State, 5–7, 17, 17n–18n, 178,
  182
Ungerman, Halinka, 52
Ungerman, Sala, 52
Union of the Proletariat of Town and
  Country, 196
USSR, *see* Soviet Union

Vatican, 140–42
  see also Catholic church
Veksler (Moscow Philharmonic staff
  member), 205n
Veterans Administration (ZBOWiD),
  238–39
Vilna (place), 198n, 199n
Voluntary Reserves of the Citizens' Militia
  (ORMO), 14n, 227, 235
Voroshilov, Kliment, 9
Vyshinsky, Andrei, 11
Vyspreva (Moscow Philharmonic staff
  member), 205n

Wałęsa, Lech, 10, 30n
Wallenberg, Raoul, 236n
Warsaw (place)
  assembling Holocaust documentation,
    170
  beginning of uprising, 171–72
  Communist gains in, 198n, 199n
  employment discrimination, 66n
  liberation by Red Army, 14
  splitting between Soviet and Nazi zones,
    3n
  uprising, 10–12, 71, 171–73
Wasersztajn, Szmul, 37, 253
Wasilewska, Wanda, 240
Wasilków (place), 41
Wąsosz (place), 42
Wat, Aleksander, 189n
Weiner, Amir, 204, 210
Weinreich, Max, 194
Werfel, Roman, 242n
Werth, Aleksander, 212
Wertheim, Stanisław, 182n
Wilno (place), 170, 184, 194
Wiślicz-Iwańczyk, Eugeniusz, 97
Wiślicz (place), 93n, 136
Witaszewski, Comrade, 123

Witlich (place), 248
Witnesses (movie), 165
Włodawa (place), 31, 49, 51, 62n
Włoszczowa (place), 112, 113
Wojewodzki Urząd Bezpieczeństwa
  Publicznego, *see* WUPB (Voivodeship
  Office of Public Security)
Woźniak, Jan, 75
Wrocław (place), 48–49, 113
Wrona, Zenon, 86, 151
Wrzeszcz, Jan, 90–91, 99
WUPB (Voivodeship Office of Public
  Security), 229, 238
Wurm, Mathilde, 195
Wyka, Kazimierz, 129–30, 132, 252
Wyrzykowska, Antonina, 55
Wysokie Mazowieckie (place), 183
Wyszyński, Stefan, 148

Yalta Conference, 14–18
Yampolski (Moscow Philharmonic staff
  member), 205n
Yaroslavtsev (Moscow Philharmonic staff
  member), 205n
Yelkhaninova (Moscow Philharmonic staff
  member), 205n
Yeltsin, Boris, 10
YIVO Institute for Jewish Research, 194

Zachariasz, Szymon, 63
Zagórski, Sergeant, 83, 84, 161
Zając (policeman), 84, 161
Zajdman, Hanna, 82
Zak (Moscow Philharmonic staff member),
  205n
Zakopane orphanage, 70
Zaręby Kościelne (place), 183
ZBOWiD (Veterans Administration),
  238–39
Żegota (organization), 6, 178, 182n
Zelek, Roman, 135, 143n
Zelicki, Mr., 218
Zertal, Idith, 29n
Zhdanov, Andrei, 25, 208, 209, 220n
Znaniecki, Florian, 194
ŻOB (Jewish Fighting Organization), 102
Zoppott (place), 152
ZPP (Association of Polish Patriots), 213,
  215n, 240
Żrałek, Mr., 232
Zuckerman, Yitzhak, 102
żydokomuna (Judeo-Communism), xii,
  192–243, 245, 259
Żydowska Organizacja Bojowa (ŻOB), 102
Zylberger, Michał, 135n
Zylbersztejn, Israel, 60n
Zyskind, Mr., 61
Żywczyński, Mieczysław, 142

JAN T. GROSS was a 2001 National Book Award nominee for his widely acclaimed *Neighbors: The Destruction of the Jewish Community in Jedwabne, Poland*. He teaches history at Princeton University, where he is the Norman B. Tomlinson '16 and '48 Professor of War and Society.